I used to really hate doing color illustrations, but these days I enjoy them. They still take me f̶o̶r̶e̶v̶e̶r̶ though!

—Naoshi Komi

NAOSHI KOMI was born in Kochi Prefecture, Japan, on March 28, 1986. His first serialized work in *Weekly Shonen Jump* was the series *Double Arts*. His current series, *Nisekoi*, is serialized in *Weekly Shonen Jump*.

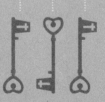

NISEKOI:
False Love
VOLUME 4
SHONEN JUMP Manga Edition

Story and Art by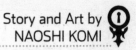
NAOSHI KOMI

Translation ✐ Camellia Nieh
Touch-Up Art & Lettering ✐ Stephen Dutro
Design ✐ Fawn Lau
Shonen Jump Series Editor ✐ John Bae
Graphic Novel Editor ✐ Amy Yu

NISEKOI © 2011 by Naoshi Komi
All rights reserved.
First published in Japan in 2011
by SHUEISHA Inc., Tokyo.
English translation rights arranged
by SHUEISHA Inc.

Printed in the U.S.A.

Published by VIZ Media, LLC
P.O. Box 77010
San Francisco, CA 94107

10 9 8 7 6 5 3 4 2 1
First printing, July 2014

www.shonenjump.com   www.viz.com

NISEKOI

False Love

vol. 4: Making Sure

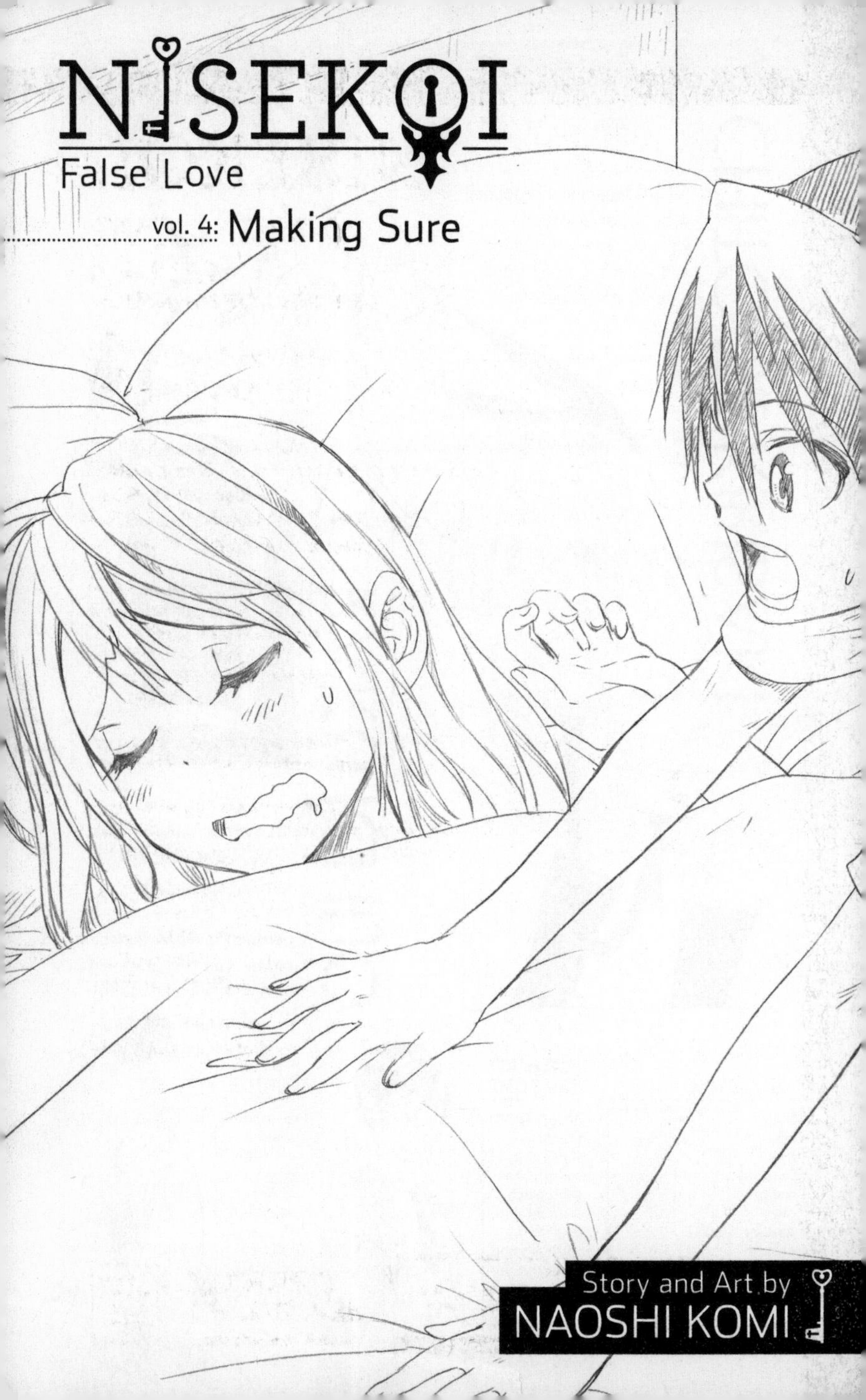

Story and Art by

NAOSHI KOMI

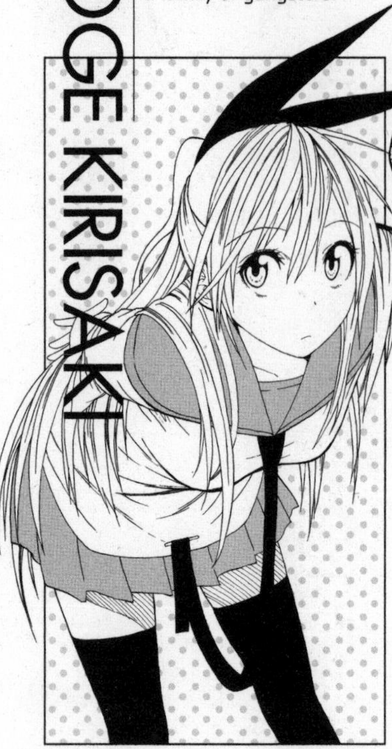

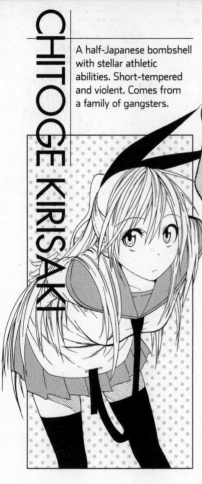

CHITOGE KIRISAKI

A half-Japanese bombshell with stellar athletic abilities. Short-tempered and violent. Comes from a family of gangsters.

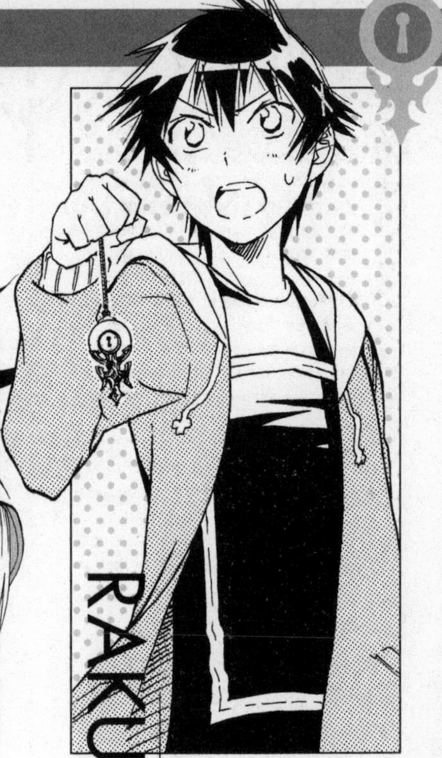

RAKU ICHIJO

A normal teen whose family happens to be yakuza. Cherishes a pendant given to him by a girl he met ten years ago. Has a crush on Kosaki.

SHU MAIKO

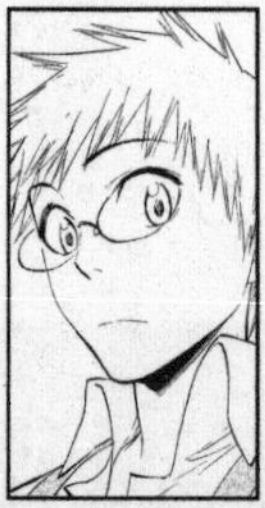

Raku's best friend. Outgoing and girl-crazy. Always tuned in to the latest gossip at school.

SEISHIRO TSUGUMI

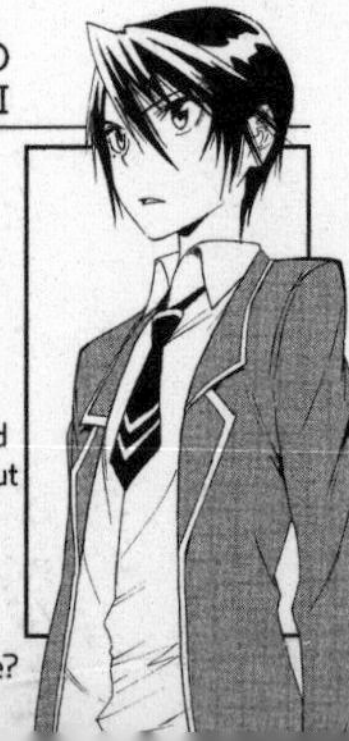

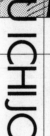

Adopted by Claude as a young child and raised as a top-notch assassin, Seishiro is 100% devoted to Chitoge. But is there more to Chitoge's new body-guard than meets the eye?

CLAUDE

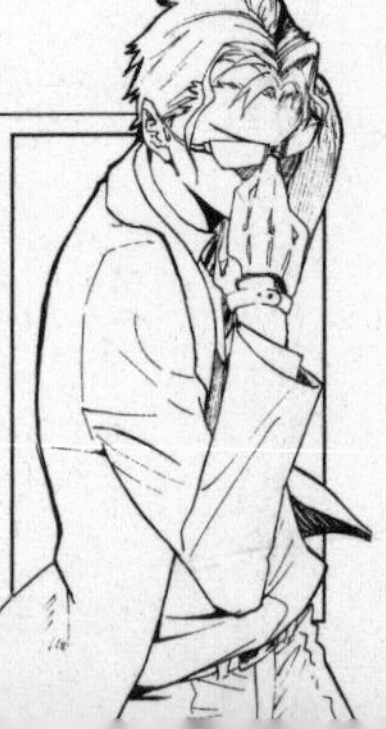

Executive member of the Beehive and protector of Chitoge. Suspicious of Raku and Chitoge's relationship.

THE STORY THUS FAR

Raku Ichijo is an ordinary teen...who just happens to come from a family of yakuza! His most treasured item is a pendant he was given ten years ago by a girl whom he promised to meet again one day and marry.

When super-babe Chitoge Kirisaki transfers into Raku's class, it's clear from the get-go that they don't get along. Unfortunately, thanks to family circumstances, Raku and Chitoge are forced to pretend to be a couple—even at school! The ever-suspicious Claude sends his protégé, a feared assassin named Seishiro, to keep tabs on the couple. Seishiro is extremely hostile toward Raku at first, but begins to soften as she gets to know him.

When Seishiro reminds Chitoge of her first crush ten years ago, Chitoge begins searching for clues as to her crush's identity and finds an old key nestled in the diary she kept when she was little. A class trip with Raku and the rest of the gang interrupts her detective work, but leads to a shocking new discovery—Raku has a scar just like the boy in her diary! And why does Chitoge's key give Raku a weird sense of déjà vu? The false couple grows closer on the school trip, and by the end, they're finally on a first-name basis.

KOSAKI ONODERA

A girl Raku has a crush on. Beautiful and sweet, Kosaki has no shortage of admirers. She's a terrible cook but makes food that *looks* amazing.

CHITOGE'S FATHER

Leader of the Beehive, a gang with designs on the Shuei-Gumi's turf.

RAKU'S FATHER

Leader of the Shuei-Gumi, the yakuza syndicate at war with the Beehive.

RURI MIYAMOTO

Kosaki's best gal pal. Comes off as aloof, but is actually a devoted and highly intuitive friend.

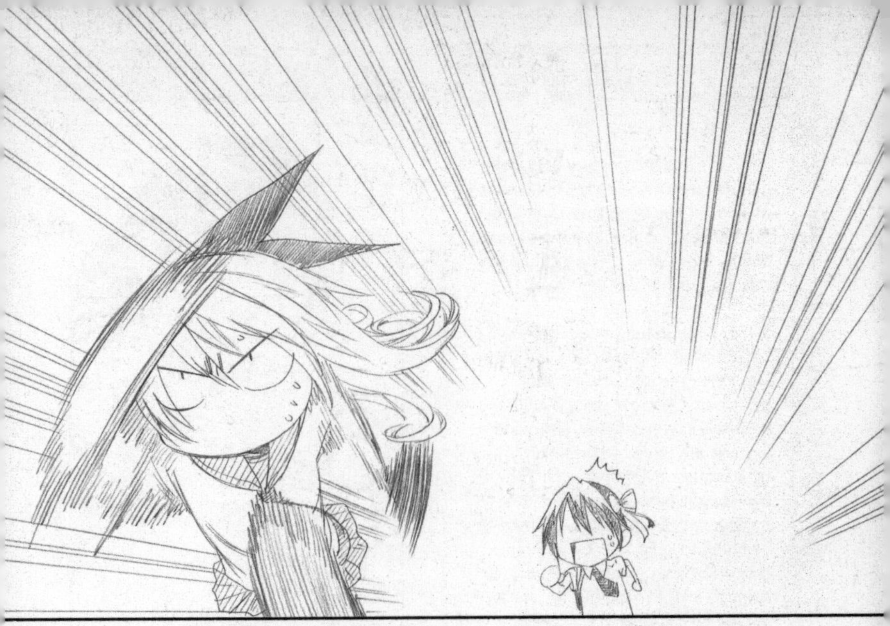

NISEKOI
False Love
vol. 4: Making Sure

TABLE OF CONTENTS

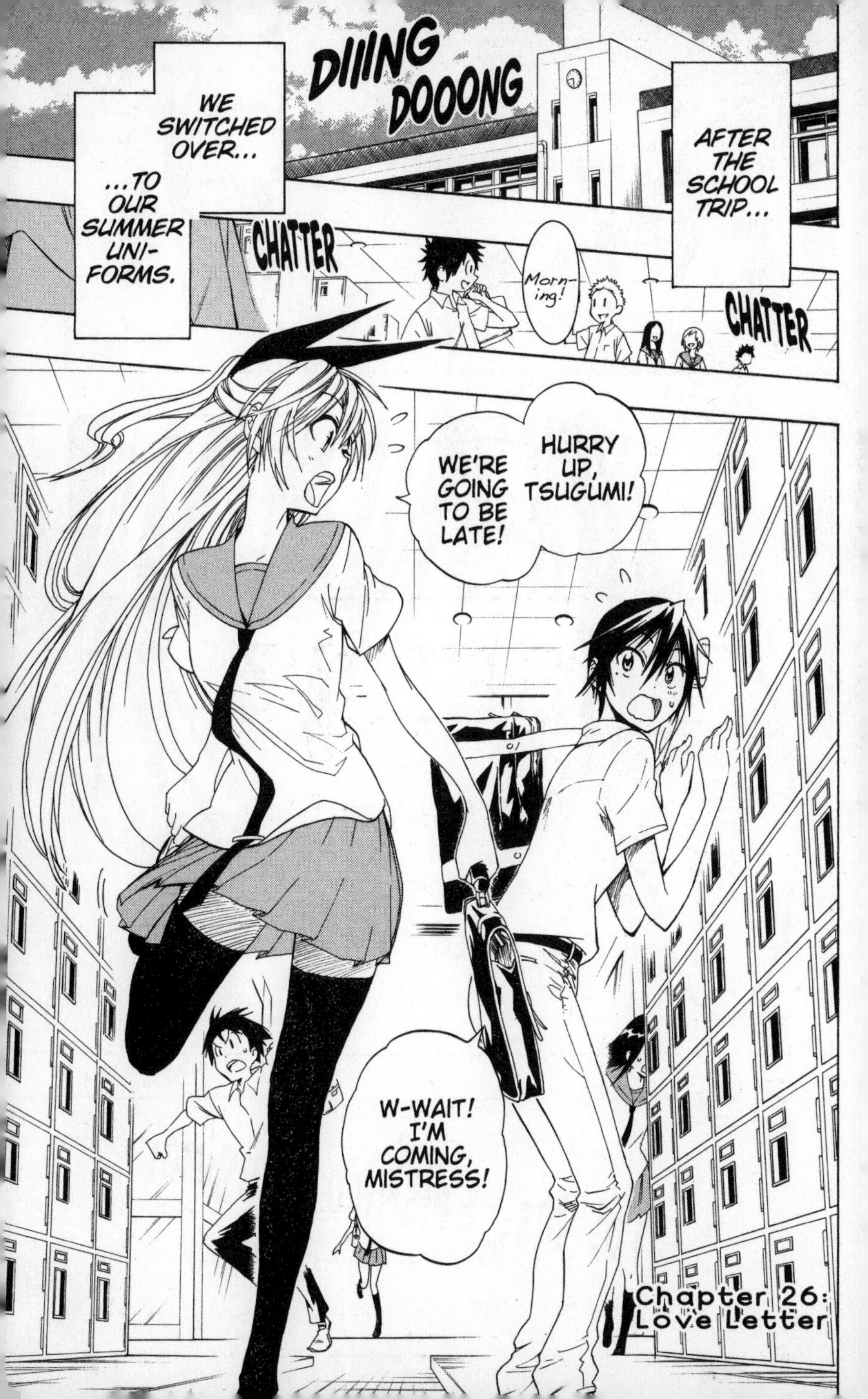
AFTER THE SCHOOL TRIP...
DIIING DOOONG
WE SWITCHED OVER...
...TO OUR SUMMER UNI-FORMS.
CHATTER
Morn-ing!
CHATTER
HURRY UP, TSUGUMI!
WE'RE GOING TO BE LATE!
W-WAIT! I'M COMING, MISTRESS!
Chapter 26: Love Letter

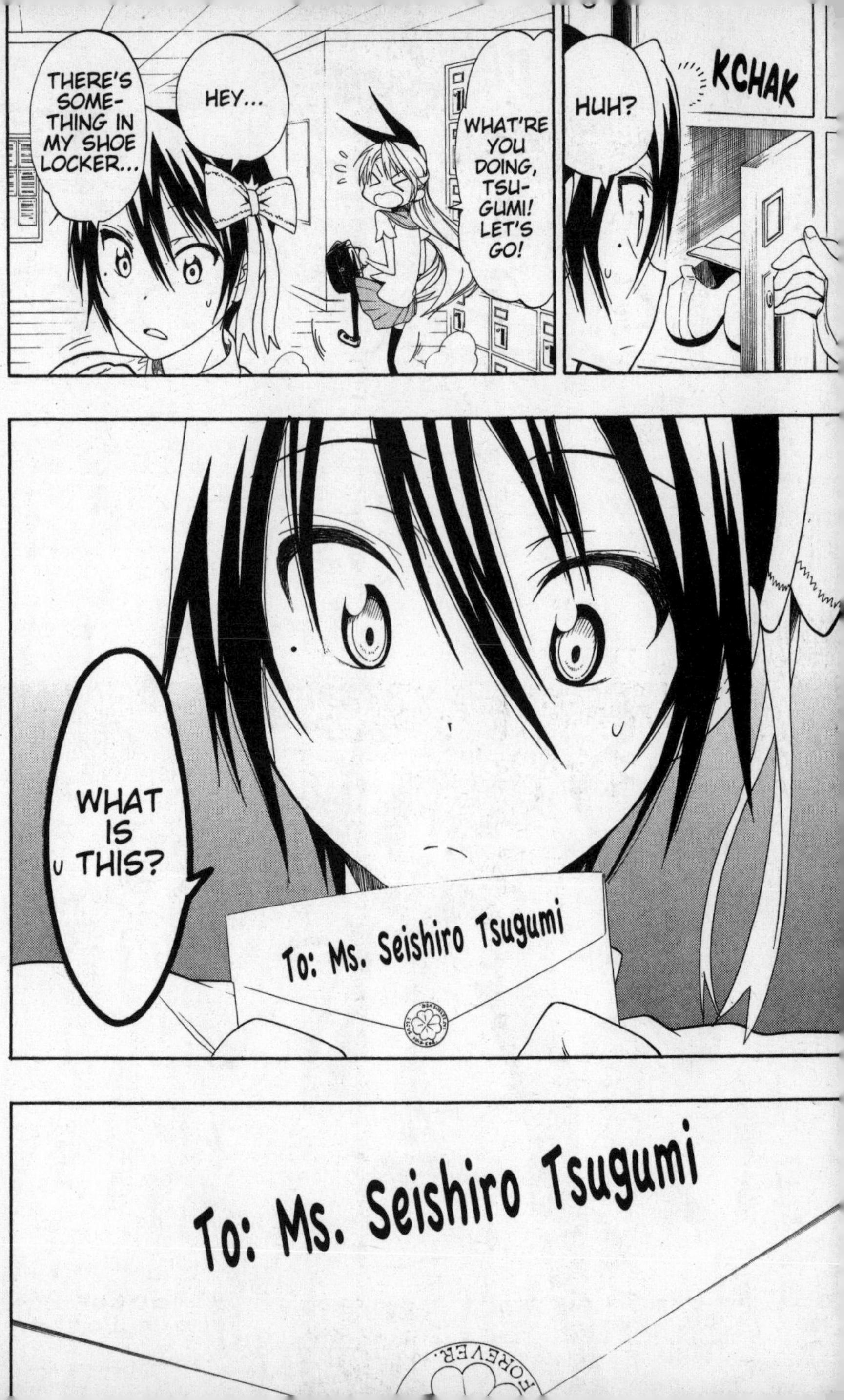
KCHAK
HUH?
WHAT'RE YOU DOING, TSUGUMI! LET'S GO!
HEY...
THERE'S SOMETHING IN MY SHOE LOCKER...
WHAT IS THIS?
To: Ms. Seishiro Tsugumi
To: Ms. Seishiro Tsugumi
FOREVER.

Chapter 26: Love Letter

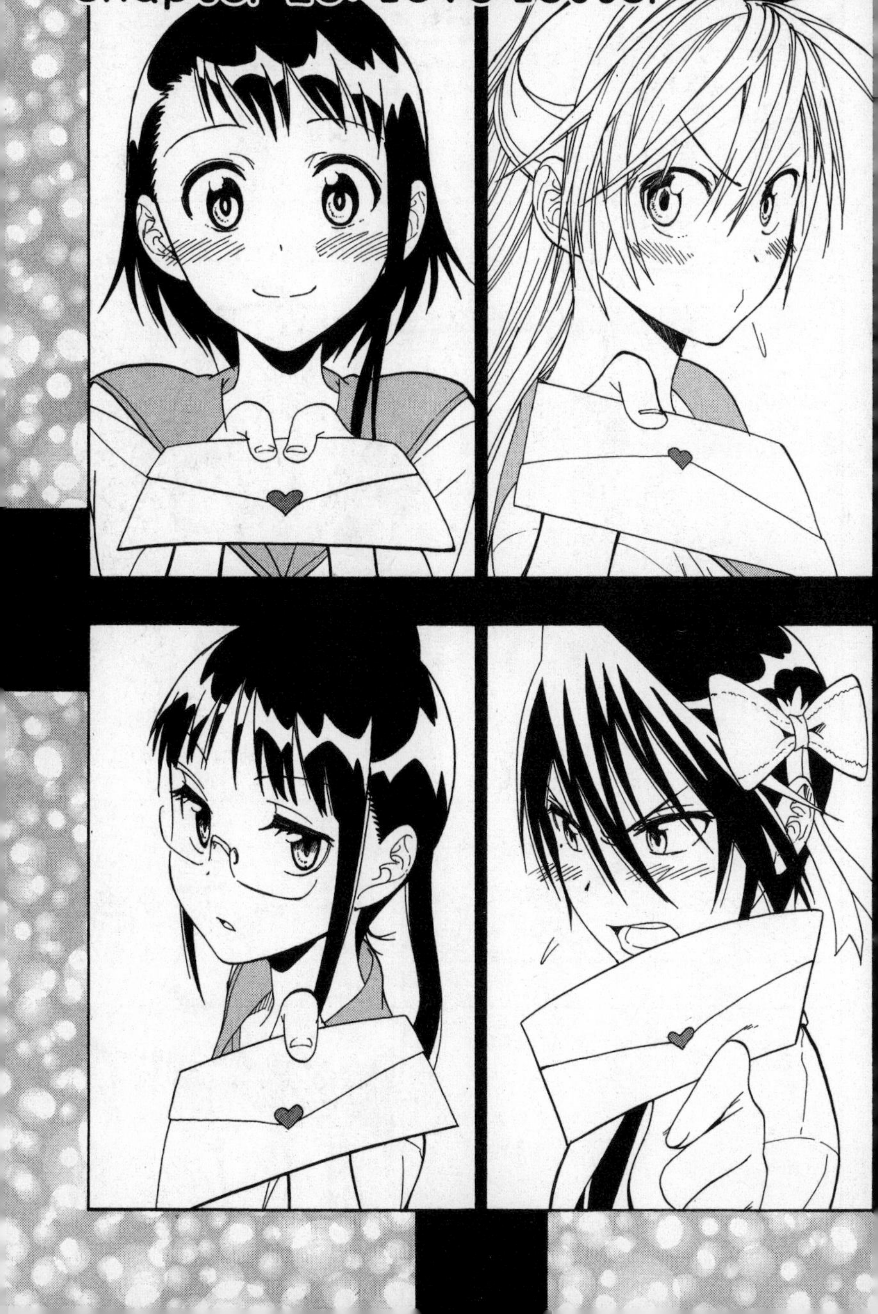

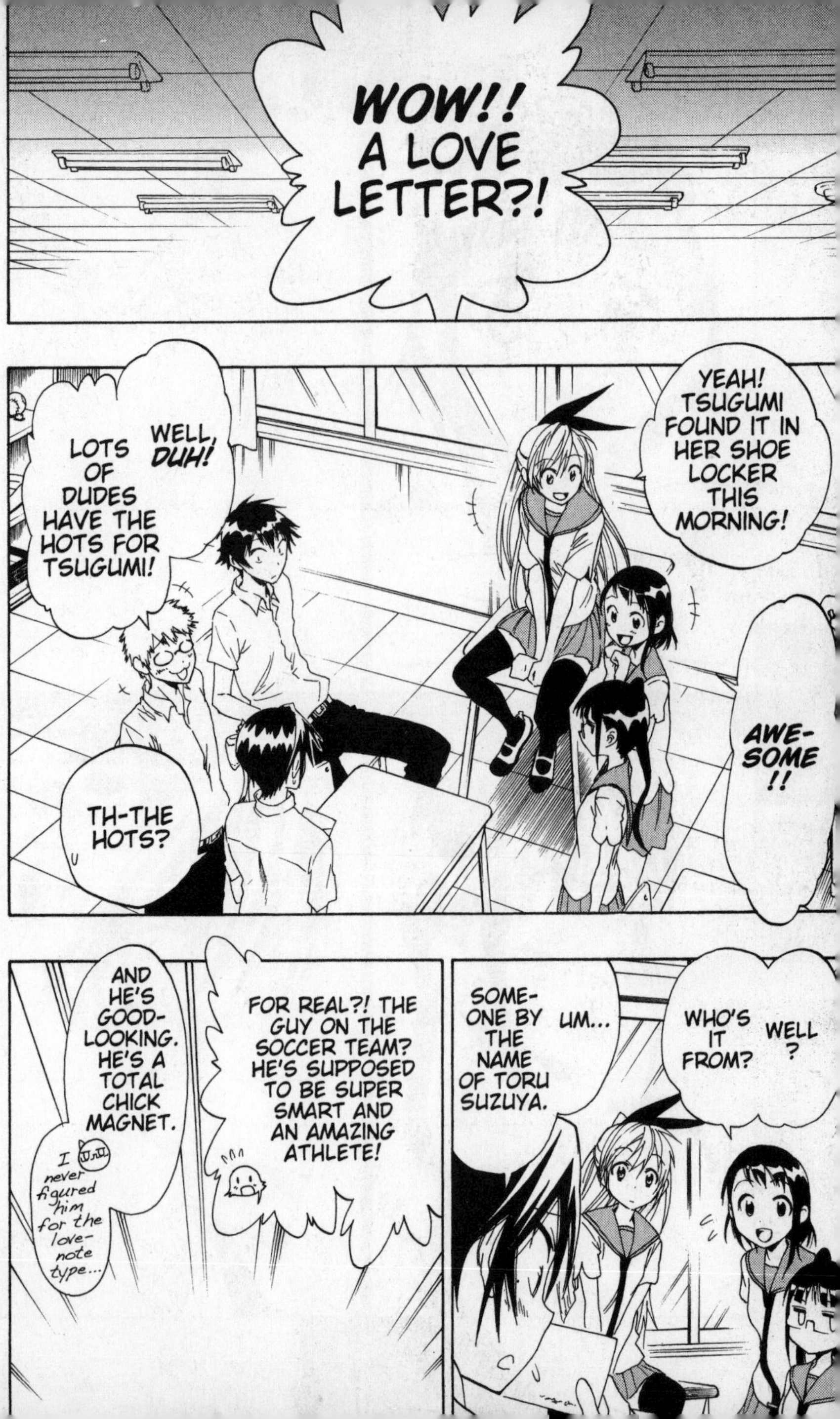
WOW!! A LOVE LETTER?!
YEAH! TSUGUMI FOUND IT IN HER SHOE LOCKER THIS MORNING!
AWE-SOME!!
WELL, DUH! LOTS OF DUDES HAVE THE HOTS FOR TSUGUMI!
TH-THE HOTS?
WELL?
WHO'S IT FROM?
UM...
SOME-ONE BY THE NAME OF TORU SUZUYA.
FOR REAL?! THE GUY ON THE SOCCER TEAM? HE'S SUPPOSED TO BE SUPER SMART AND AN AMAZING ATHLETE!
AND HE'S GOOD-LOOKING. HE'S A TOTAL CHICK MAGNET.
I never figured him for the love-note type...

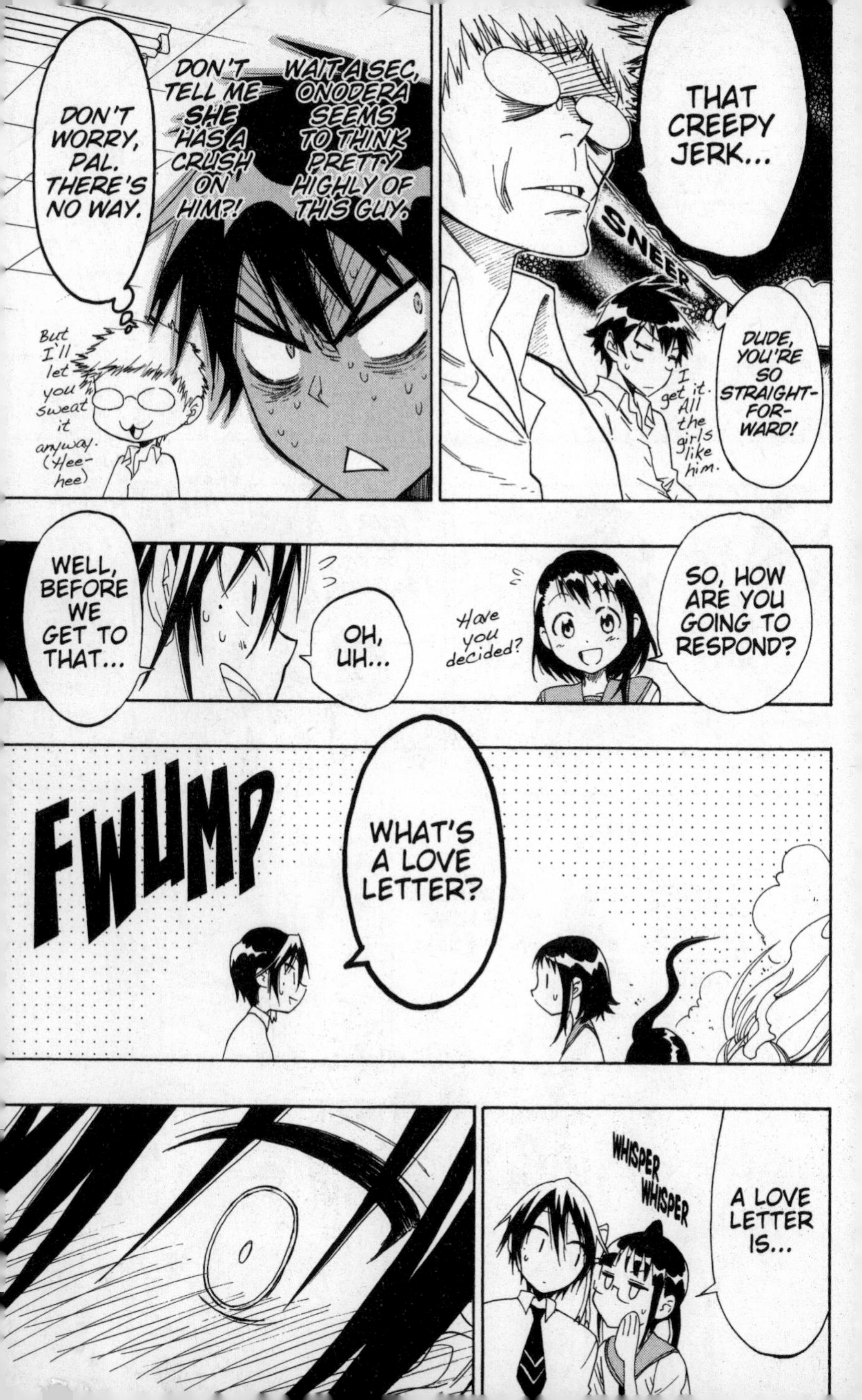
THAT CREEPY JERK...
SNEER
DUDE, YOU'RE SO STRAIGHT-FOR-WARD!
I get it. All the girls like him.
WAIT A SEC, ONODERA SEEMS TO THINK PRETTY HIGHLY OF THIS GUY.
DON'T TELL ME SHE HAS A CRUSH ON HIM?!
DON'T WORRY, PAL. THERE'S NO WAY.
But I'll let you sweat it anyway. (Hee-hee)
SO, HOW ARE YOU GOING TO RESPOND?
Have you decided?
OH, UH...
WELL, BEFORE WE GET TO THAT...
WHAT'S A LOVE LETTER?
FWUMP
A LOVE LETTER IS...
WHISPER WHISPER

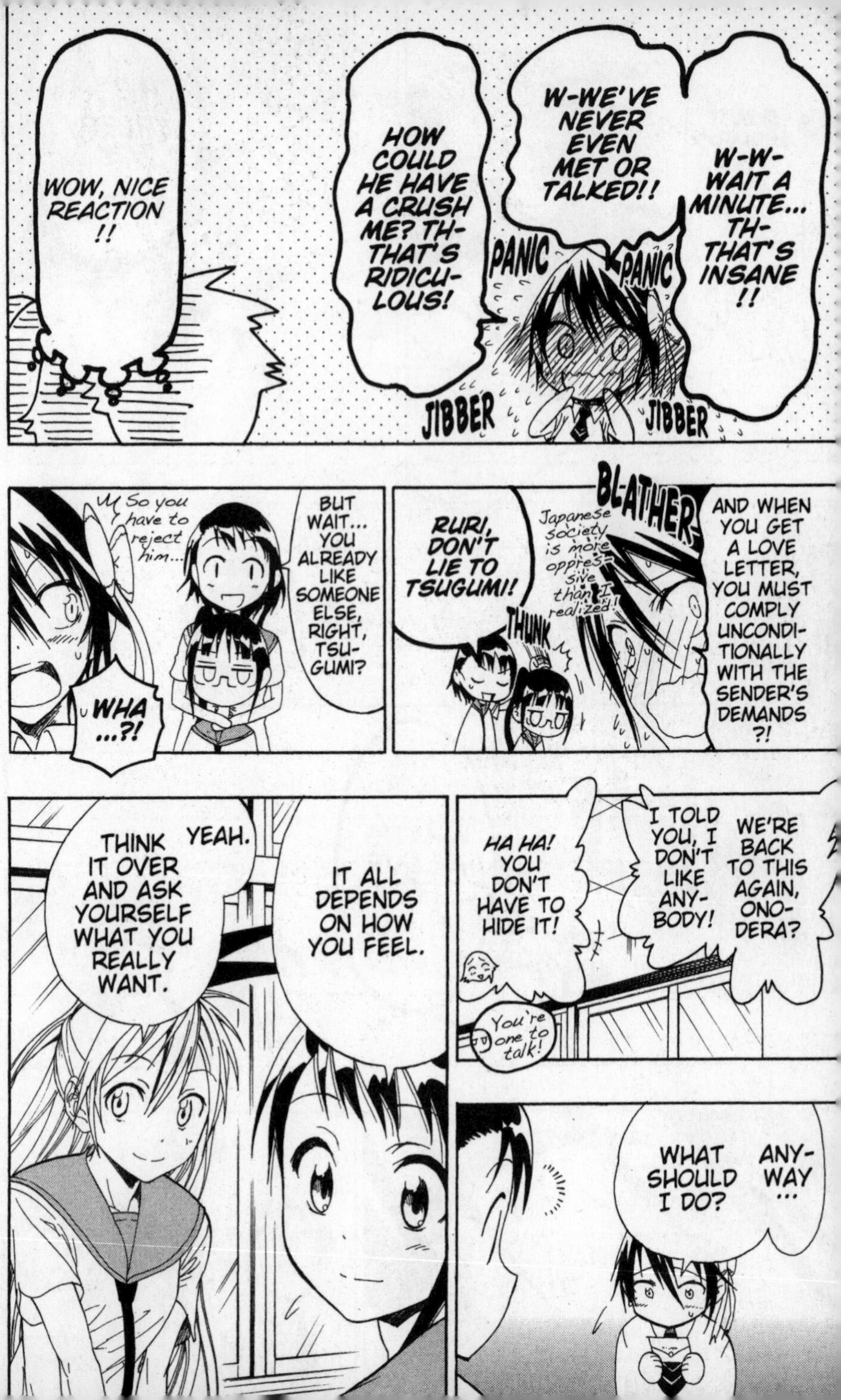
W-W-WAIT A MINUTE... TH-THAT'S INSANE!!
W-WE'VE NEVER EVEN MET OR TALKED!!
PANIC
PANIC
HOW COULD HE HAVE A CRUSH ME? TH-THAT'S RIDICULOUS!
JIBBER
JIBBER
WOW, NICE REACTION!!
BLATHER
AND WHEN YOU GET A LOVE LETTER, YOU MUST COMPLY UNCONDITIONALLY WITH THE SENDER'S DEMANDS?!
Japanese society is more oppressive than I realized!
RURI, DON'T LIE TO TSUGUMI!
THUNK
BUT WAIT... YOU ALREADY LIKE SOMEONE ELSE, RIGHT, TSUGUMI?
So you have to reject him...
WHA...?!
WE'RE BACK TO THIS AGAIN, ONODERA?
I TOLD YOU, I DON'T LIKE ANYBODY!
HA HA! YOU DON'T HAVE TO HIDE IT!
You're one to talk!
ANYWAY...
WHAT SHOULD I DO?
IT ALL DEPENDS ON HOW YOU FEEL.
YEAH.
THINK IT OVER AND ASK YOURSELF WHAT YOU REALLY WANT.

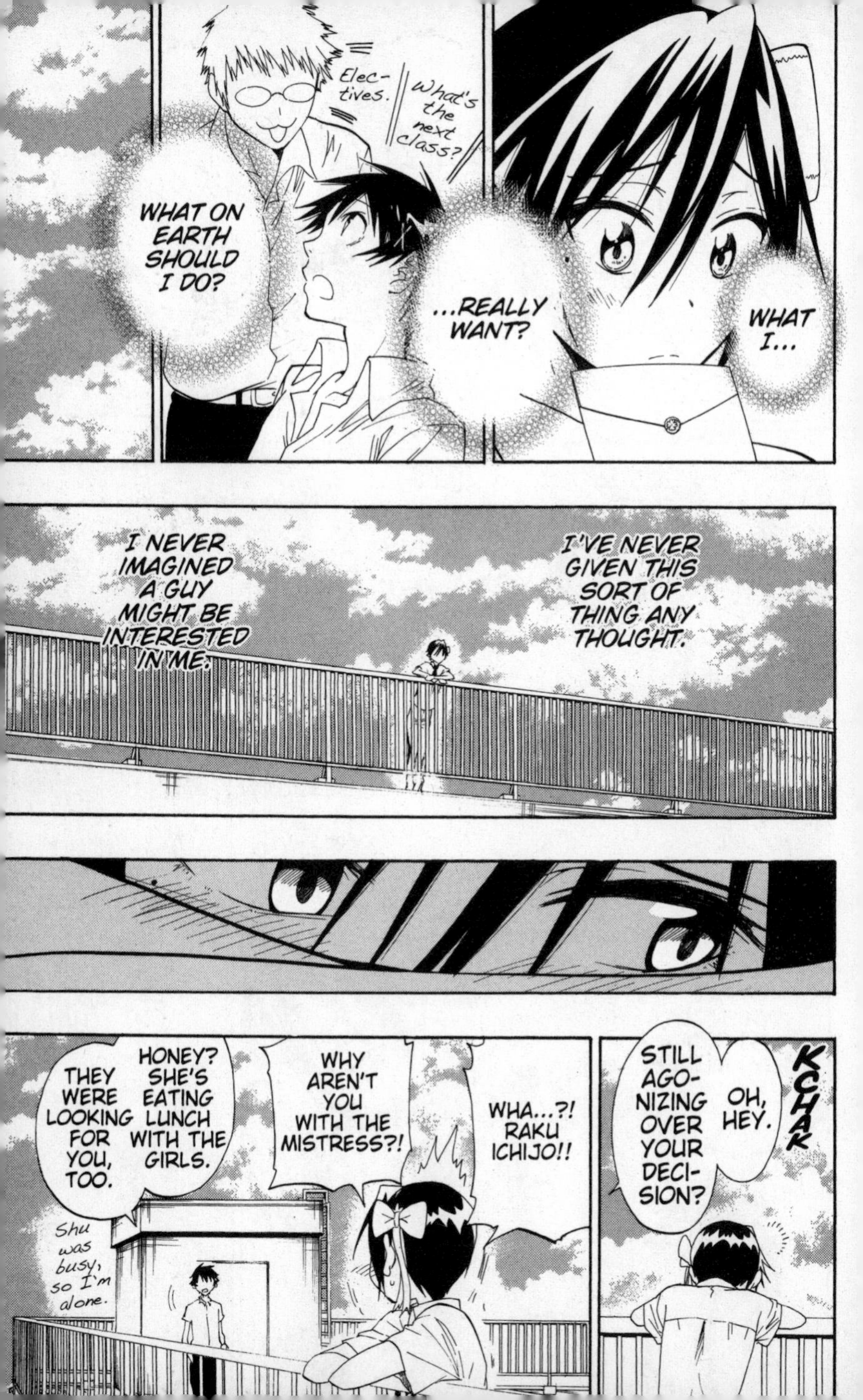
WHAT I...
...REALLY WANT?
What's the next class?
Electives.
WHAT ON EARTH SHOULD I DO?
I'VE NEVER GIVEN THIS SORT OF THING ANY THOUGHT.
I NEVER IMAGINED A GUY MIGHT BE INTERESTED IN ME.
KCHAK
OH, HEY.
STILL AGONIZING OVER YOUR DECISION?
WHA...?! RAKU ICHIJO!!
WHY AREN'T YOU WITH THE MISTRESS?!
HONEY? SHE'S EATING LUNCH WITH THE GIRLS.
THEY WERE LOOKING FOR YOU, TOO.
Shu was busy, so I'm alone.

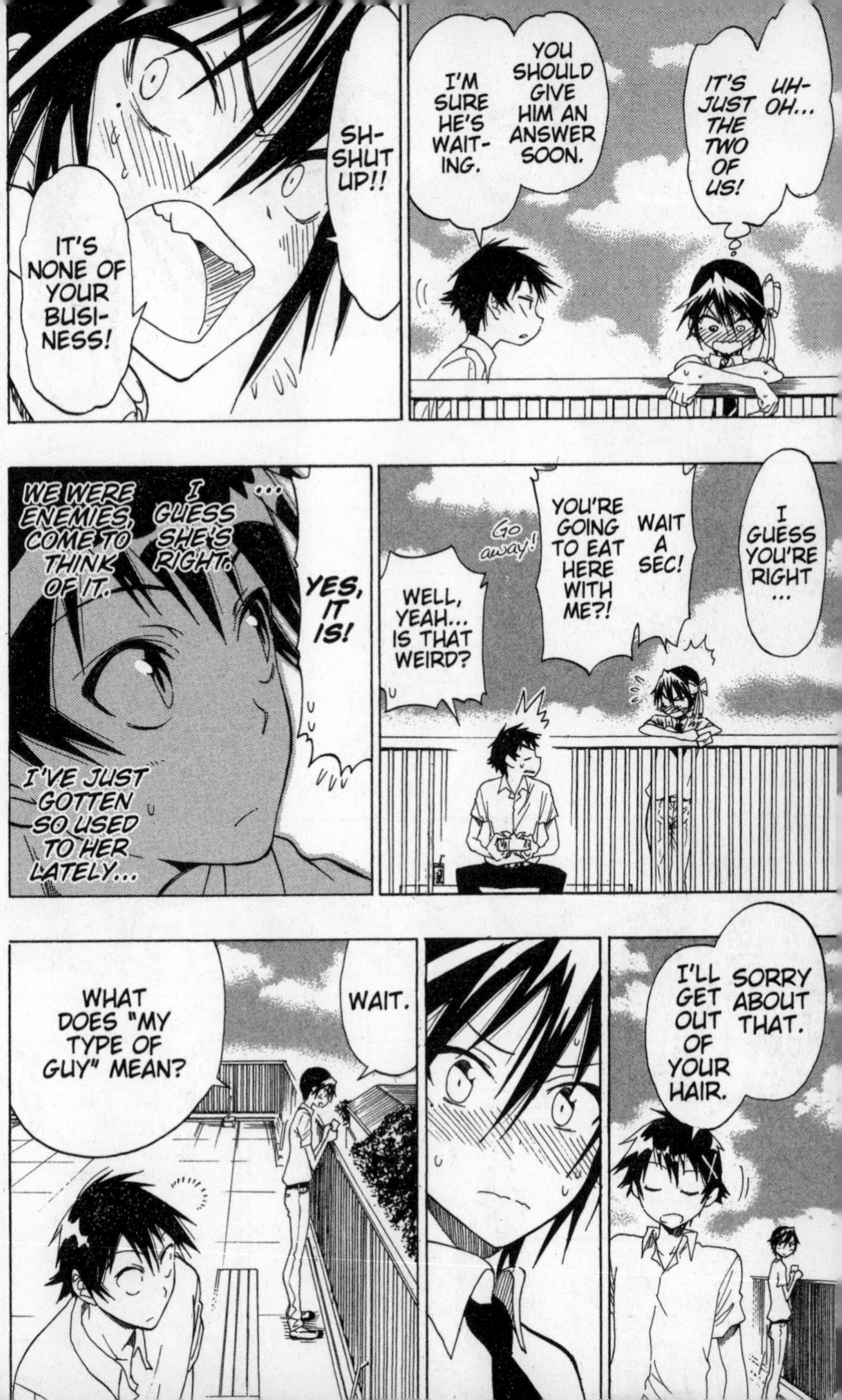
UH-OH...
IT'S JUST THE TWO OF US!
YOU SHOULD GIVE HIM AN ANSWER SOON.
I'M SURE HE'S WAIT-ING.
SH-SHUT UP!!
IT'S NONE OF YOUR BUSI-NESS!
I GUESS YOU'RE RIGHT...
WAIT A SEC!
YOU'RE GOING TO EAT HERE WITH ME?!
Go away!
WELL, YEAH... IS THAT WEIRD?
YES, IT IS!
... I GUESS SHE'S RIGHT.
WE WERE ENEMIES, COME TO THINK OF IT.
I'VE JUST GOTTEN SO USED TO HER LATELY...
SORRY ABOUT THAT.
I'LL GET OUT OF YOUR HAIR.
WAIT.
WHAT DOES "MY TYPE OF GUY" MEAN?

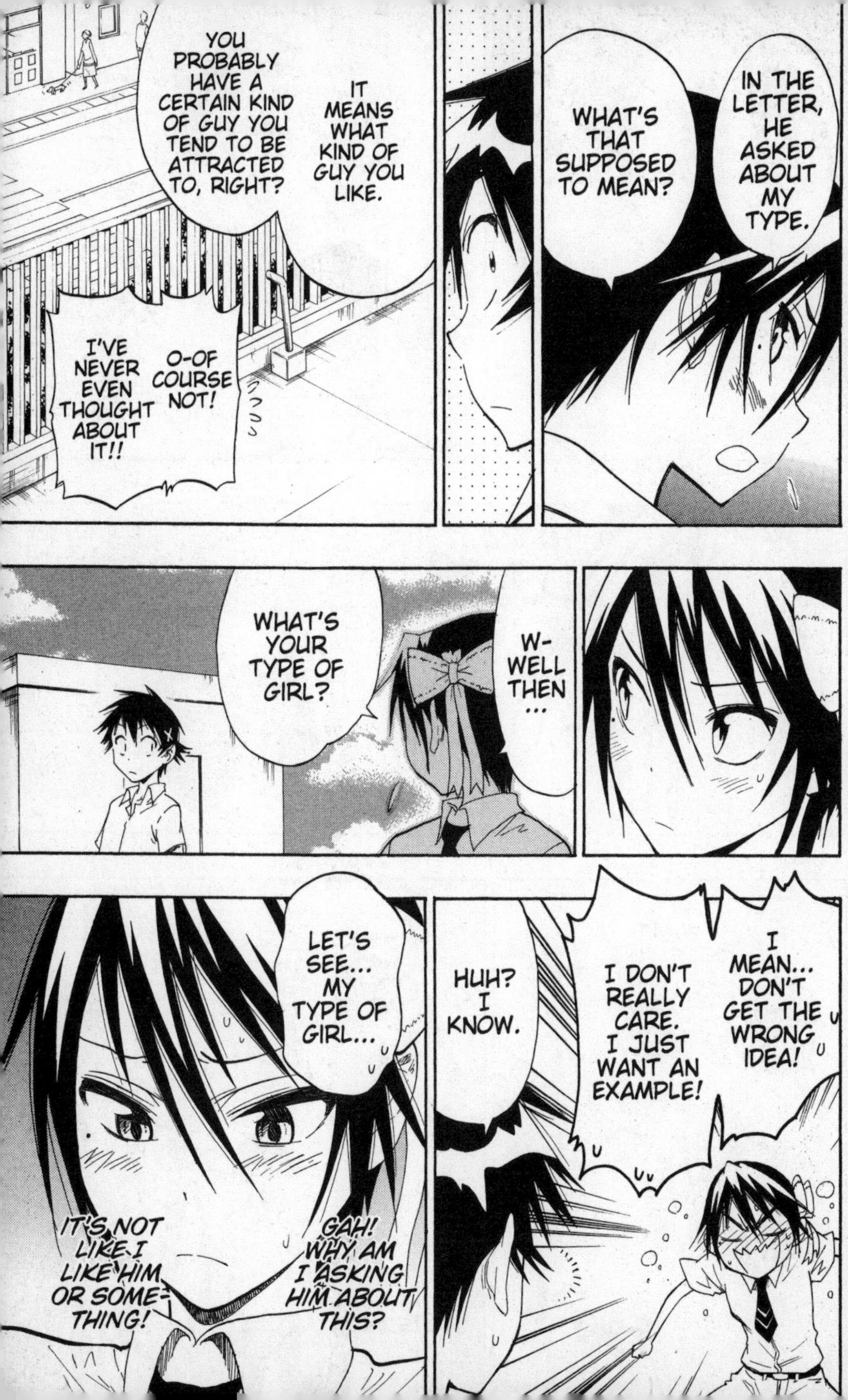
IN THE LETTER, HE ASKED ABOUT MY TYPE.
WHAT'S THAT SUPPOSED TO MEAN?
IT MEANS WHAT KIND OF GUY YOU LIKE.
YOU PROBABLY HAVE A CERTAIN KIND OF GUY YOU TEND TO BE ATTRACTED TO, RIGHT?
O-OF COURSE NOT!
I'VE NEVER EVEN THOUGHT ABOUT IT!!
W-WELL THEN...
WHAT'S YOUR TYPE OF GIRL?
I MEAN... DON'T GET THE WRONG IDEA!
I DON'T REALLY CARE. I JUST WANT AN EXAMPLE!
HUH? I KNOW.
LET'S SEE... MY TYPE OF GIRL...
GAH! WHY AM I ASKING HIM ABOUT THIS?
IT'S NOT LIKE I LIKE HIM OR SOME-THING!

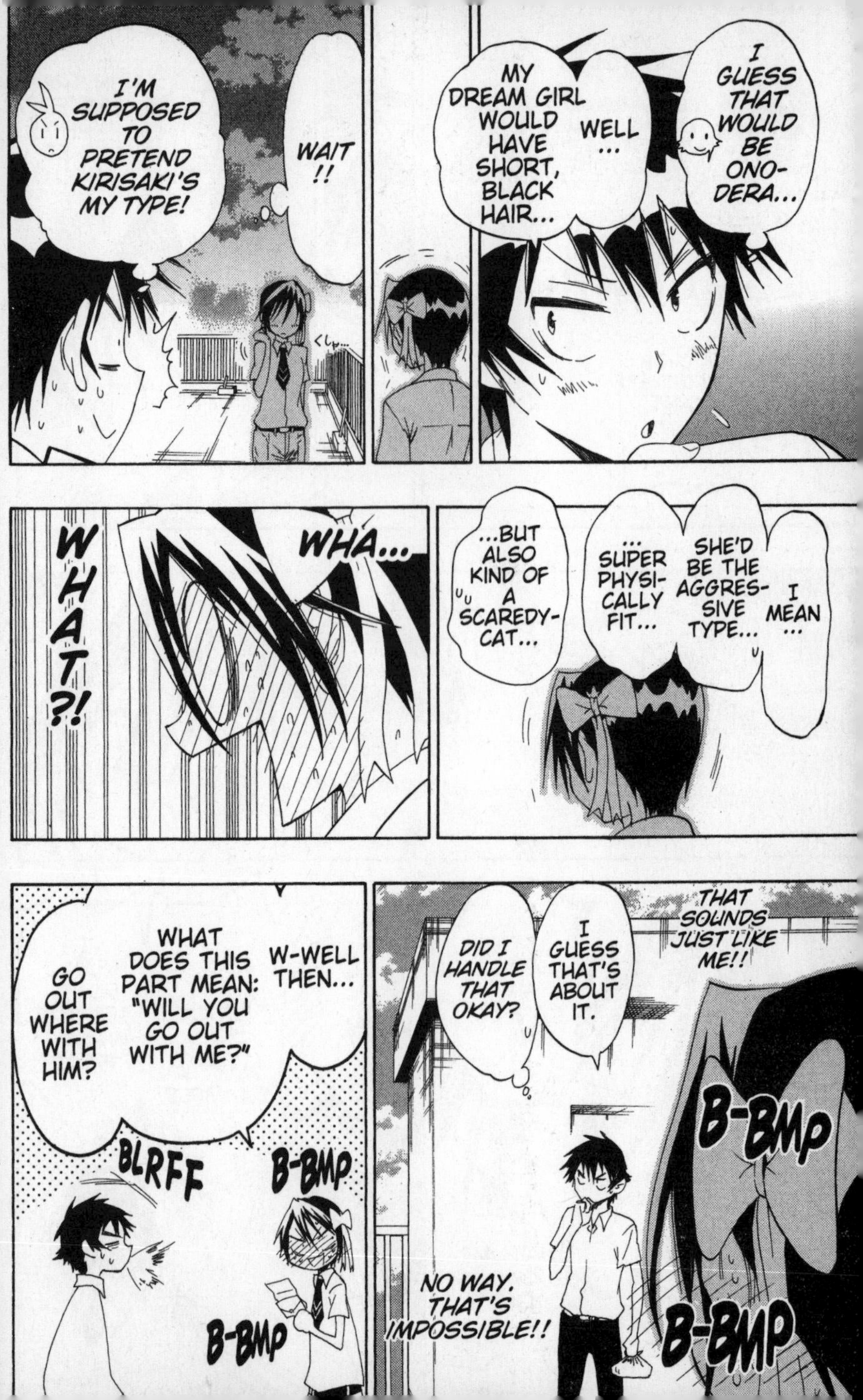
I GUESS THAT WOULD BE ONODERA...
WELL...
MY DREAM GIRL WOULD HAVE SHORT, BLACK HAIR...
くしゃ...
WAIT!!
I'M SUPPOSED TO PRETEND KIRISAKI'S MY TYPE!
I MEAN...
SHE'D BE THE AGGRESSIVE TYPE...
...SUPER PHYSICALLY FIT...
...BUT ALSO KIND OF A SCAREDY-CAT...
WHA...
WHAT?!
THAT SOUNDS JUST LIKE ME!!
I GUESS THAT'S ABOUT IT.
DID I HANDLE THAT OKAY?
B-BMP
NO WAY. THAT'S IMPOSSIBLE!!
B-BMP
W-WELL THEN...
WHAT DOES THIS PART MEAN: "WILL YOU GO OUT WITH ME?"
GO OUT WHERE WITH HIM?
B-BMP
BLRFF
B-BMP

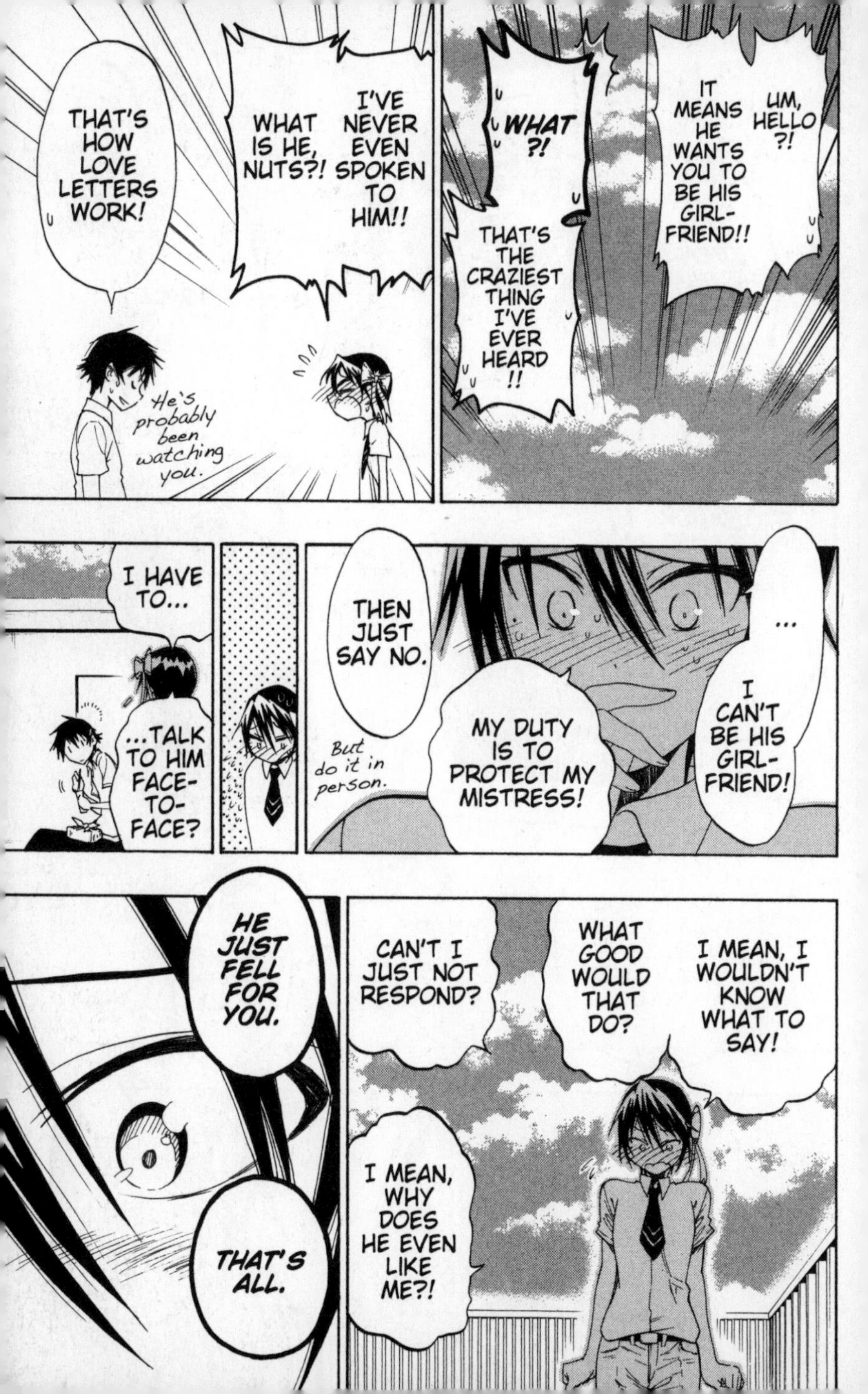
UM, HELLO?!
IT MEANS HE WANTS YOU TO BE HIS GIRL-FRIEND!!
WHAT?!
THAT'S THE CRAZIEST THING I'VE EVER HEARD!!
I'VE NEVER EVEN SPOKEN TO HIM!!
WHAT IS HE, NUTS?!
THAT'S HOW LOVE LETTERS WORK!
He's probably been watching you.
...
I CAN'T BE HIS GIRL-FRIEND!
MY DUTY IS TO PROTECT MY MISTRESS!
THEN JUST SAY NO.
But do it in person.
I HAVE TO...
...TALK TO HIM FACE-TO-FACE?
I MEAN, I WOULDN'T KNOW WHAT TO SAY!
WHAT GOOD WOULD THAT DO?
CAN'T I JUST NOT RESPOND?
I MEAN, WHY DOES HE EVEN LIKE ME?!
HE JUST FELL FOR YOU.
THAT'S ALL.

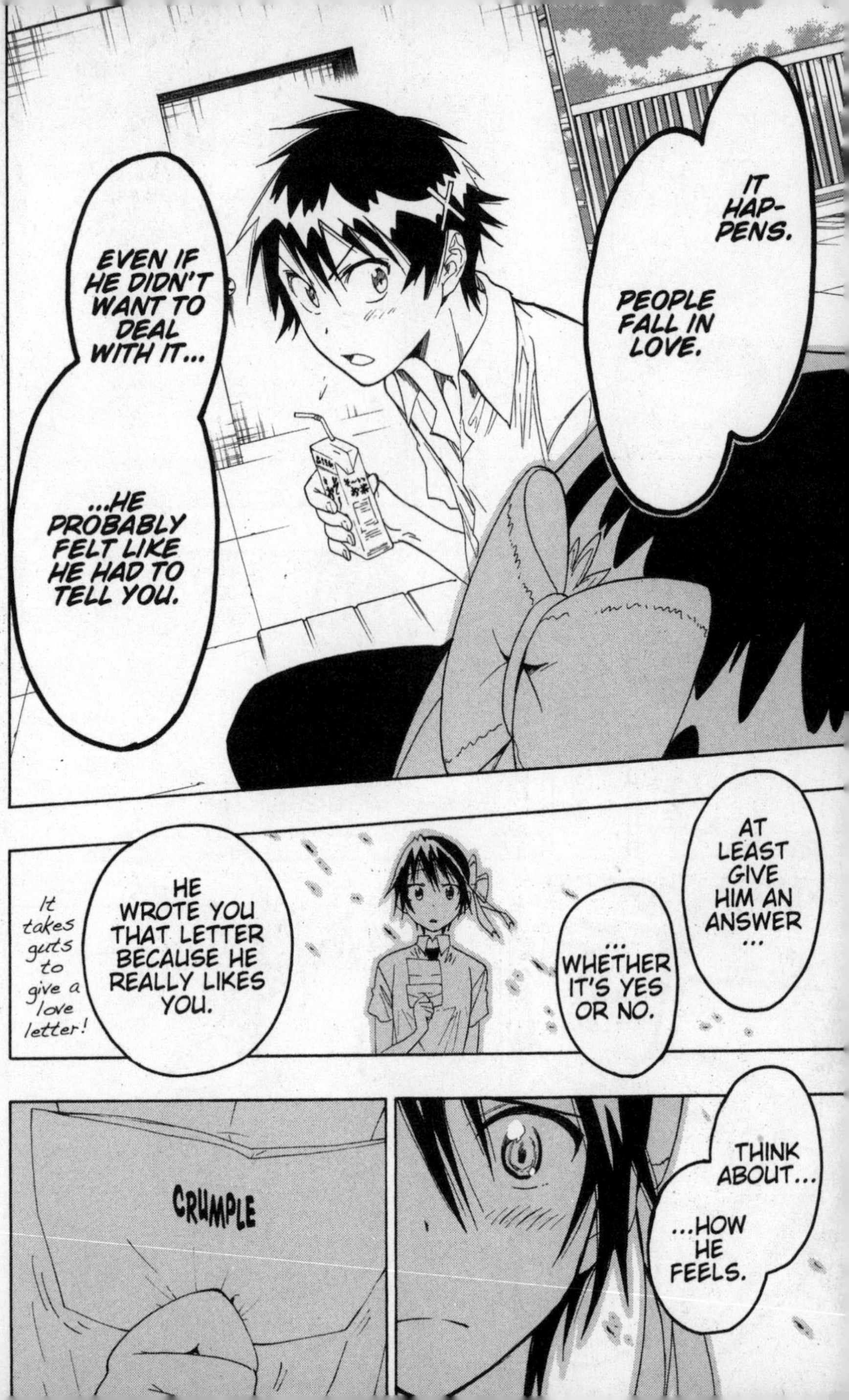
IT HAPPENS.
PEOPLE FALL IN LOVE.
EVEN IF HE DIDN'T WANT TO DEAL WITH IT...
...HE PROBABLY FELT LIKE HE HAD TO TELL YOU.
AT LEAST GIVE HIM AN ANSWER...
...WHETHER IT'S YES OR NO.
HE WROTE YOU THAT LETTER BECAUSE HE REALLY LIKES YOU.
It takes guts to give a love letter!
THINK ABOUT...
...HOW HE FEELS.
CRUMPLE

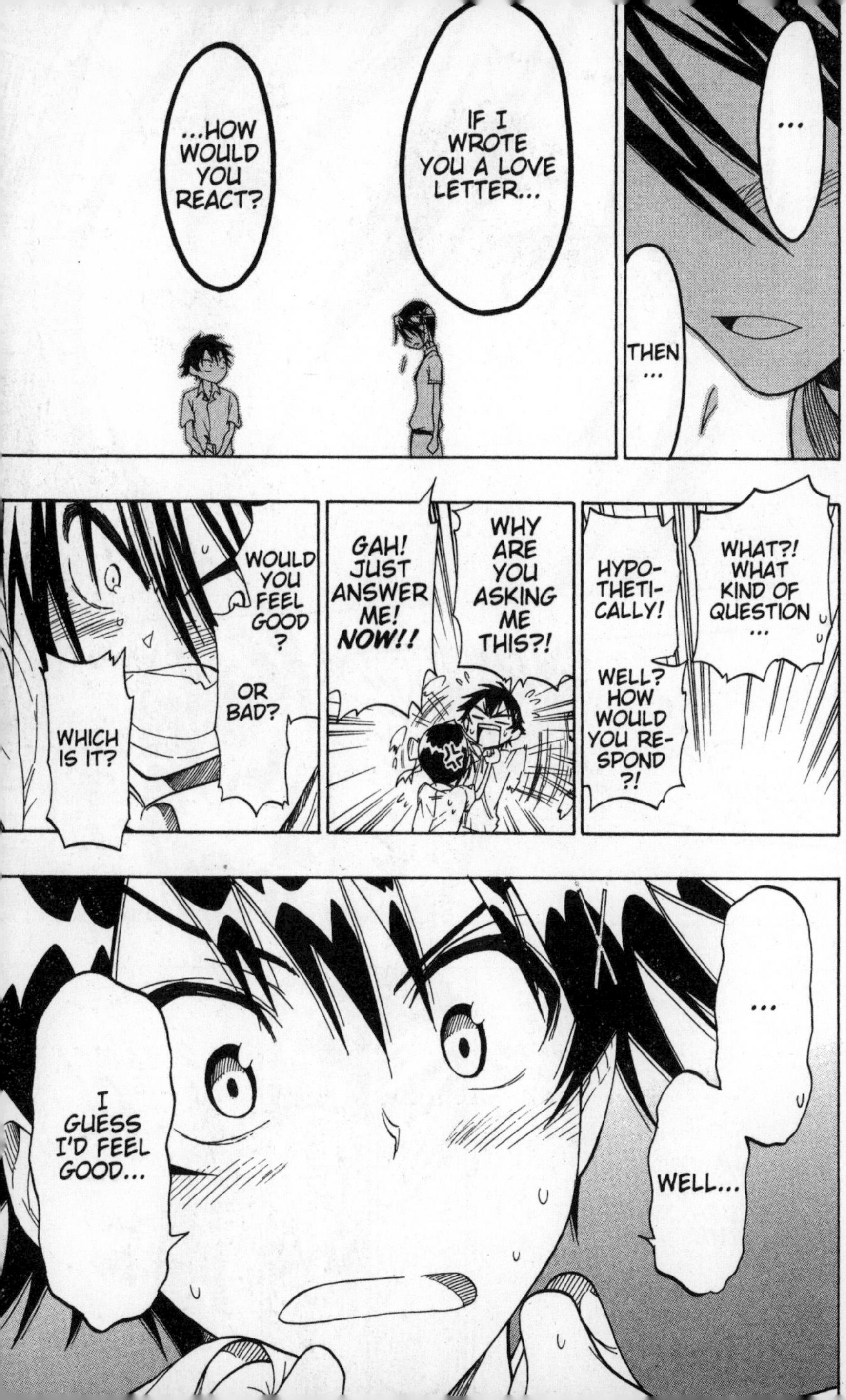
...
THEN...
IF I WROTE YOU A LOVE LETTER...
...HOW WOULD YOU REACT?
WHAT?! WHAT KIND OF QUESTION...
HYPO-THETI-CALLY!
WELL? HOW WOULD YOU RE-SPOND?!
WHY ARE YOU ASKING ME THIS?!
GAH! JUST ANSWER ME! *NOW!!*
WOULD YOU FEEL GOOD?
OR BAD?
WHICH IS IT?
...
WELL...
I GUESS I'D FEEL GOOD...

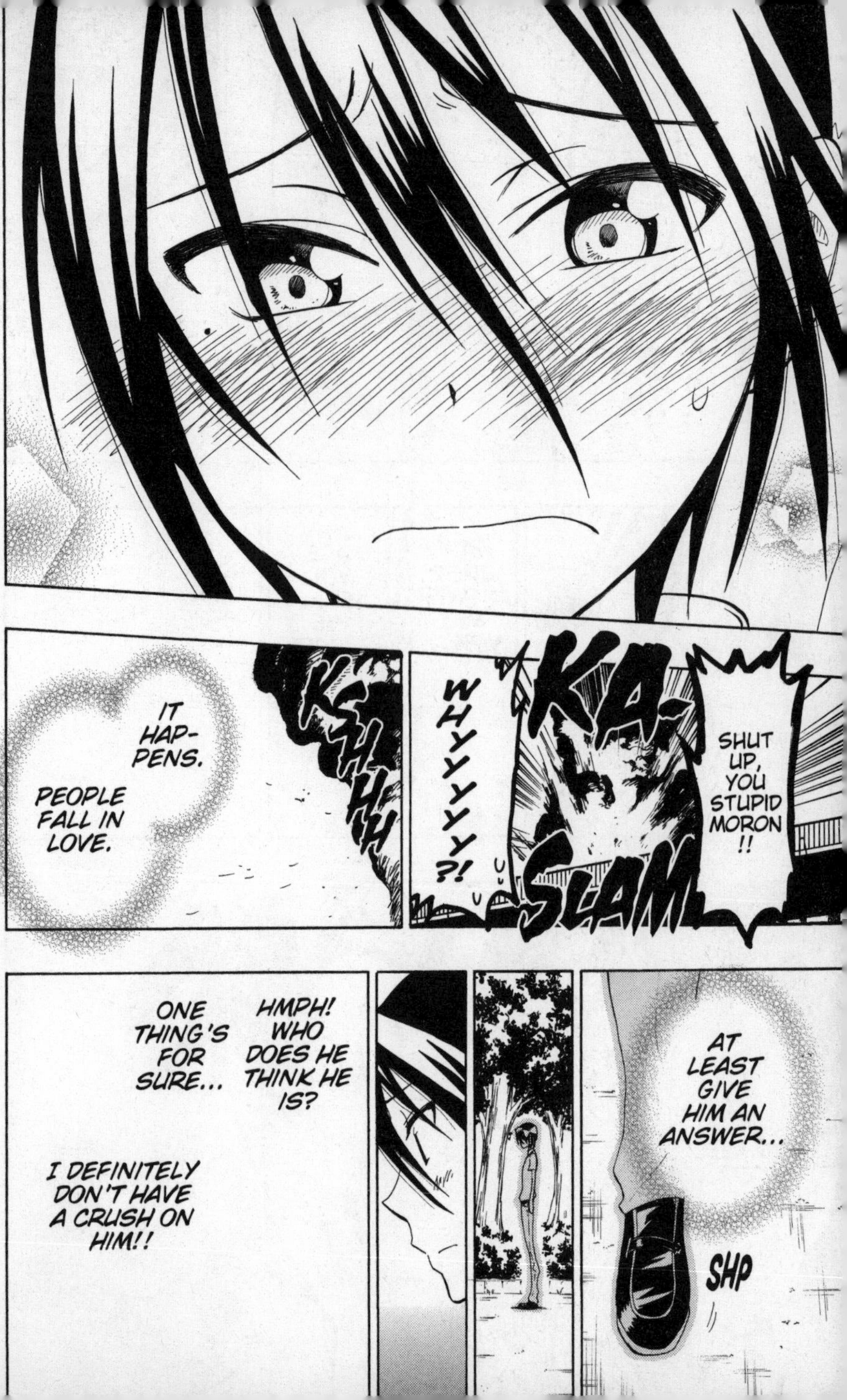
SHUT UP, YOU STUPID MORON!!
KA-SLAM
WHYYYYYYY?!
IT HAP-PENS.
PEOPLE FALL IN LOVE.
AT LEAST GIVE HIM AN ANSWER...
SHP
HMPH! WHO DOES HE THINK HE IS?
ONE THING'S FOR SURE...
I DEFINITELY DON'T HAVE A CRUSH ON HIM!!

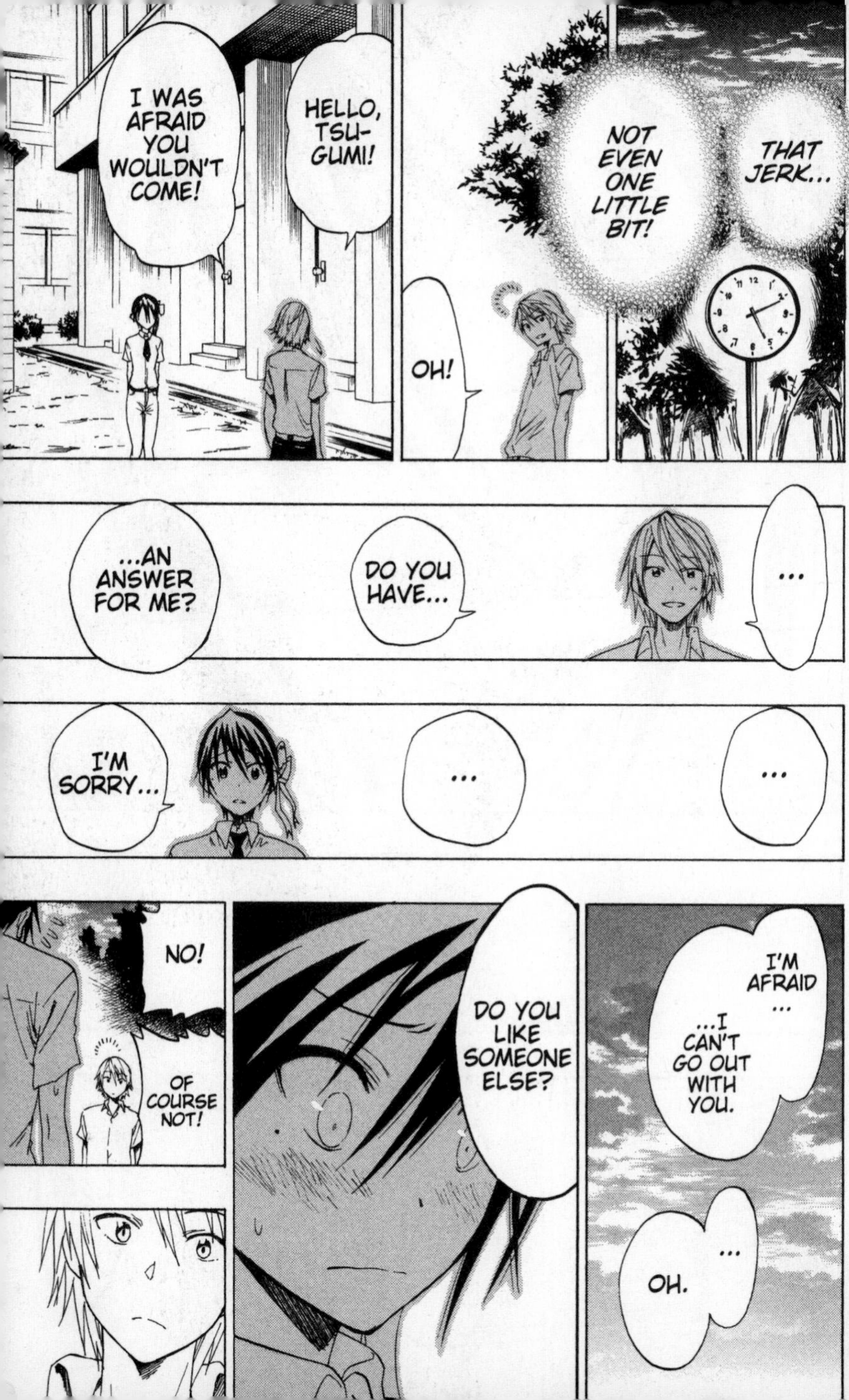
THAT JERK...
NOT EVEN ONE LITTLE BIT!
OH!
HELLO, TSUGUMI!
I WAS AFRAID YOU WOULDN'T COME!
...
DO YOU HAVE...
...AN ANSWER FOR ME?
...
...
I'M SORRY...
I'M AFRAID ...
...I CAN'T GO OUT WITH YOU.
...
OH.
DO YOU LIKE SOMEONE ELSE?
NO!
OF COURSE NOT!

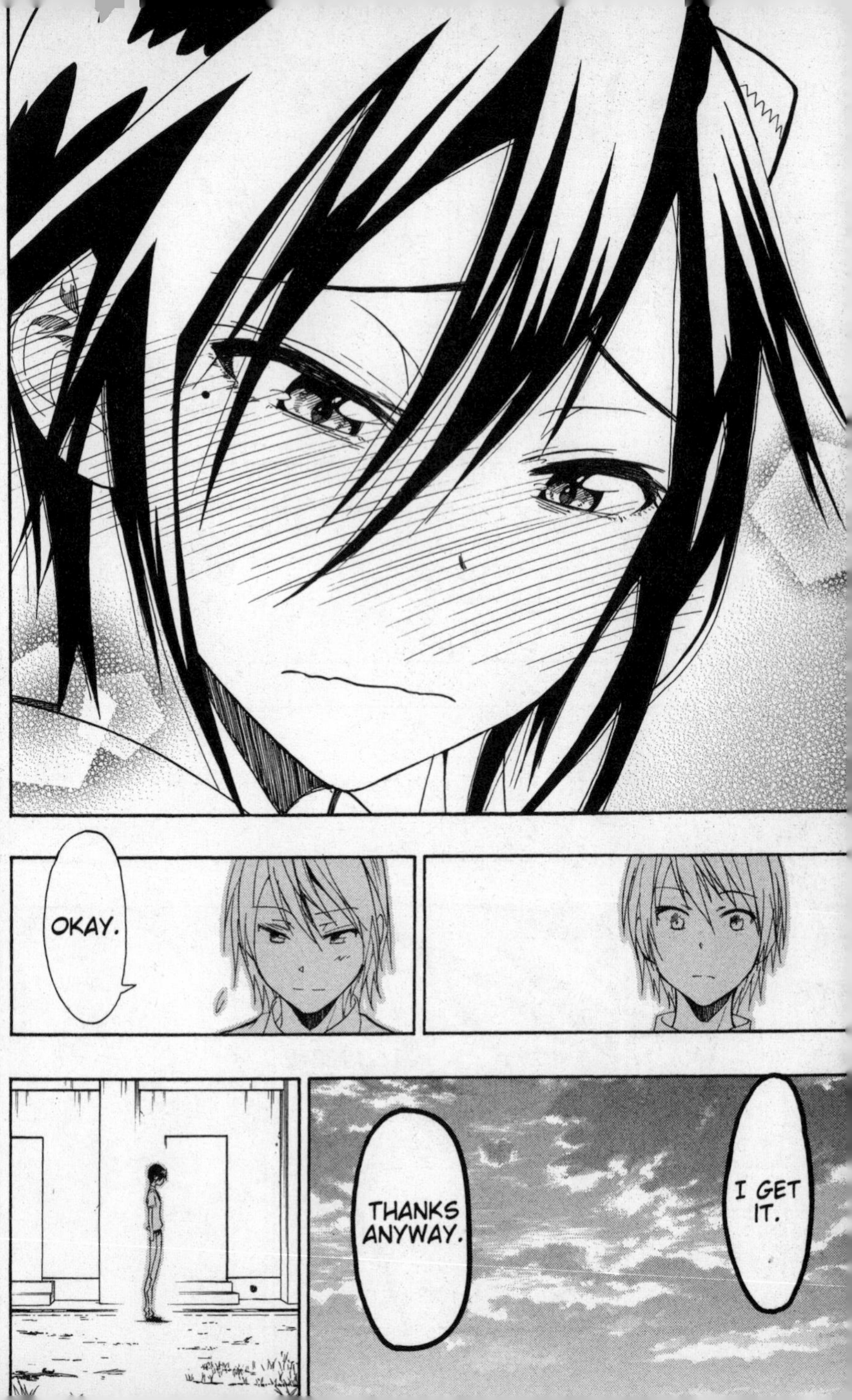
OKAY.
I GET IT.
THANKS ANYWAY.

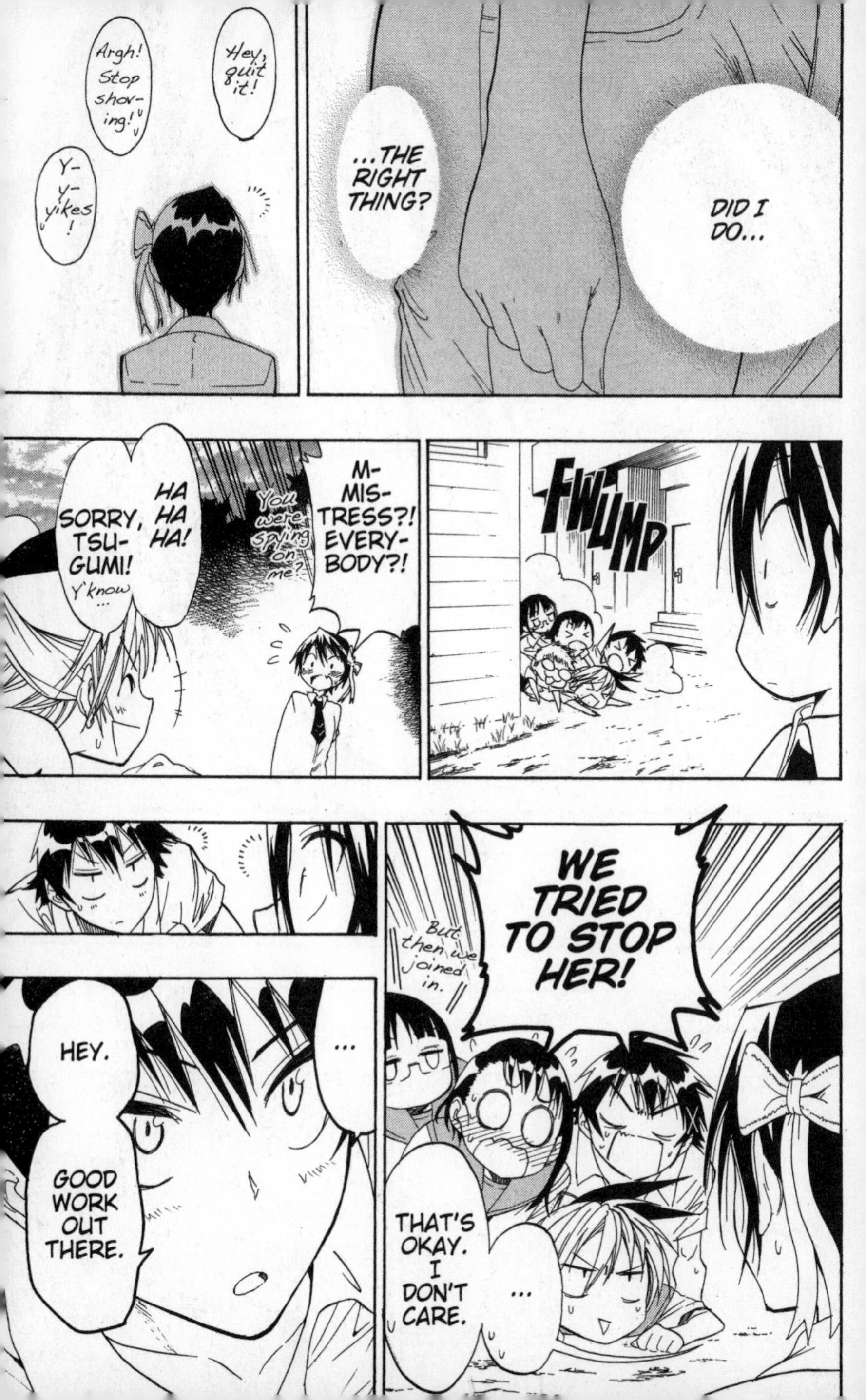
DID I DO...
...THE RIGHT THING?
Hey, quit it!
Argh! Stop shov-ing!
Y-y-yikes!
FWUMP
M-MIS-TRESS?! EVERY-BODY?!
You were spying on me?
HA HA HA!
SORRY, TSU-GUMI! Y'know...
WE TRIED TO STOP HER!
But then we joined in.
...
THAT'S OKAY. I DON'T CARE.
...
HEY.
GOOD WORK OUT THERE.

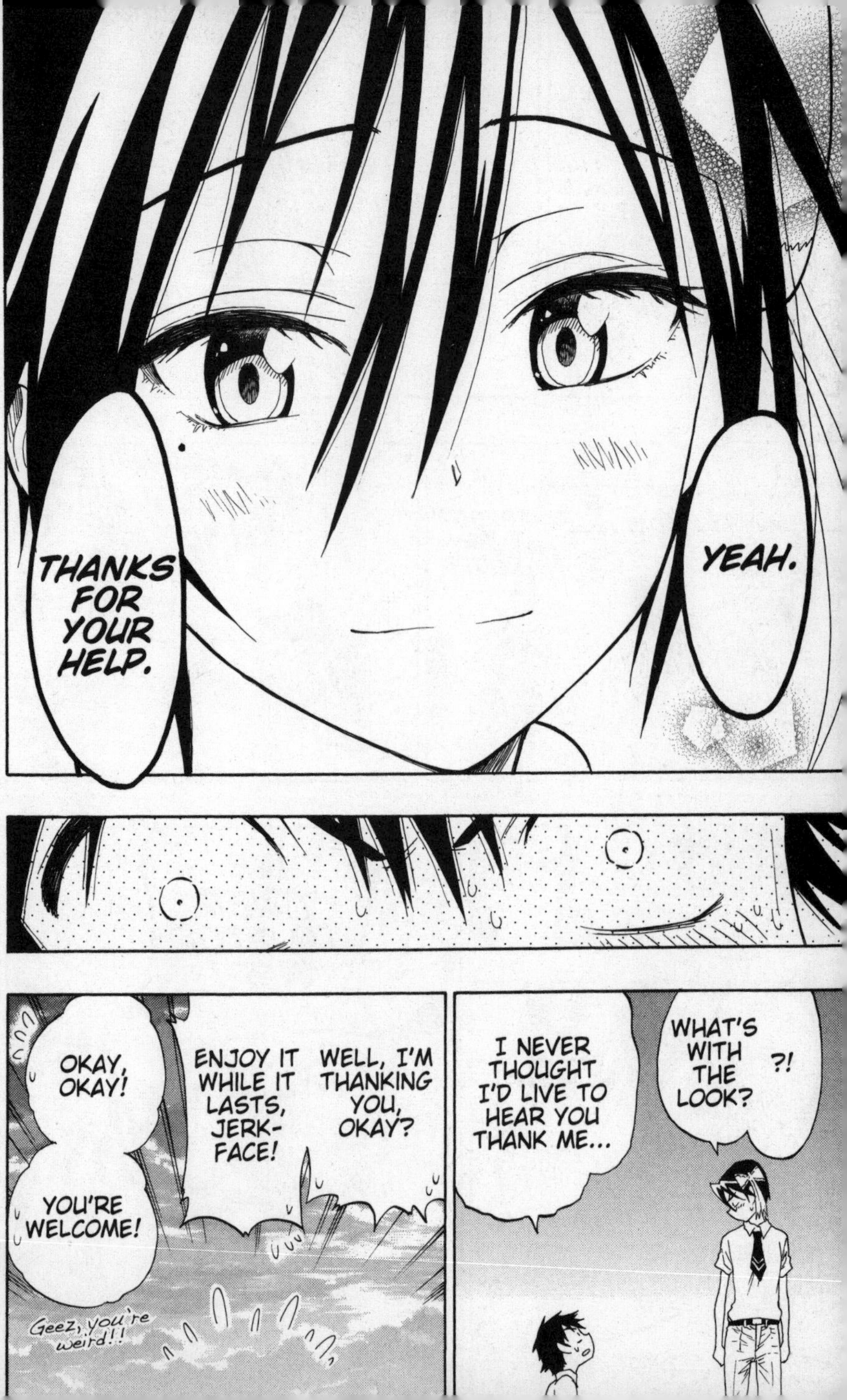
YEAH.
THANKS FOR YOUR HELP.
?!
WHAT'S WITH THE LOOK?
I NEVER THOUGHT I'D LIVE TO HEAR YOU THANK ME...
WELL, I'M THANKING YOU, OKAY?
ENJOY IT WHILE IT LASTS, JERK-FACE!
OKAY, OKAY!
YOU'RE WELCOME!
Geez, you're weird!!

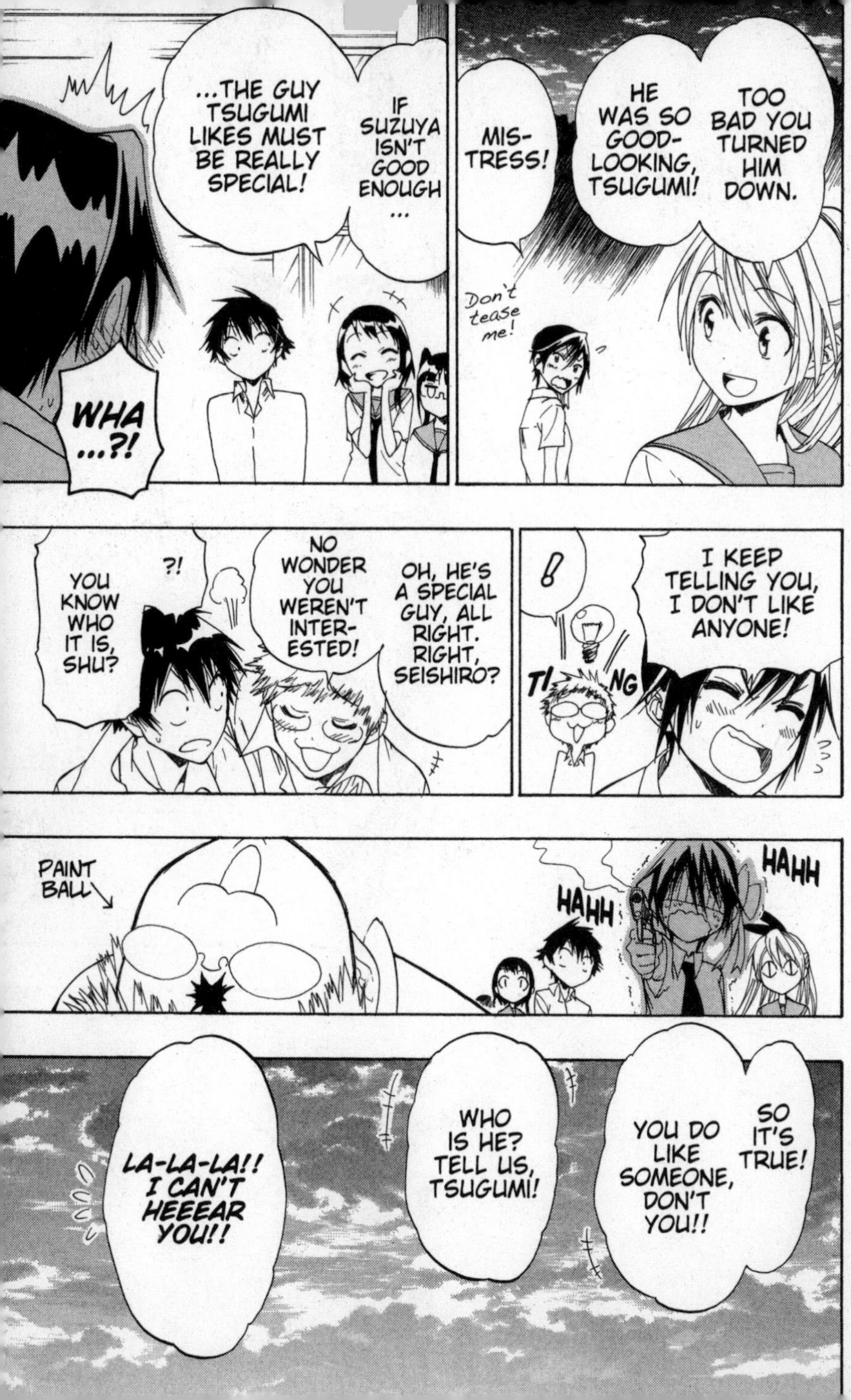
TOO BAD YOU TURNED HIM DOWN.
HE WAS SO GOOD-LOOKING, TSUGUMI!
MIS-TRESS!
Don't tease me!
IF SUZUYA ISN'T GOOD ENOUGH ...
...THE GUY TSUGUMI LIKES MUST BE REALLY SPECIAL!
WHA ...?!
I KEEP TELLING YOU, I DON'T LIKE ANYONE!
!
TING
OH, HE'S A SPECIAL GUY, ALL RIGHT. RIGHT, SEISHIRO?
NO WONDER YOU WEREN'T INTER-ESTED!
?!
YOU KNOW WHO IT IS, SHU?
HAHH
HAHH
PAINT BALL
SO IT'S TRUE!
YOU DO LIKE SOMEONE, DON'T YOU!!
WHO IS HE? TELL US, TSUGUMI!
LA-LA-LA!! I CAN'T HEEEAR YOU!!

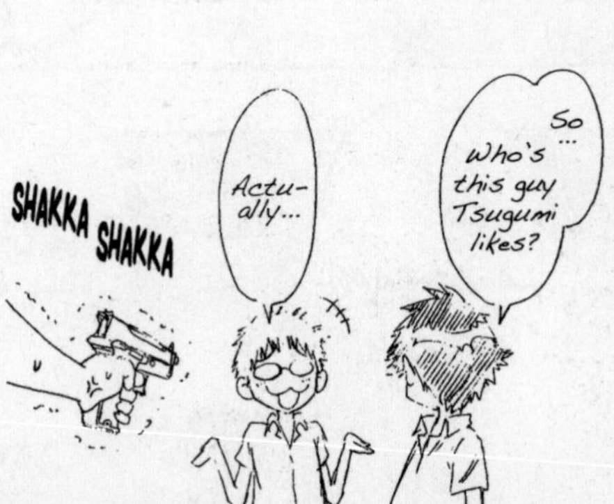
So... Who's this guy Tsugumi likes?
Actu-ally...
SHAKKA SHAKKA

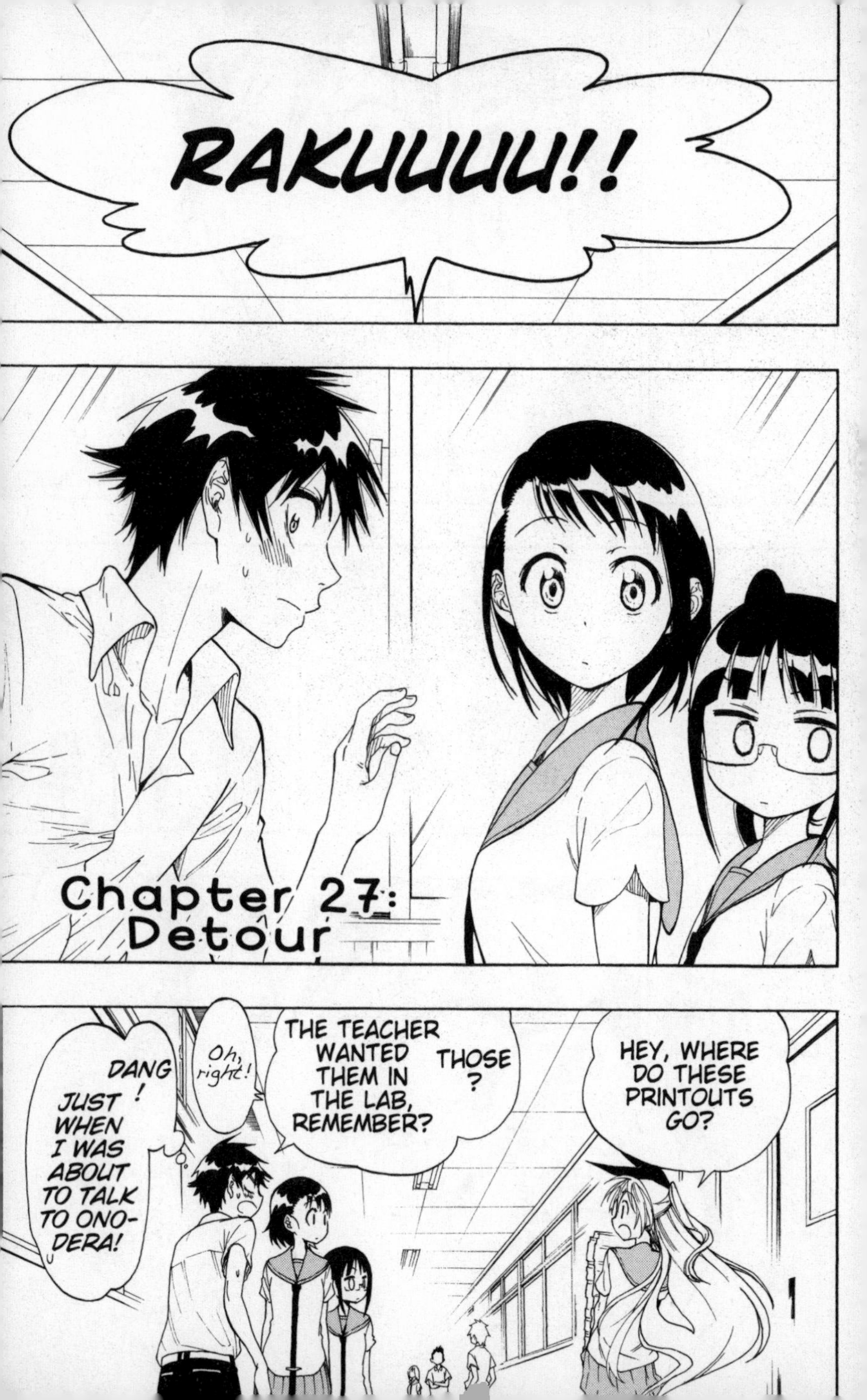
RAKUUUUU!!
Chapter 27: Detour
HEY, WHERE DO THESE PRINTOUTS GO?
THOSE?
THE TEACHER WANTED THEM IN THE LAB, REMEMBER?
Oh, right!
DANG! JUST WHEN I WAS ABOUT TO TALK TO ONO-DERA!

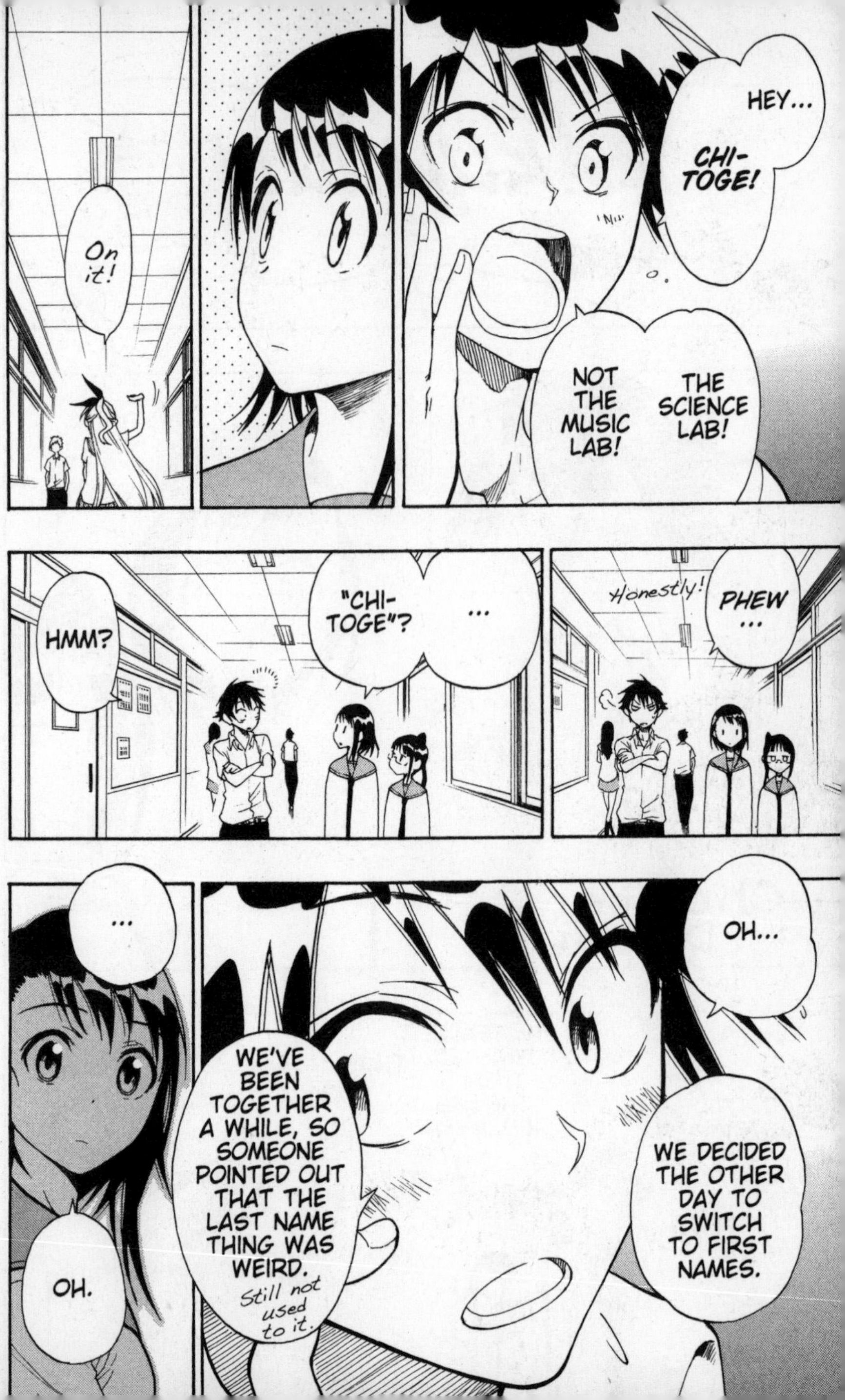
HEY... CHI-TOGE!
THE SCIENCE LAB!
NOT THE MUSIC LAB!
On it!
PHEW ...
Honestly!
...
"CHI-TOGE"?
HMM?
OH...
WE DECIDED THE OTHER DAY TO SWITCH TO FIRST NAMES.
WE'VE BEEN TOGETHER A WHILE, SO SOMEONE POINTED OUT THAT THE LAST NAME THING WAS WEIRD.
Still not used to it.
...
OH.

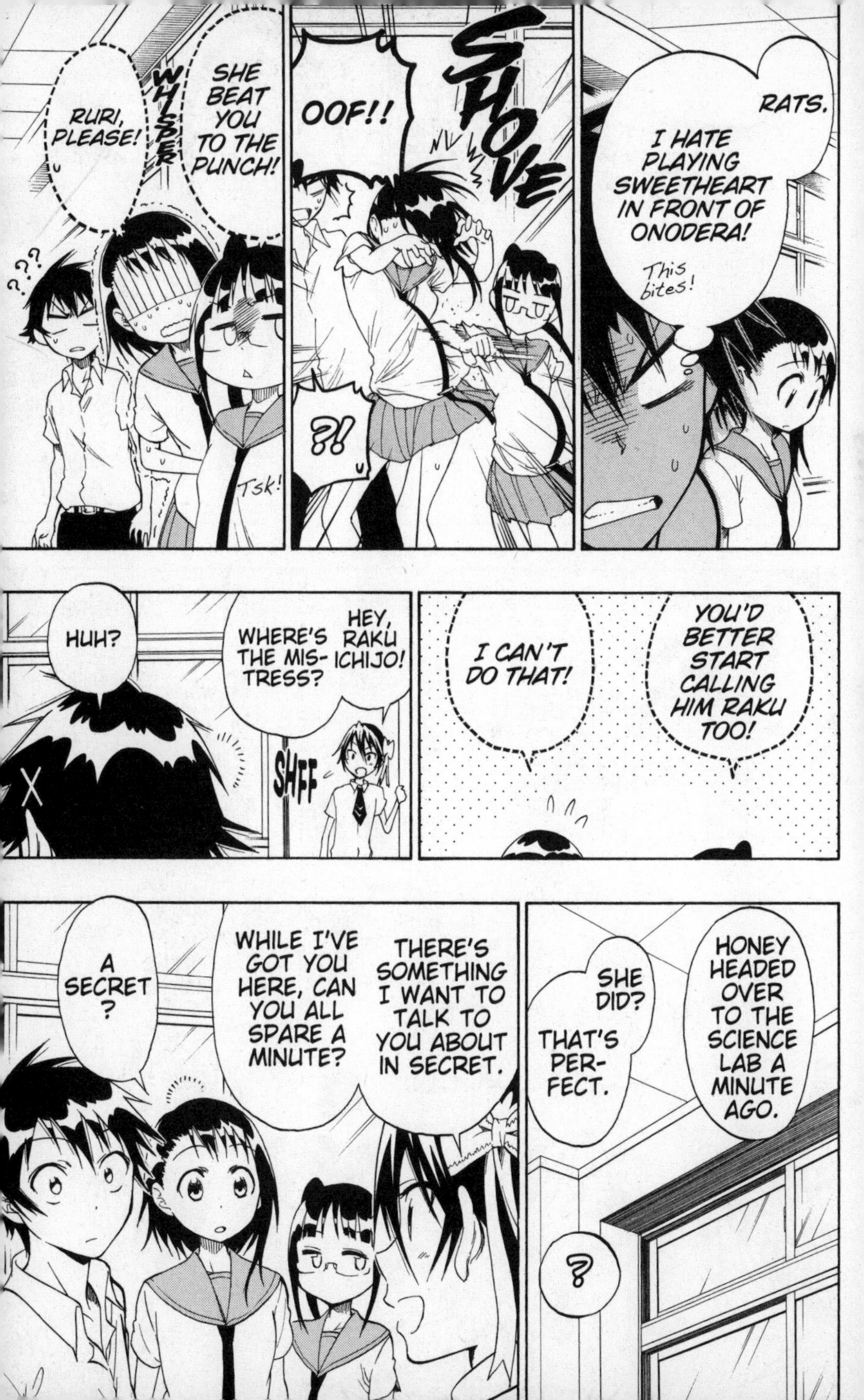
RATS.
I HATE PLAYING SWEETHEART IN FRONT OF ONODERA!
This bites!
SHOVE
OOF!!
?!
SHE BEAT YOU TO THE PUNCH!
WHISPER
RURI, PLEASE!
???
Tsk!
YOU'D BETTER START CALLING HIM RAKU TOO!
I CAN'T DO THAT!
HEY, RAKU ICHIJO!
WHERE'S THE MISTRESS?
SHFF
HUH?
HONEY HEADED OVER TO THE SCIENCE LAB A MINUTE AGO.
SHE DID?
THAT'S PERFECT.
?
THERE'S SOMETHING I WANT TO TALK TO YOU ABOUT IN SECRET.
WHILE I'VE GOT YOU HERE, CAN YOU ALL SPARE A MINUTE?
A SECRET?

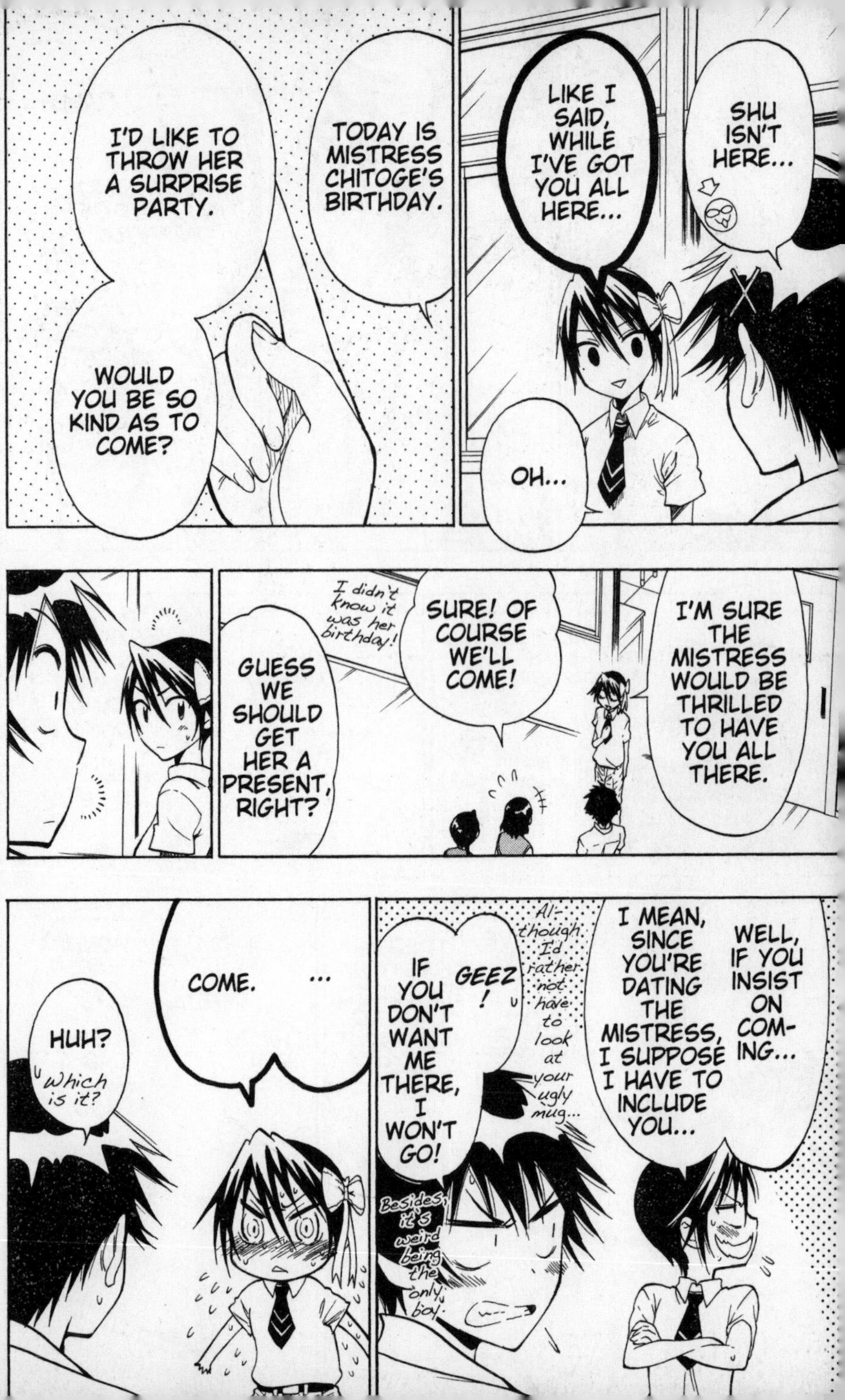
SHU ISN'T HERE...
LIKE I SAID, WHILE I'VE GOT YOU ALL HERE...
OH...
TODAY IS MISTRESS CHITOGE'S BIRTHDAY.
I'D LIKE TO THROW HER A SURPRISE PARTY.
WOULD YOU BE SO KIND AS TO COME?
I'M SURE THE MISTRESS WOULD BE THRILLED TO HAVE YOU ALL THERE.
SURE! OF COURSE WE'LL COME!
I didn't know it was her birthday!
GUESS WE SHOULD GET HER A PRESENT, RIGHT?
WELL, IF YOU INSIST ON COMING...
I MEAN, SINCE YOU'RE DATING THE MISTRESS, I SUPPOSE I HAVE TO INCLUDE YOU...
Although I'd rather not have to look at your ugly mug...
GEEZ!
IF YOU DON'T WANT ME THERE, I WON'T GO!
Besides, it's weird being the only boy.
COME. ...
HUH?
Which is it?

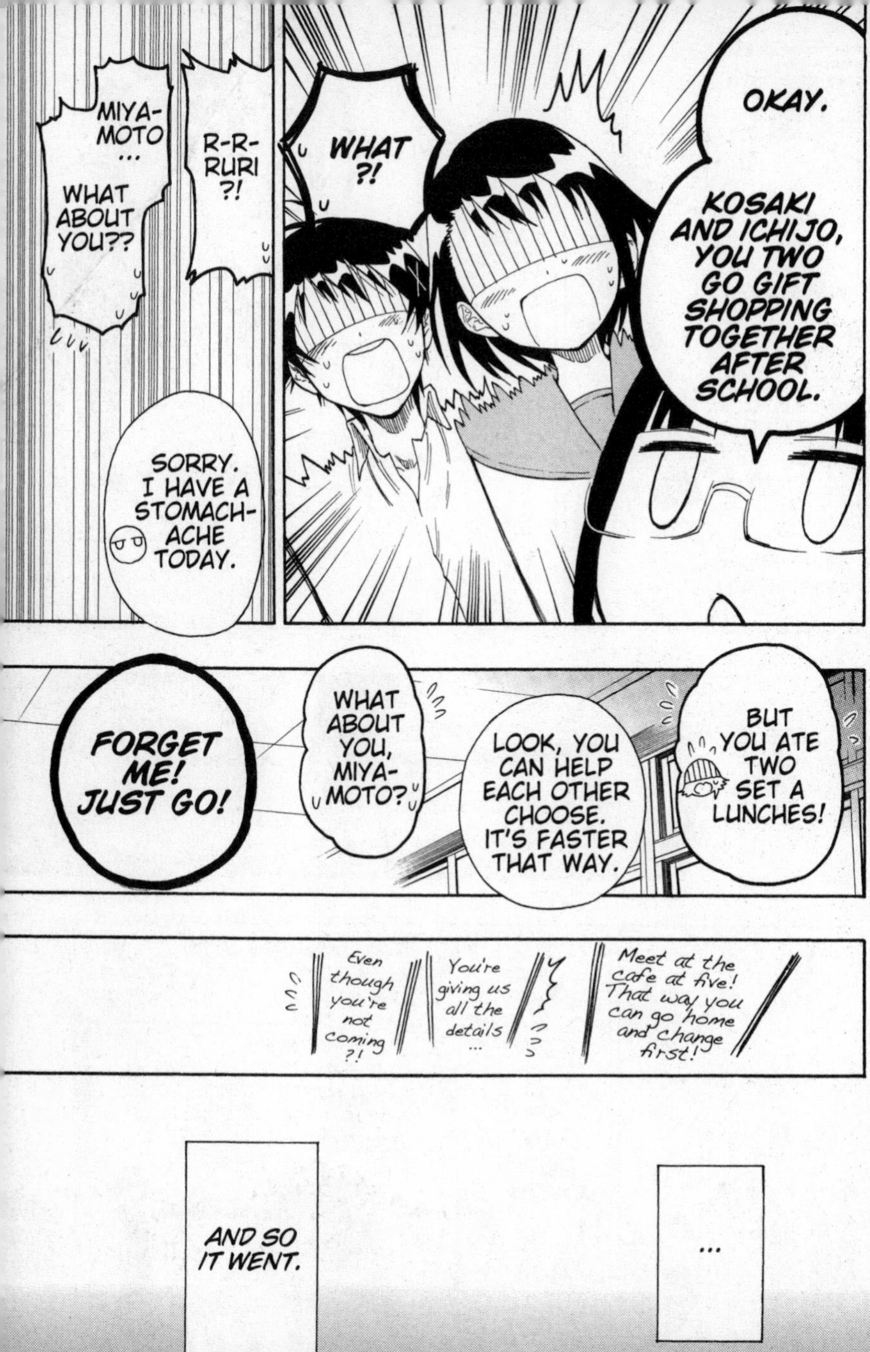
OKAY.
KOSAKI AND ICHIJO, YOU TWO GO GIFT SHOPPING TOGETHER AFTER SCHOOL.
WHAT?!
R-R-RURI?!
MIYA-MOTO... WHAT ABOUT YOU??
SORRY. I HAVE A STOMACH-ACHE TODAY.
BUT YOU ATE TWO SET A LUNCHES!
LOOK, YOU CAN HELP EACH OTHER CHOOSE. IT'S FASTER THAT WAY.
WHAT ABOUT YOU, MIYA-MOTO?
FORGET ME! JUST GO!
Meet at the cafe at five! That way you can go home and change first!
You're giving us all the details...
Even though you're not coming?!
...
AND SO IT WENT.

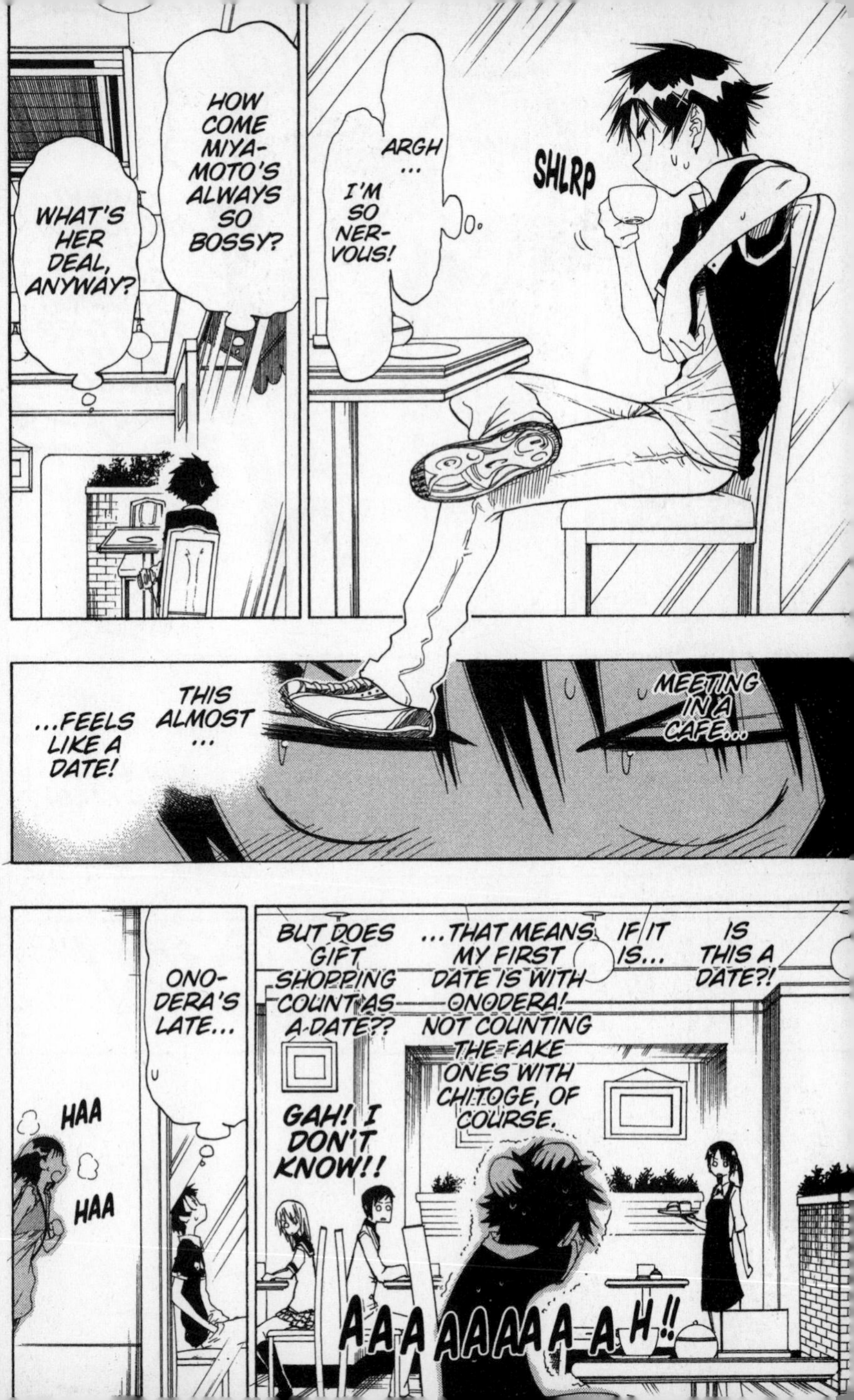
SHLRP
ARGH ... I'M SO NERVOUS!
HOW COME MIYAMOTO'S ALWAYS SO BOSSY?
WHAT'S HER DEAL, ANYWAY?
MEETING IN A CAFE...
THIS ALMOST ...
...FEELS LIKE A DATE!
IS THIS A DATE?!
IF IT IS...
...THAT MEANS MY FIRST DATE IS WITH ONODERA! NOT COUNTING THE FAKE ONES WITH CHITOGE, OF COURSE.
BUT DOES GIFT SHOPPING COUNT AS A DATE??
GAH! I DON'T KNOW!!
AAAAAAAAAH!!
ONODERA'S LATE...
HAA
HAA

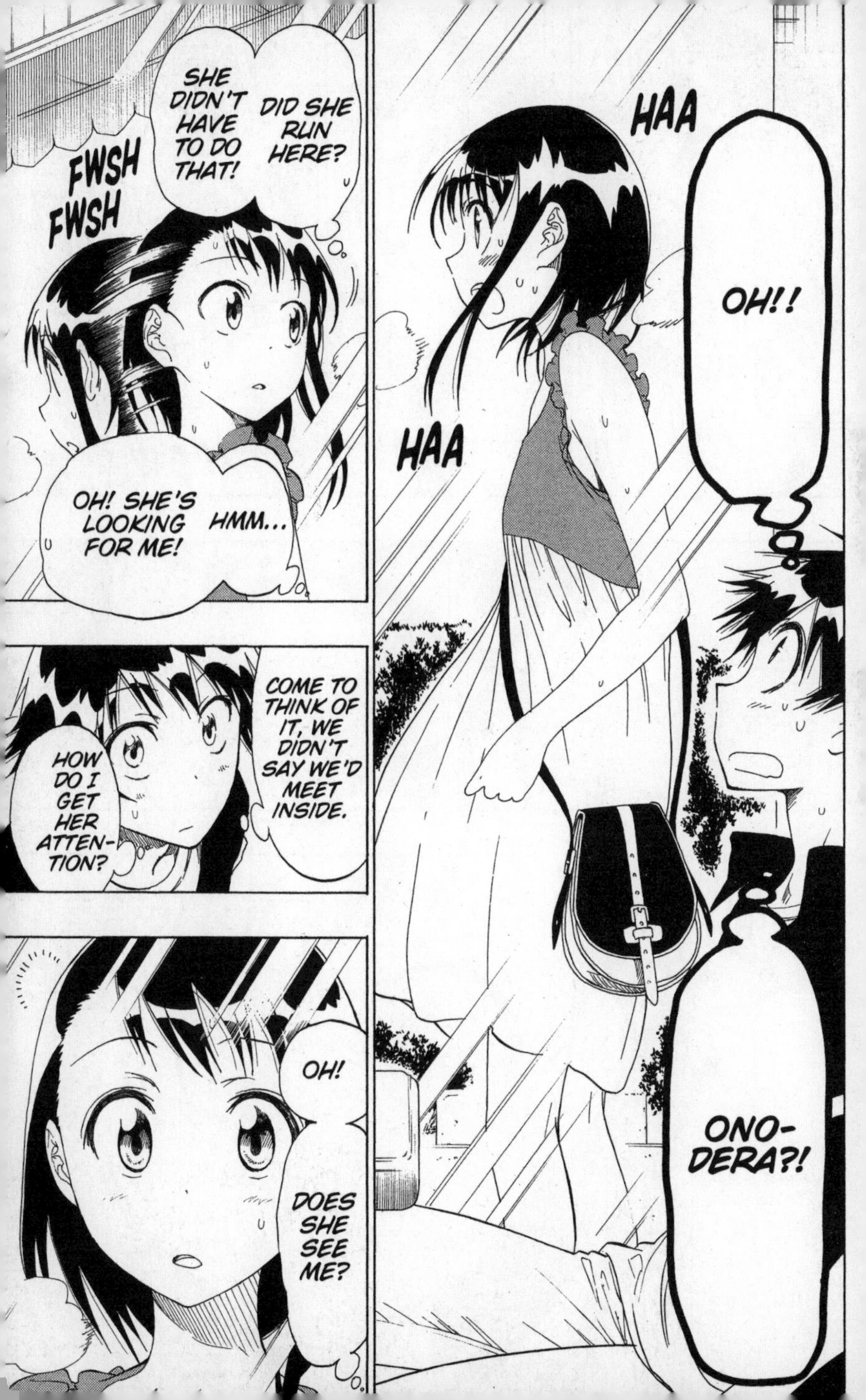
HAA
OH!!
HAA
ONO-DERA?!
DID SHE RUN HERE?
SHE DIDN'T HAVE TO DO THAT!
FWSH FWSH
HMM...
OH! SHE'S LOOKING FOR ME!
COME TO THINK OF IT, WE DIDN'T SAY WE'D MEET INSIDE.
HOW DO I GET HER ATTENTION?
OH!
DOES SHE SEE ME?

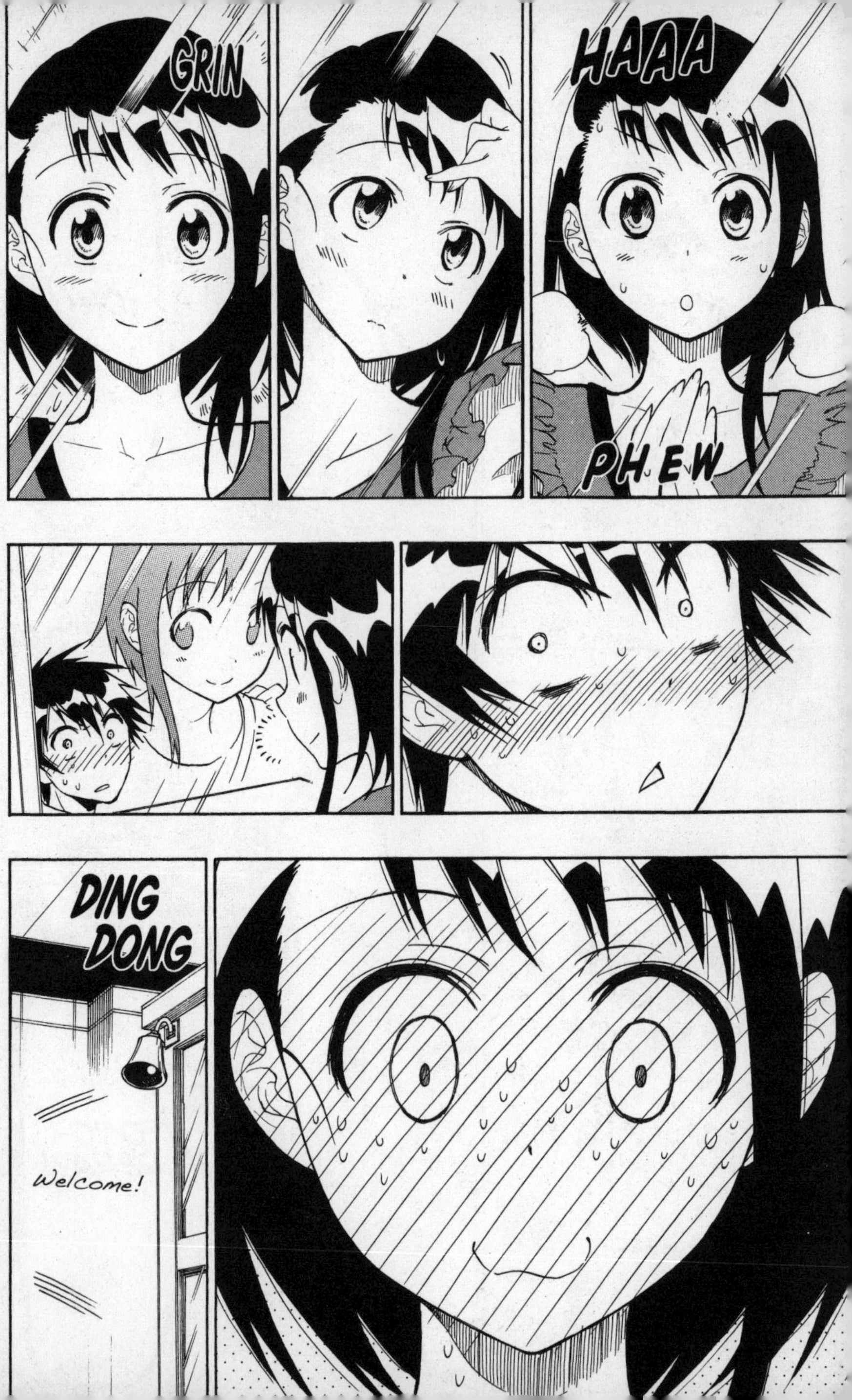
HAAA
PHEW
GRIN
DING DONG
Welcome!

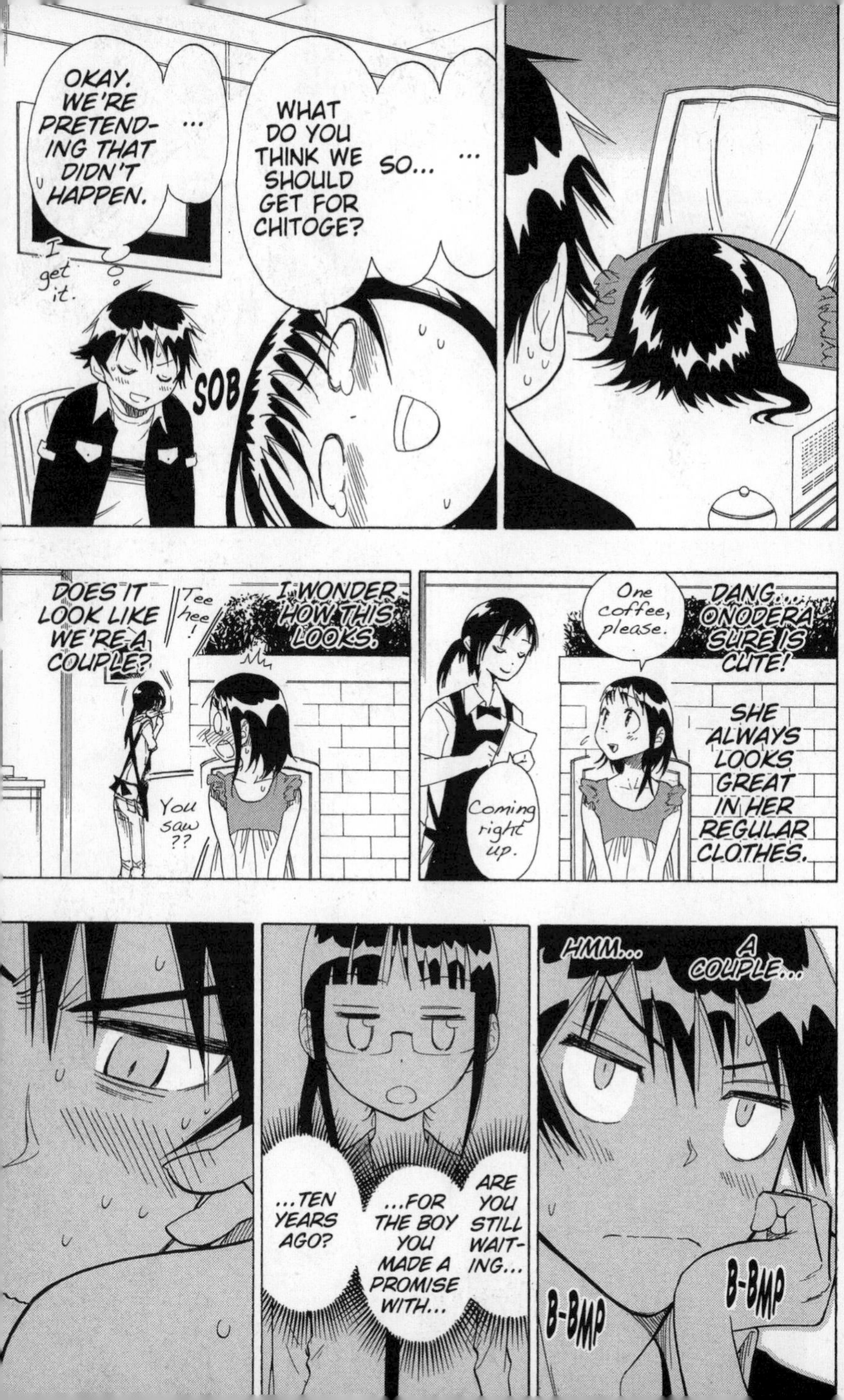
...
SO...
WHAT DO YOU THINK WE SHOULD GET FOR CHITOGE?
...
OKAY. WE'RE PRETENDING THAT DIDN'T HAPPEN.
I get it.
SOB
DANG... ONODERA SURE IS CUTE!
SHE ALWAYS LOOKS GREAT IN HER REGULAR CLOTHES.
One coffee, please.
Coming right up.
I WONDER HOW THIS LOOKS.
Tee hee!
DOES IT LOOK LIKE WE'RE A COUPLE?
You saw??
A COUPLE...
HMM...
B-BMP
B-BMP
ARE YOU STILL WAITING...
...FOR THE BOY YOU MADE A PROMISE WITH...
...TEN YEARS AGO?

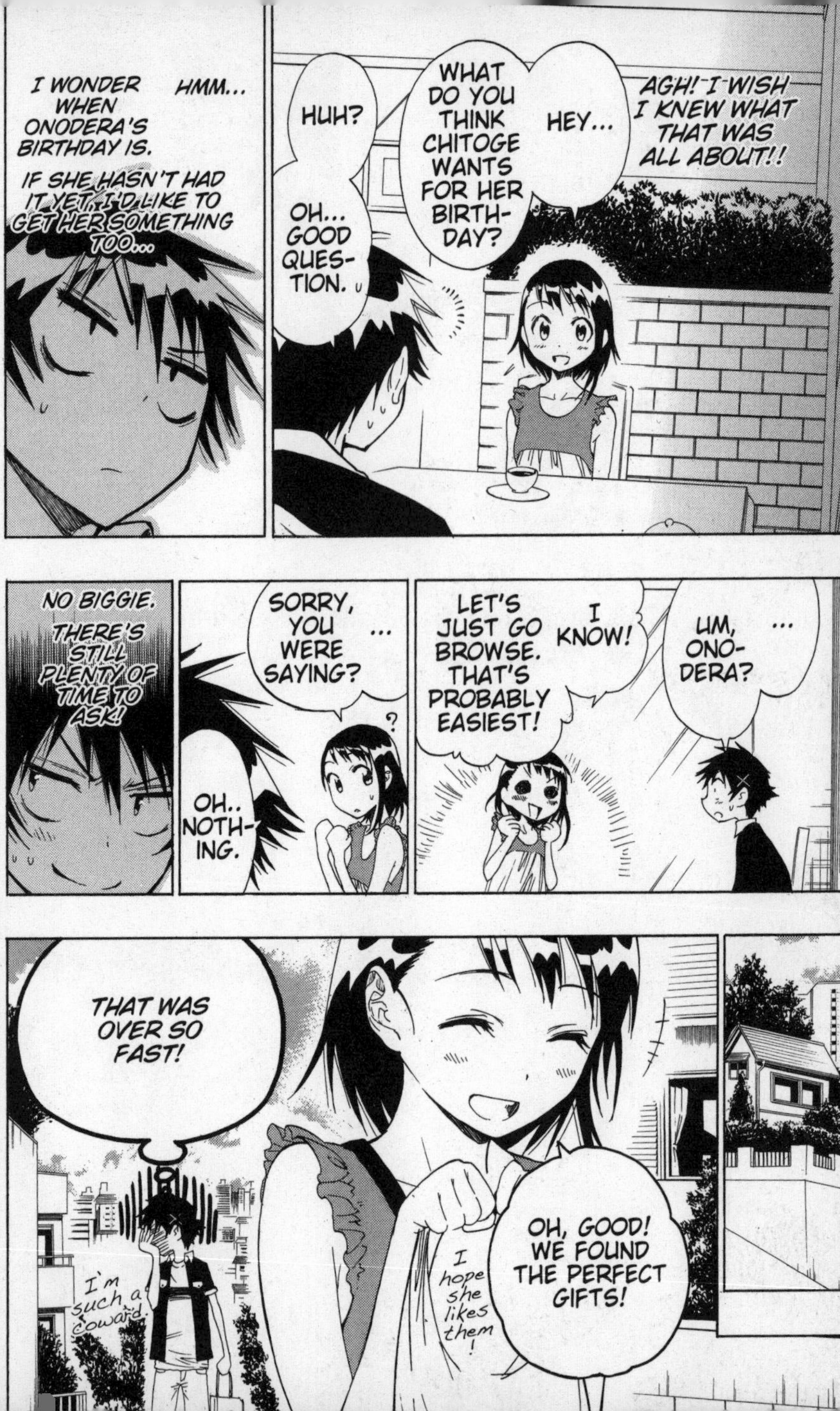
AGH! I WISH I KNEW WHAT THAT WAS ALL ABOUT!!
HEY...
WHAT DO YOU THINK CHITOGE WANTS FOR HER BIRTHDAY?
HUH?
OH... GOOD QUESTION.
HMM...
I WONDER WHEN ONODERA'S BIRTHDAY IS.
IF SHE HASN'T HAD IT YET, I'D LIKE TO GET HER SOMETHING TOO...
...
UM, ONODERA?
I KNOW!
LET'S JUST GO BROWSE. THAT'S PROBABLY EASIEST!
...
SORRY, YOU WERE SAYING?
?
OH.. NOTHING.
NO BIGGIE. THERE'S STILL PLENTY OF TIME TO ASK!
OH, GOOD! WE FOUND THE PERFECT GIFTS!
I hope she likes them!
THAT WAS OVER SO FAST!
I'm such a coward.

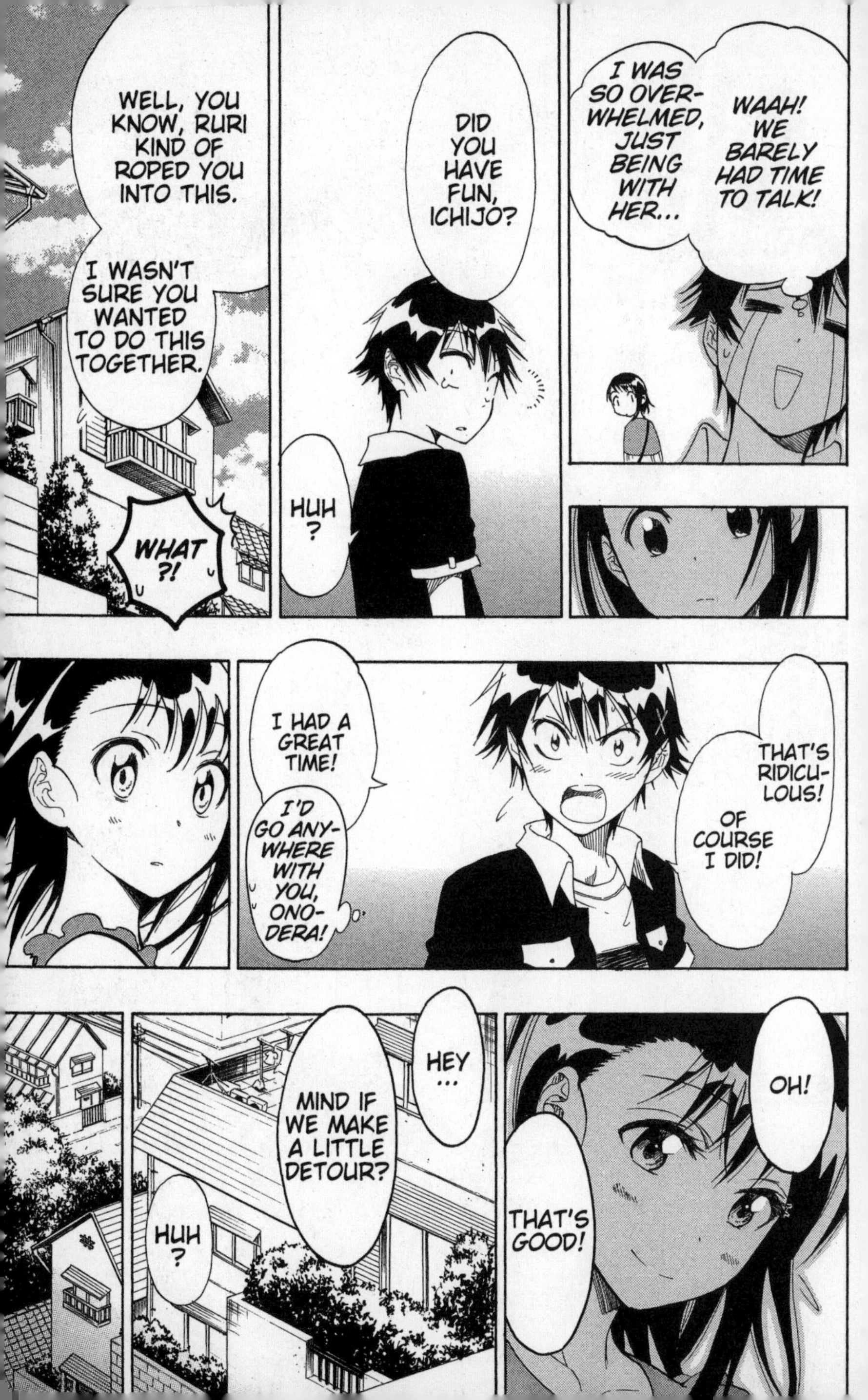
WAAH! WE BARELY HAD TIME TO TALK!
I WAS SO OVER-WHELMED, JUST BEING WITH HER...
DID YOU HAVE FUN, ICHIJO?
HUH?
WELL, YOU KNOW, RURI KIND OF ROPED YOU INTO THIS.
I WASN'T SURE YOU WANTED TO DO THIS TOGETHER.
WHAT?!
THAT'S RIDICULOUS!
OF COURSE I DID!
I HAD A GREAT TIME!
I'D GO ANY-WHERE WITH YOU, ONO-DERA!
OH!
THAT'S GOOD!
HEY...
MIND IF WE MAKE A LITTLE DETOUR?
HUH?

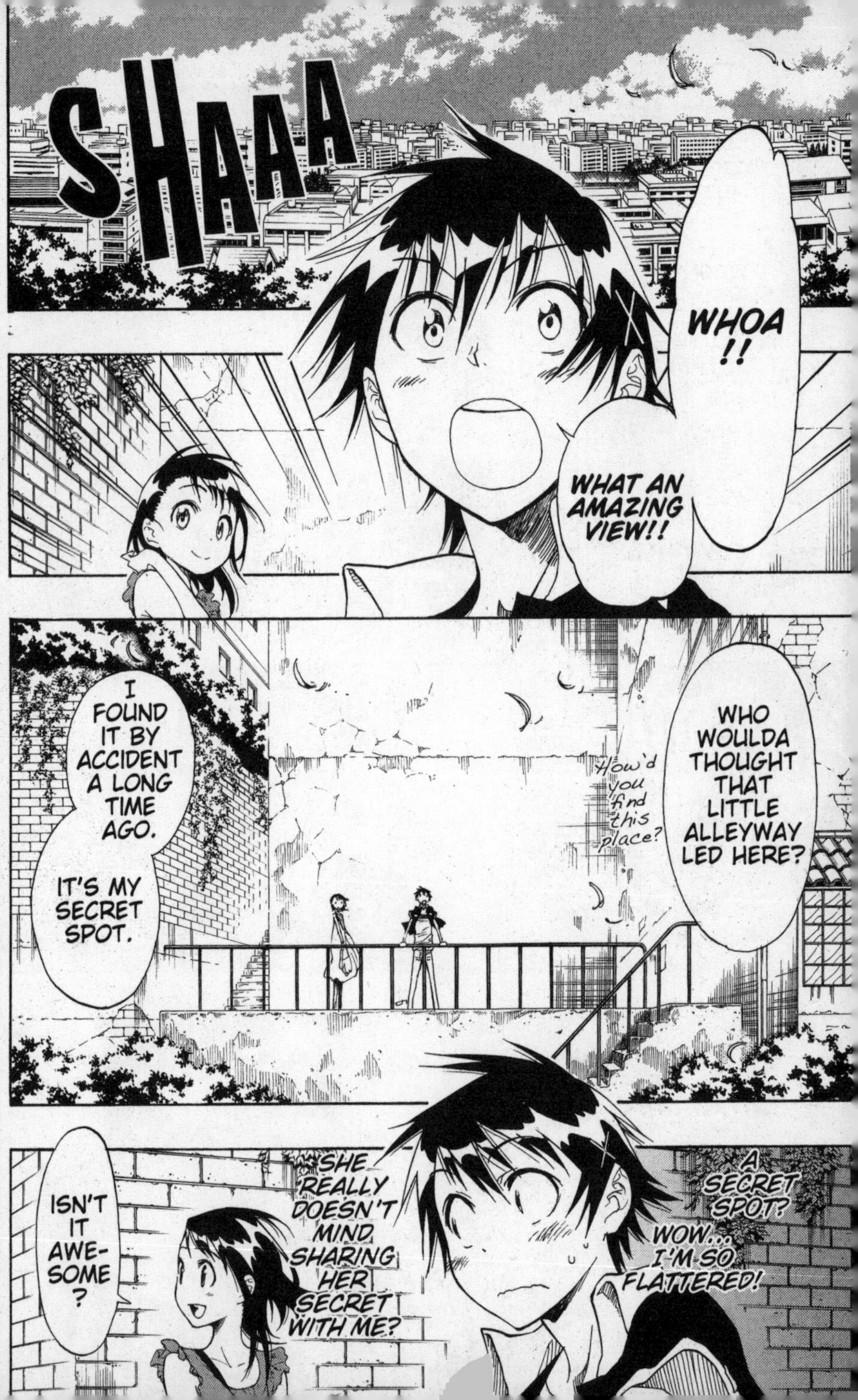
SHAAA
WHOA!!
WHAT AN AMAZING VIEW!!
WHO WOULDA THOUGHT THAT LITTLE ALLEYWAY LED HERE?
How'd you find this place?
I FOUND IT BY ACCIDENT A LONG TIME AGO.
IT'S MY SECRET SPOT.
A SECRET SPOT?
WOW... I'M SO FLATTERED!
SHE REALLY DOESN'T MIND SHARING HER SECRET WITH ME?
ISN'T IT AWESOME?

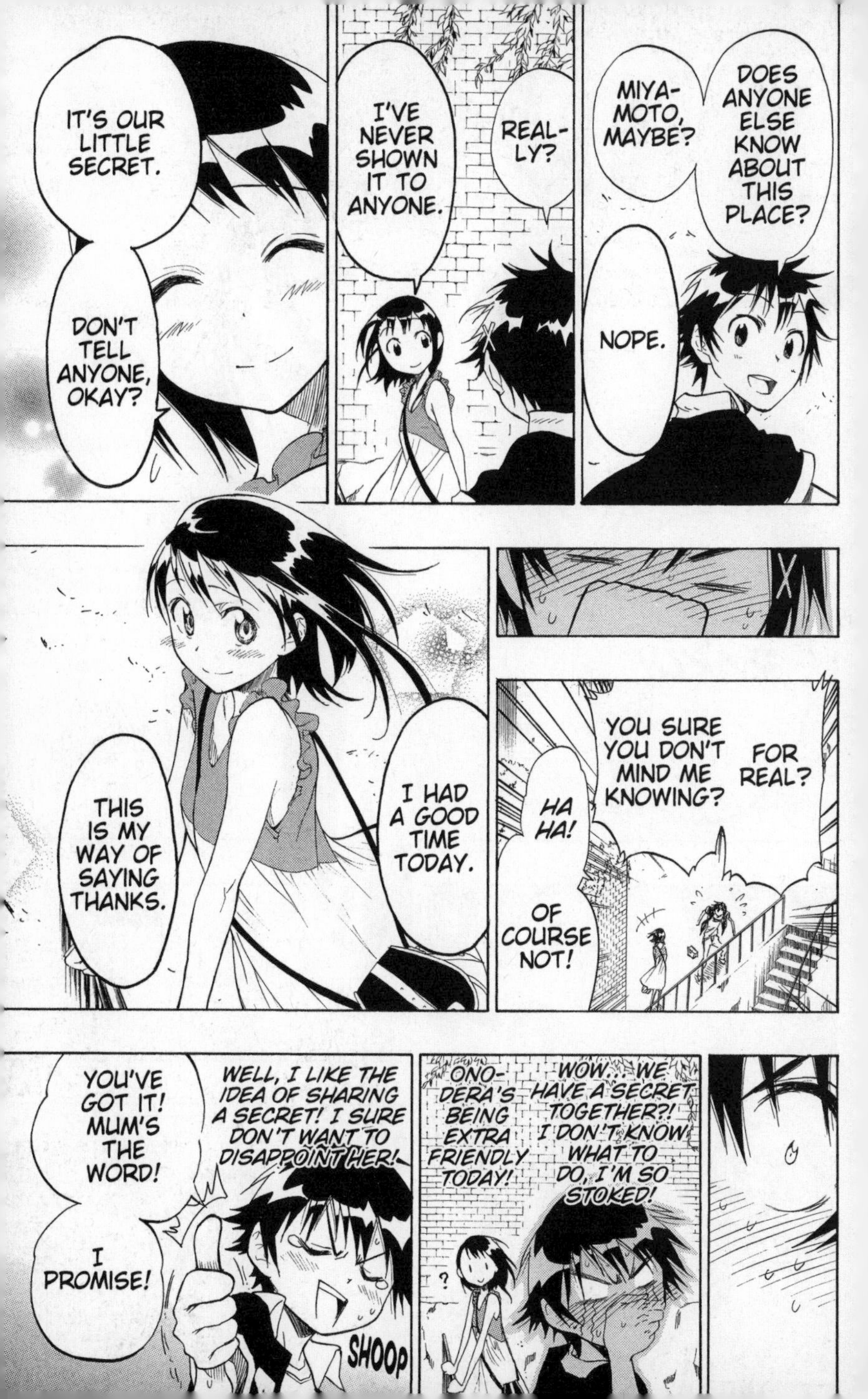
DOES ANYONE ELSE KNOW ABOUT THIS PLACE?
MIYA-MOTO, MAYBE?
NOPE.
REAL-LY?
I'VE NEVER SHOWN IT TO ANYONE.
IT'S OUR LITTLE SECRET.
DON'T TELL ANYONE, OKAY?
FOR REAL?
YOU SURE YOU DON'T MIND ME KNOWING?
HA HA!
OF COURSE NOT!
I HAD A GOOD TIME TODAY.
THIS IS MY WAY OF SAYING THANKS.
WOW... WE HAVE A SECRET TOGETHER?! I DON'T KNOW WHAT TO DO, I'M SO STOKED!
ONO-DERA'S BEING EXTRA FRIENDLY TODAY!
?
WELL, I LIKE THE IDEA OF SHARING A SECRET! I SURE DON'T WANT TO DISAPPOINT HER!
YOU'VE GOT IT! MUM'S THE WORD!
I PROMISE!
SHOOP

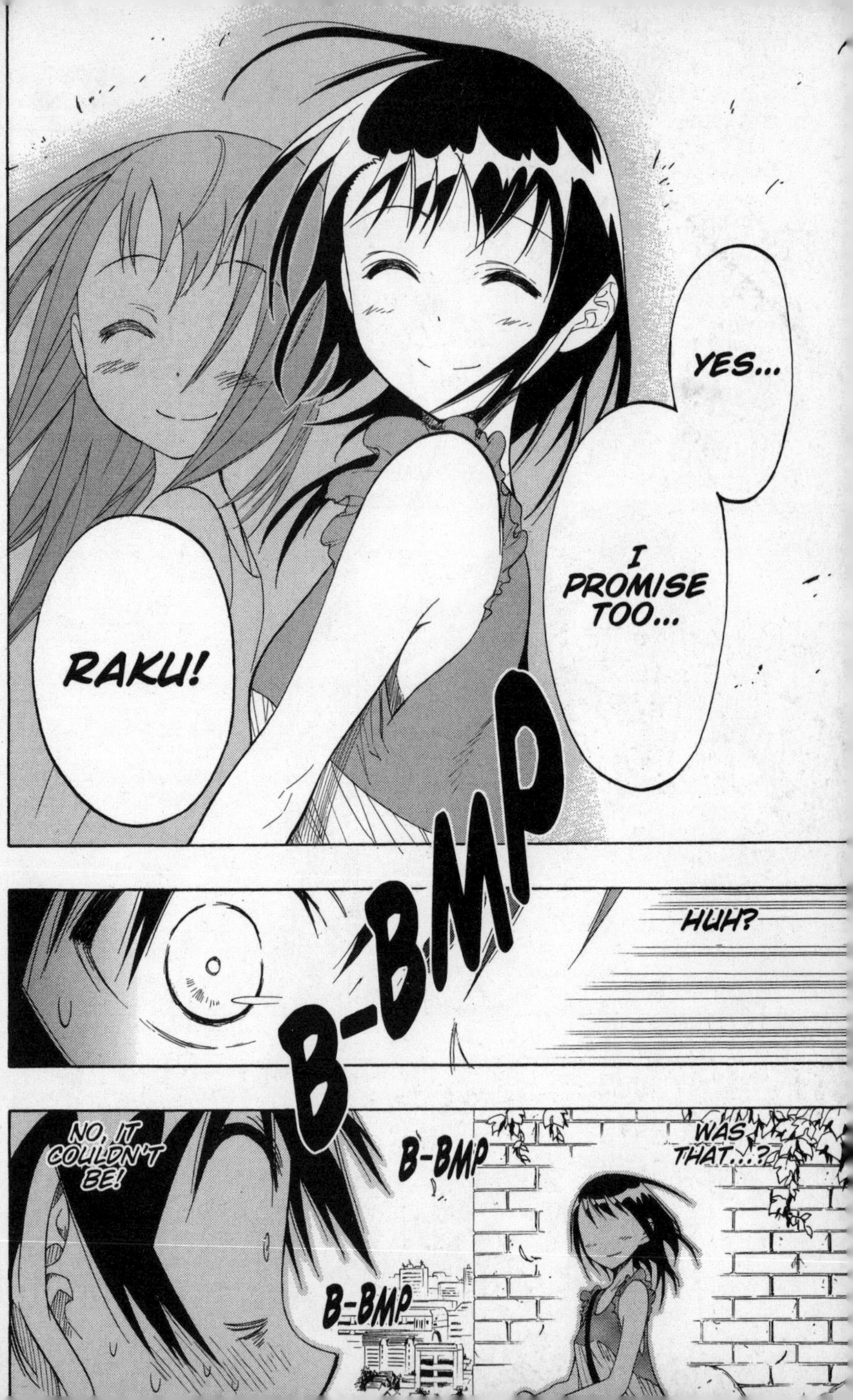
YES...
I PROMISE TOO...
RAKU!
HUH?
B-BMP
WAS THAT...?
NO, IT COULDN'T BE!
B-BMP
B-BMP

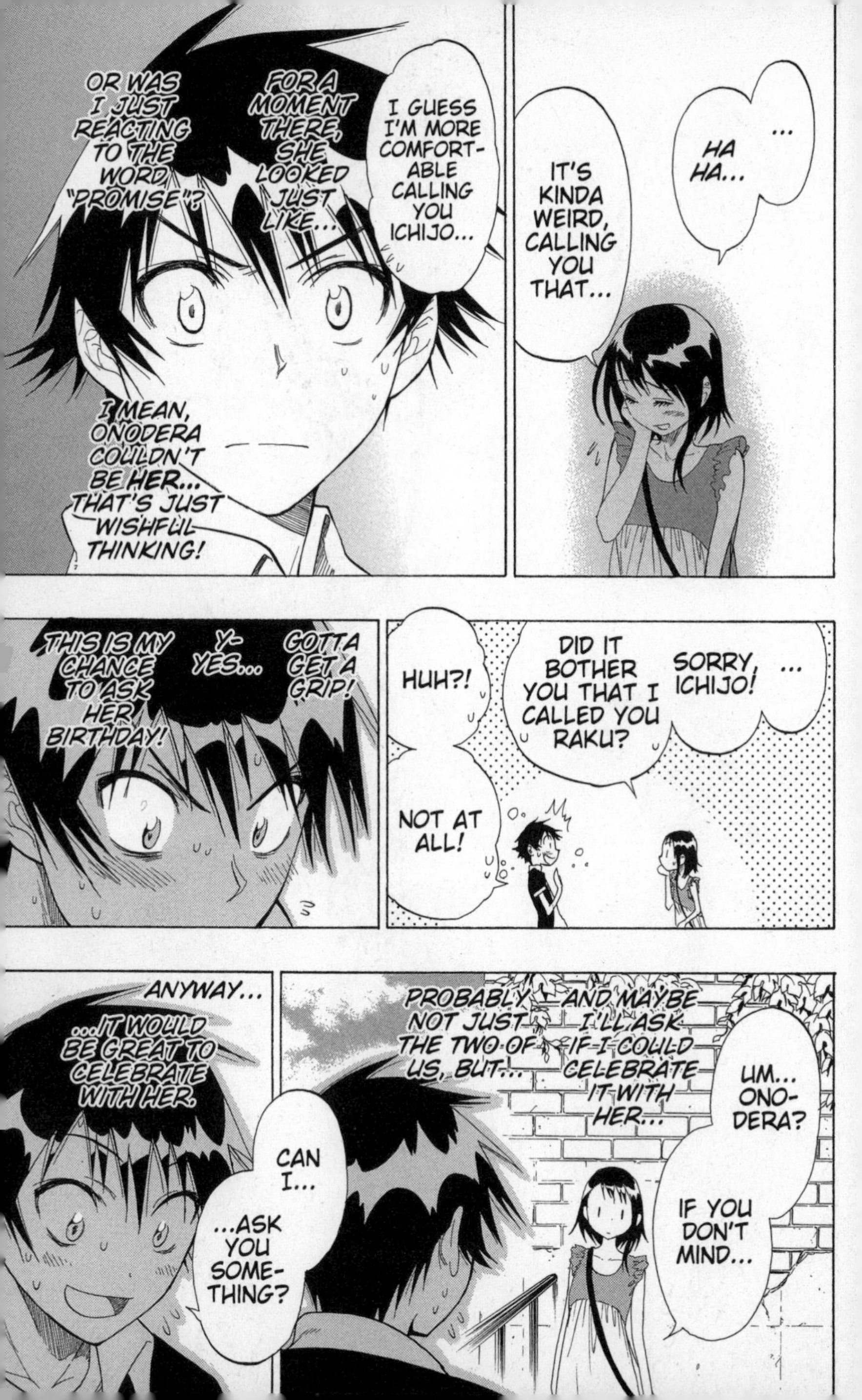
...
HA HA...
IT'S KINDA WEIRD, CALLING YOU THAT...
I GUESS I'M MORE COMFORTABLE CALLING YOU ICHIJO...
FOR A MOMENT THERE, SHE LOOKED JUST LIKE...
OR WAS I JUST REACTING TO THE WORD "PROMISE"?
I MEAN, ONODERA COULDN'T BE HER... THAT'S JUST WISHFUL THINKING!
...
SORRY, ICHIJO!
DID IT BOTHER YOU THAT I CALLED YOU RAKU?
HUH?!
NOT AT ALL!
GOTTA GET A GRIP!
Y-YES...
THIS IS MY CHANCE TO ASK HER BIRTHDAY!
AND MAYBE I'LL ASK IF I COULD CELEBRATE IT WITH HER...
PROBABLY NOT JUST THE TWO OF US, BUT...
UM... ONODERA?
IF YOU DON'T MIND...
CAN I...
...ASK YOU SOMETHING?
ANYWAY...
...IT WOULD BE GREAT TO CELEBRATE WITH HER.

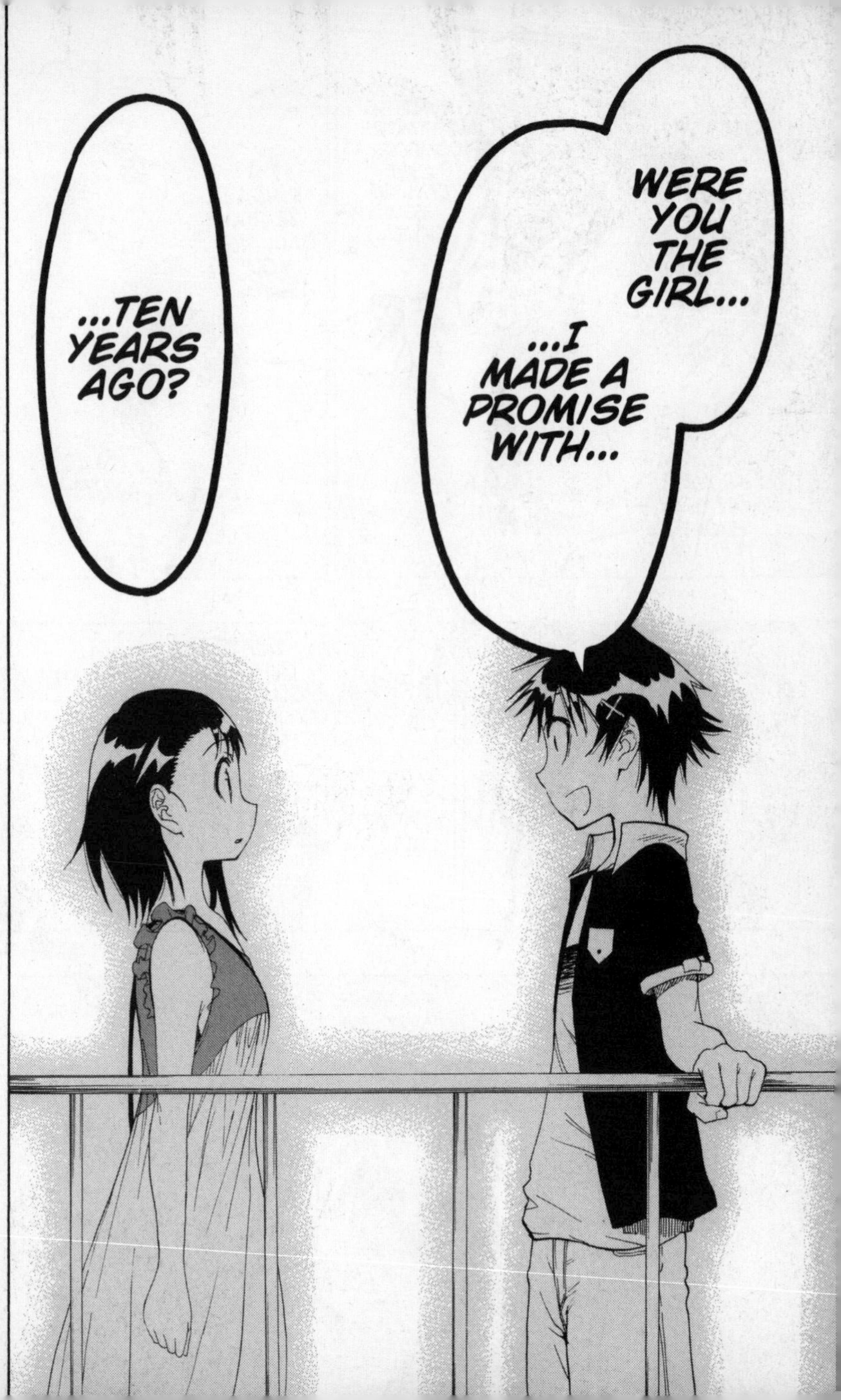
WERE YOU THE GIRL...
...I MADE A PROMISE WITH...
...TEN YEARS AGO?

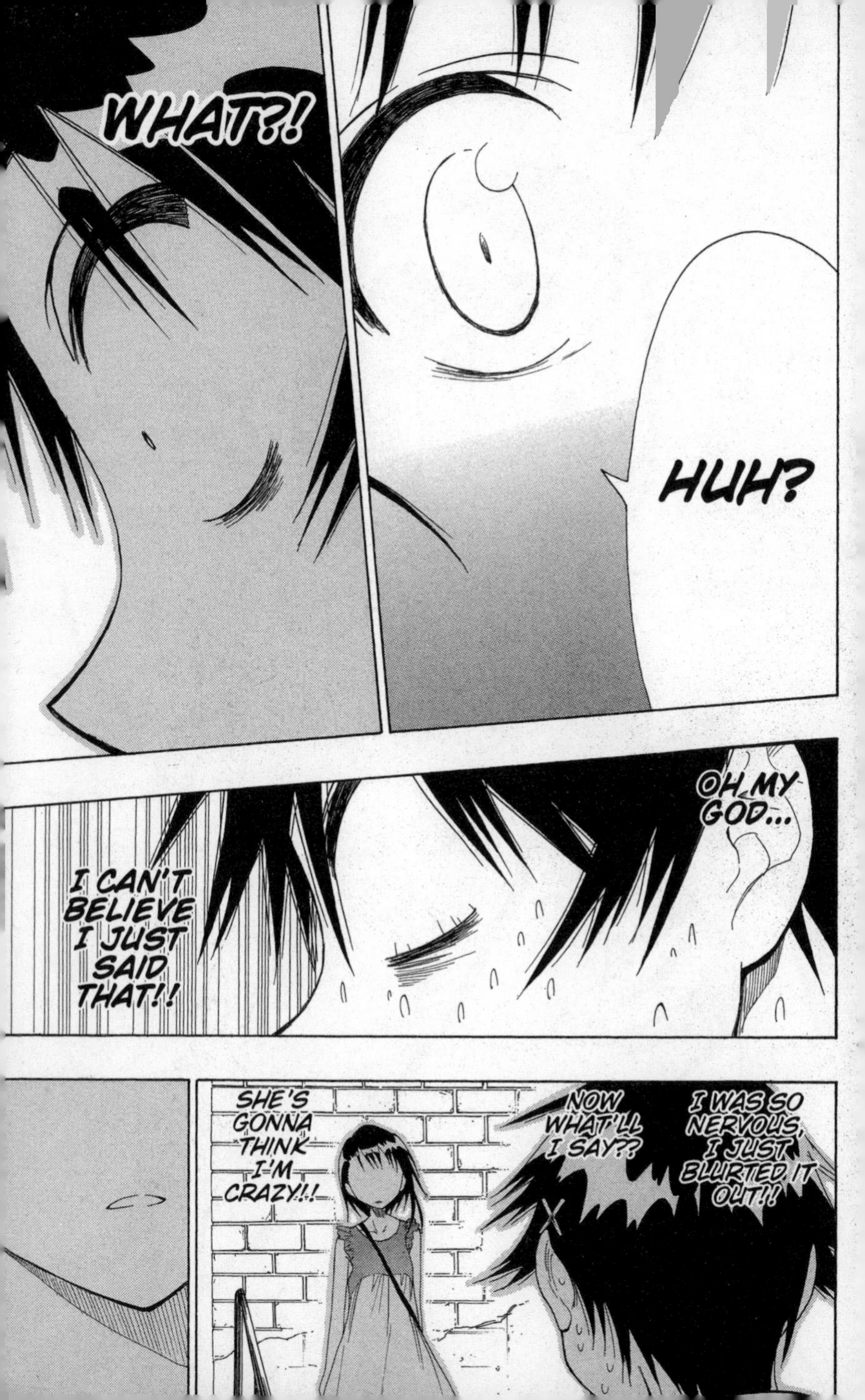
HUH?
WHAT?!
OH MY GOD...
I CAN'T BELIEVE I JUST SAID THAT!!
I WAS SO NERVOUS, I JUST BLURTED IT OUT!!
NOW WHAT'LL I SAY??
SHE'S GONNA THINK I'M CRAZY!!

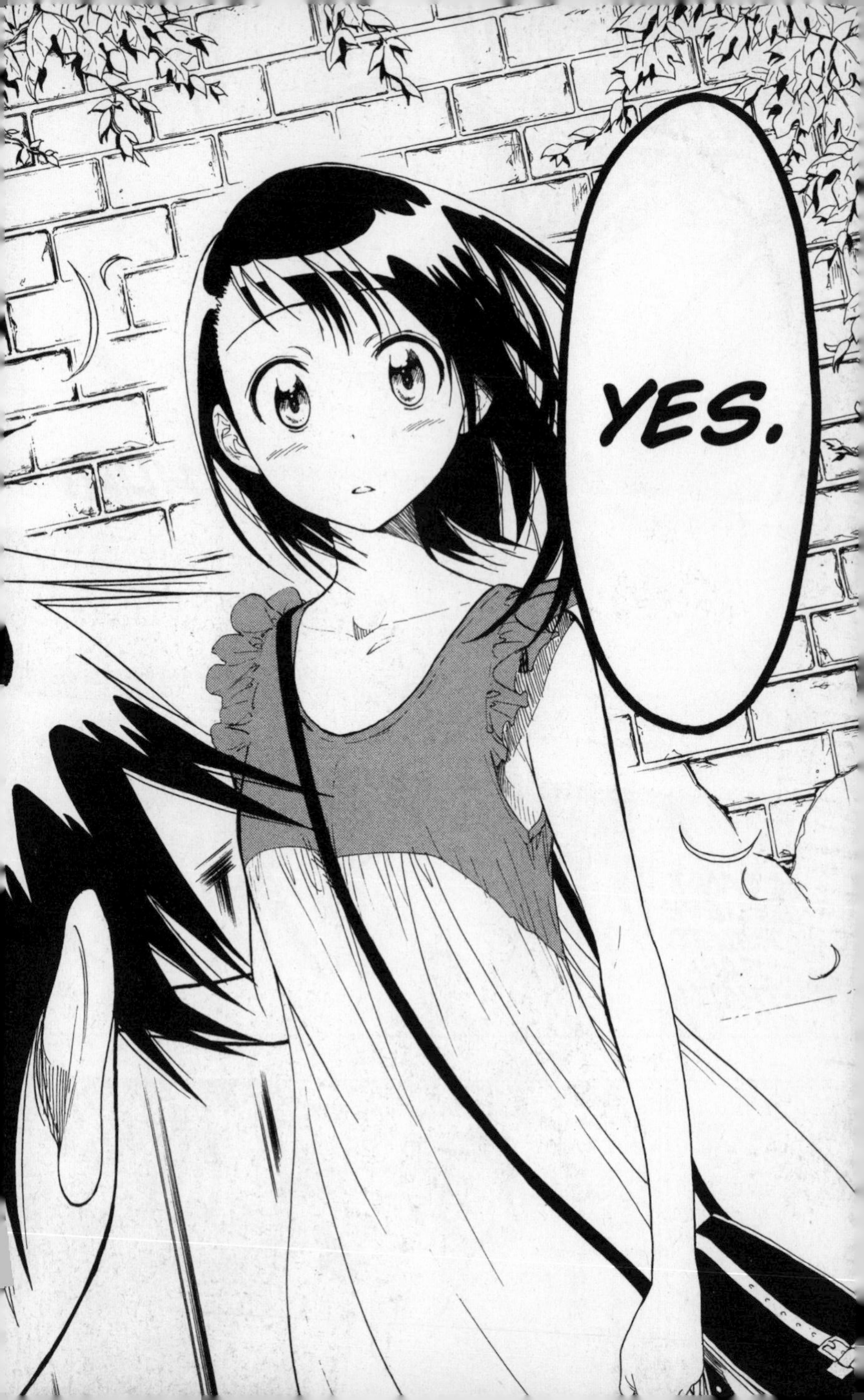
YES.

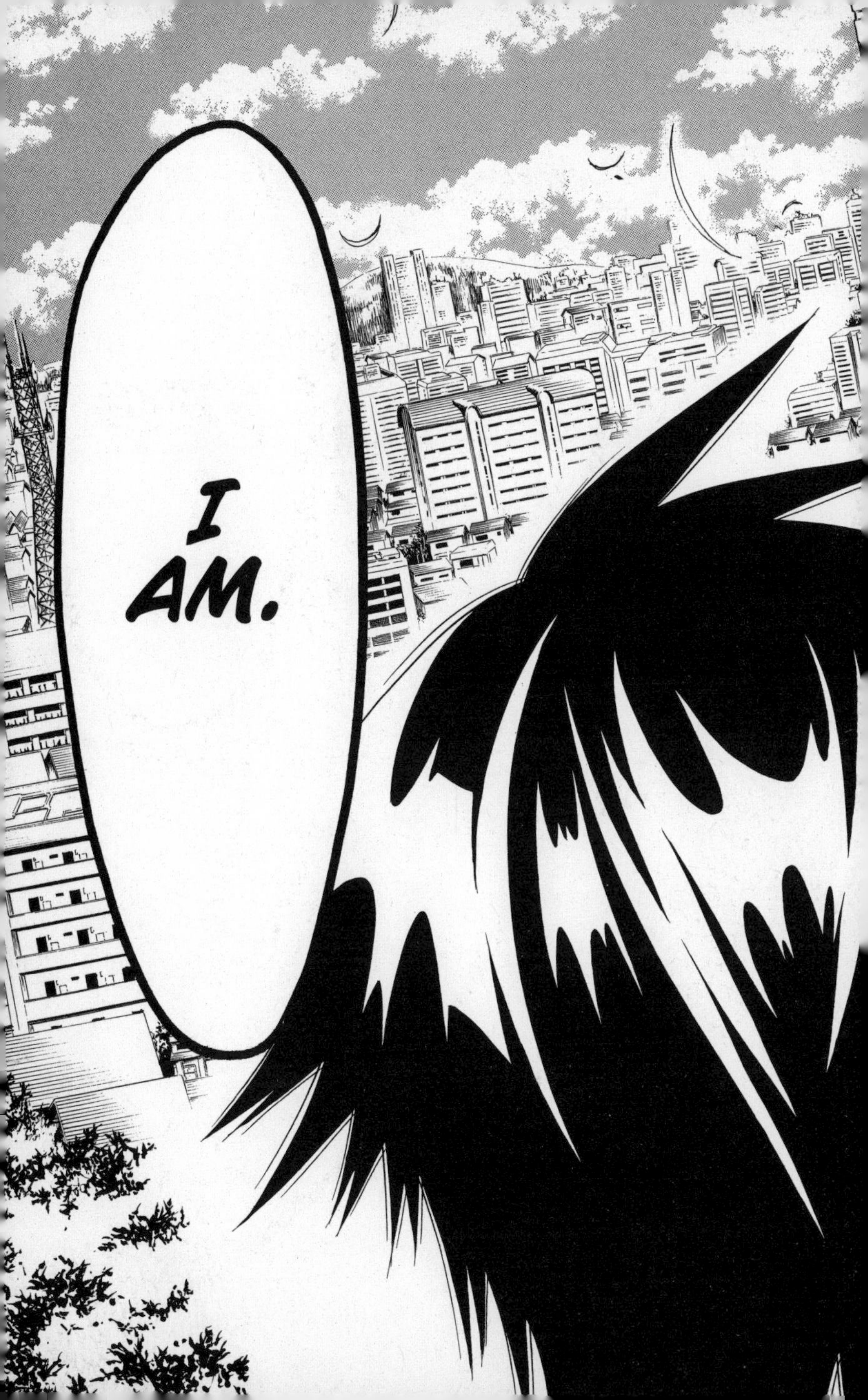
I AM.

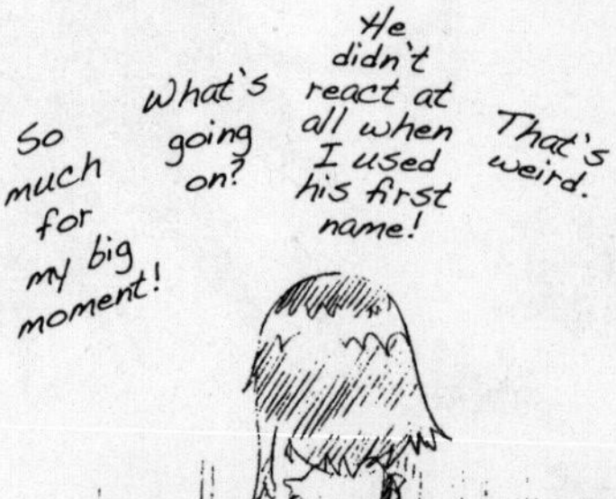
That's weird.
He didn't react at all when I used his first name!
What's going on?
So much for my big moment!

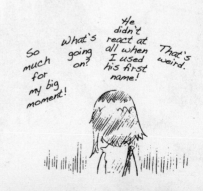

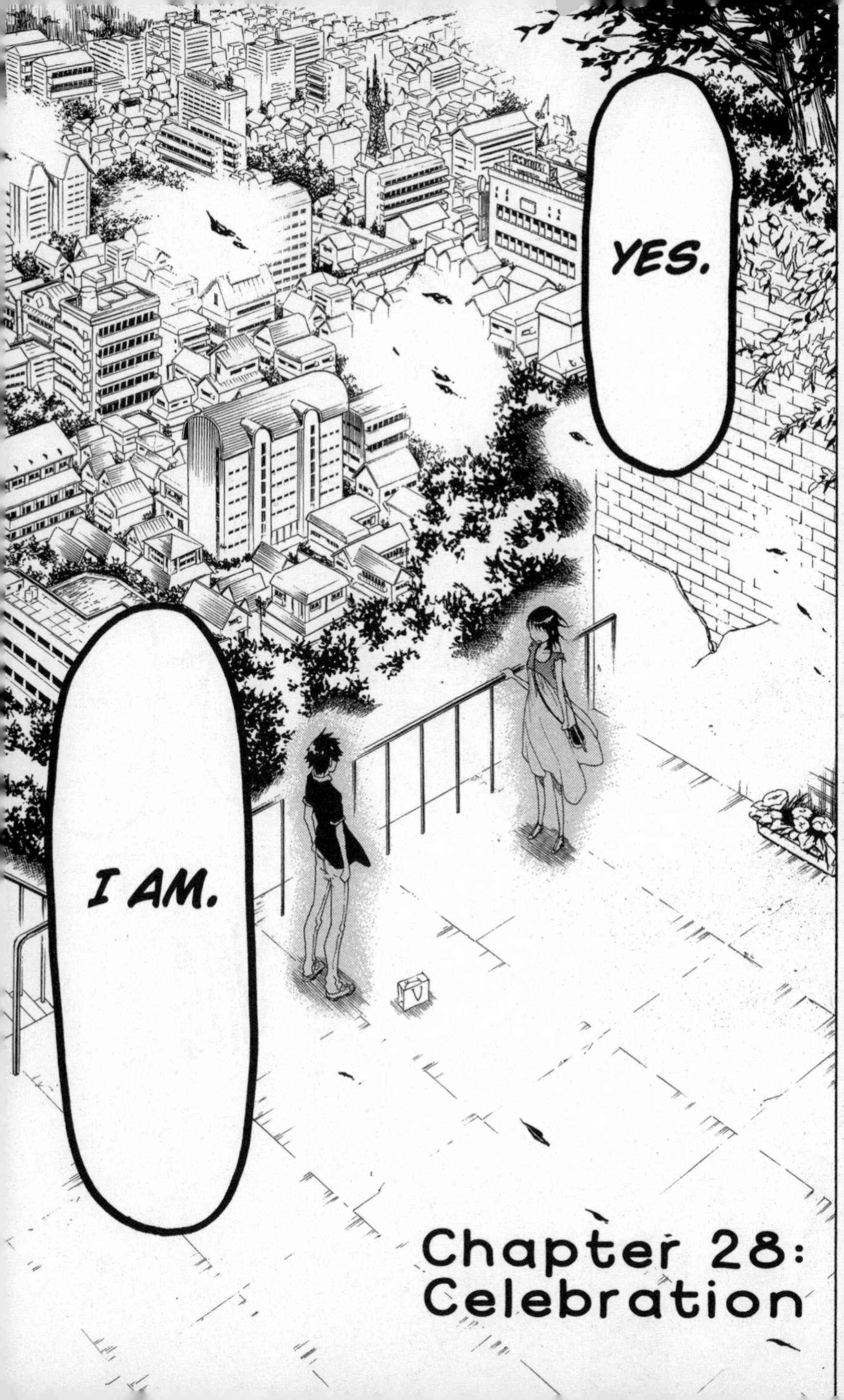
YES.
I AM.

Chapter 28: Celebration

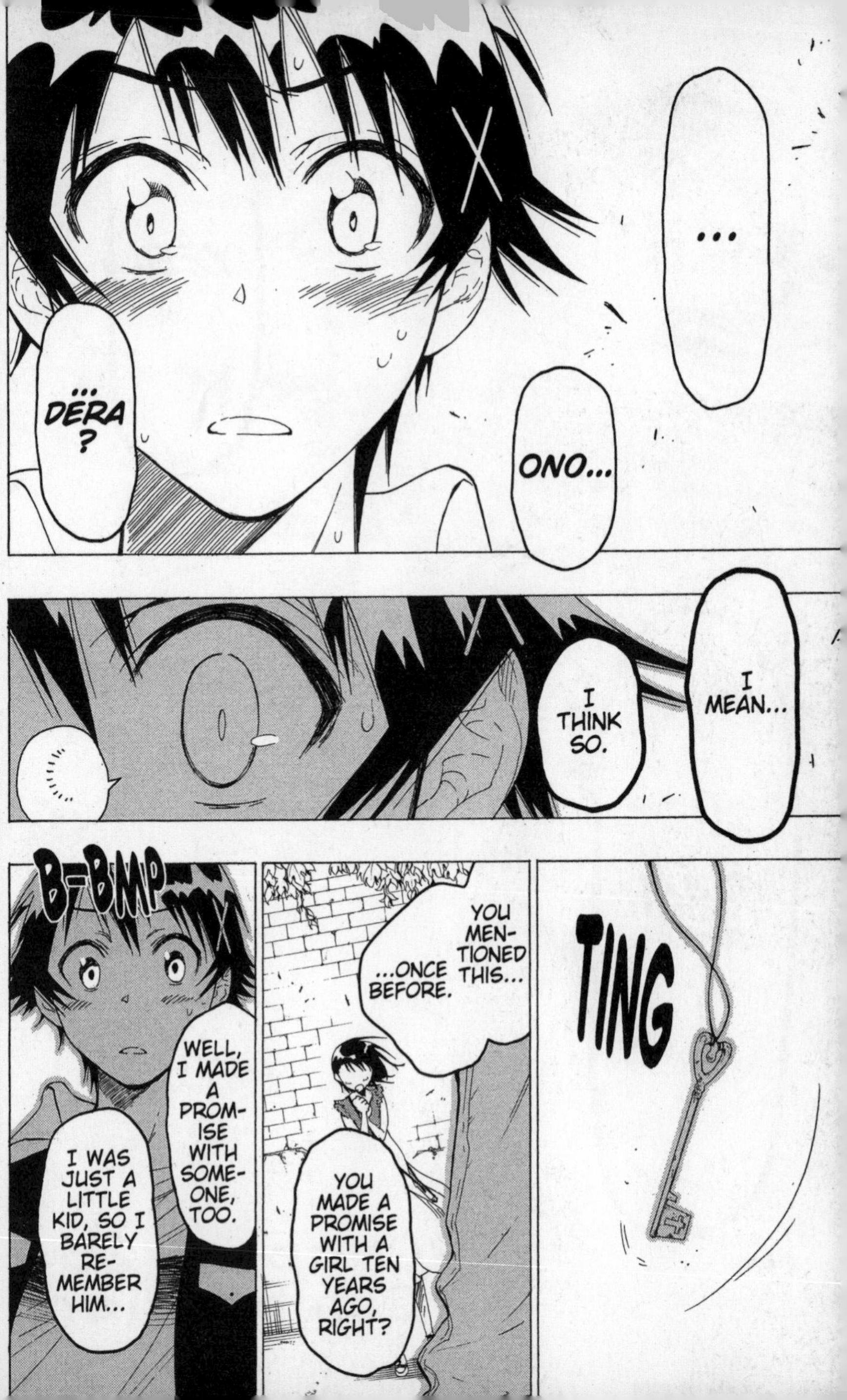
...
ONO...
...DERA?
I MEAN...
I THINK SO.
TING
YOU MENTIONED THIS...
...ONCE BEFORE.
YOU MADE A PROMISE WITH A GIRL TEN YEARS AGO, RIGHT?
B-BMP
WELL, I MADE A PROMISE WITH SOMEONE, TOO.
I WAS JUST A LITTLE KID, SO I BARELY REMEMBER HIM...

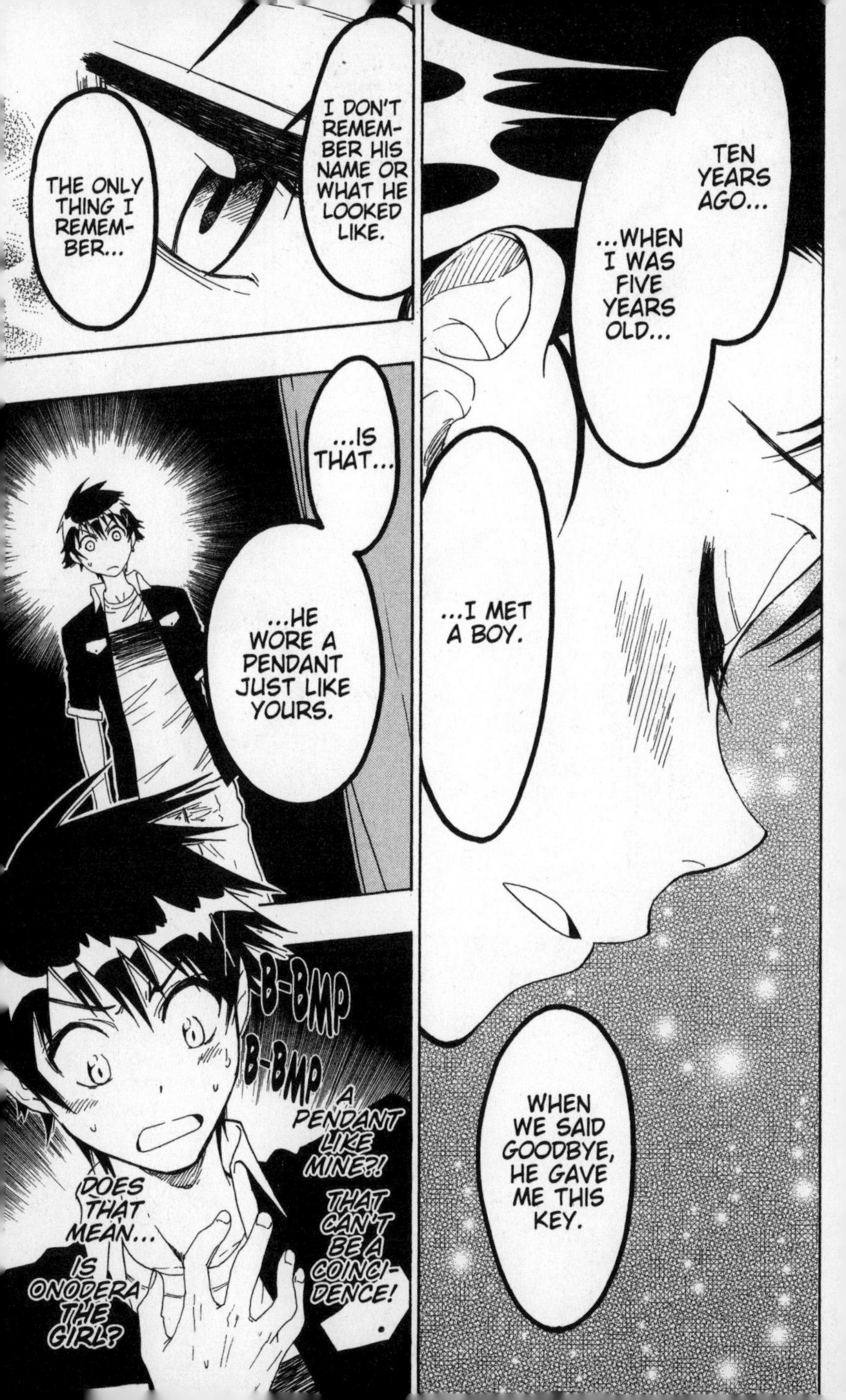
TEN YEARS AGO...
...WHEN I WAS FIVE YEARS OLD...
...I MET A BOY.
WHEN WE SAID GOODBYE, HE GAVE ME THIS KEY.
I DON'T REMEMBER HIS NAME OR WHAT HE LOOKED LIKE.
THE ONLY THING I REMEMBER...
...IS THAT...
...HE WORE A PENDANT JUST LIKE YOURS.
B-BMP
B-BMP
A PENDANT LIKE MINE?!
THAT CAN'T BE A COINCIDENCE!
DOES THAT MEAN...
IS ONODERA THE GIRL?

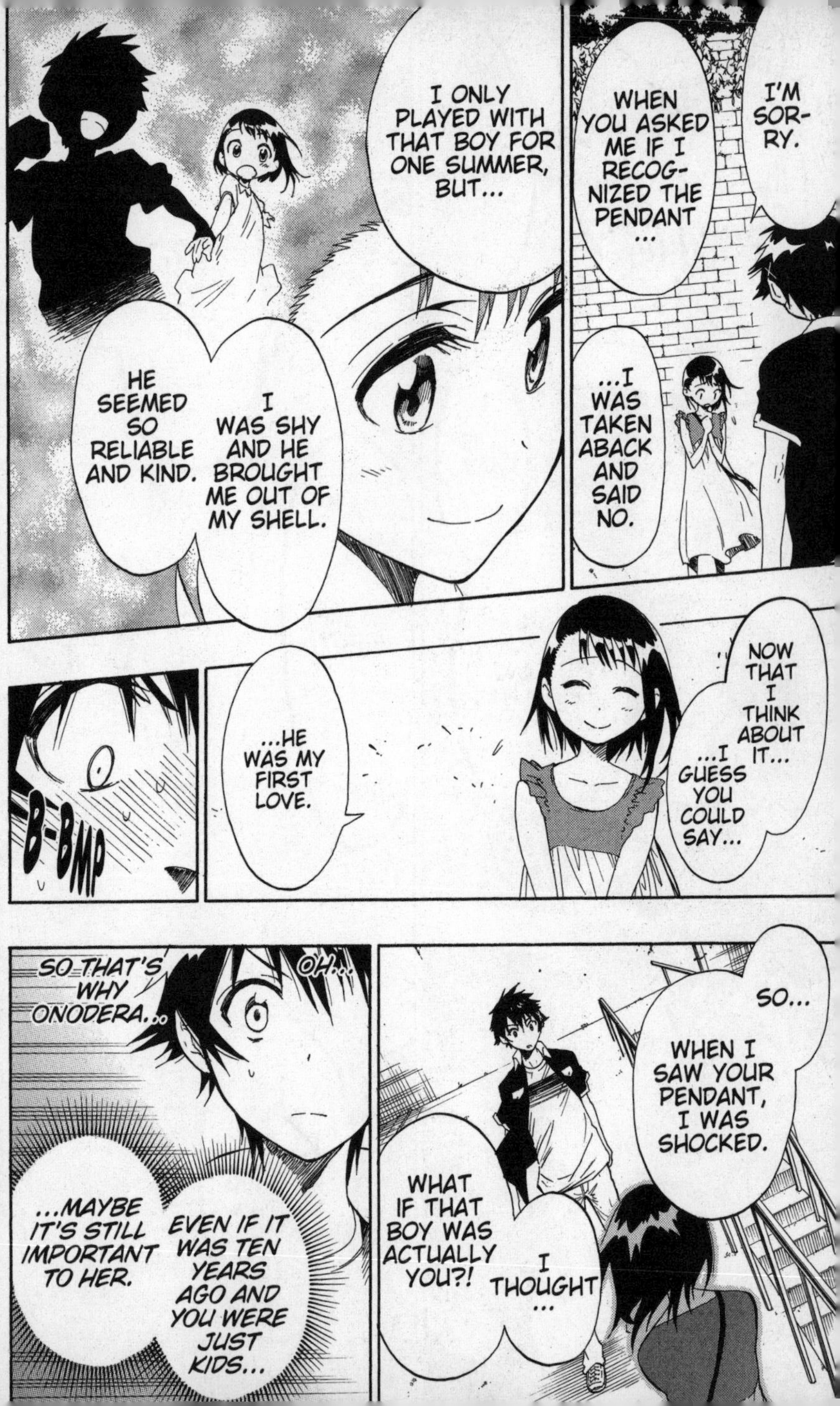
I'M SORRY.
WHEN YOU ASKED ME IF I RECOGNIZED THE PENDANT...
...I WAS TAKEN ABACK AND SAID NO.
I ONLY PLAYED WITH THAT BOY FOR ONE SUMMER, BUT...
I WAS SHY AND HE BROUGHT ME OUT OF MY SHELL.
HE SEEMED SO RELIABLE AND KIND.
NOW THAT I THINK ABOUT IT...
...I GUESS YOU COULD SAY...
...HE WAS MY FIRST LOVE.
B-BMP
SO...
WHEN I SAW YOUR PENDANT, I WAS SHOCKED.
I THOUGHT...
WHAT IF THAT BOY WAS ACTUALLY YOU?!
OH...
SO THAT'S WHY ONODERA...
EVEN IF IT WAS TEN YEARS AGO AND YOU WERE JUST KIDS...
...MAYBE IT'S STILL IMPORTANT TO HER.

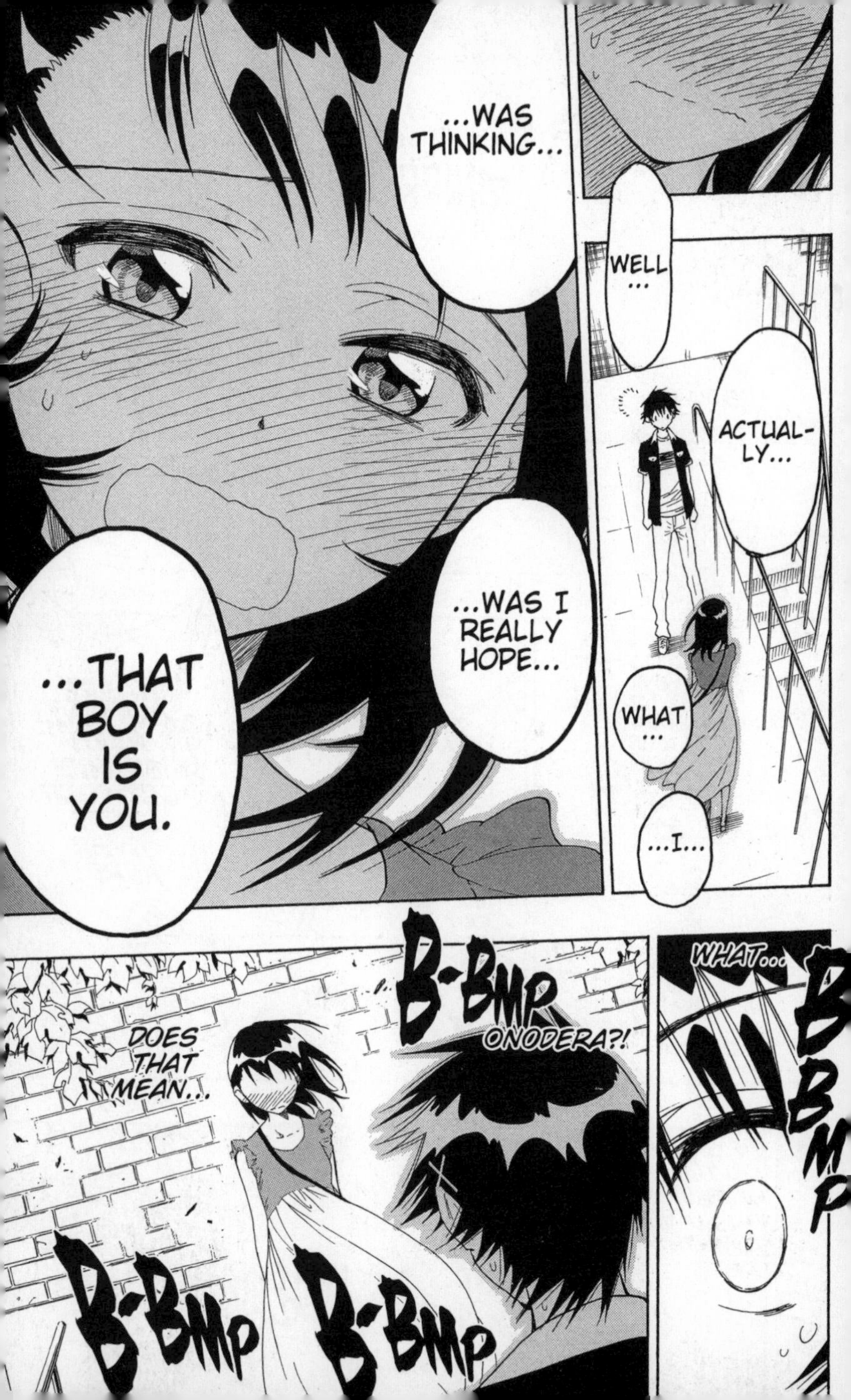
WELL...
ACTUAL-LY...
WHAT...
...I...
...WAS THINKING...
...WAS I REALLY HOPE...
...THAT BOY IS YOU.
WHAT...
BBMP
B-BMP
ONODERA?!
DOES THAT MEAN...
B-BMP
B-BMP

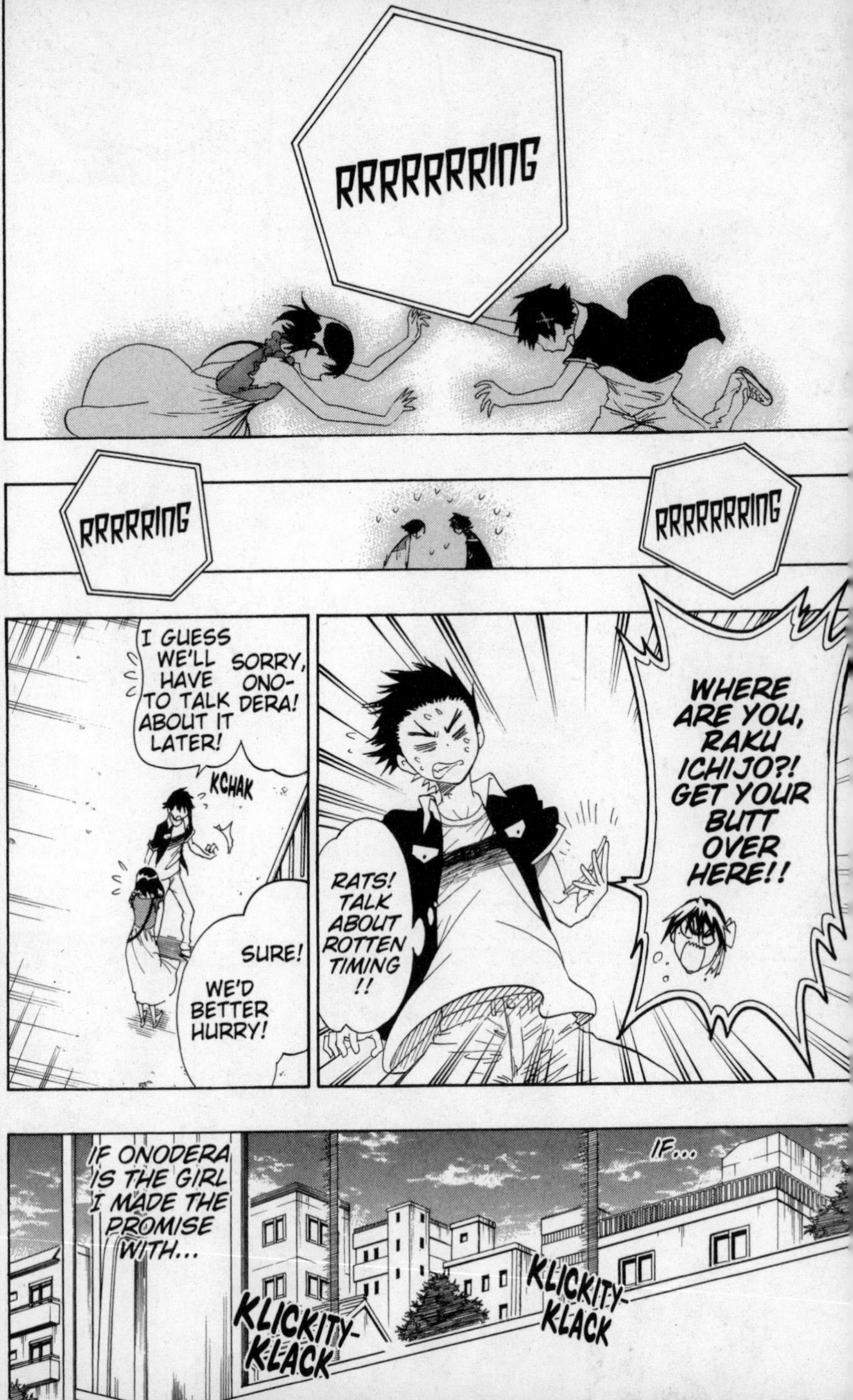
RRRRRRRING
RRRRRRRING
RRRRRING
WHERE ARE YOU, RAKU ICHIJO?! GET YOUR BUTT OVER HERE!!
RATS! TALK ABOUT ROTTEN TIMING!!
SORRY, ONODERA!
I GUESS WE'LL HAVE TO TALK ABOUT IT LATER!
KCHAK
SURE!
WE'D BETTER HURRY!
IF...
KLICKITY-KLACK
IF ONODERA IS THE GIRL I MADE THE PROMISE WITH...
KLICKITY-KLACK

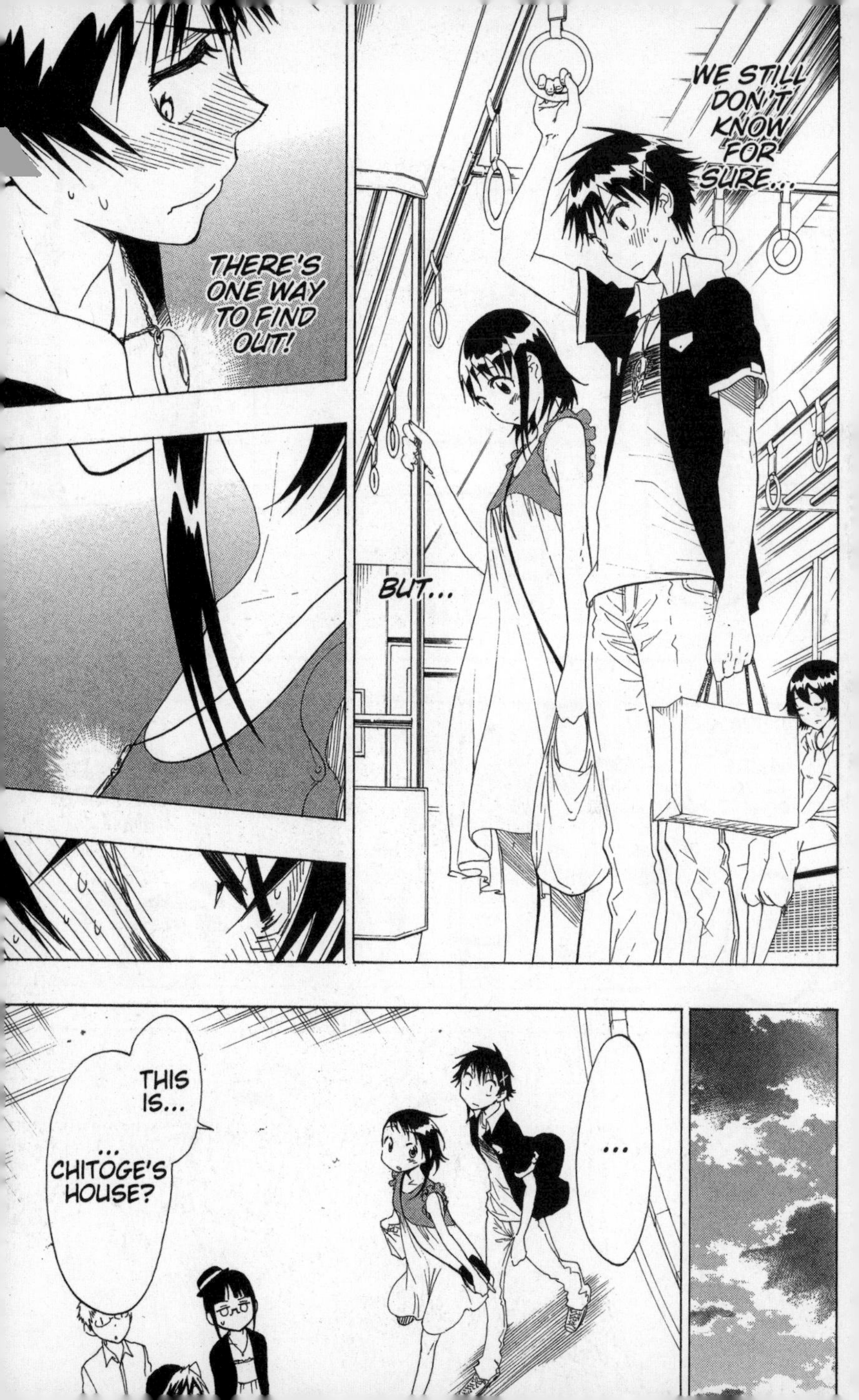
WE STILL DON'T KNOW FOR SURE...
BUT...
THERE'S ONE WAY TO FIND OUT!
...
THIS IS...
... CHITOGE'S HOUSE?

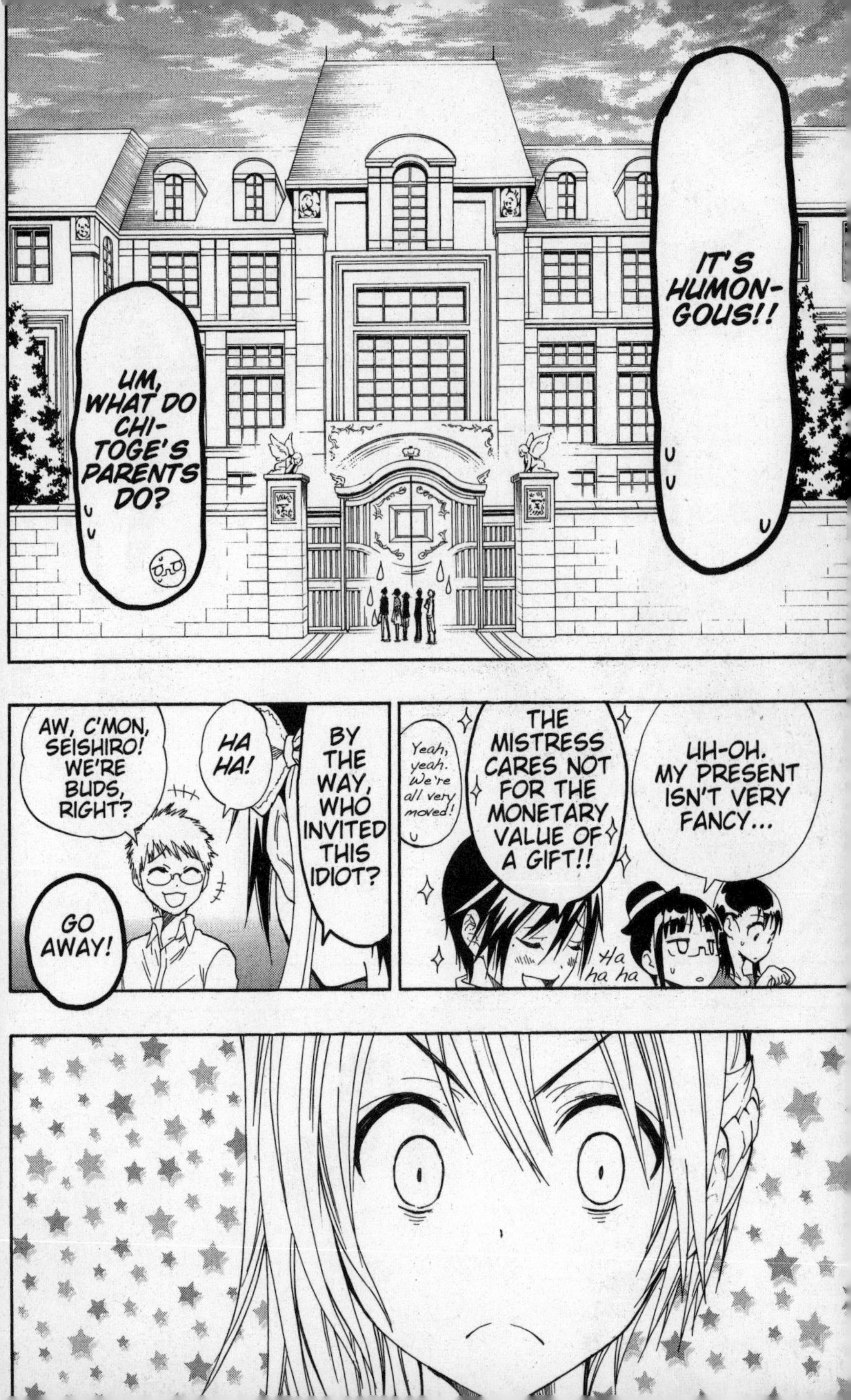
IT'S HUMON-GOUS!!
UM, WHAT DO CHI-TOGE'S PARENTS DO?
UH-OH. MY PRESENT ISN'T VERY FANCY...
THE MISTRESS CARES NOT FOR THE MONETARY VALUE OF A GIFT!!
Yeah, yeah. We're all very moved!
Ha ha ha
BY THE WAY, WHO INVITED THIS IDIOT?
HA HA!
AW, C'MON, SEISHIRO! WE'RE BUDS, RIGHT?
GO AWAY!

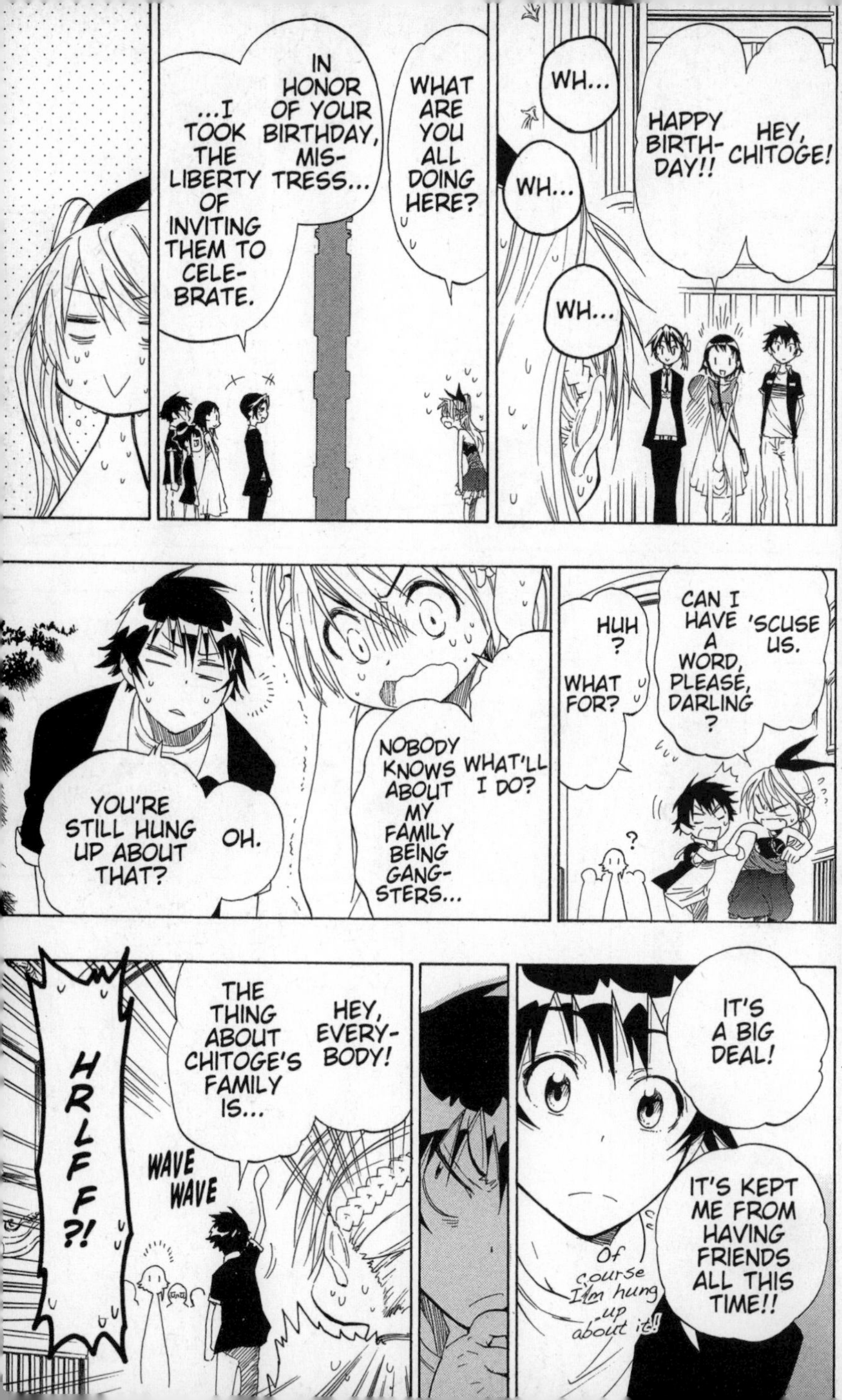
HEY, CHITOGE!
HAPPY BIRTH-DAY!!
WH...
WH...
WH...
WHAT ARE YOU ALL DOING HERE?
IN HONOR OF YOUR BIRTHDAY, MIS-TRESS...
...I TOOK THE LIBERTY OF INVITING THEM TO CELE-BRATE.
'SCUSE US.
CAN I HAVE A WORD, PLEASE, DARLING?
HUH? WHAT FOR?
WHAT'LL I DO?
NOBODY KNOWS ABOUT MY FAMILY BEING GANG-STERS...
OH.
YOU'RE STILL HUNG UP ABOUT THAT?
IT'S A BIG DEAL!
IT'S KEPT ME FROM HAVING FRIENDS ALL THIS TIME!!
Of course I'm hung up about it!!
HEY, EVERY-BODY!
THE THING ABOUT CHITOGE'S FAMILY IS...
WAVE WAVE
HRLFF?!

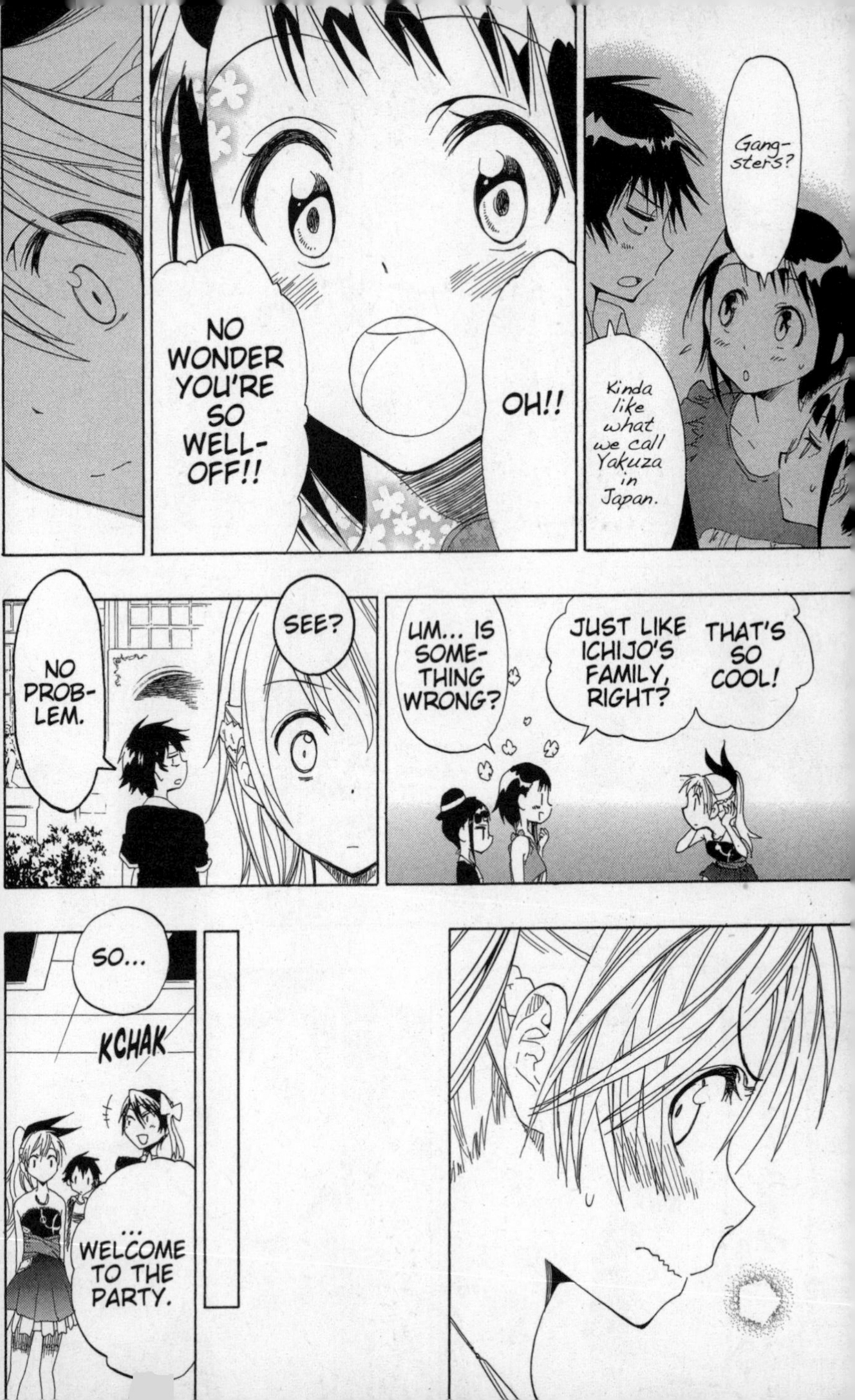
Gang-sters?
Kinda like what we call Yakuza in Japan.
OH!!
NO WONDER YOU'RE SO WELL-OFF!!
THAT'S SO COOL!
JUST LIKE ICHIJO'S FAMILY, RIGHT?
UM... IS SOME-THING WRONG?
SEE?
NO PROB-LEM.
SO...
KCHAK
...WELCOME TO THE PARTY.

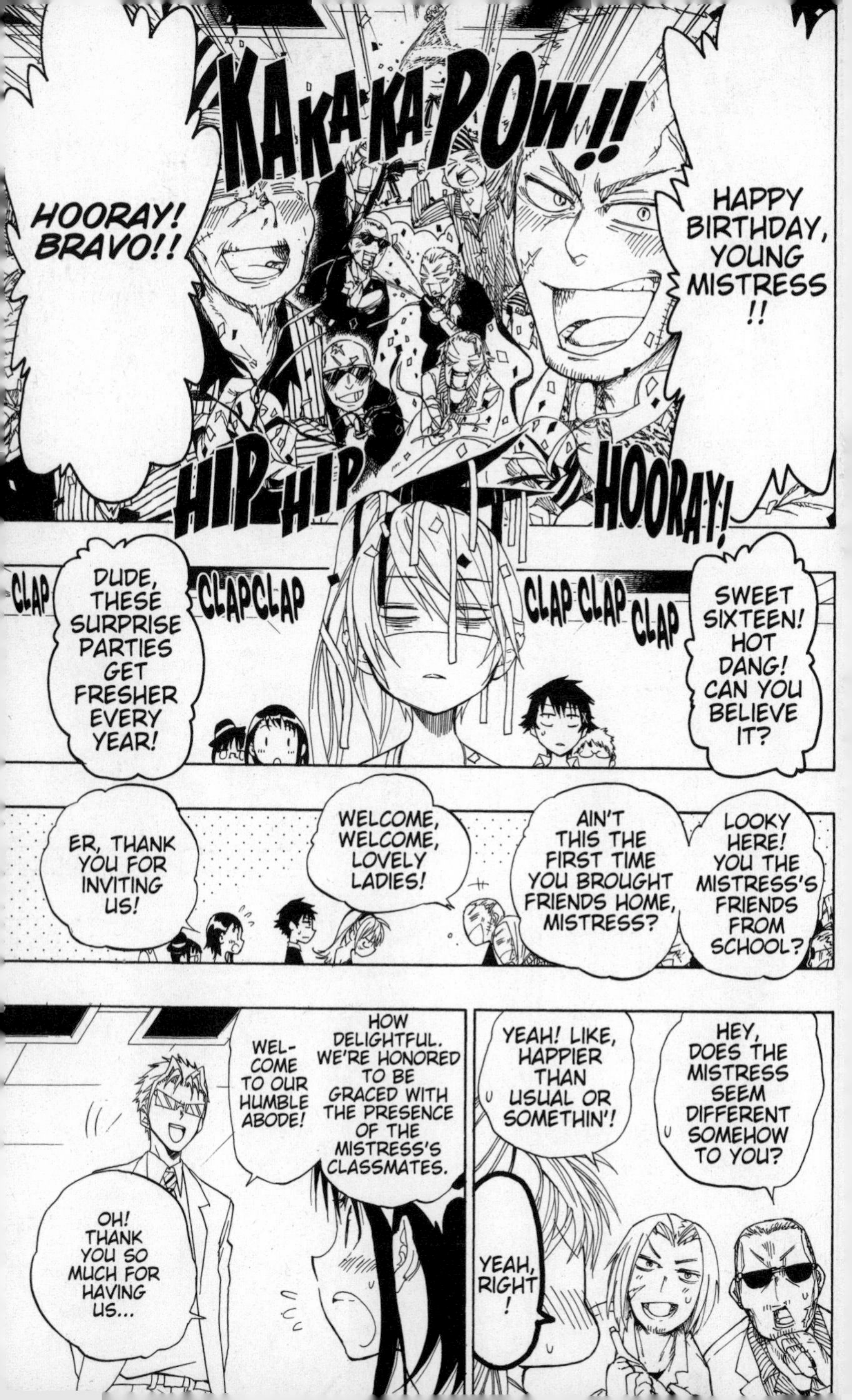
HAPPY BIRTHDAY, YOUNG MISTRESS !!
KAKAKAPOW!!
HOORAY! BRAVO!!
HIP HIP HOORAY!
SWEET SIXTEEN! HOT DANG! CAN YOU BELIEVE IT?
CLAP CLAP CLAP
CLAPCLAP
DUDE, THESE SURPRISE PARTIES GET FRESHER EVERY YEAR!
CLAP
LOOKY HERE! YOU THE MISTRESS'S FRIENDS FROM SCHOOL?
AIN'T THIS THE FIRST TIME YOU BROUGHT FRIENDS HOME, MISTRESS?
WELCOME, WELCOME, LOVELY LADIES!
ER, THANK YOU FOR INVITING US!
HEY, DOES THE MISTRESS SEEM DIFFERENT SOMEHOW TO YOU?
YEAH! LIKE, HAPPIER THAN USUAL OR SOMETHIN'!
YEAH, RIGHT!
HOW DELIGHTFUL. WE'RE HONORED TO BE GRACED WITH THE PRESENCE OF THE MISTRESS'S CLASSMATES.
WEL-COME TO OUR HUMBLE ABODE!
OH! THANK YOU SO MUCH FOR HAVING US...

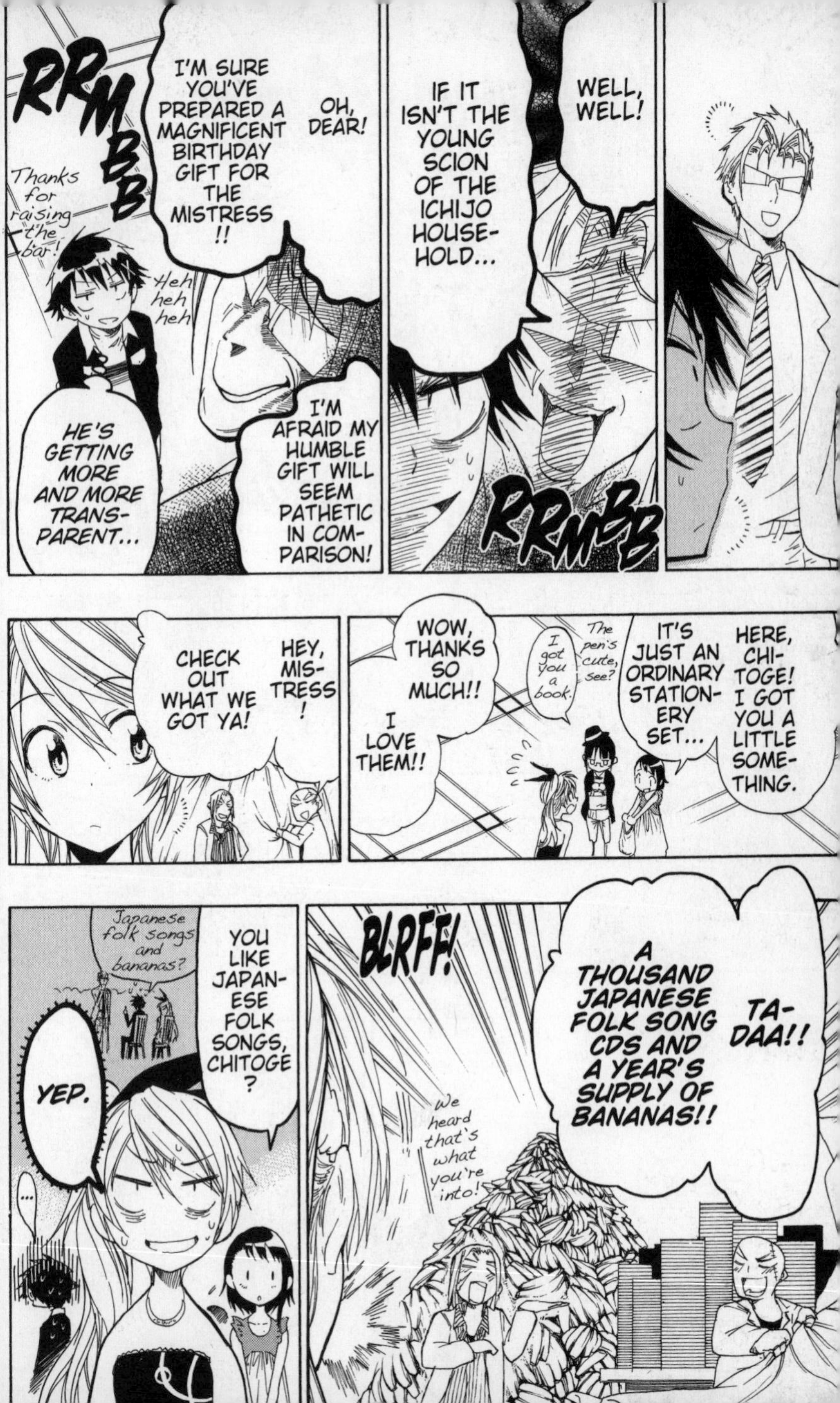
WELL, WELL!
IF IT ISN'T THE YOUNG SCION OF THE ICHIJO HOUSE-HOLD...
RRMBB
OH, DEAR!
I'M SURE YOU'VE PREPARED A MAGNIFICENT BIRTHDAY GIFT FOR THE MISTRESS!!
I'M AFRAID MY HUMBLE GIFT WILL SEEM PATHETIC IN COM-PARISON!
RRMBB
Heh heh heh
Thanks for raising the bar!
HE'S GETTING MORE AND MORE TRANS-PARENT...
HERE, CHI-TOGE! I GOT YOU A LITTLE SOME-THING.
IT'S JUST AN ORDINARY STATION-ERY SET...
The pen's cute, see?
I got you a book.
WOW, THANKS SO MUCH!!
I LOVE THEM!!
HEY, MIS-TRESS!
CHECK OUT WHAT WE GOT YA!
TA-DAA!!
A THOUSAND JAPANESE FOLK SONG CDS AND A YEAR'S SUPPLY OF BANANAS!!
BLRFF!
We heard that's what you're into!
Japanese folk songs and bananas?
YOU LIKE JAPAN-ESE FOLK SONGS, CHITOGE?
YEP.
...

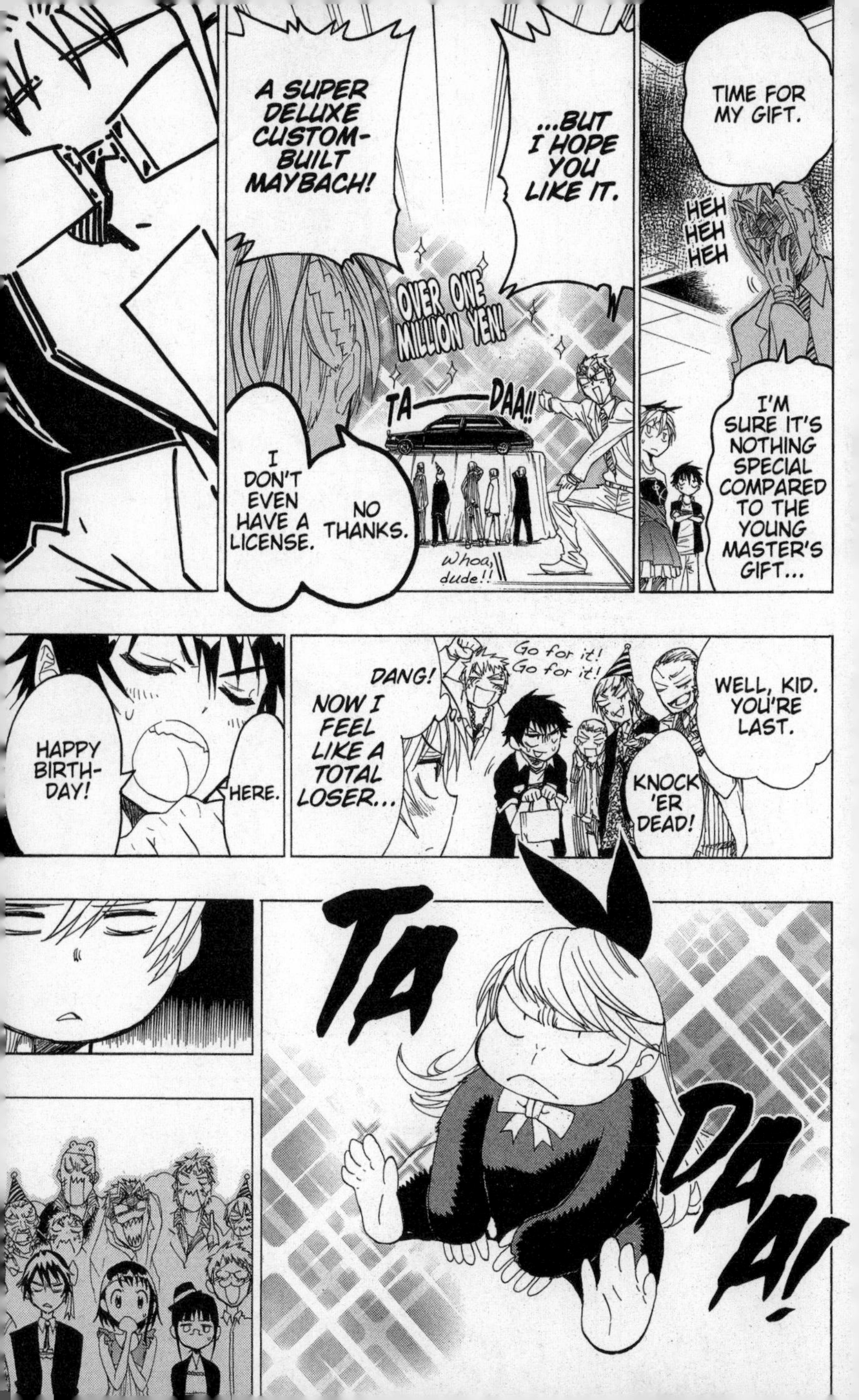
TIME FOR MY GIFT.
HEH HEH HEH
I'M SURE IT'S NOTHING SPECIAL COMPARED TO THE YOUNG MASTER'S GIFT...
...BUT I HOPE YOU LIKE IT.
A SUPER DELUXE CUSTOM-BUILT MAYBACH!
OVER ONE MILLION YEN!
TA—DAA!!
Whoa, dude!!
NO THANKS.
I DON'T EVEN HAVE A LICENSE.
WELL, KID. YOU'RE LAST.
Go for it! Go for it!
KNOCK 'ER DEAD!
DANG! NOW I FEEL LIKE A TOTAL LOSER...
HERE.
HAPPY BIRTH-DAY!
TA DAA!

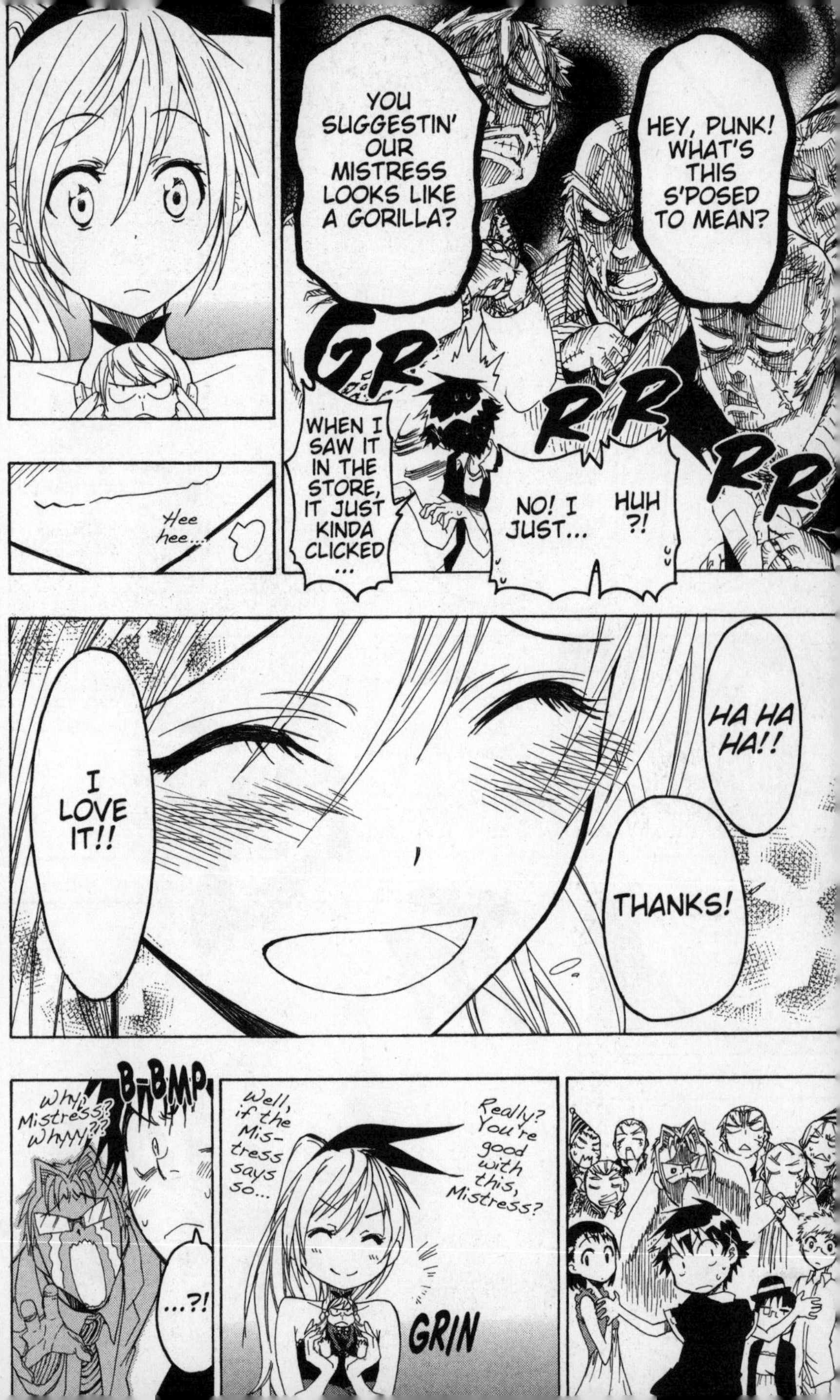
HEY, PUNK! WHAT'S THIS S'POSED TO MEAN?
YOU SUGGESTIN' OUR MISTRESS LOOKS LIKE A GORILLA?
GRRRR
HUH ?!
NO! I JUST...
WHEN I SAW IT IN THE STORE, IT JUST KINDA CLICKED ...
Hee hee...
HA HA HA!!
THANKS!
I LOVE IT!!
Really? You're good with this, Mistress?
Well, if the Mistress says so...
GRIN
B-BMP
...?!
Why, Mistress? Whyyy?!

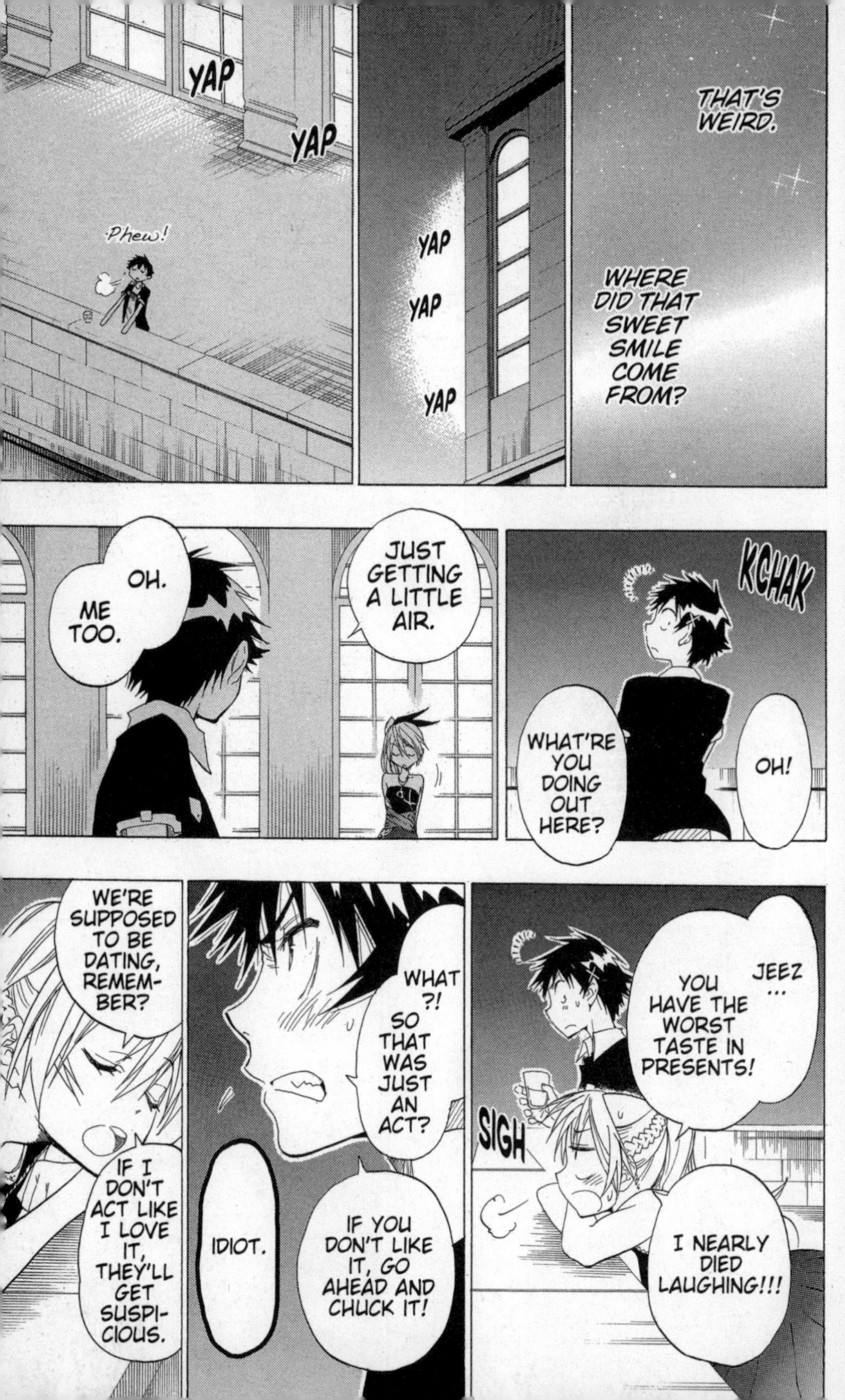
THAT'S WEIRD.
WHERE DID THAT SWEET SMILE COME FROM?
YAP
YAP
YAP
YAP
YAP
Phew!
KCHAK
OH!
WHAT'RE YOU DOING OUT HERE?
JUST GETTING A LITTLE AIR.
OH. ME TOO.
JEEZ...
YOU HAVE THE WORST TASTE IN PRESENTS!
SIGH
I NEARLY DIED LAUGHING!!!
WHAT?!
SO THAT WAS JUST AN ACT?
IF YOU DON'T LIKE IT, GO AHEAD AND CHUCK IT!
IDIOT.
WE'RE SUPPOSED TO BE DATING, REMEMBER?
IF I DON'T ACT LIKE I LOVE IT, THEY'LL GET SUSPICIOUS.

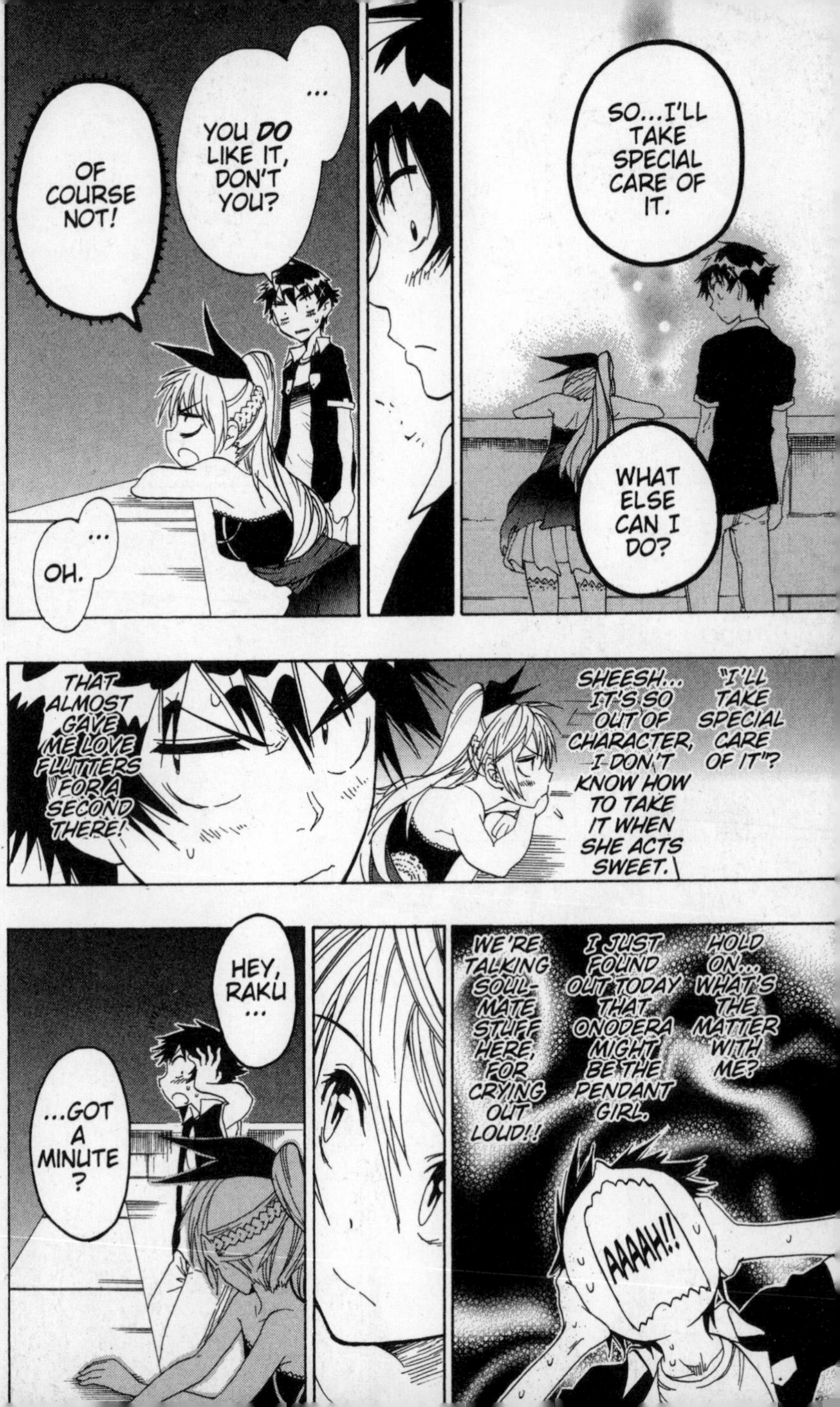
SO...I'LL TAKE SPECIAL CARE OF IT.
WHAT ELSE CAN I DO?
...
YOU DO LIKE IT, DON'T YOU?
OF COURSE NOT!
... OH.
"I'LL TAKE SPECIAL CARE OF IT"?
SHEESH... IT'S SO OUT OF CHARACTER, I DON'T KNOW HOW TO TAKE IT WHEN SHE ACTS SWEET.
THAT ALMOST GAVE ME LOVE FLUTTERS FOR A SECOND THERE!
HOLD ON... WHAT'S THE MATTER WITH ME?
I JUST FOUND OUT TODAY THAT ONODERA MIGHT BE THE PENDANT GIRL.
WE'RE TALKING SOUL-MATE STUFF HERE, FOR CRYING OUT LOUD!!
AAAAH!!
HEY, RAKU...
...GOT A MINUTE?

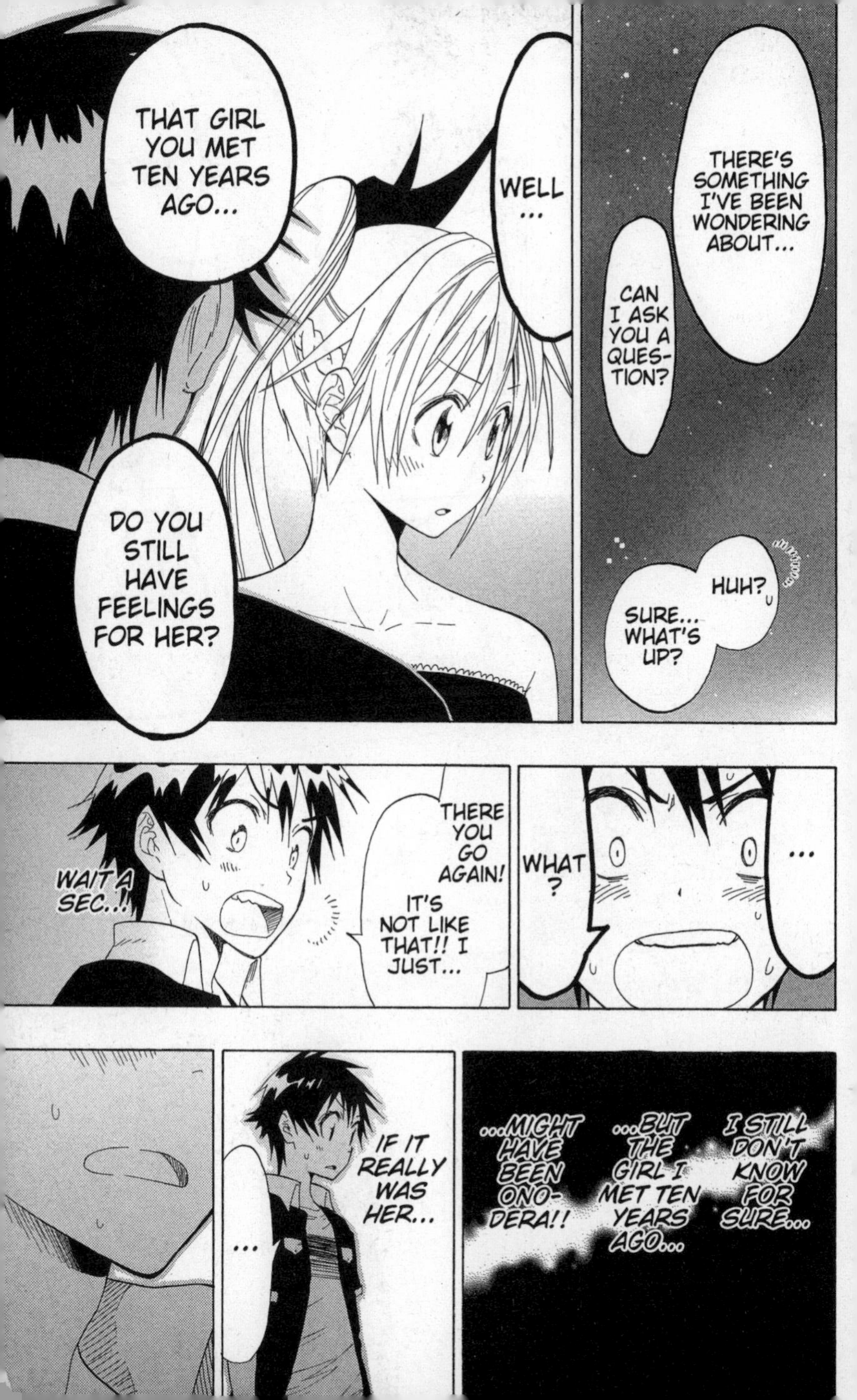
THERE'S SOMETHING I'VE BEEN WONDERING ABOUT...
CAN I ASK YOU A QUESTION?
HUH?
SURE... WHAT'S UP?
WELL...
THAT GIRL YOU MET TEN YEARS AGO...
DO YOU STILL HAVE FEELINGS FOR HER?
...
WHAT?
THERE YOU GO AGAIN!
IT'S NOT LIKE THAT!! I JUST...
WAIT A SEC..!
I STILL DON'T KNOW FOR SURE...
...BUT THE GIRL I MET TEN YEARS AGO...
...MIGHT HAVE BEEN ONODERA!!
IF IT REALLY WAS HER...
...

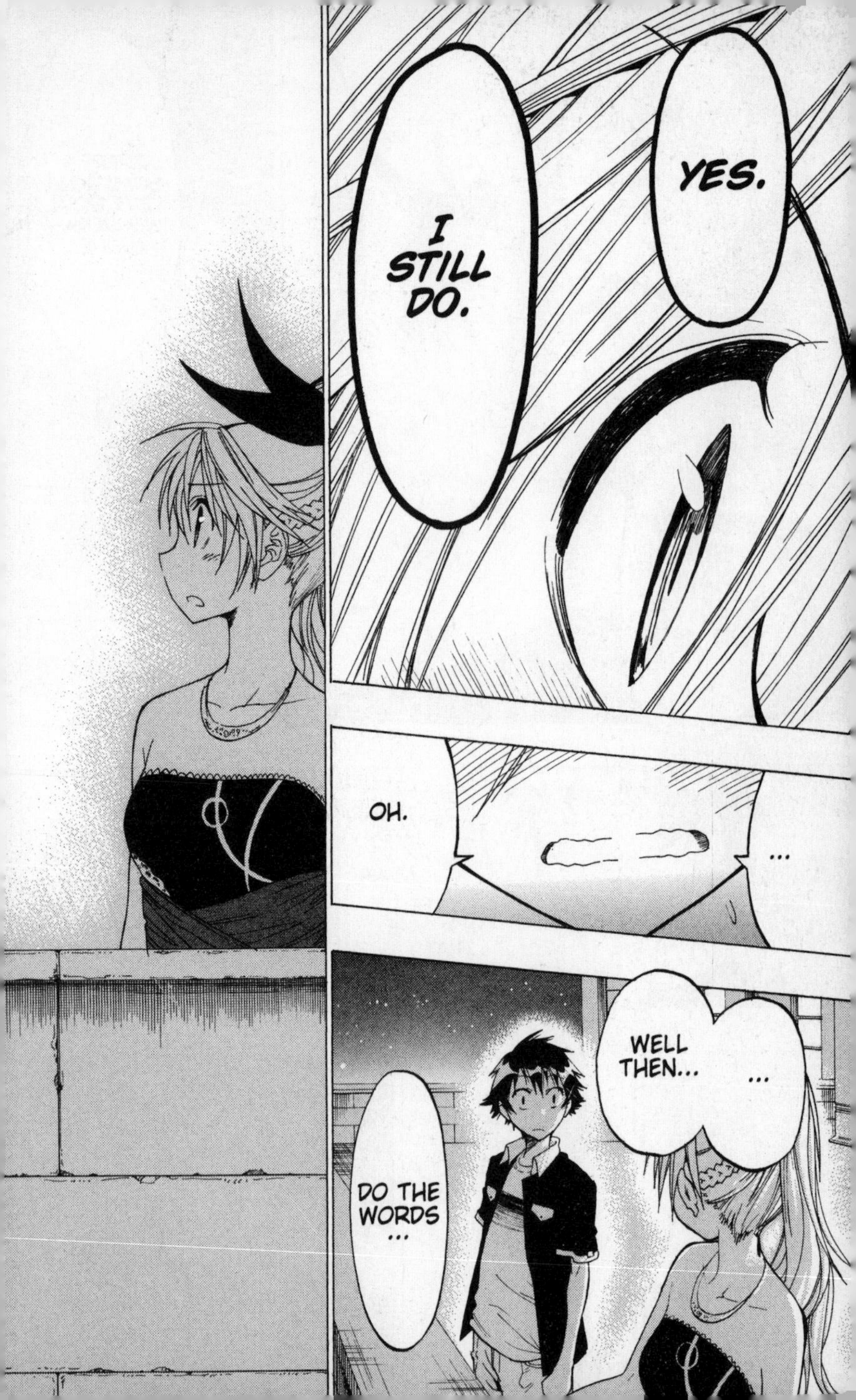

YES.
I STILL DO.
...
OH.
WELL THEN... ...
DO THE WORDS ...

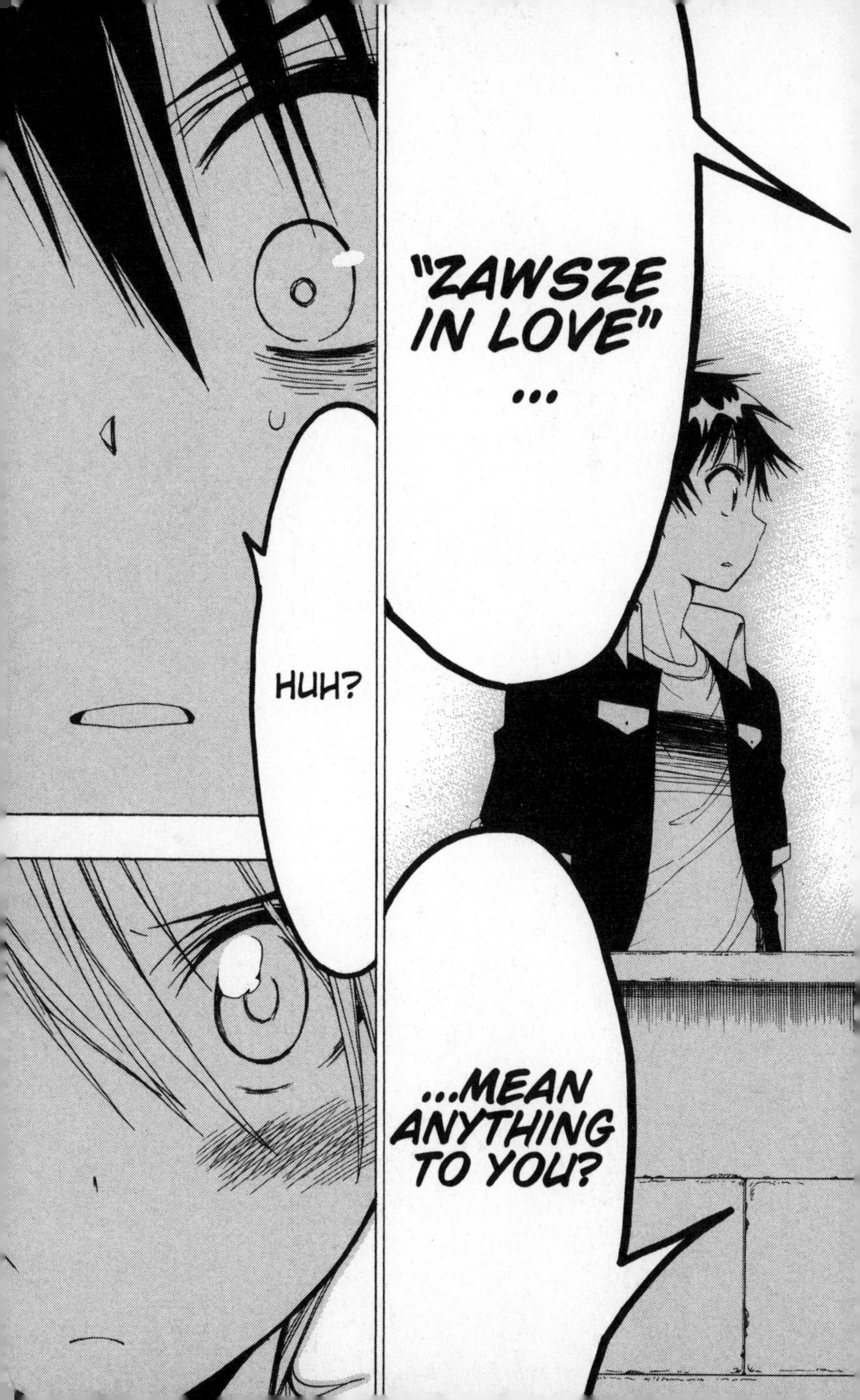
"ZAWSZE IN LOVE" ...
...MEAN ANYTHING TO YOU?
HUH?

The Shopping Trip

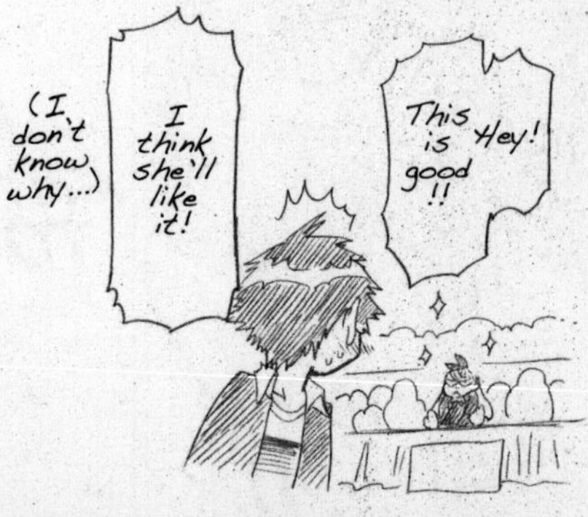
Hey!
This is good!!
I think she'll like it!
(I don't know why...)

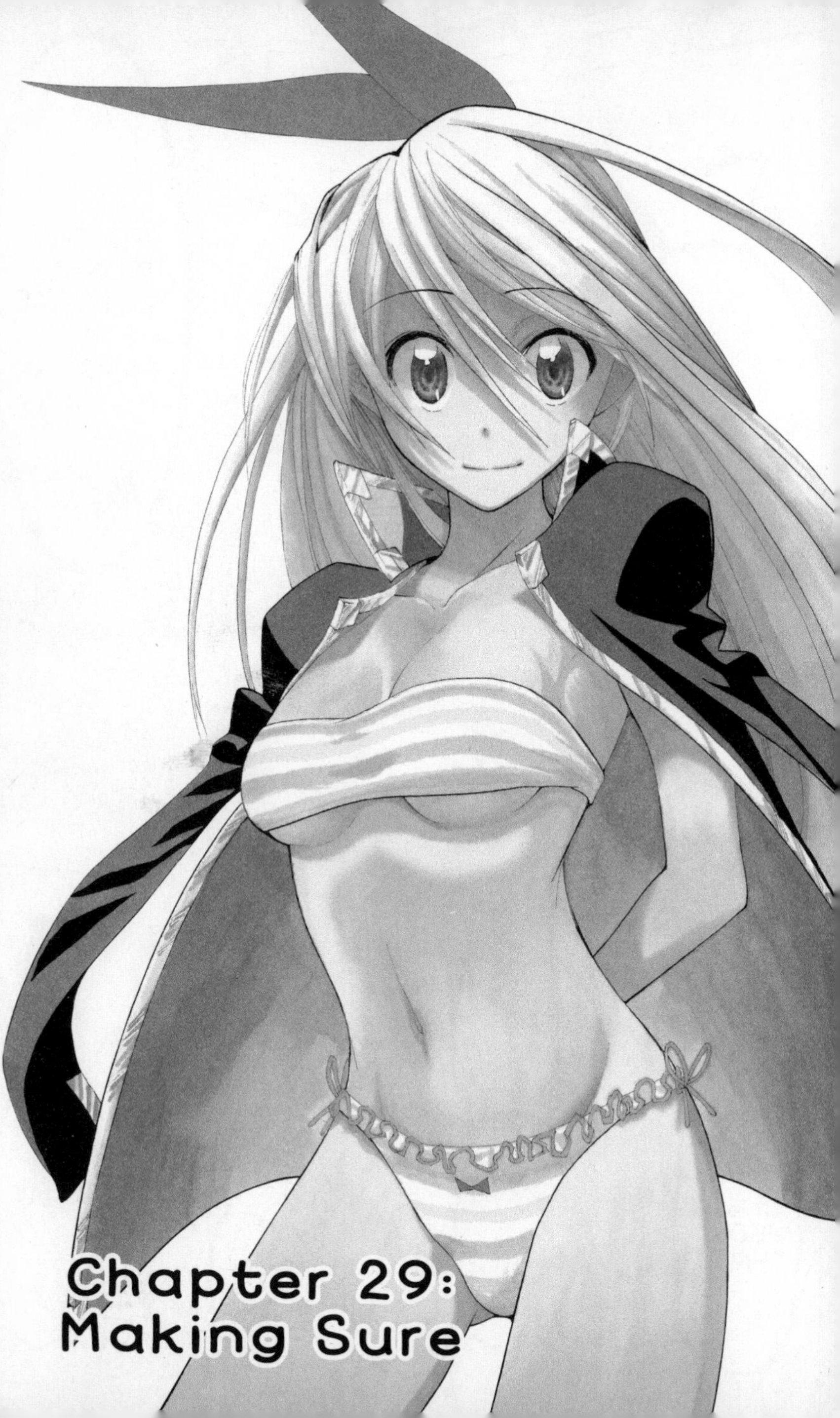

Chapter 29: Making Sure

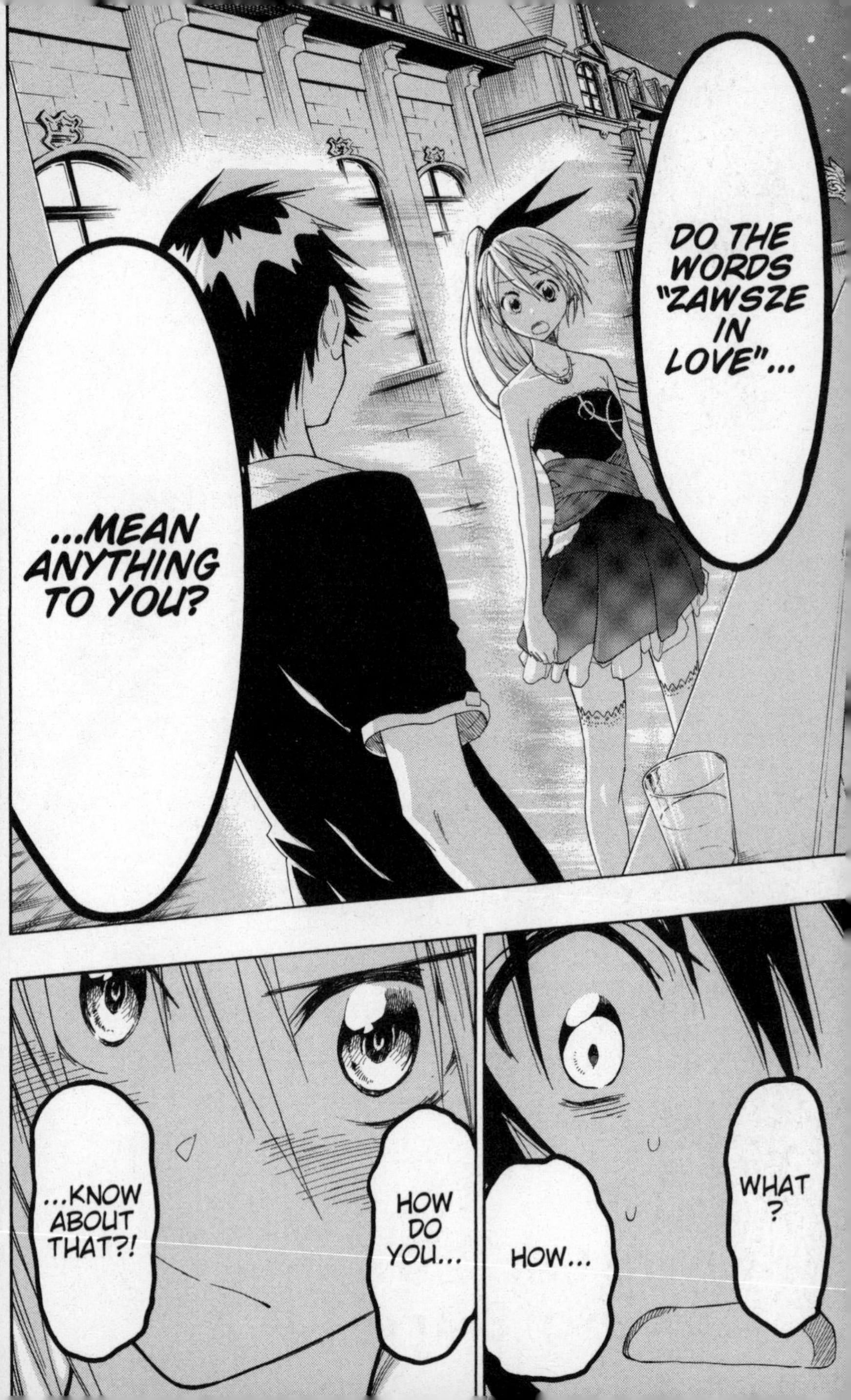
DO THE WORDS "ZAWSZE IN LOVE"...
...MEAN ANYTHING TO YOU?
WHAT?
HOW...
HOW DO YOU...
...KNOW ABOUT THAT?!

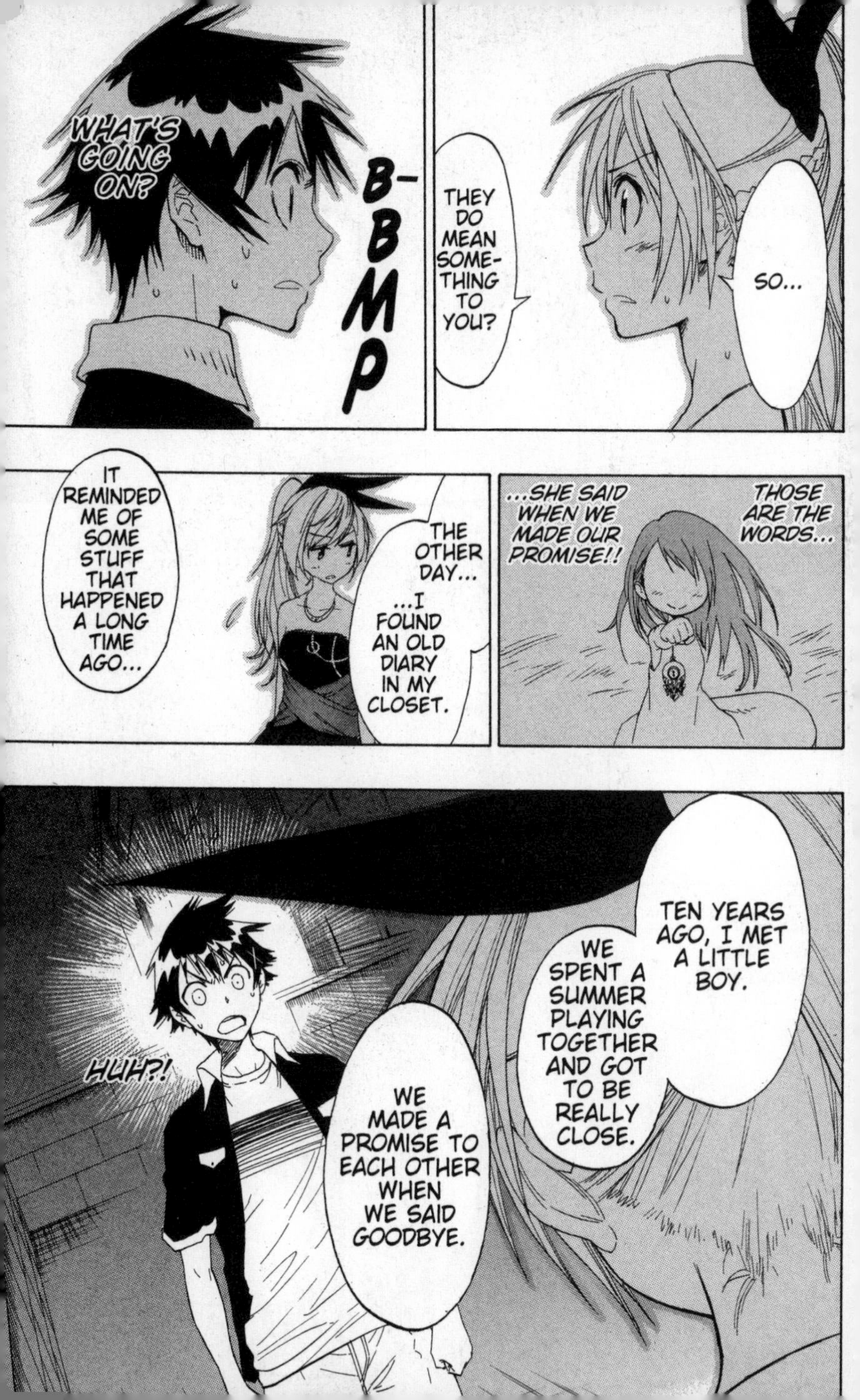
SO...
THEY DO MEAN SOMETHING TO YOU?
B-BBMP
WHAT'S GOING ON?
THOSE ARE THE WORDS...
...SHE SAID WHEN WE MADE OUR PROMISE!!
THE OTHER DAY...
...I FOUND AN OLD DIARY IN MY CLOSET.
IT REMINDED ME OF SOME STUFF THAT HAPPENED A LONG TIME AGO...
TEN YEARS AGO, I MET A LITTLE BOY.
WE SPENT A SUMMER PLAYING TOGETHER AND GOT TO BE REALLY CLOSE.
WE MADE A PROMISE TO EACH OTHER WHEN WE SAID GOODBYE.
HUH?!

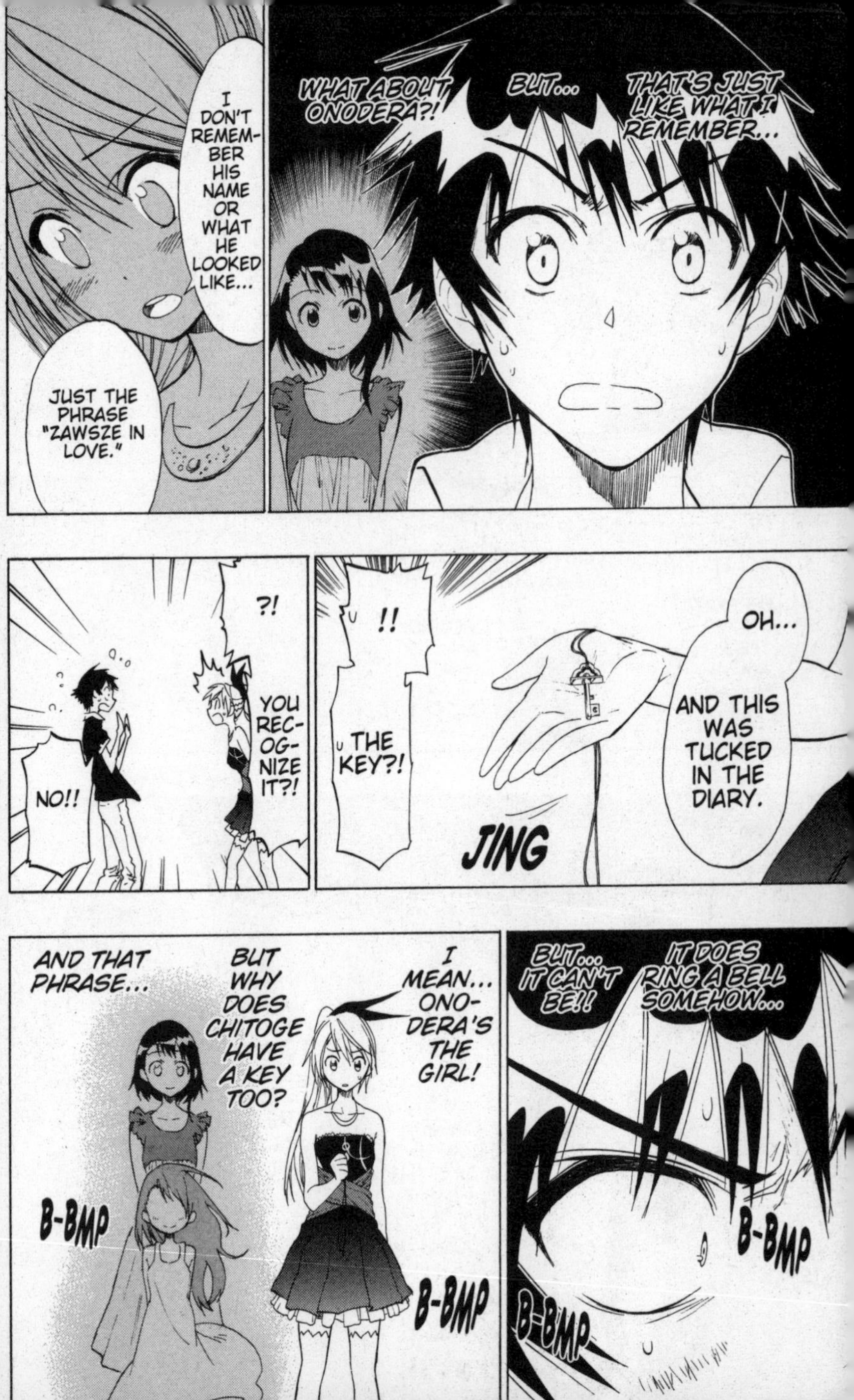
THAT'S JUST LIKE WHAT I REMEMBER...
BUT...
WHAT ABOUT ONODERA?!
I DON'T REMEMBER HIS NAME OR WHAT HE LOOKED LIKE...
JUST THE PHRASE "ZAWSZE IN LOVE."
OH...
AND THIS WAS TUCKED IN THE DIARY.
JING
!!
THE KEY?!
?!
YOU RECOGNIZE IT?!
NO!!
IT DOES RING A BELL SOMEHOW...
BUT... IT CAN'T BE!!
B-BMP
B-BMP
I MEAN... ONODERA'S THE GIRL!
BUT WHY DOES CHITOGE HAVE A KEY TOO?
AND THAT PHRASE...
B-BMP
B-BMP

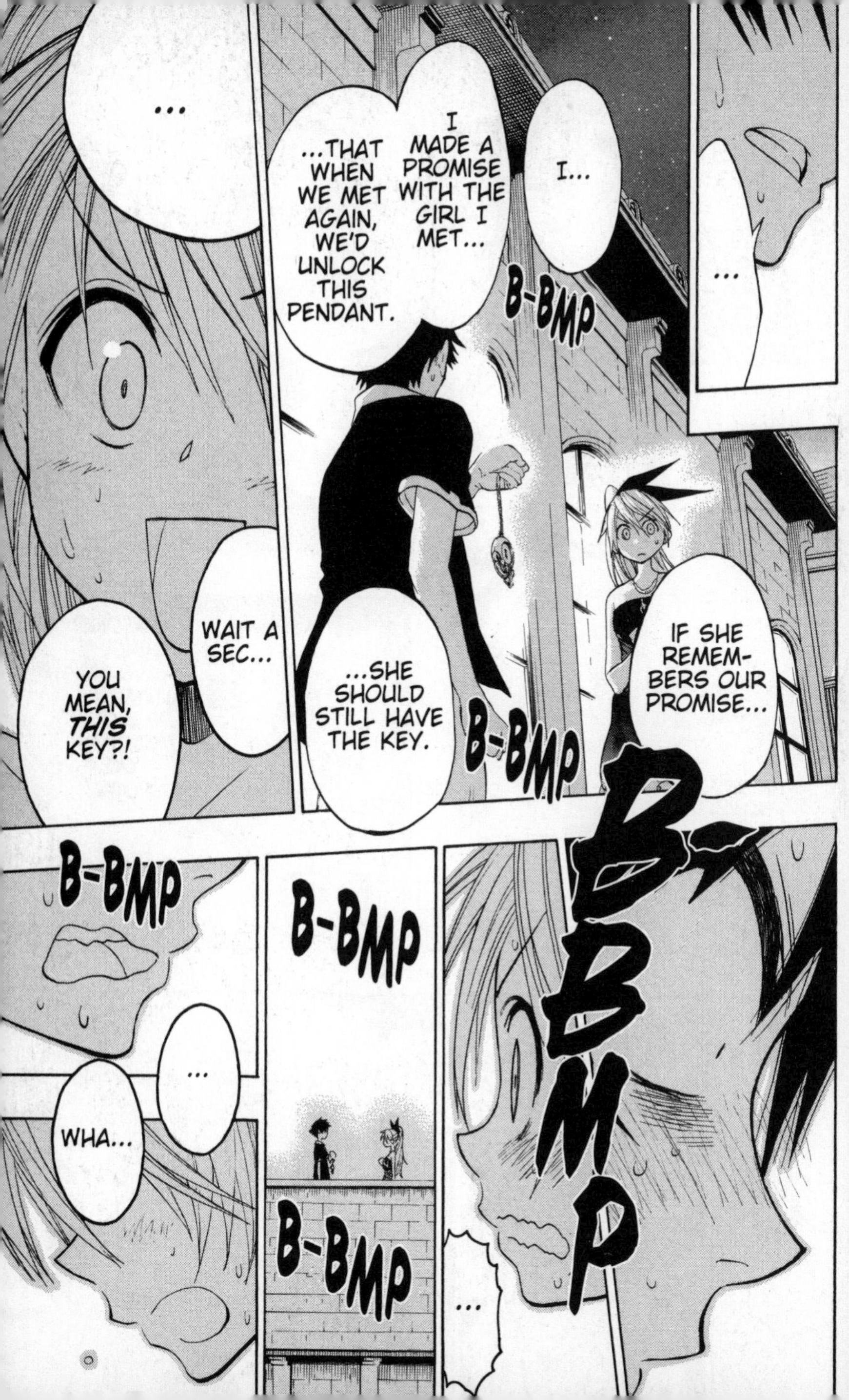
...
I...
I MADE A PROMISE WITH THE GIRL I MET...
...THAT WHEN WE MET AGAIN, WE'D UNLOCK THIS PENDANT.
B-BMP
IF SHE REMEMBERS OUR PROMISE...
...SHE SHOULD STILL HAVE THE KEY.
B-BMP
...
WAIT A SEC...
YOU MEAN, *THIS* KEY?!
BBMP
...
B-BMP
B-BMP
B-BMP
...
WHA...

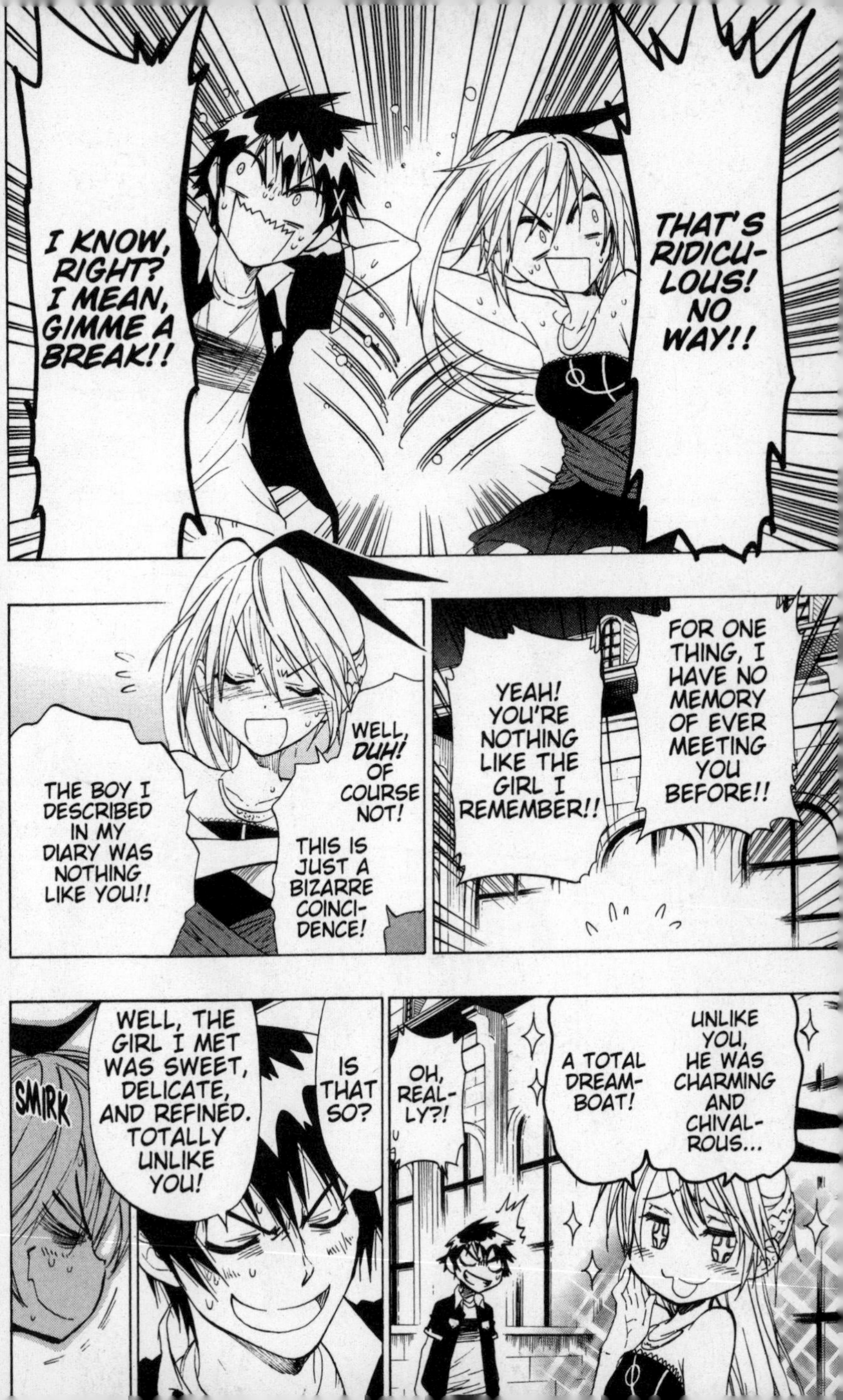
THAT'S RIDICULOUS! NO WAY!!
I KNOW, RIGHT? I MEAN, GIMME A BREAK!!
FOR ONE THING, I HAVE NO MEMORY OF EVER MEETING YOU BEFORE!!
YEAH! YOU'RE NOTHING LIKE THE GIRL I REMEMBER!!
WELL, DUH! OF COURSE NOT!
THIS IS JUST A BIZARRE COINCIDENCE!
THE BOY I DESCRIBED IN MY DIARY WAS NOTHING LIKE YOU!!
UNLIKE YOU, HE WAS CHARMING AND CHIVALROUS...
A TOTAL DREAMBOAT!
OH, REALLY?!
IS THAT SO?
WELL, THE GIRL I MET WAS SWEET, DELICATE, AND REFINED. TOTALLY UNLIKE YOU!
SMIRK

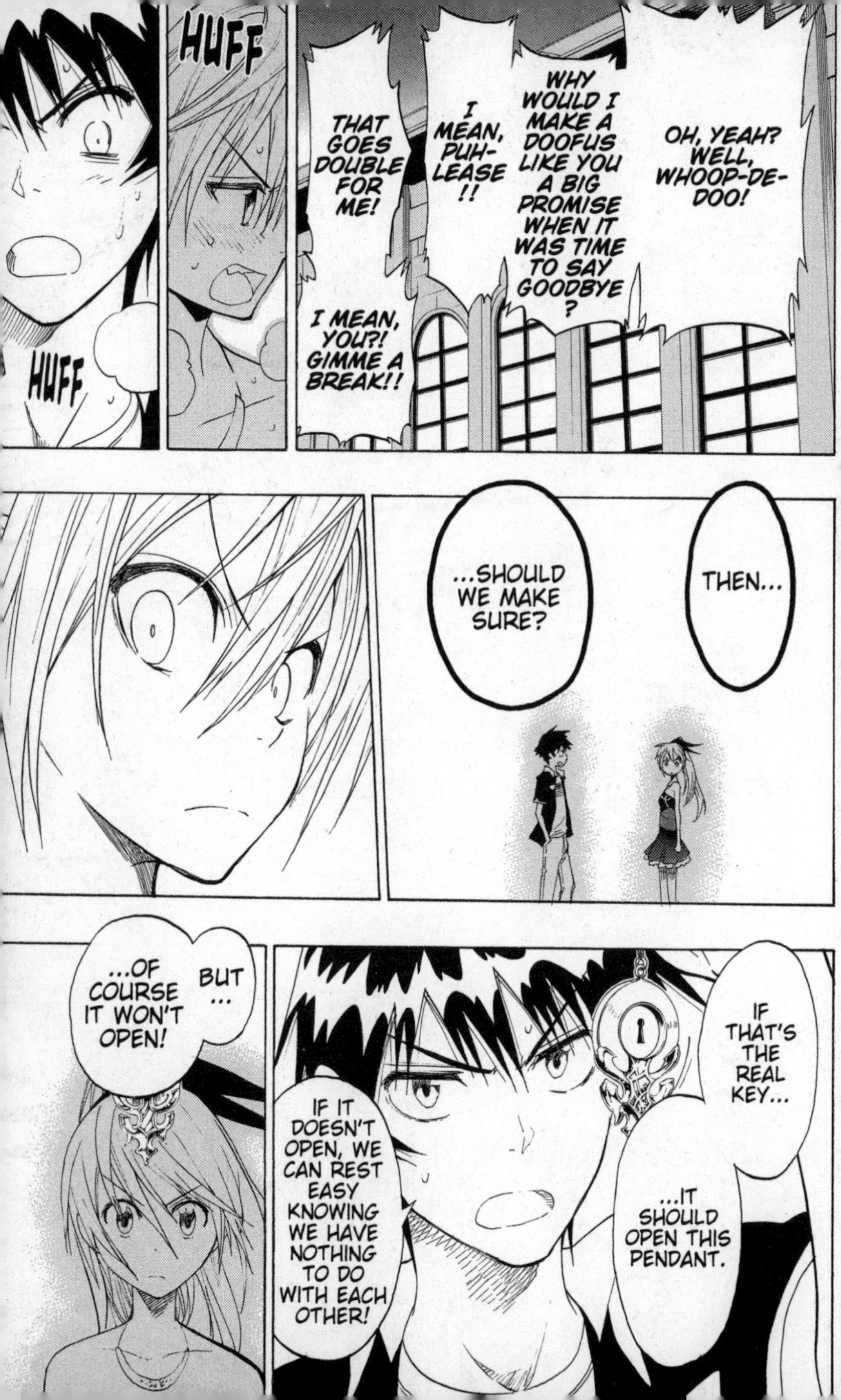
OH, YEAH? WELL, WHOOP-DE-DOO!
WHY WOULD I MAKE A DOOFUS LIKE YOU A BIG PROMISE WHEN IT WAS TIME TO SAY GOODBYE?
I MEAN, PUH-LEASE!!
THAT GOES DOUBLE FOR ME!
I MEAN, YOU?! GIMME A BREAK!!
HUFF
HUFF
THEN...
...SHOULD WE MAKE SURE?
IF THAT'S THE REAL KEY...
...IT SHOULD OPEN THIS PENDANT.
IF IT DOESN'T OPEN, WE CAN REST EASY KNOWING WE HAVE NOTHING TO DO WITH EACH OTHER!
BUT...
...OF COURSE IT WON'T OPEN!

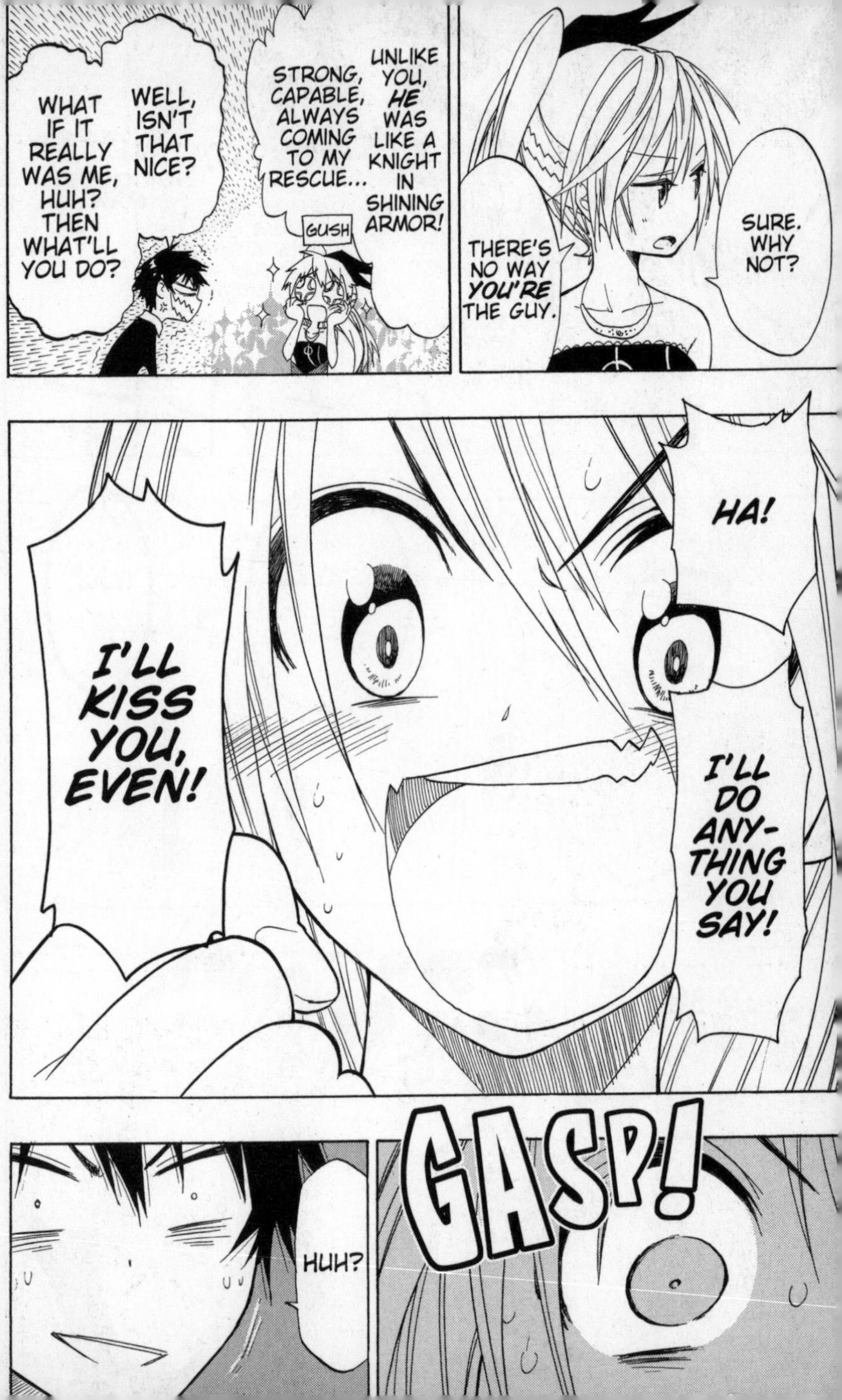
SURE. WHY NOT?
THERE'S NO WAY YOU'RE THE GUY.
UNLIKE YOU, HE WAS LIKE A KNIGHT IN SHINING ARMOR!
STRONG, CAPABLE, ALWAYS COMING TO MY RESCUE...
GUSH
WELL, ISN'T THAT NICE?
WHAT IF IT REALLY WAS ME, HUH? THEN WHAT'LL YOU DO?
HA!
I'LL DO ANYTHING YOU SAY!
I'LL KISS YOU, EVEN!
GASP!
HUH?

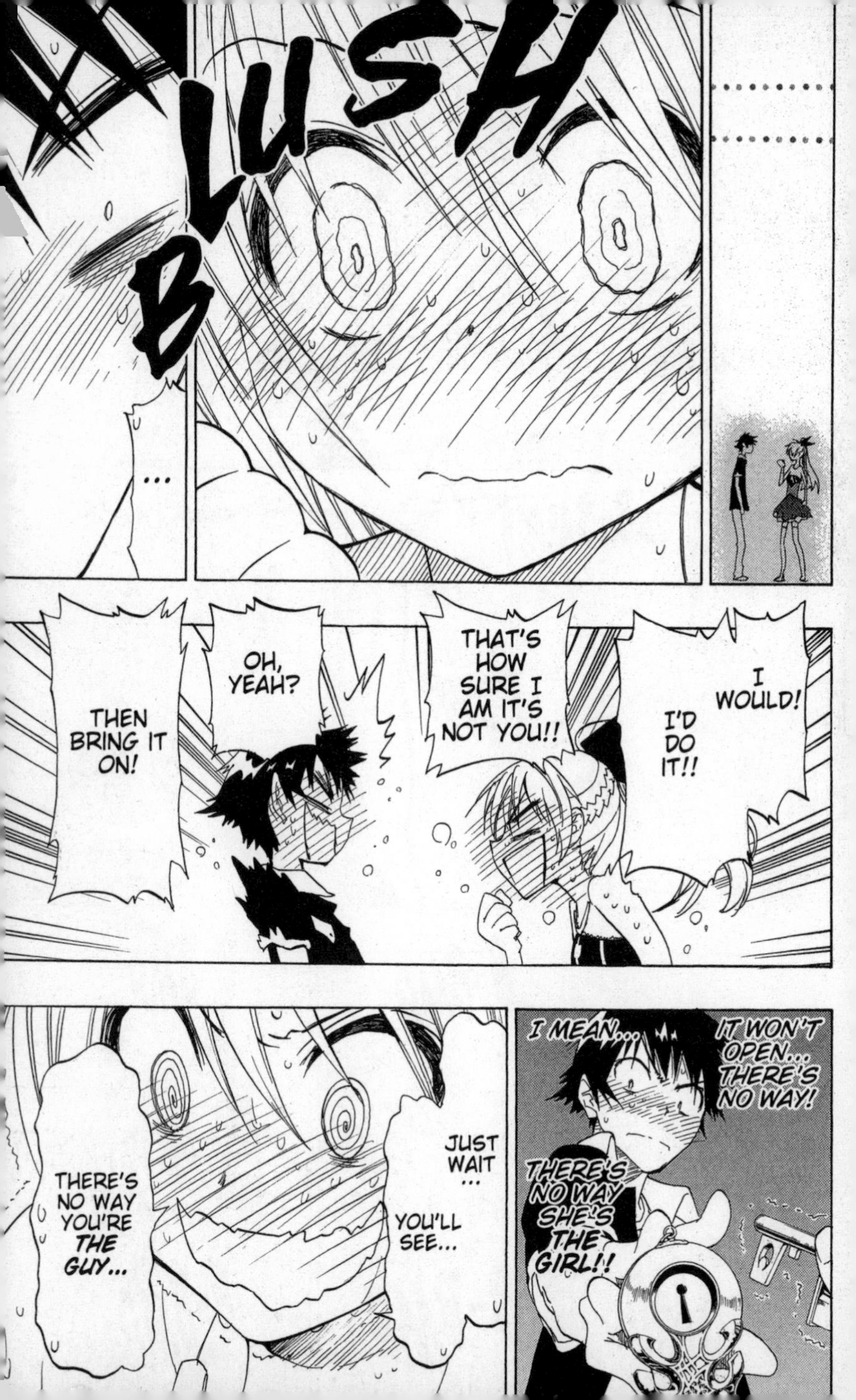
......
......
BLUSH
...
I WOULD!
I'D DO IT!!
THAT'S HOW SURE I AM IT'S NOT YOU!!
OH, YEAH?
THEN BRING IT ON!
IT WON'T OPEN... THERE'S NO WAY!
I MEAN...
THERE'S NO WAY SHE'S THE GIRL!!
JUST WAIT ...
YOU'LL SEE...
THERE'S NO WAY YOU'RE THE GUY...

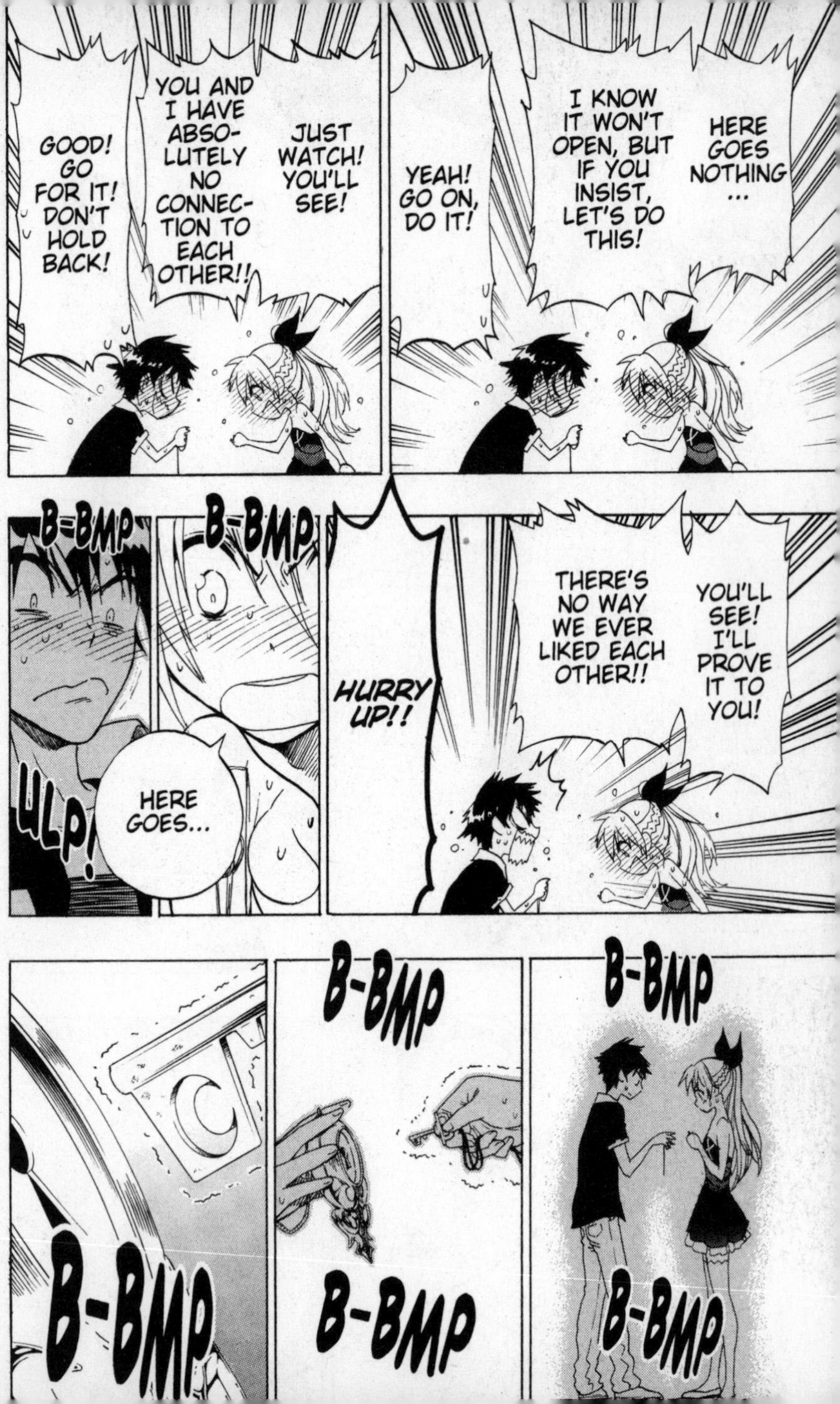
HERE GOES NOTHING...
I KNOW IT WON'T OPEN, BUT IF YOU INSIST, LET'S DO THIS!
YEAH! GO ON, DO IT!
JUST WATCH! YOU'LL SEE!
YOU AND I HAVE ABSOLUTELY NO CONNECTION TO EACH OTHER!!
GOOD! GO FOR IT! DON'T HOLD BACK!
YOU'LL SEE! I'LL PROVE IT TO YOU!
THERE'S NO WAY WE EVER LIKED EACH OTHER!!
HURRY UP!!
B-BMP
B-BMP
HERE GOES...
ULP!
B-BMP
B-BMP
B-BMP
B-BMP
B-BMP

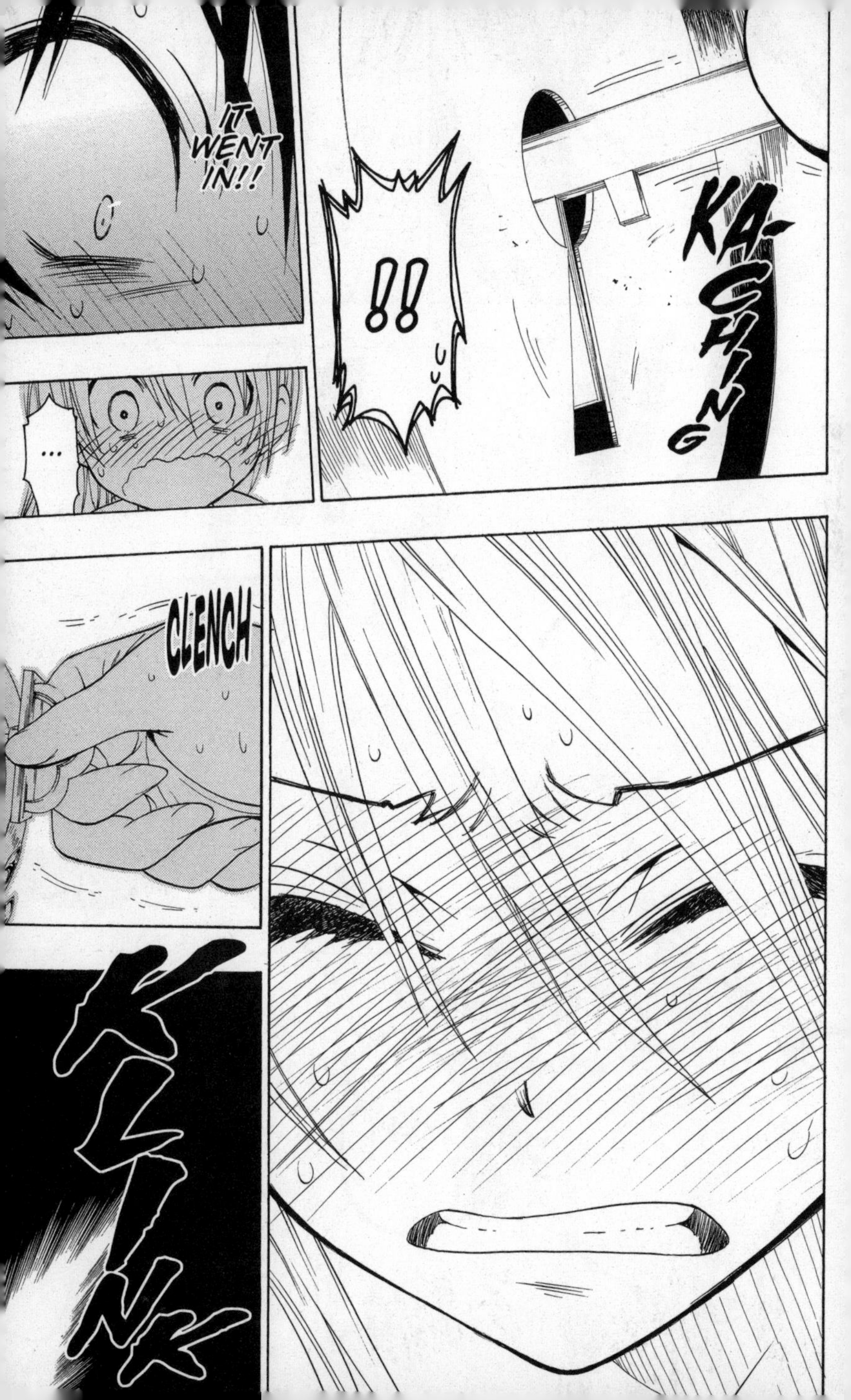
KA-CHING
!!
IT WENT IN!!
...
CLENCH
KLUNK

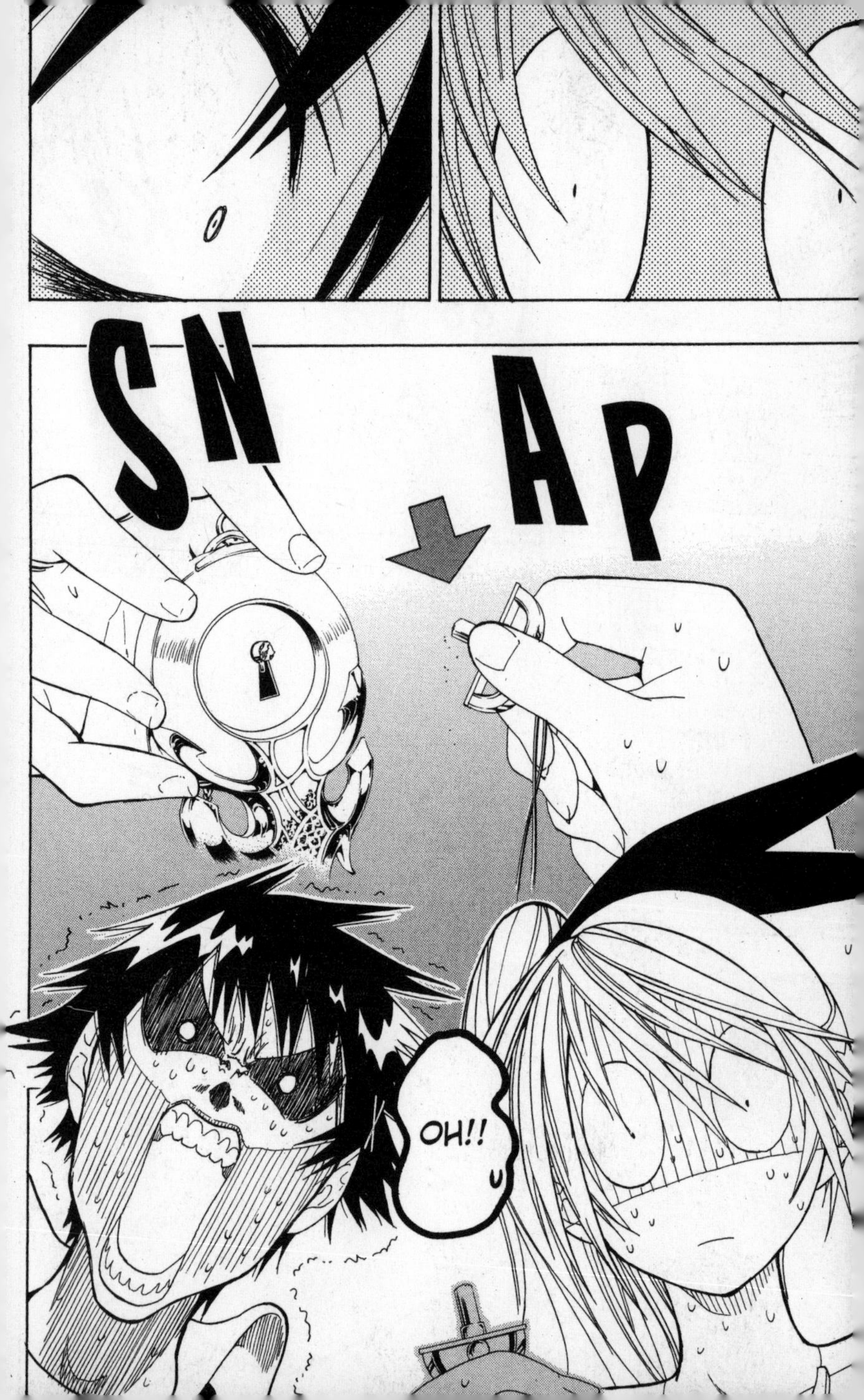
SNAP
OH!!

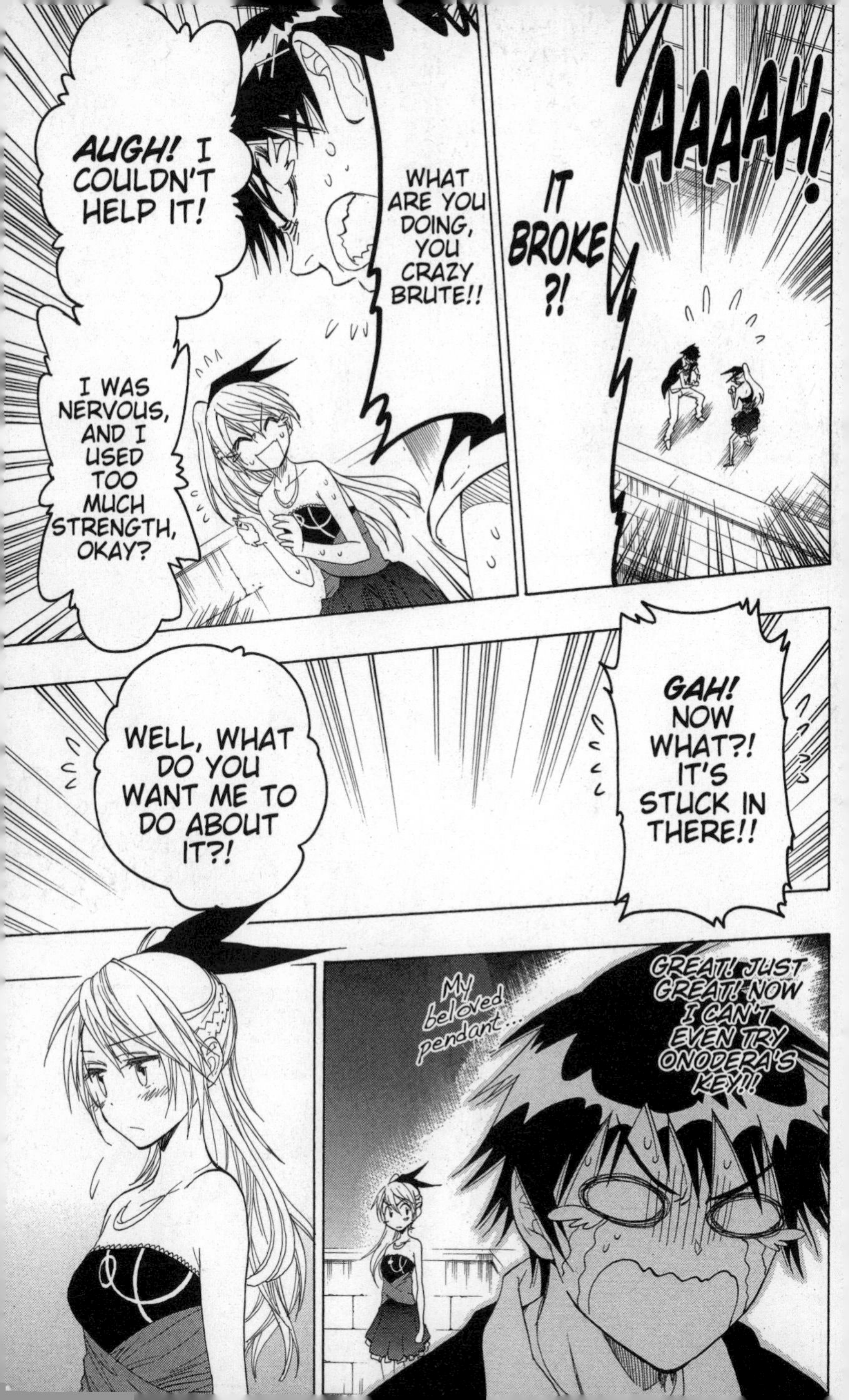
AAAAH!
IT BROKE?!
WHAT ARE YOU DOING, YOU CRAZY BRUTE!!
AUGH! I COULDN'T HELP IT!
I WAS NERVOUS, AND I USED TOO MUCH STRENGTH, OKAY?
GAH! NOW WHAT?! IT'S STUCK IN THERE!!
WELL, WHAT DO YOU WANT ME TO DO ABOUT IT?!
GREAT! JUST GREAT! NOW I CAN'T EVEN TRY ONODERA'S KEY!!
My beloved pendant...

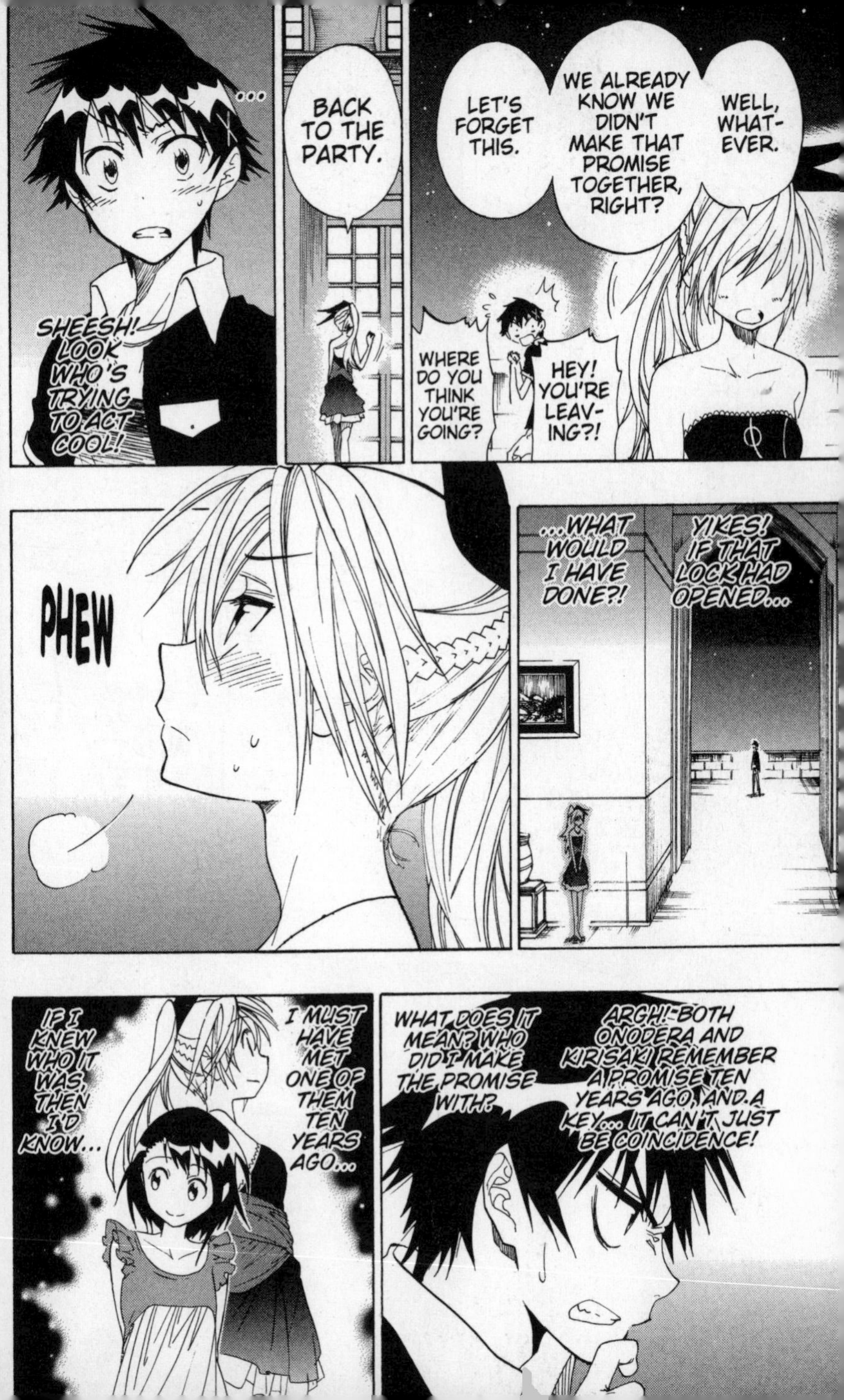
WELL, WHATEVER.
WE ALREADY KNOW WE DIDN'T MAKE THAT PROMISE TOGETHER, RIGHT?
LET'S FORGET THIS.
HEY! YOU'RE LEAVING?!
WHERE DO YOU THINK YOU'RE GOING?
BACK TO THE PARTY.
...
SHEESH! LOOK WHO'S TRYING TO ACT COOL!
YIKES! IF THAT LOCK HAD OPENED...
...WHAT WOULD I HAVE DONE?!
PHEW
ARGH! BOTH ONODERA AND KIRISAKI REMEMBER A PROMISE TEN YEARS AGO, AND A KEY... IT CAN'T JUST BE COINCIDENCE!
WHAT DOES IT MEAN? WHO DID I MAKE THE PROMISE WITH?
I MUST HAVE MET ONE OF THEM TEN YEARS AGO...
IF I KNEW WHO IT WAS, THEN I'D KNOW...

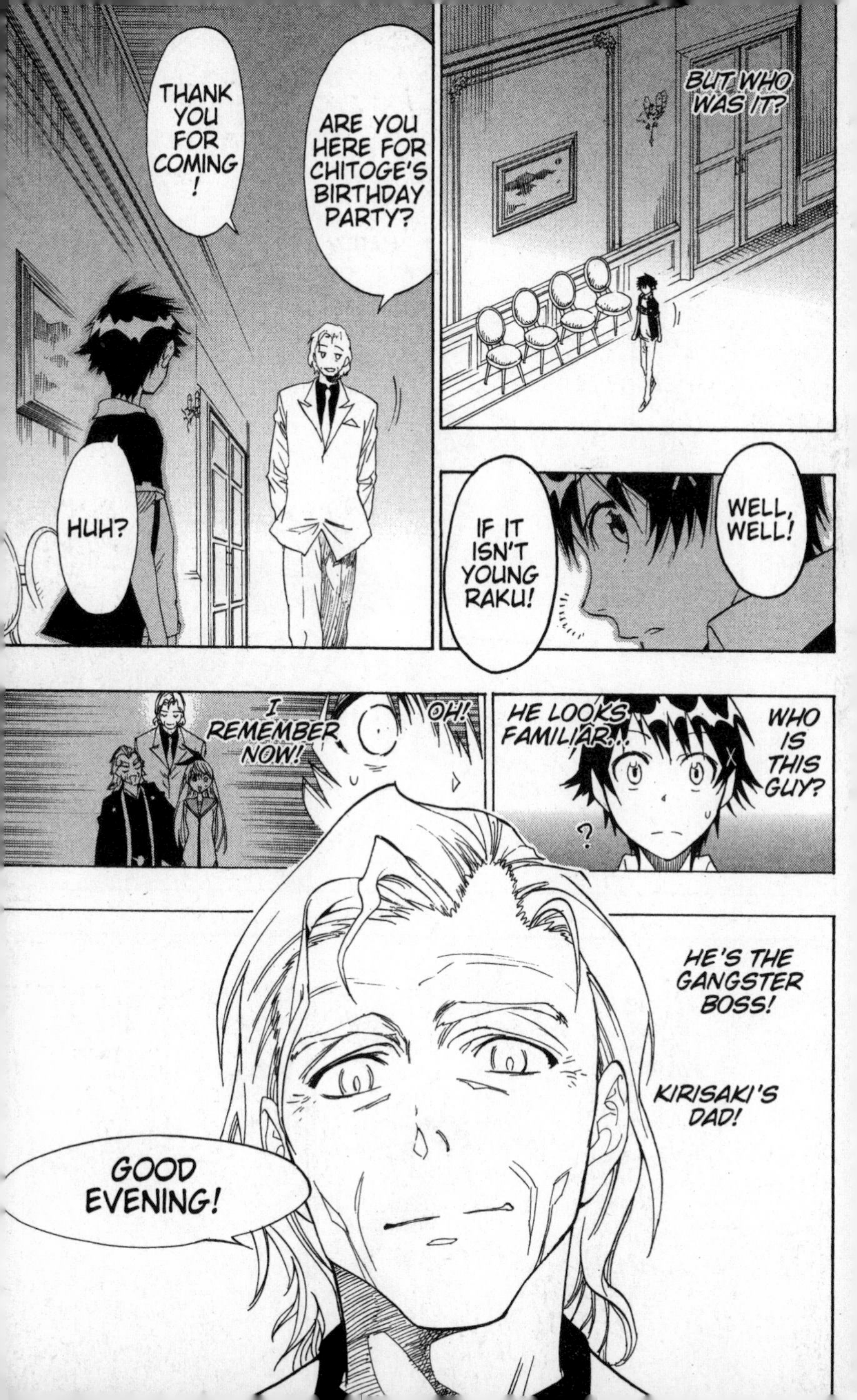
BUT WHO WAS IT?
WELL, WELL!
IF IT ISN'T YOUNG RAKU!
ARE YOU HERE FOR CHITOGE'S BIRTHDAY PARTY?
THANK YOU FOR COMING!
HUH?
WHO IS THIS GUY?
HE LOOKS FAMILIAR...
OH!
I REMEMBER NOW!
HE'S THE GANGSTER BOSS!
KIRISAKI'S DAD!
GOOD EVENING!

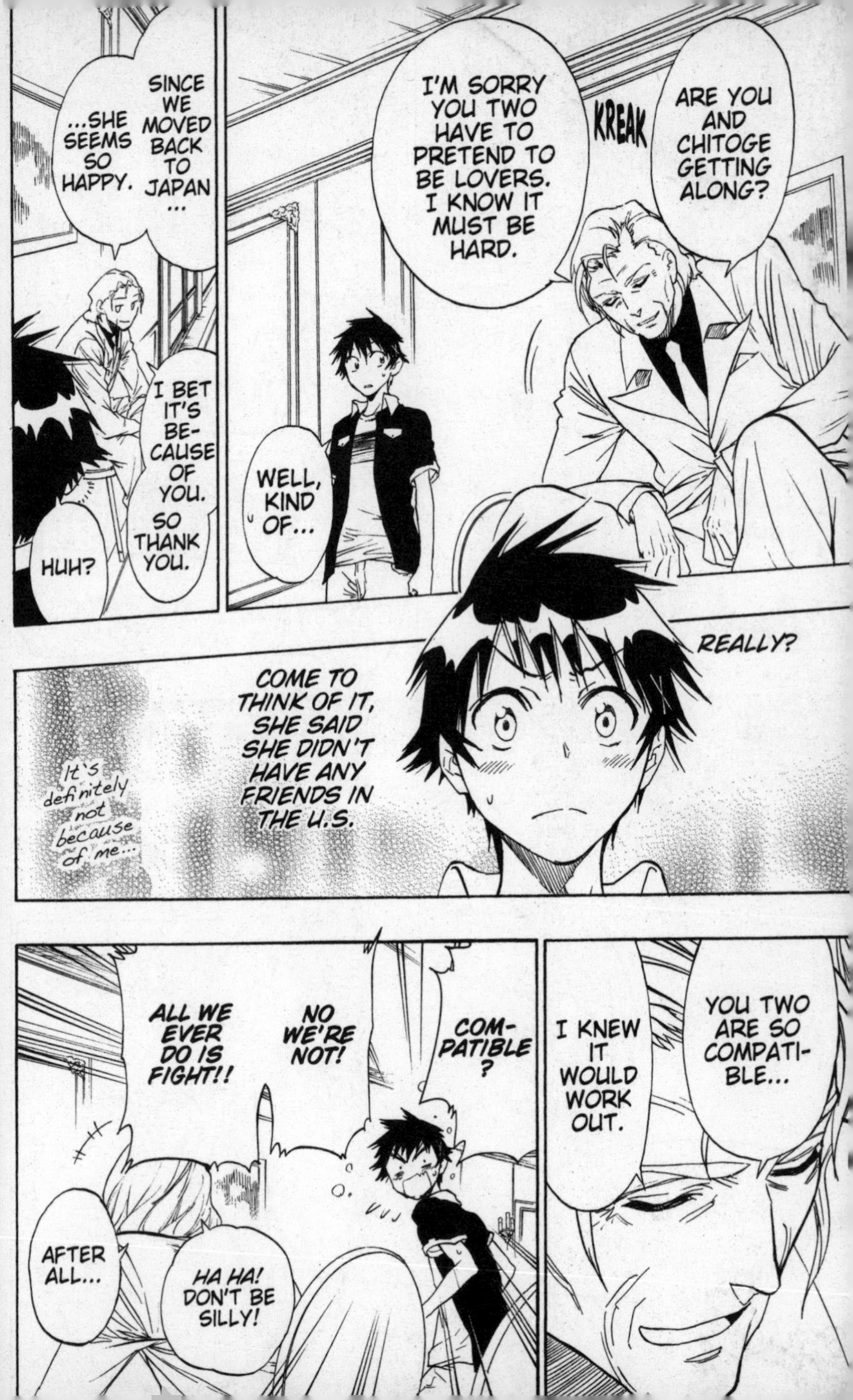

ARE YOU AND CHITOGE GETTING ALONG?
KREAK
I'M SORRY YOU TWO HAVE TO PRETEND TO BE LOVERS. I KNOW IT MUST BE HARD.
WELL, KIND OF...
SINCE WE MOVED BACK TO JAPAN...
...SHE SEEMS SO HAPPY.
I BET IT'S BE-CAUSE OF YOU.
SO THANK YOU.
HUH?
REALLY?
COME TO THINK OF IT, SHE SAID SHE DIDN'T HAVE ANY FRIENDS IN THE U.S.
It's definitely not because of me...
YOU TWO ARE SO COMPATI-BLE...
I KNEW IT WOULD WORK OUT.
COM-PATIBLE?
NO WE'RE NOT!
ALL WE EVER DO IS FIGHT!!
HA HA! DON'T BE SILLY!
AFTER ALL...

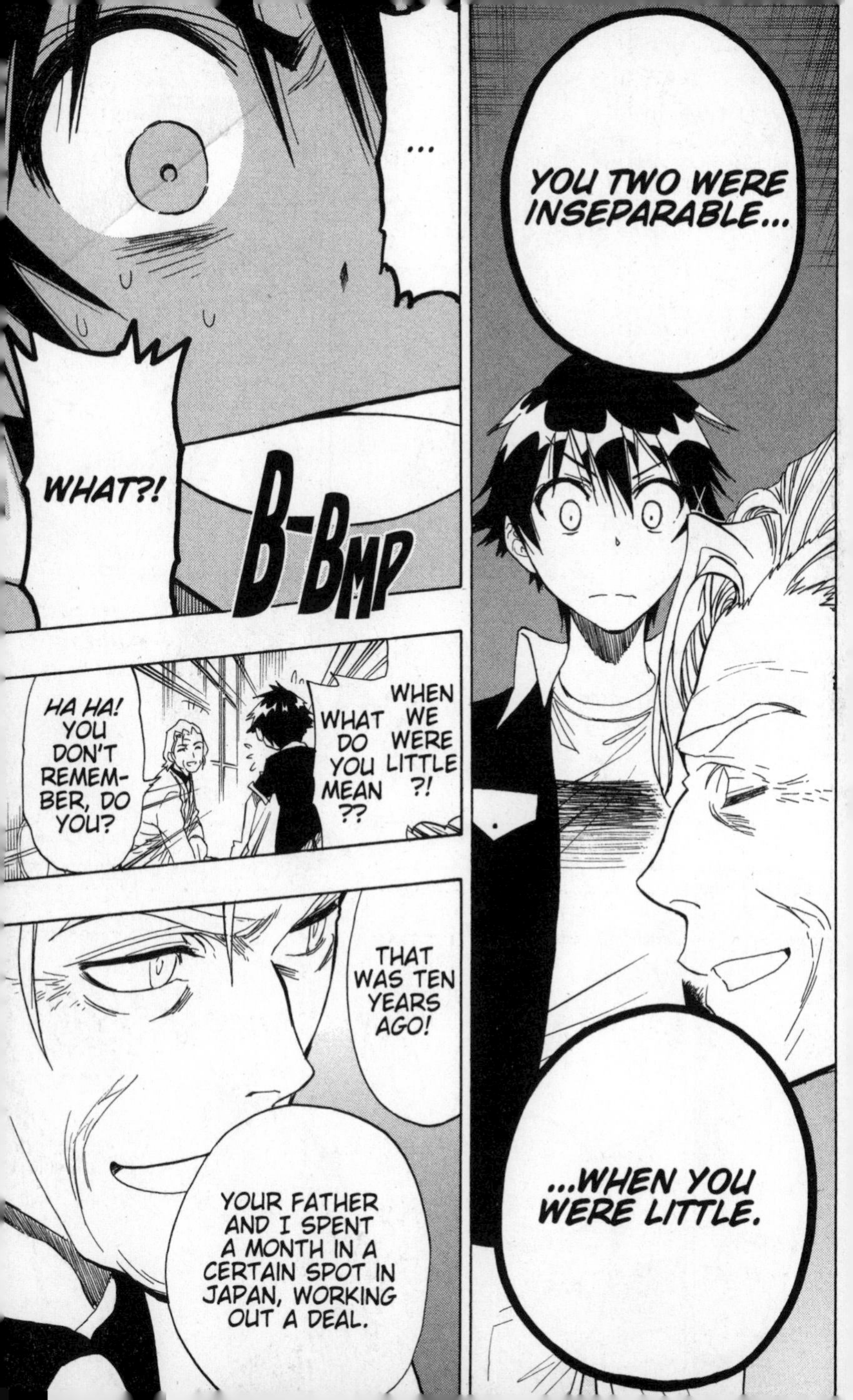
YOU TWO WERE INSEPARABLE...
...WHEN YOU WERE LITTLE.
...
WHAT?!
B-BMP
WHEN WE WERE LITTLE ?!
WHAT DO YOU MEAN ??
HA HA! YOU DON'T REMEM-BER, DO YOU?
THAT WAS TEN YEARS AGO!
YOUR FATHER AND I SPENT A MONTH IN A CERTAIN SPOT IN JAPAN, WORKING OUT A DEAL.

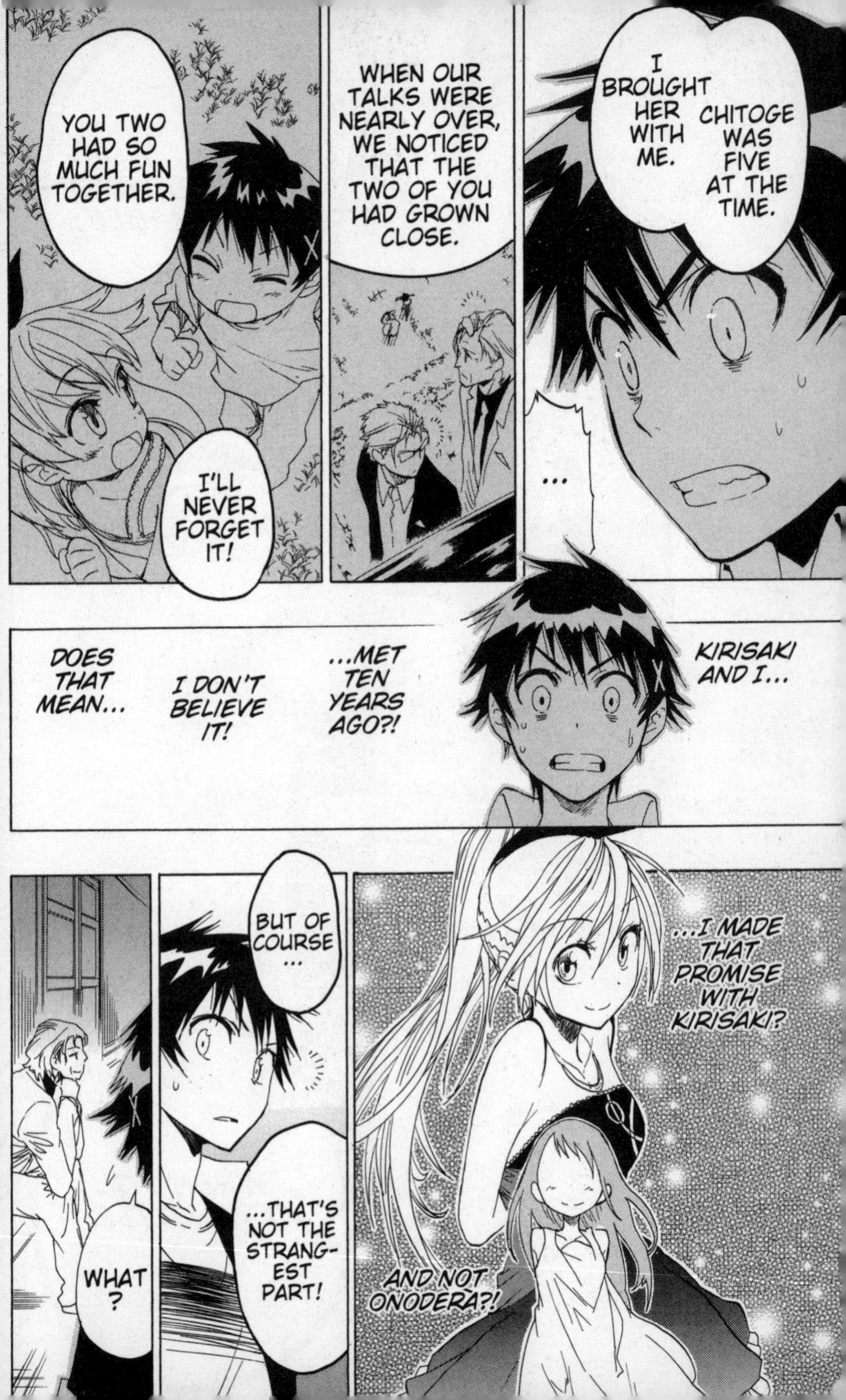
CHITOGE WAS FIVE AT THE TIME.
I BROUGHT HER WITH ME.
...
WHEN OUR TALKS WERE NEARLY OVER, WE NOTICED THAT THE TWO OF YOU HAD GROWN CLOSE.
YOU TWO HAD SO MUCH FUN TOGETHER.
I'LL NEVER FORGET IT!
KIRISAKI AND I...
...MET TEN YEARS AGO?!
I DON'T BELIEVE IT!
DOES THAT MEAN...
...I MADE THAT PROMISE WITH KIRISAKI?
AND NOT ONODERA?!
BUT OF COURSE...
...THAT'S NOT THE STRANGEST PART!
WHAT?

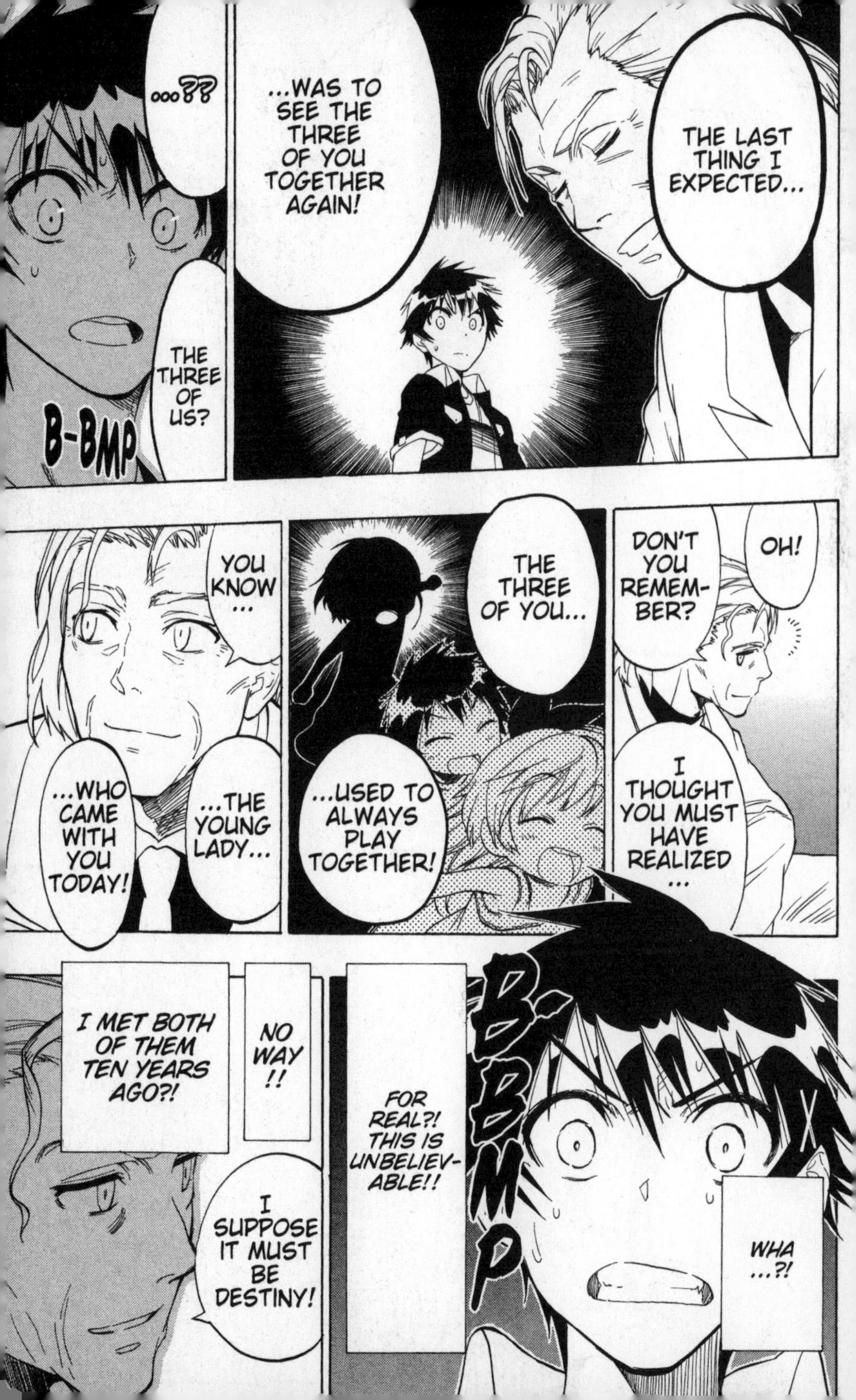
THE LAST THING I EXPECTED...
...WAS TO SEE THE THREE OF YOU TOGETHER AGAIN!
ooo??
THE THREE OF US?
B-BMP
OH!
DON'T YOU REMEMBER?
I THOUGHT YOU MUST HAVE REALIZED...
THE THREE OF YOU...
...USED TO ALWAYS PLAY TOGETHER!
YOU KNOW...
...THE YOUNG LADY...
...WHO CAME WITH YOU TODAY!
BDBMP
WHA...?!
FOR REAL?! THIS IS UNBELIEV-ABLE!!
NO WAY!!
I MET BOTH OF THEM TEN YEARS AGO?!
I SUPPOSE IT MUST BE DESTINY!

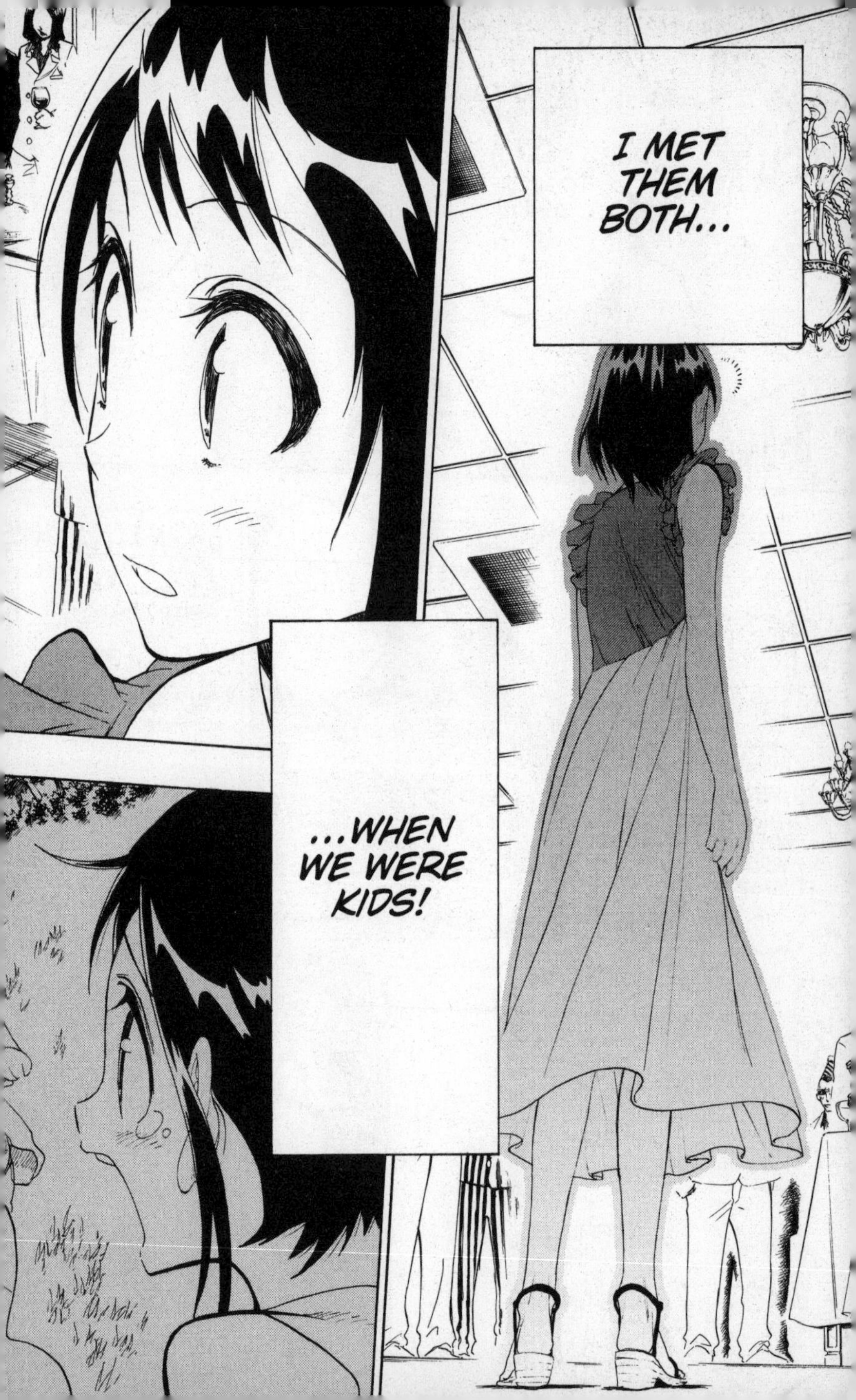
I MET THEM BOTH...
...WHEN WE WERE KIDS!

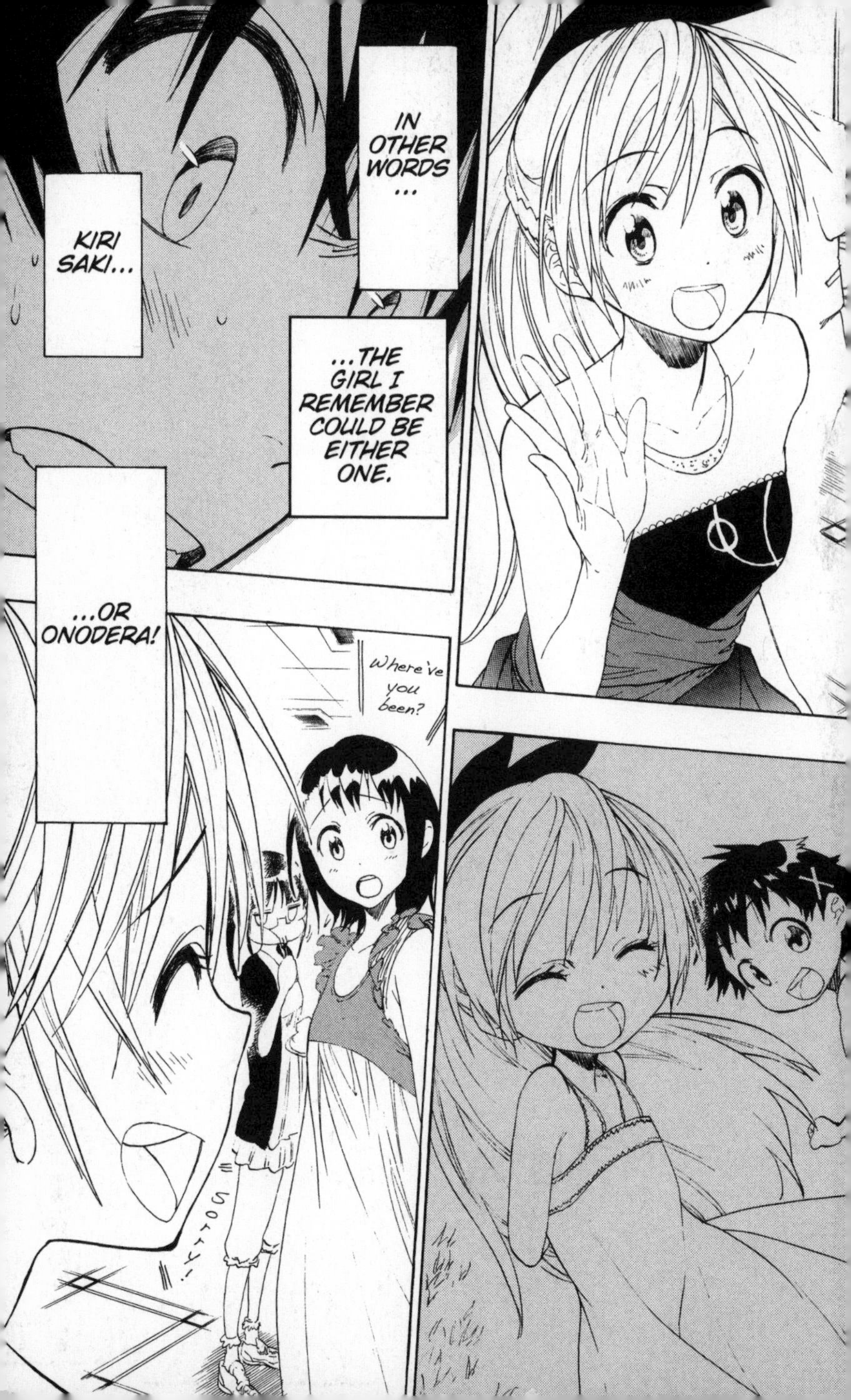
IN OTHER WORDS...
...THE GIRL I REMEMBER COULD BE EITHER ONE.
KIRI SAKI...
...OR ONODERA!
Where've you been?
Sorry!

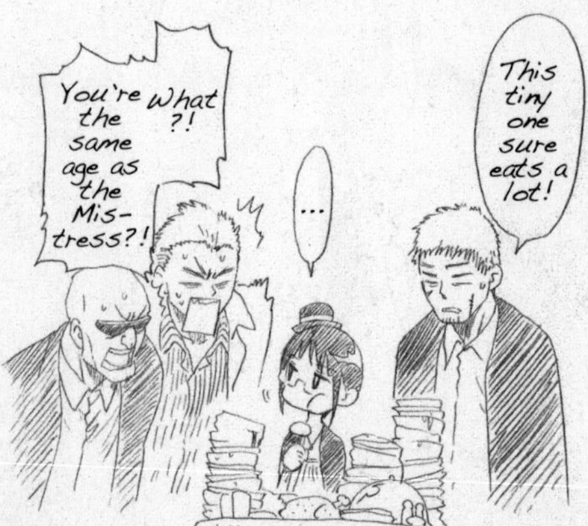
This tiny one sure eats a lot!
...
What?!
You're the same age as the Mis-tress?!

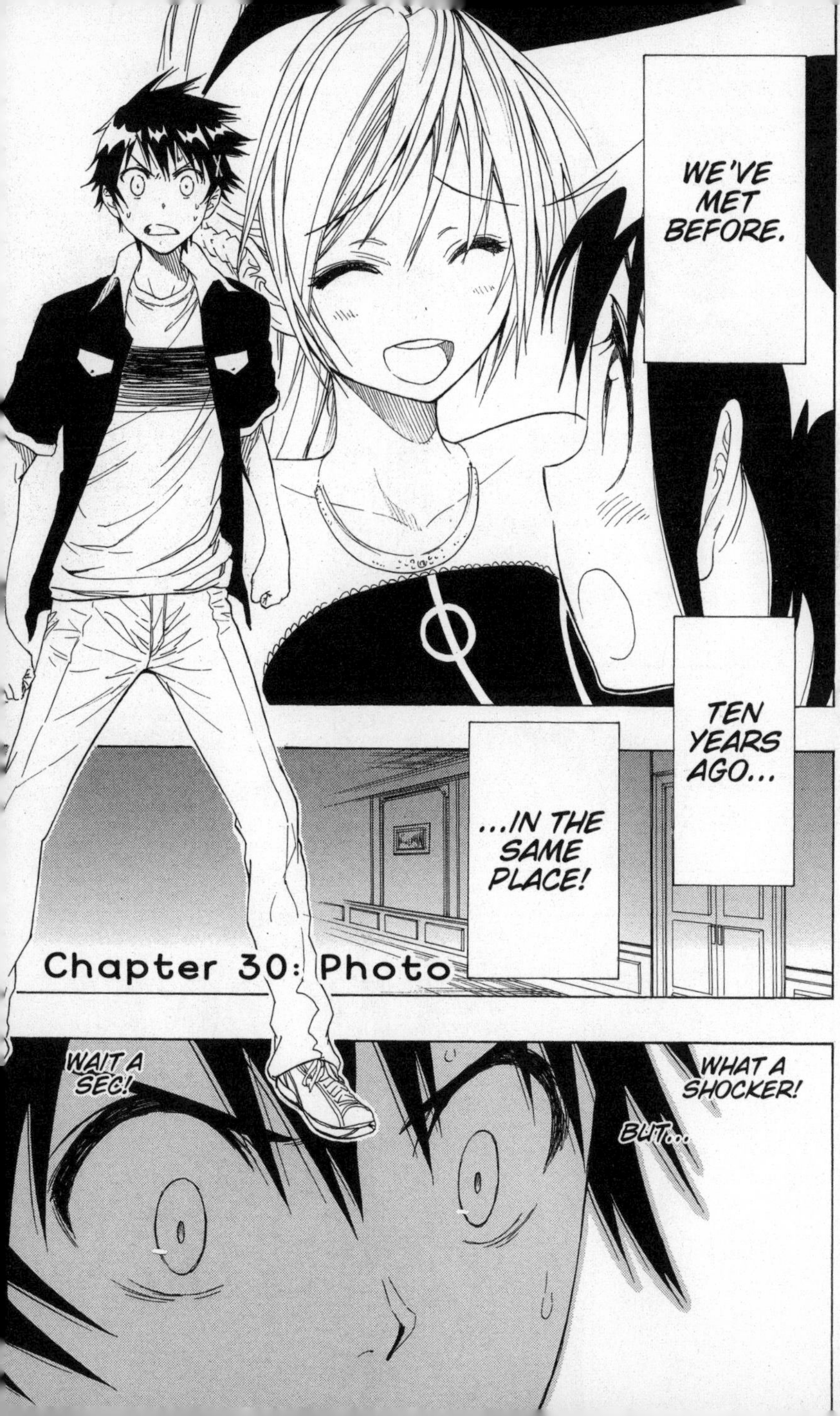
WE'VE MET BEFORE.
TEN YEARS AGO...
...IN THE SAME PLACE!
Chapter 30: Photo
WHAT A SHOCKER!
BUT...
WAIT A SEC!

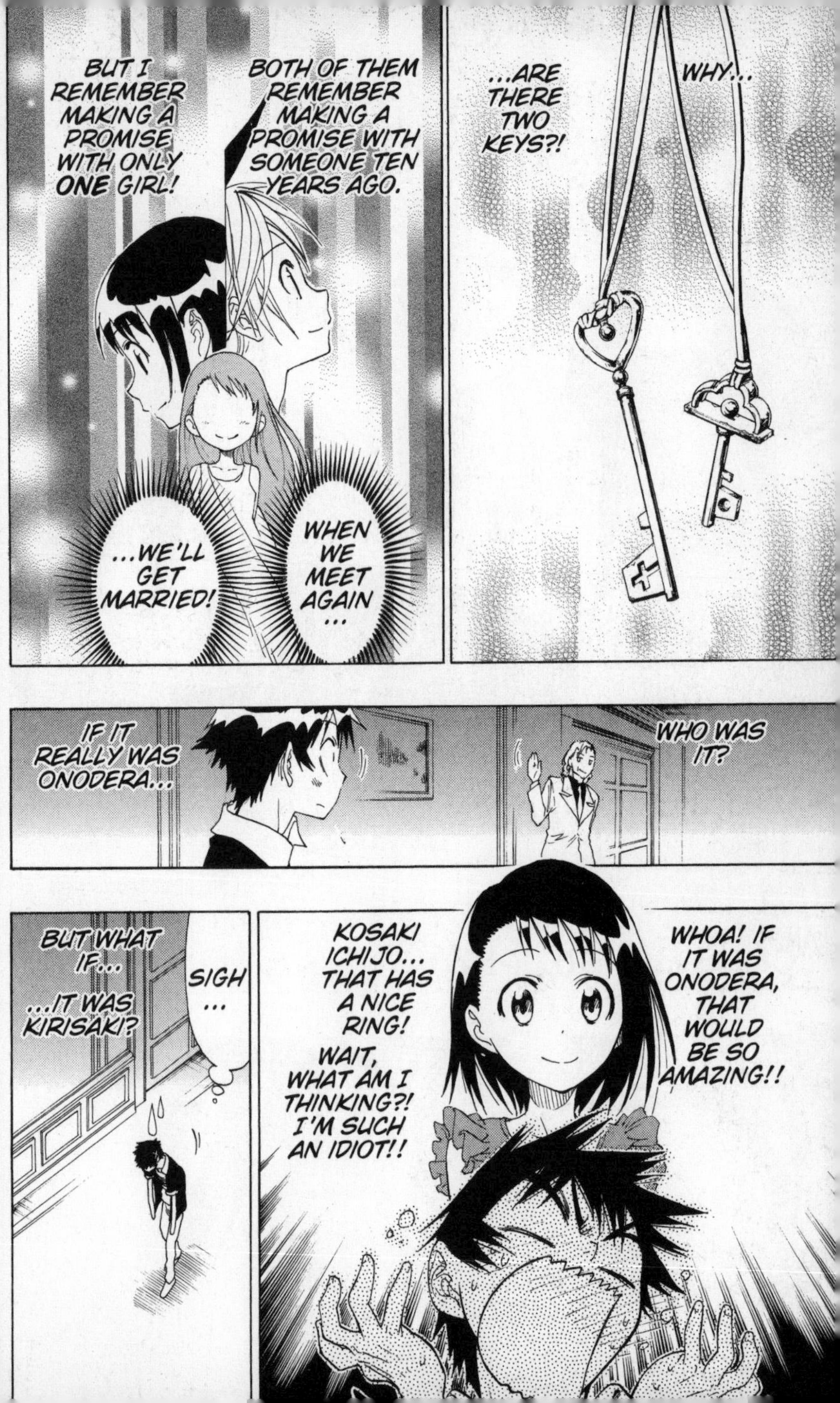
WHY...
...ARE THERE TWO KEYS?!
BOTH OF THEM REMEMBER MAKING A PROMISE WITH SOMEONE TEN YEARS AGO.
BUT I REMEMBER MAKING A PROMISE WITH ONLY ONE GIRL!
WHEN WE MEET AGAIN...
...WE'LL GET MARRIED!
WHO WAS IT?
IF IT REALLY WAS ONODERA...
WHOA! IF IT WAS ONODERA, THAT WOULD BE SO AMAZING!!
KOSAKI ICHIJO... THAT HAS A NICE RING!
WAIT, WHAT AM I THINKING?! I'M SUCH AN IDIOT!!
SIGH...
BUT WHAT IF...
...IT WAS KIRISAKI?

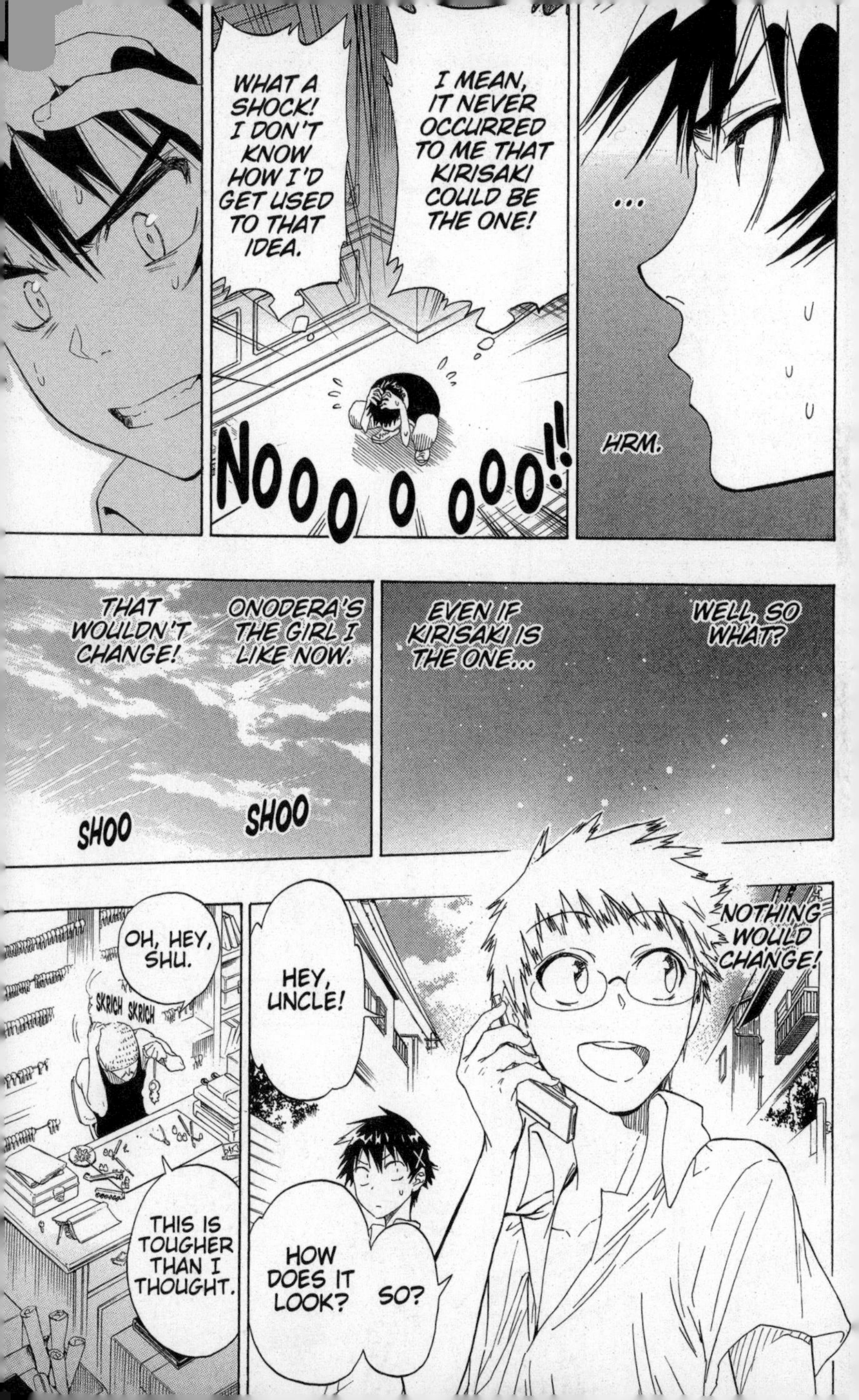
...
HRM.
I MEAN, IT NEVER OCCURRED TO ME THAT KIRISAKI COULD BE THE ONE!
WHAT A SHOCK! I DON'T KNOW HOW I'D GET USED TO THAT IDEA.
NOOO O OOO!!
WELL, SO WHAT?
EVEN IF KIRISAKI IS THE ONE...
ONODERA'S THE GIRL I LIKE NOW.
THAT WOULDN'T CHANGE!
SHOO
SHOO
NOTHING WOULD CHANGE!
HEY, UNCLE!
SO?
HOW DOES IT LOOK?
OH, HEY, SHU.
SKRICH SKRICH
THIS IS TOUGHER THAN I THOUGHT.

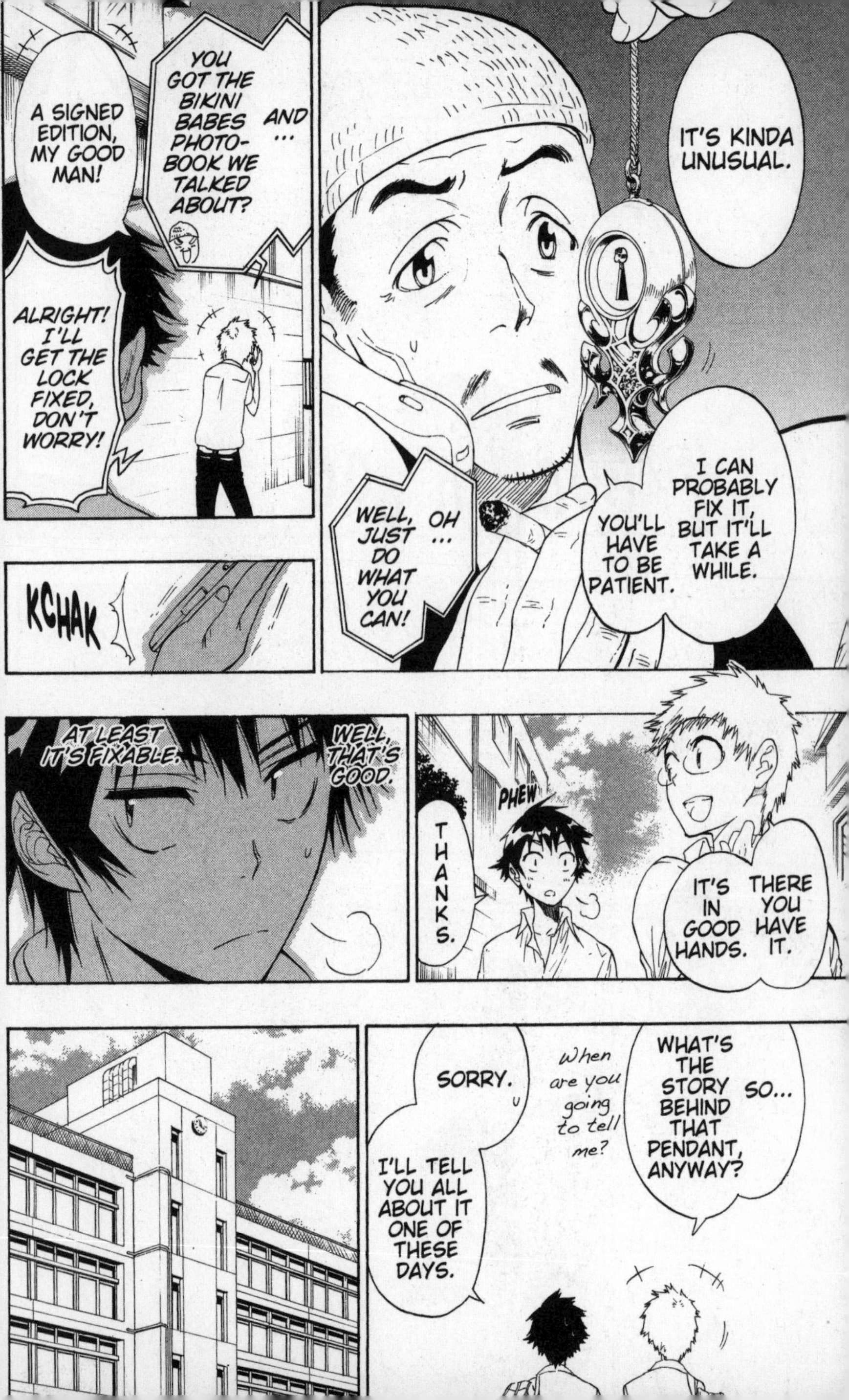
IT'S KINDA UNUSUAL.
I CAN PROBABLY FIX IT, BUT IT'LL TAKE A WHILE.
YOU'LL HAVE TO BE PATIENT.
OH ...
WELL, JUST DO WHAT YOU CAN!
YOU GOT THE BIKINI BABES PHOTO-BOOK WE TALKED ABOUT?
AND ...
A SIGNED EDITION, MY GOOD MAN!
ALRIGHT! I'LL GET THE LOCK FIXED, DON'T WORRY!
KCHAK
THERE YOU HAVE IT.
IT'S IN GOOD HANDS.
PHEW
THANKS.
WELL, THAT'S GOOD.
AT LEAST IT'S FIXABLE.
SO...
WHAT'S THE STORY BEHIND THAT PENDANT, ANYWAY?
When are you going to tell me?
SORRY.
I'LL TELL YOU ALL ABOUT IT ONE OF THESE DAYS.

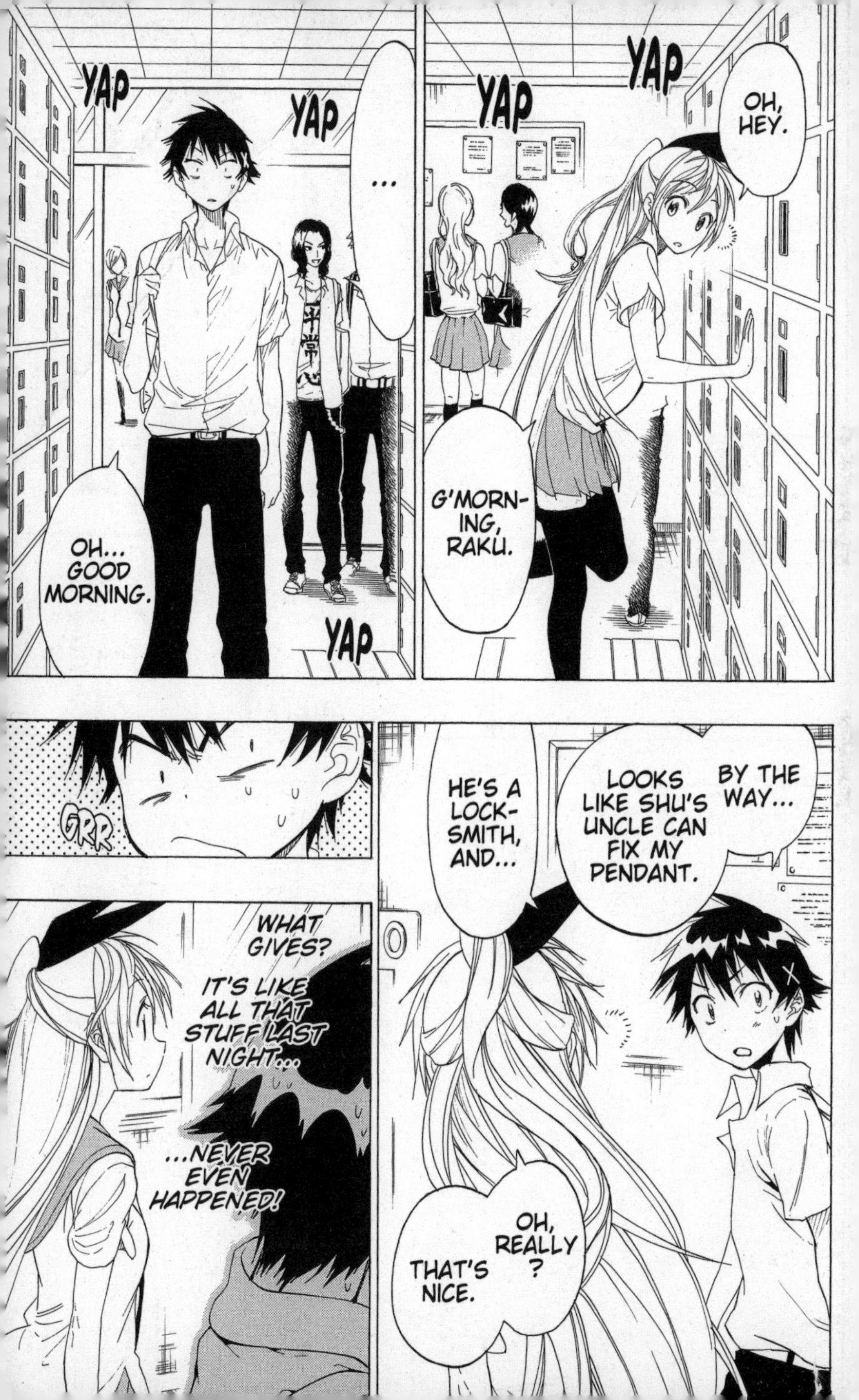
YAP
OH, HEY.
YAP
G'MORNING, RAKU.
YAP
YAP
...
OH... GOOD MORNING.
YAP
BY THE WAY...
LOOKS LIKE SHU'S UNCLE CAN FIX MY PENDANT.
HE'S A LOCKSMITH, AND...
OH, REALLY?
THAT'S NICE.
GRR
WHAT GIVES?
IT'S LIKE ALL THAT STUFF LAST NIGHT...
...NEVER EVEN HAPPENED!

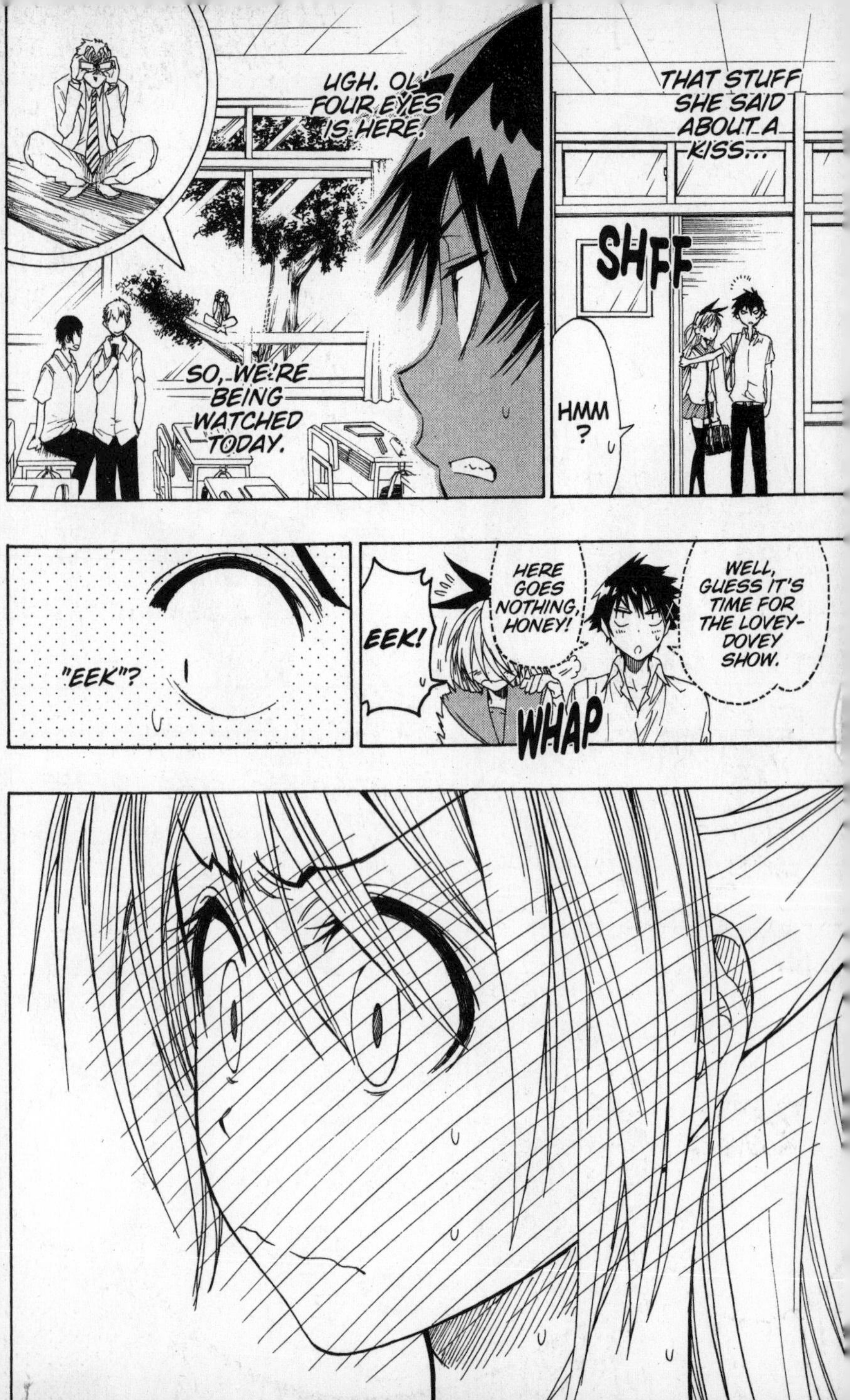
THAT STUFF SHE SAID ABOUT A KISS...
SHFF
HMM?
UGH. OL' FOUR EYES IS HERE.
SO, WE'RE BEING WATCHED TODAY.
WELL, GUESS IT'S TIME FOR THE LOVEY-DOVEY SHOW.
HERE GOES NOTHING, HONEY!
EEK!
WHAP
"EEK"?

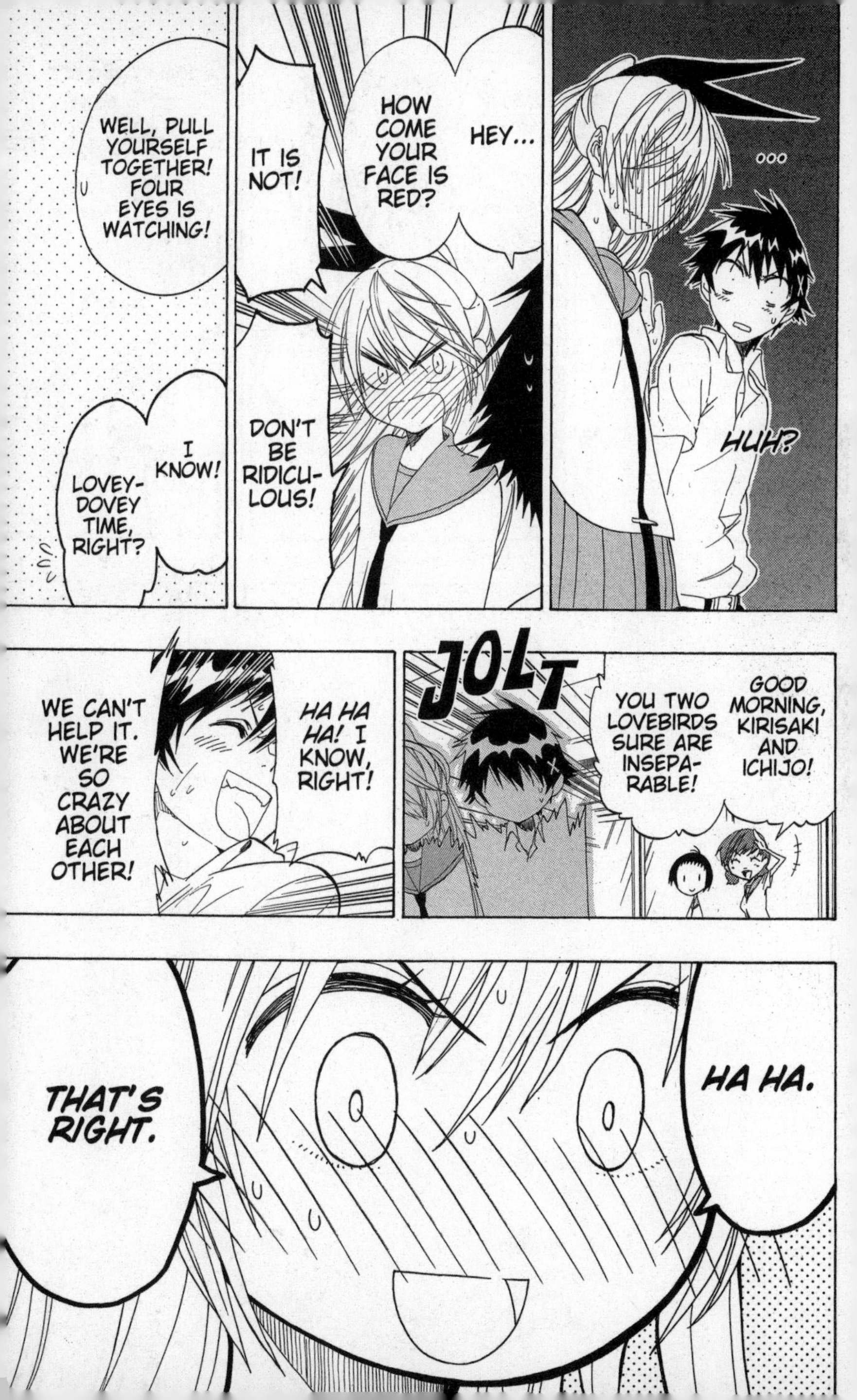

ooo
HUH?
HEY...
HOW COME YOUR FACE IS RED?
IT IS NOT!
DON'T BE RIDICULOUS!
WELL, PULL YOURSELF TOGETHER! FOUR EYES IS WATCHING!
I KNOW!
LOVEY-DOVEY TIME, RIGHT?
GOOD MORNING, KIRISAKI AND ICHIJO!
YOU TWO LOVEBIRDS SURE ARE INSEPA-RABLE!
JOLT
HA HA HA! I KNOW, RIGHT!
WE CAN'T HELP IT. WE'RE SO CRAZY ABOUT EACH OTHER!
HA HA.
THAT'S RIGHT.

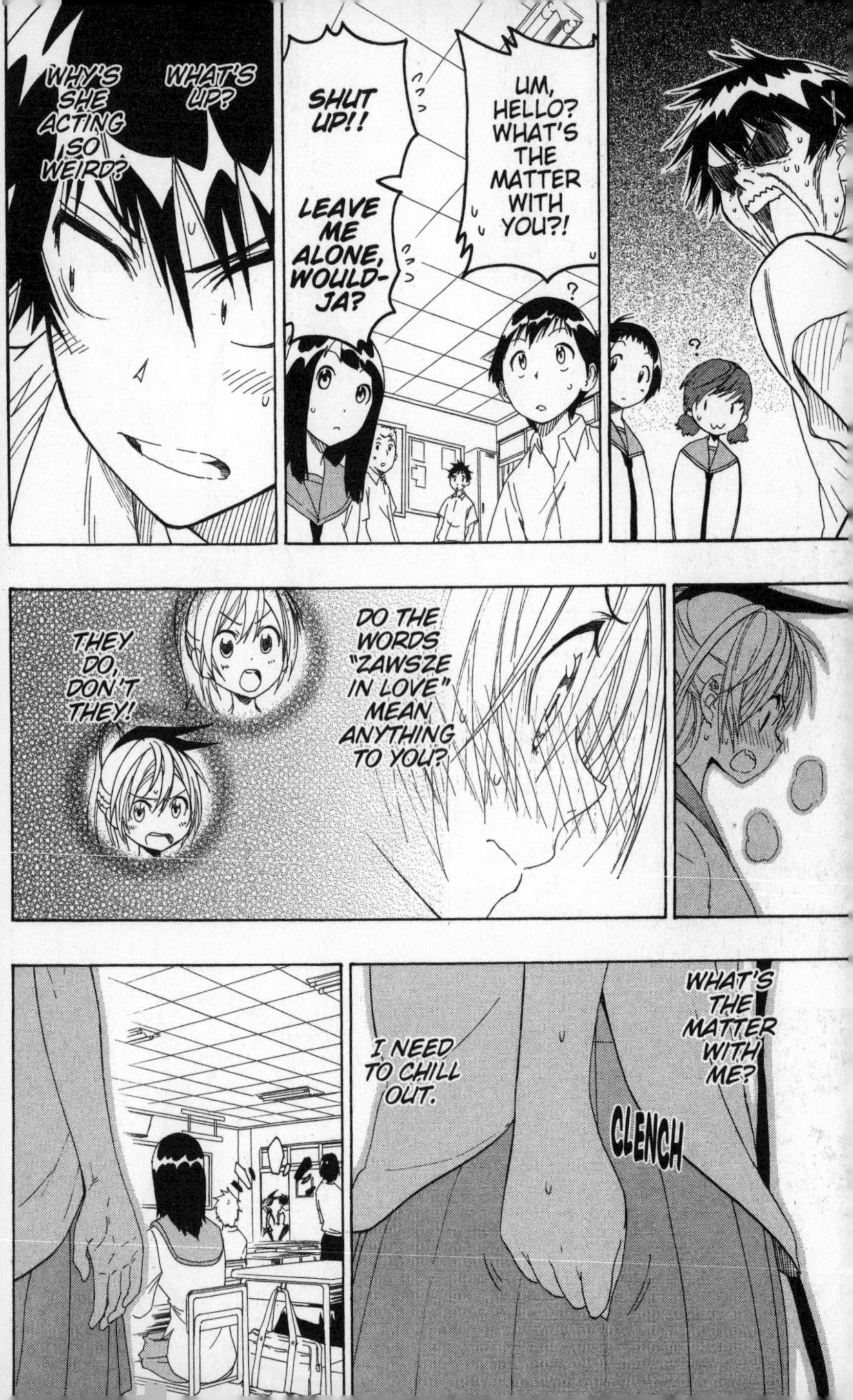
UM, HELLO? WHAT'S THE MATTER WITH YOU?!
SHUT UP!!
LEAVE ME ALONE, WOULD-JA?
WHAT'S UP?
WHY'S SHE ACTING SO WEIRD?
DO THE WORDS "ZAWSZE IN LOVE" MEAN ANYTHING TO YOU?
THEY DO, DON'T THEY!
WHAT'S THE MATTER WITH ME?
CLENCH
I NEED TO CHILL OUT.

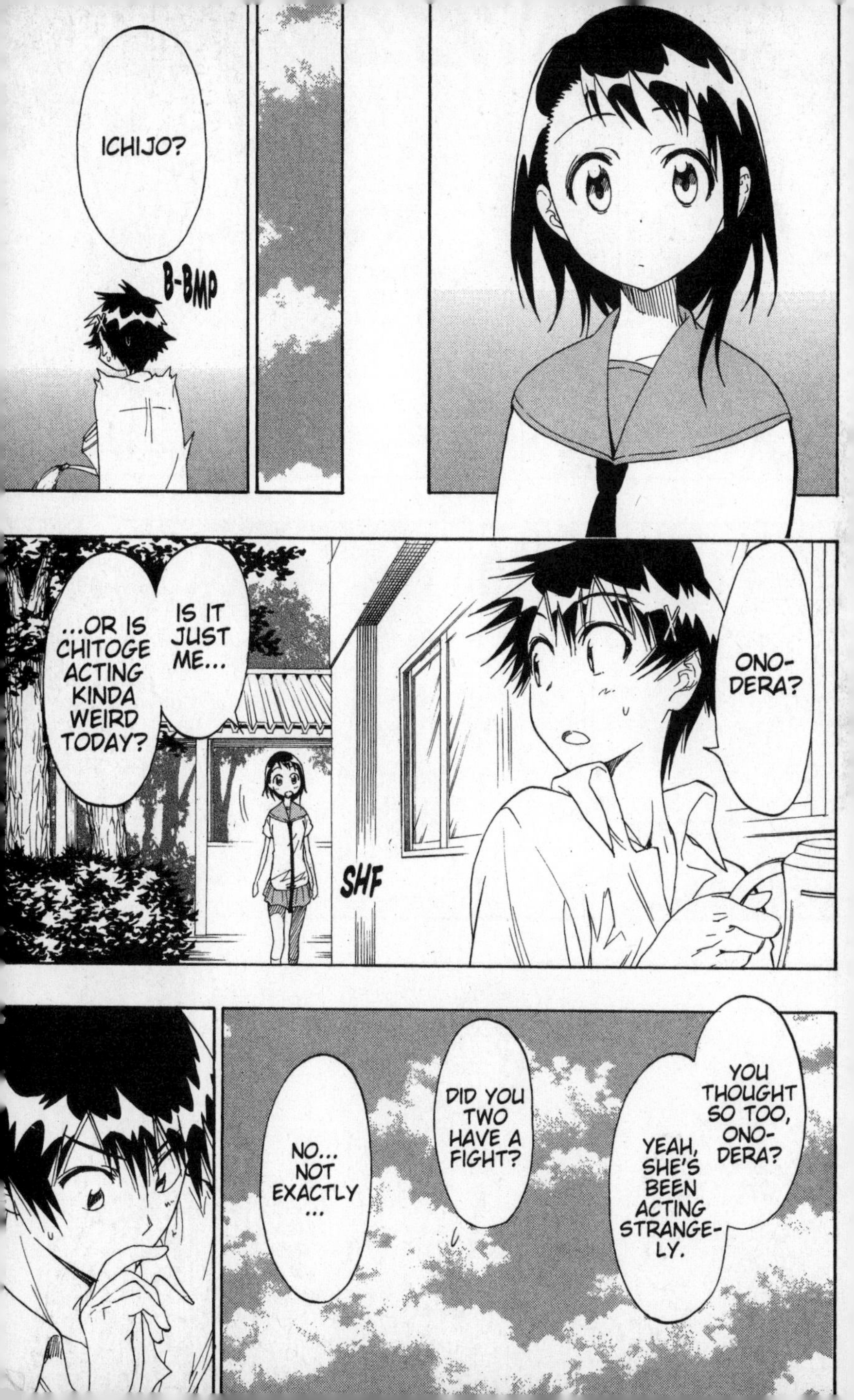
ICHIJO?
B-BMP
ONO-DERA?
SHF
IS IT JUST ME...
...OR IS CHITOGE ACTING KINDA WEIRD TODAY?
YOU THOUGHT SO TOO, ONO-DERA?
YEAH, SHE'S BEEN ACTING STRANGE-LY.
DID YOU TWO HAVE A FIGHT?
NO... NOT EXACTLY ...

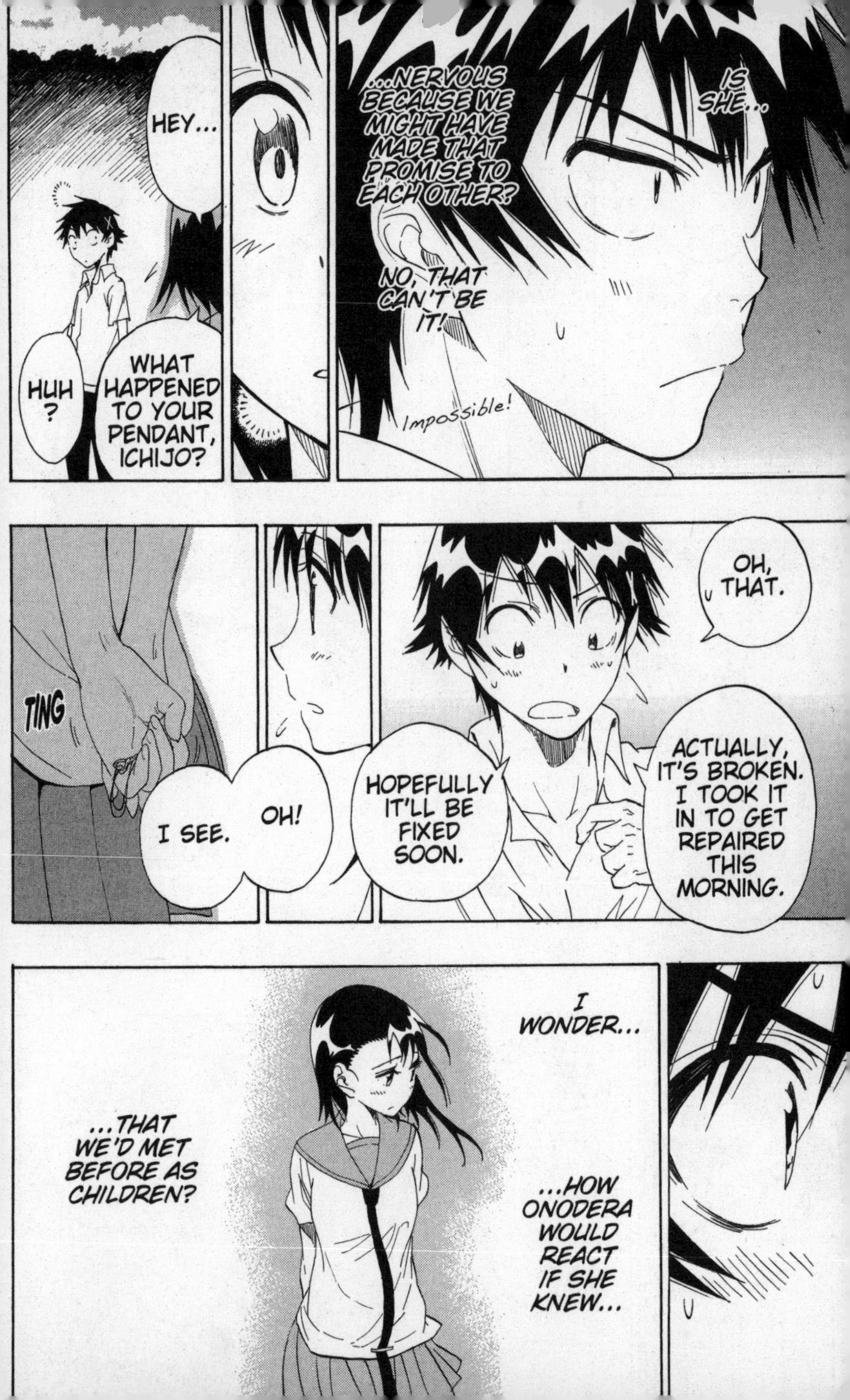
IS SHE...
...NERVOUS BECAUSE WE MIGHT HAVE MADE THAT PROMISE TO EACH OTHER?
NO, THAT CAN'T BE IT!
Impossible!
HEY...
WHAT HAPPENED TO YOUR PENDANT, ICHIJO?
HUH?
OH, THAT.
ACTUALLY, IT'S BROKEN. I TOOK IT IN TO GET REPAIRED THIS MORNING.
HOPEFULLY IT'LL BE FIXED SOON.
OH!
I SEE.
TING
I WONDER...
...HOW ONODERA WOULD REACT IF SHE KNEW...
...THAT WE'D MET BEFORE AS CHILDREN?

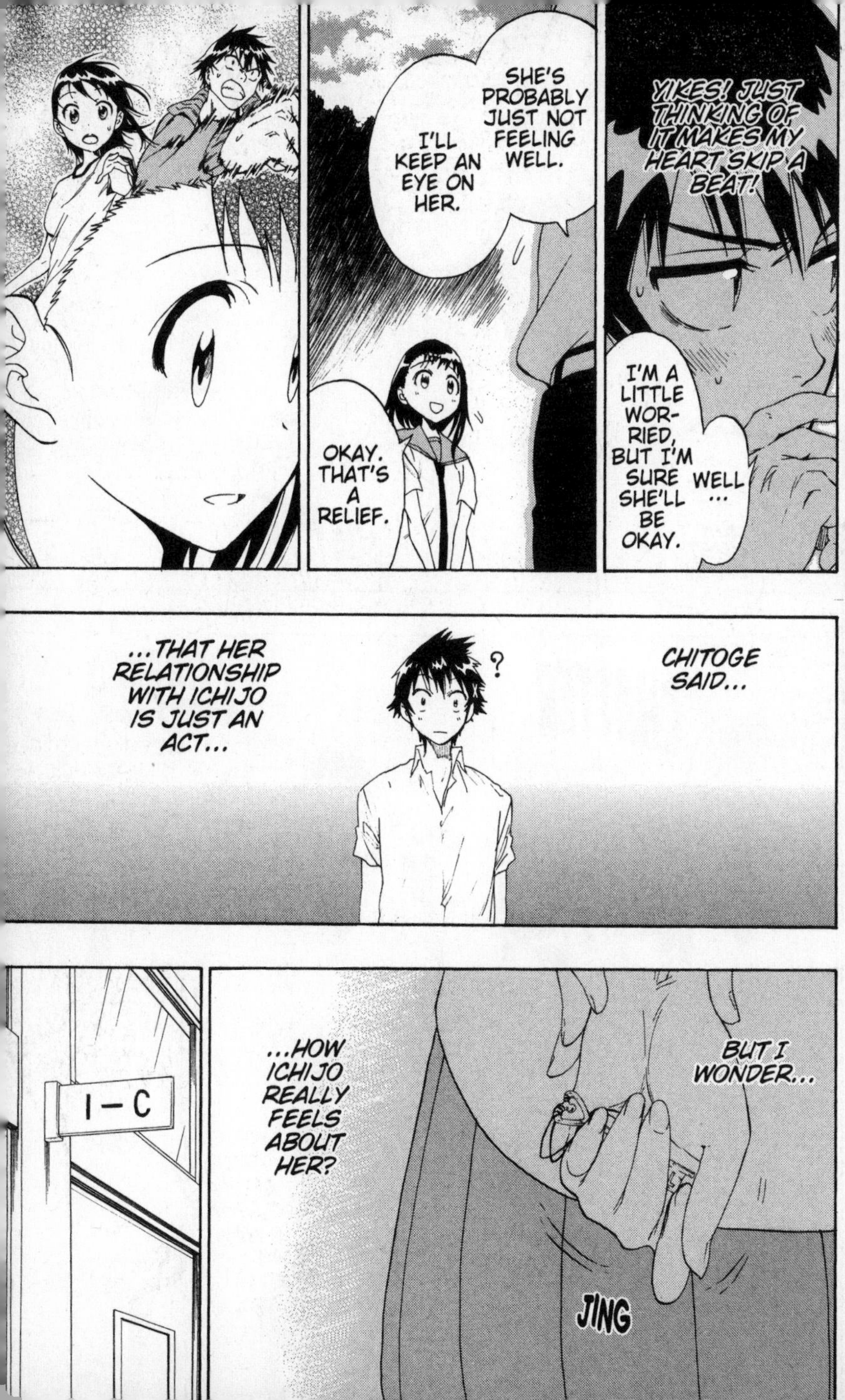
YIKES! JUST THINKING OF IT MAKES MY HEART SKIP A BEAT!
WELL...
I'M A LITTLE WOR-RIED, BUT I'M SURE SHE'LL BE OKAY.
SHE'S PROBABLY JUST NOT FEELING WELL.
I'LL KEEP AN EYE ON HER.
OKAY. THAT'S A RELIEF.
CHITOGE SAID...
?
...THAT HER RELATIONSHIP WITH ICHIJO IS JUST AN ACT...
BUT I WONDER...
...HOW ICHIJO REALLY FEELS ABOUT HER?
JING
I-C

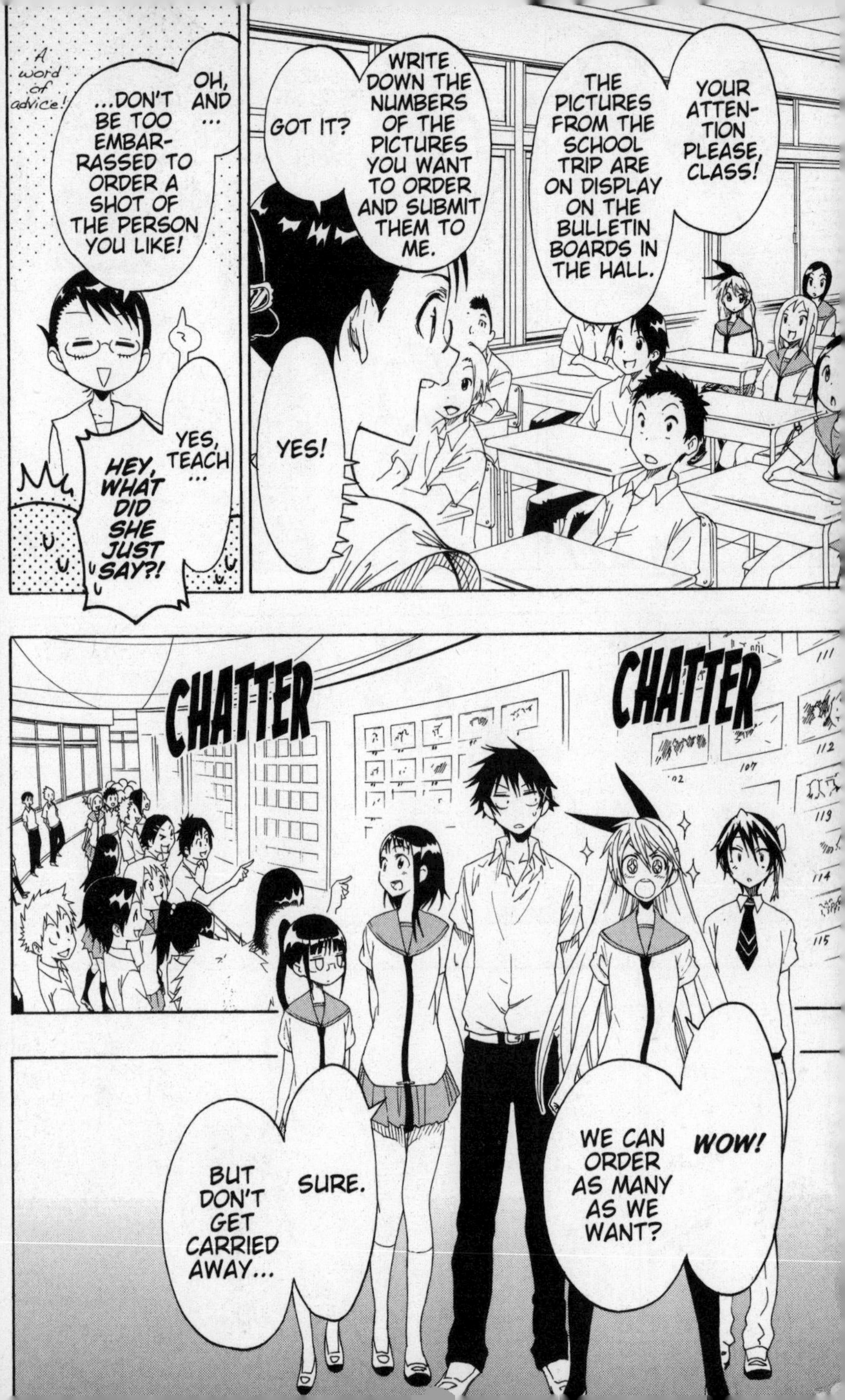
YOUR ATTENTION PLEASE, CLASS!
THE PICTURES FROM THE SCHOOL TRIP ARE ON DISPLAY ON THE BULLETIN BOARDS IN THE HALL.
WRITE DOWN THE NUMBERS OF THE PICTURES YOU WANT TO ORDER AND SUBMIT THEM TO ME.
GOT IT?
YES!
OH, AND...
...DON'T BE TOO EMBARRASSED TO ORDER A SHOT OF THE PERSON YOU LIKE!
A word of advice!
YES, TEACH...
HEY, WHAT DID SHE JUST SAY?!
CHATTER
CHATTER
WOW!
WE CAN ORDER AS MANY AS WE WANT?
SURE.
BUT DON'T GET CARRIED AWAY...

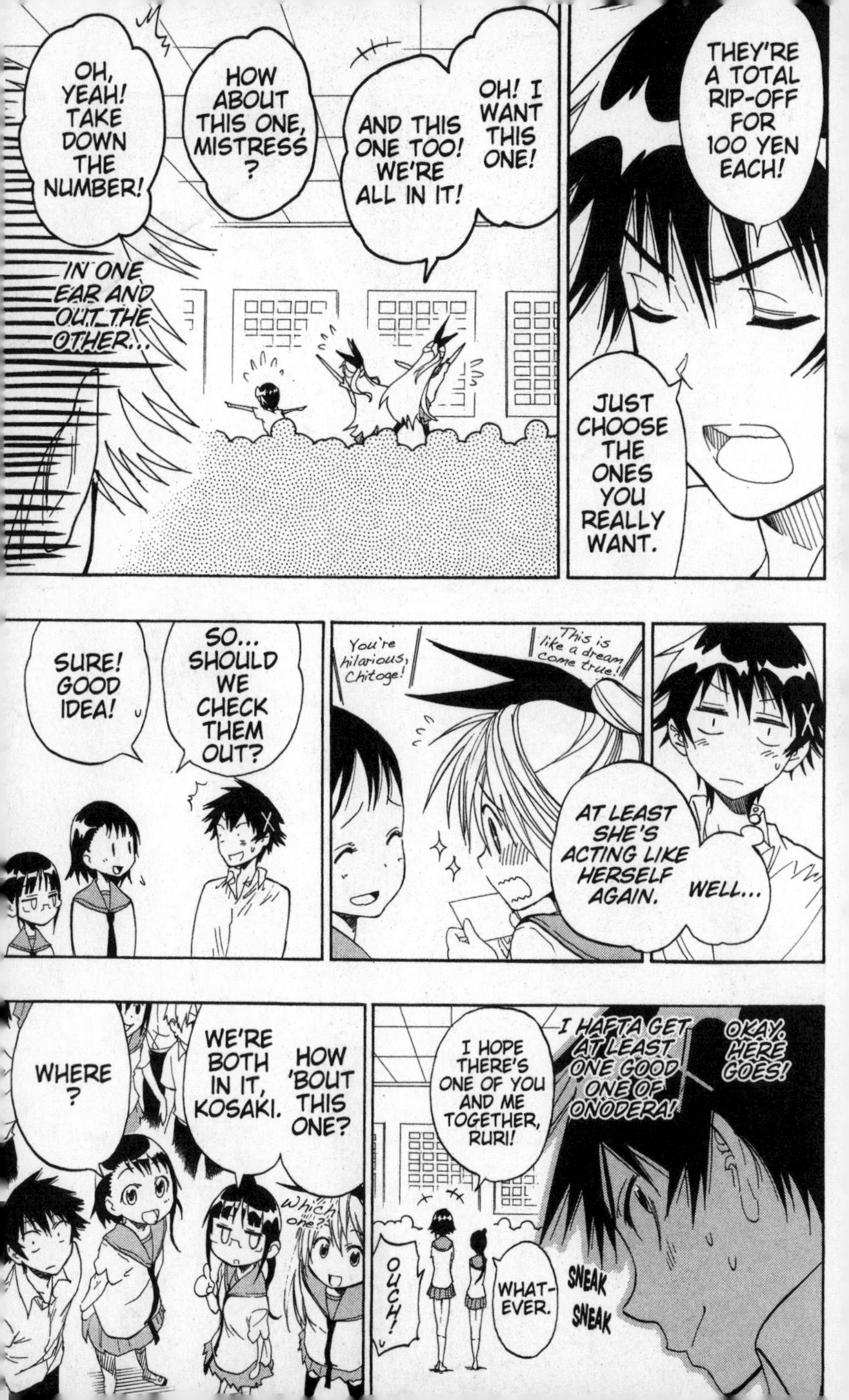
THEY'RE A TOTAL RIP-OFF FOR 100 YEN EACH!
JUST CHOOSE THE ONES YOU REALLY WANT.
OH! I WANT THIS ONE!
AND THIS ONE TOO! WE'RE ALL IN IT!
HOW ABOUT THIS ONE, MISTRESS?
OH, YEAH! TAKE DOWN THE NUMBER!
IN ONE EAR AND OUT THE OTHER...
WELL...
AT LEAST SHE'S ACTING LIKE HERSELF AGAIN.
This is like a dream come true!
You're hilarious, Chitoge!
SO... SHOULD WE CHECK THEM OUT?
SURE! GOOD IDEA!
OKAY. HERE GOES!
I HAFTA GET AT LEAST ONE GOOD ONE OF ONODERA!
SNEAK
SNEAK
I HOPE THERE'S ONE OF YOU AND ME TOGETHER, RURI!
WHATEVER.
OUCH!
HOW 'BOUT THIS ONE?
WE'RE BOTH IN IT, KOSAKI.
Which one?
WHERE?

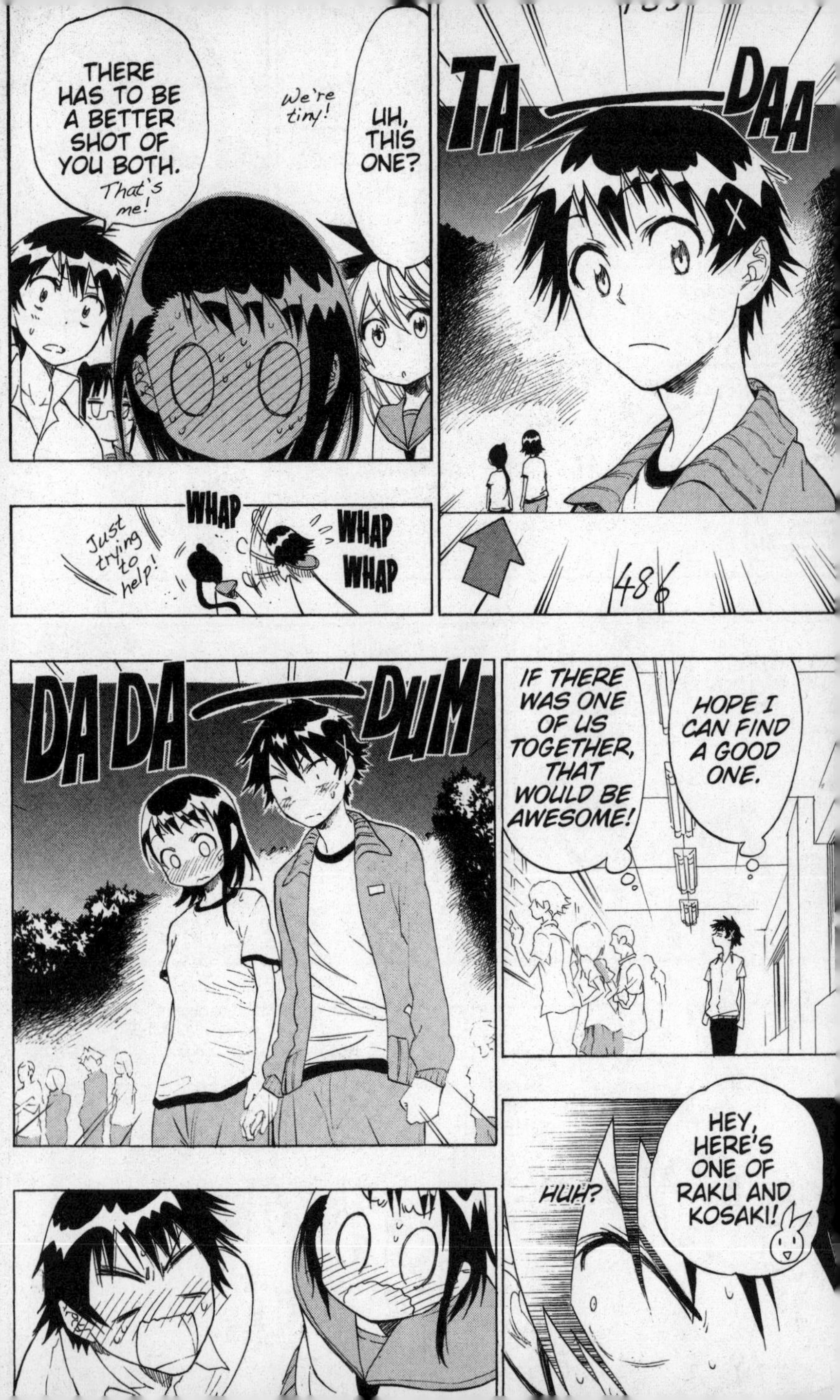
TA—DAA
We're tiny!
UH, THIS ONE?
THERE HAS TO BE A BETTER SHOT OF YOU BOTH.
That's me!
486
WHAP
WHAP WHAP
Just trying to help!
HOPE I CAN FIND A GOOD ONE.
IF THERE WAS ONE OF US TOGETHER, THAT WOULD BE AWESOME!
DA DA—DUM
HEY, HERE'S ONE OF RAKU AND KOSAKI!
HUH?

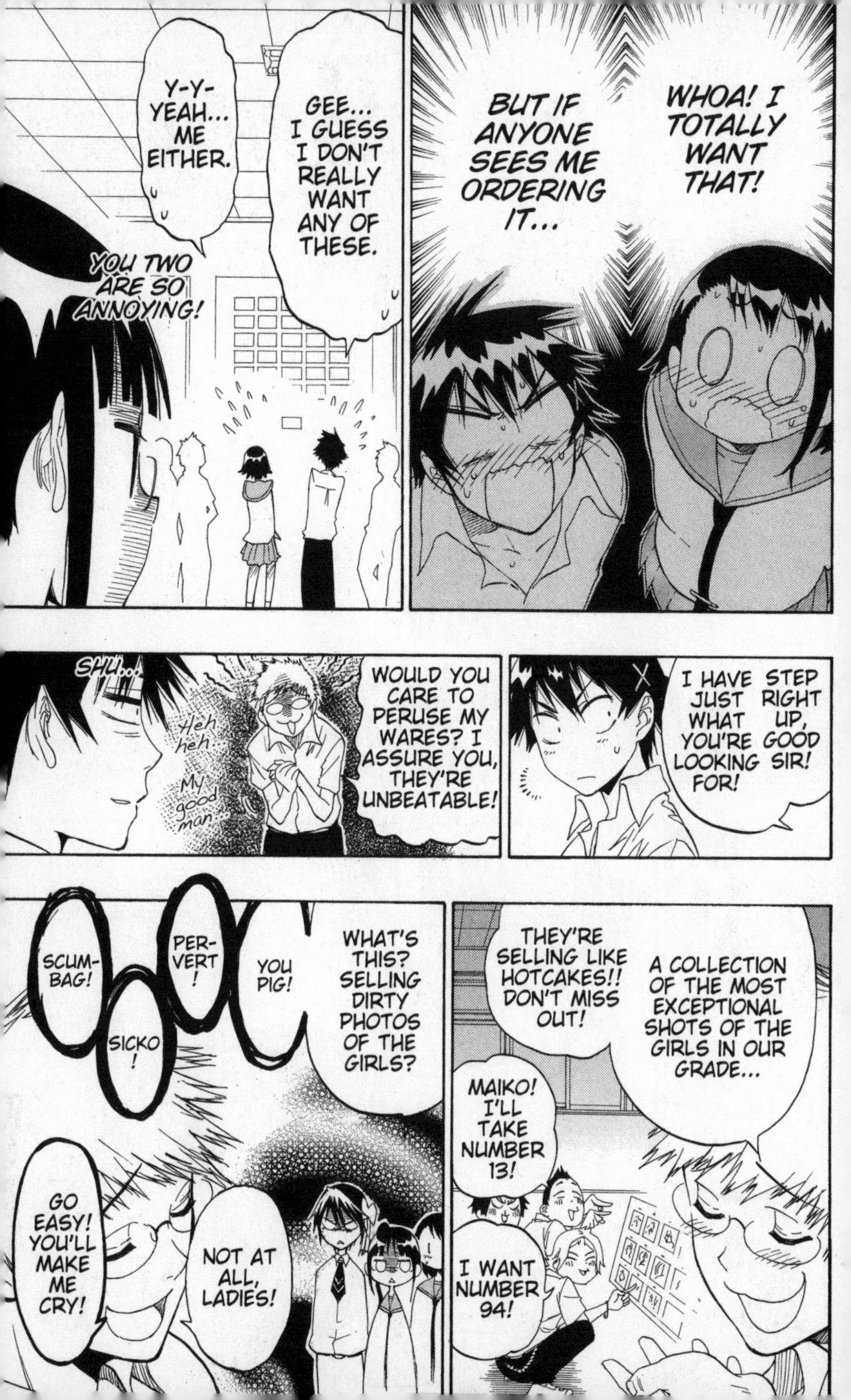
WHOA! I TOTALLY WANT THAT!
BUT IF ANYONE SEES ME ORDERING IT...
GEE... I GUESS I DON'T REALLY WANT ANY OF THESE.
Y-Y-YEAH... ME EITHER.
YOU TWO ARE SO ANNOYING!
STEP RIGHT UP, GOOD SIR!
I HAVE JUST WHAT YOU'RE LOOKING FOR!
WOULD YOU CARE TO PERUSE MY WARES? I ASSURE YOU, THEY'RE UNBEATABLE!
Heh heh... My good man...
SHU...
A COLLECTION OF THE MOST EXCEPTIONAL SHOTS OF THE GIRLS IN OUR GRADE...
THEY'RE SELLING LIKE HOTCAKES!! DON'T MISS OUT!
MAIKO! I'LL TAKE NUMBER 13!
I WANT NUMBER 94!
WHAT'S THIS? SELLING DIRTY PHOTOS OF THE GIRLS?
YOU PIG!
PER-VERT!
SCUM-BAG!
SICKO!
NOT AT ALL, LADIES!
GO EASY! YOU'LL MAKE ME CRY!

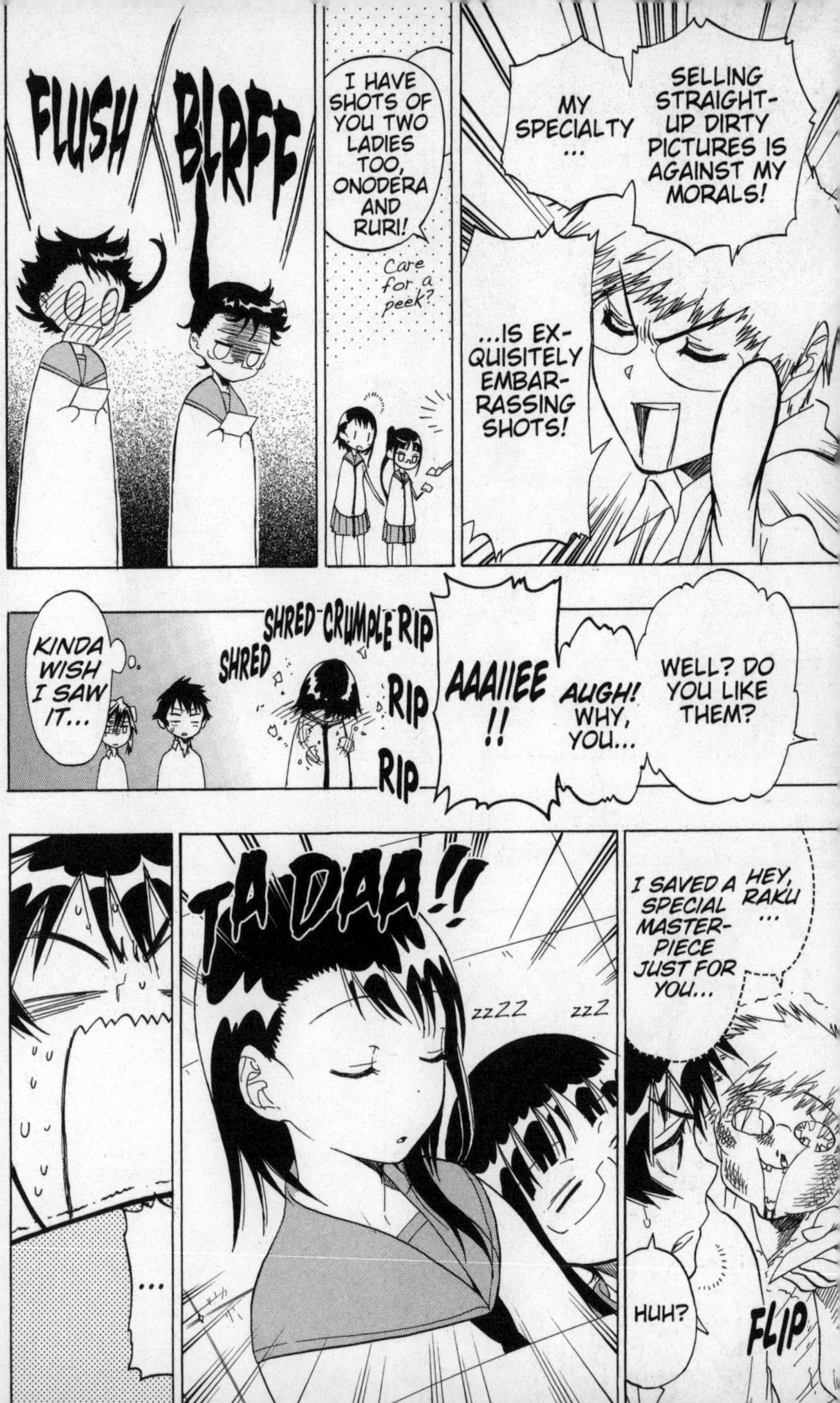
SELLING STRAIGHT-UP DIRTY PICTURES IS AGAINST MY MORALS!
MY SPECIALTY ...
...IS EXQUISITELY EMBARRASSING SHOTS!
I HAVE SHOTS OF YOU TWO LADIES TOO, ONODERA AND RURI!
Care for a peek?
BLRFF
FLUSH
WELL? DO YOU LIKE THEM?
AUGH! WHY, YOU...
AAAIIEE!!
SHRED CRUMPLE RIP
RIP
RIP
SHRED
KINDA WISH I SAW IT...
HEY, RAKU ...
I SAVED A SPECIAL MASTERPIECE JUST FOR YOU...
HUH?
FLIP
TA DAA!!
zzZZ
zzZ
...

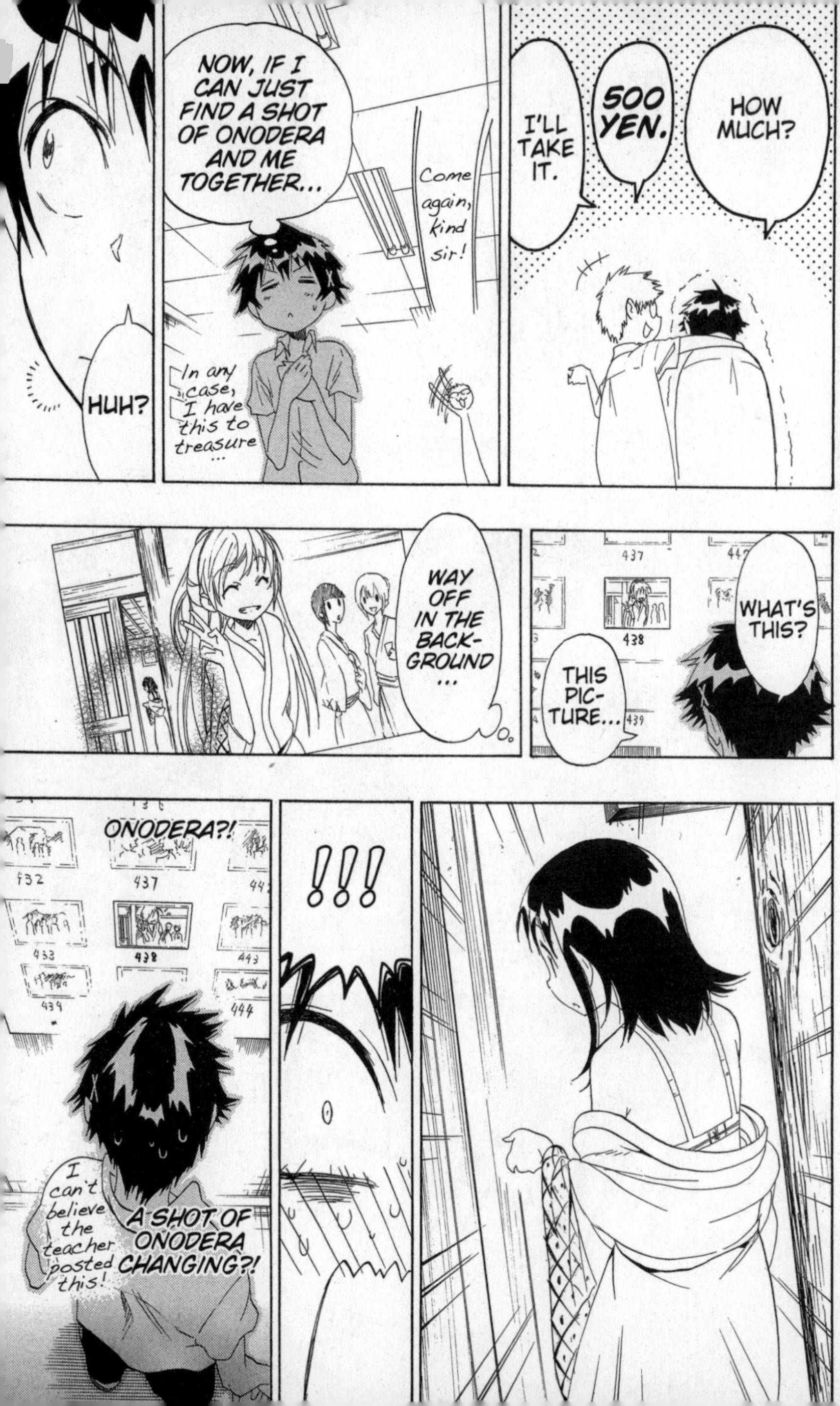
HOW MUCH?
500 YEN.
I'LL TAKE IT.
Come again, kind sir!
NOW, IF I CAN JUST FIND A SHOT OF ONODERA AND ME TOGETHER...
In any case, I have this to treasure...
HUH?
WHAT'S THIS?
THIS PICTURE...
WAY OFF IN THE BACKGROUND...
!!!
ONODERA?!
A SHOT OF ONODERA CHANGING?!
I can't believe the teacher posted this!

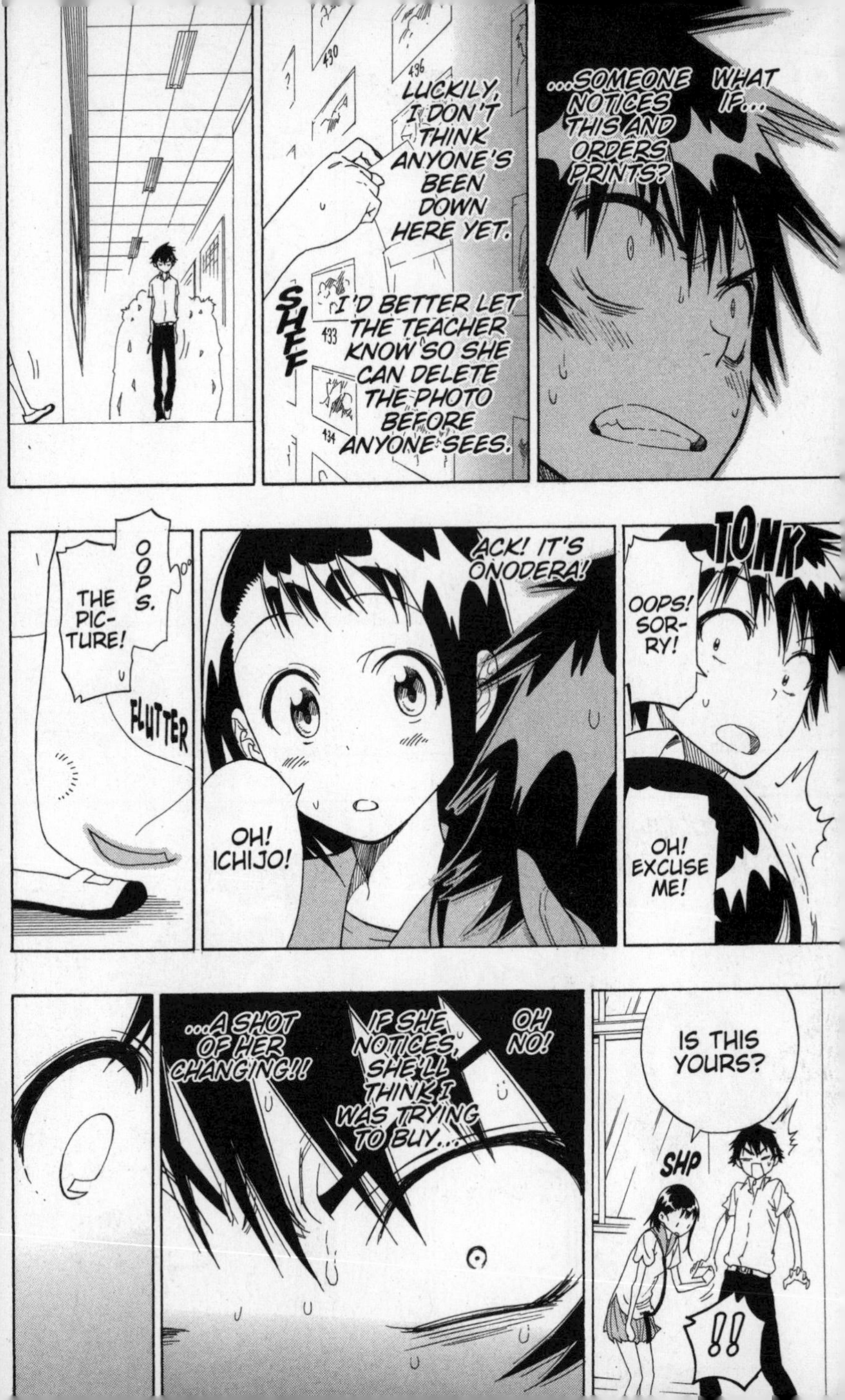
WHAT IF...
...SOMEONE NOTICES THIS AND ORDERS PRINTS?
LUCKILY, I DON'T THINK ANYONE'S BEEN DOWN HERE YET.
SHFF
I'D BETTER LET THE TEACHER KNOW SO SHE CAN DELETE THE PHOTO BEFORE ANYONE SEES.
TONK
OOPS! SORRY!
OH! EXCUSE ME!
ACK! IT'S ONODERA!
OH! ICHIJO!
OOPS. THE PICTURE!
FLUTTER
IS THIS YOURS?
SHP
!!
OH NO!
IF SHE NOTICES, SHE'LL THINK I WAS TRYING TO BUY...
...A SHOT OF HER CHANGING!!

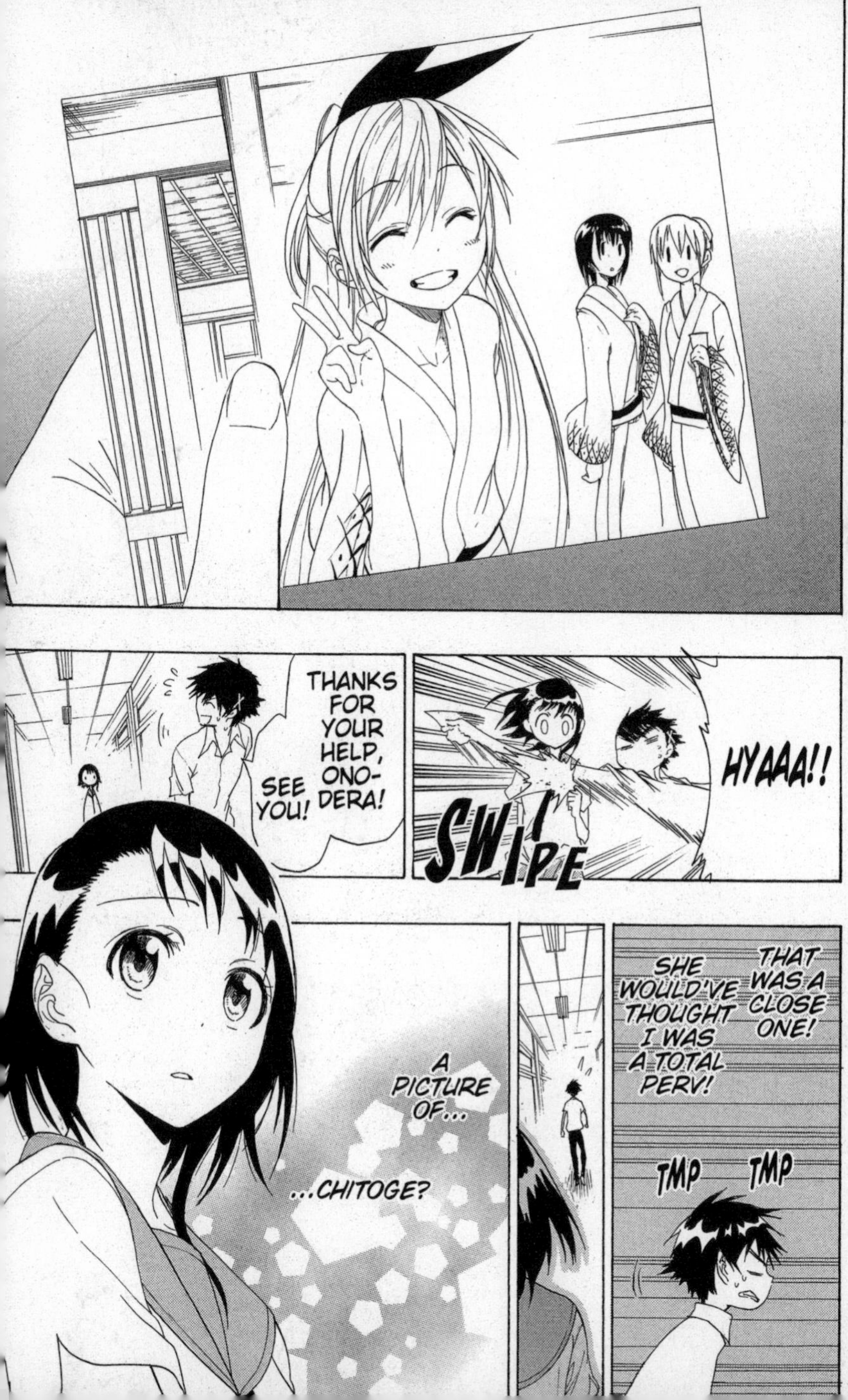
HYAAA!!
SWIPE
THANKS FOR YOUR HELP, ONO-DERA!
SEE YOU!
THAT WAS A CLOSE ONE!
SHE WOULD'VE THOUGHT I WAS A TOTAL PERV!
TMP TMP
A PICTURE OF...
...CHITOGE?

Kosaki and Ruri's
☆ Embarrassing ☆
Shots

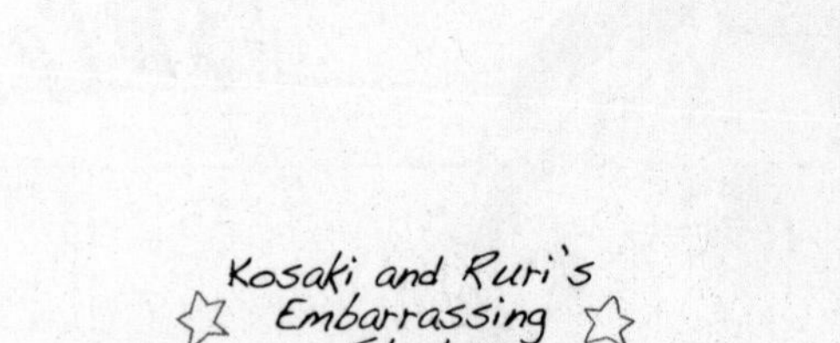

Ruri: "Why did you stuff so much food in your mouth? You look like a hamster!"
Kosaki: "The noodles were longer than I thought, okay?"

Kosaki: "At least cover your mouth, Ruri!"
Ruri: "I was sleepy, okay?"

Chapter 31: After School

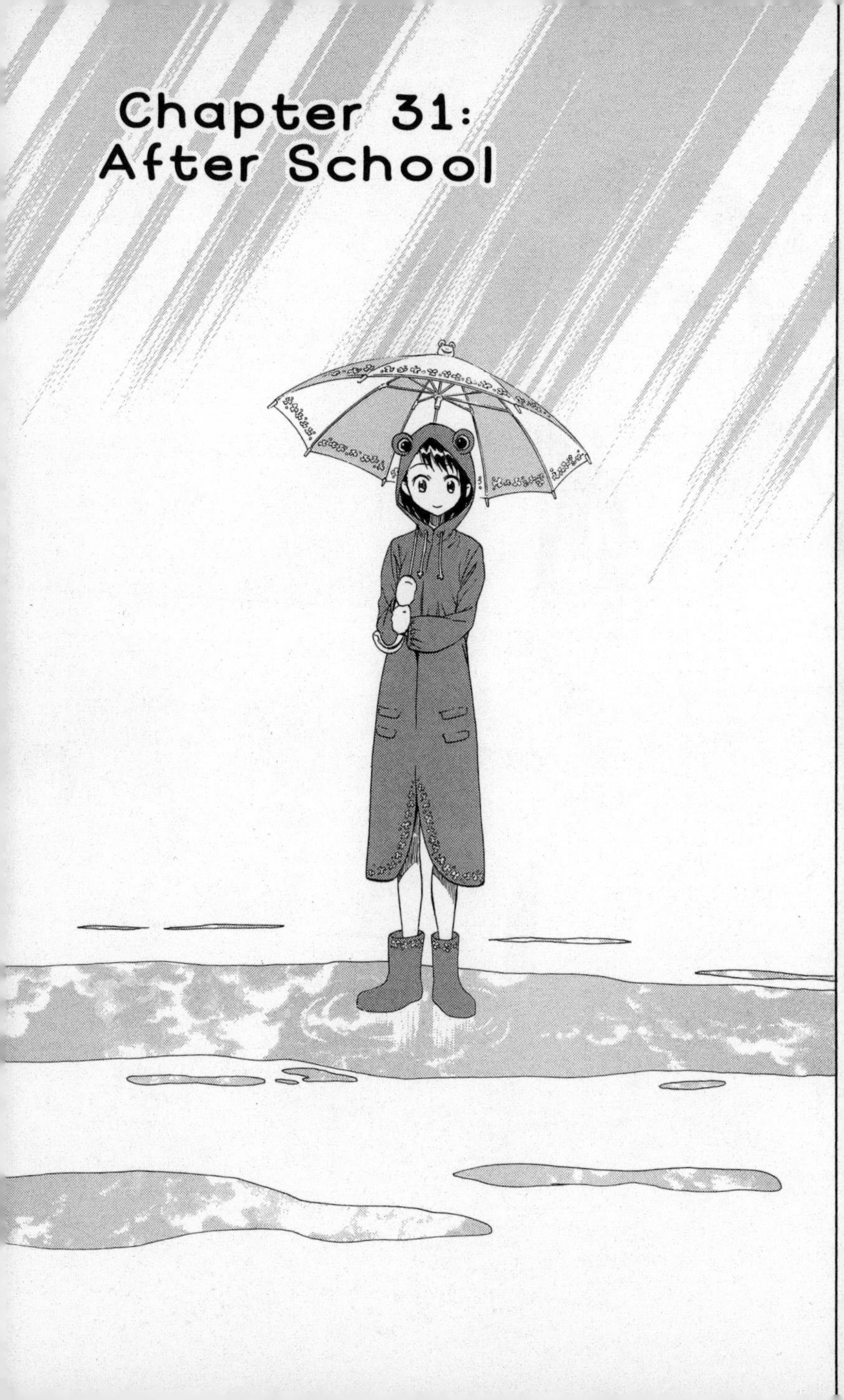

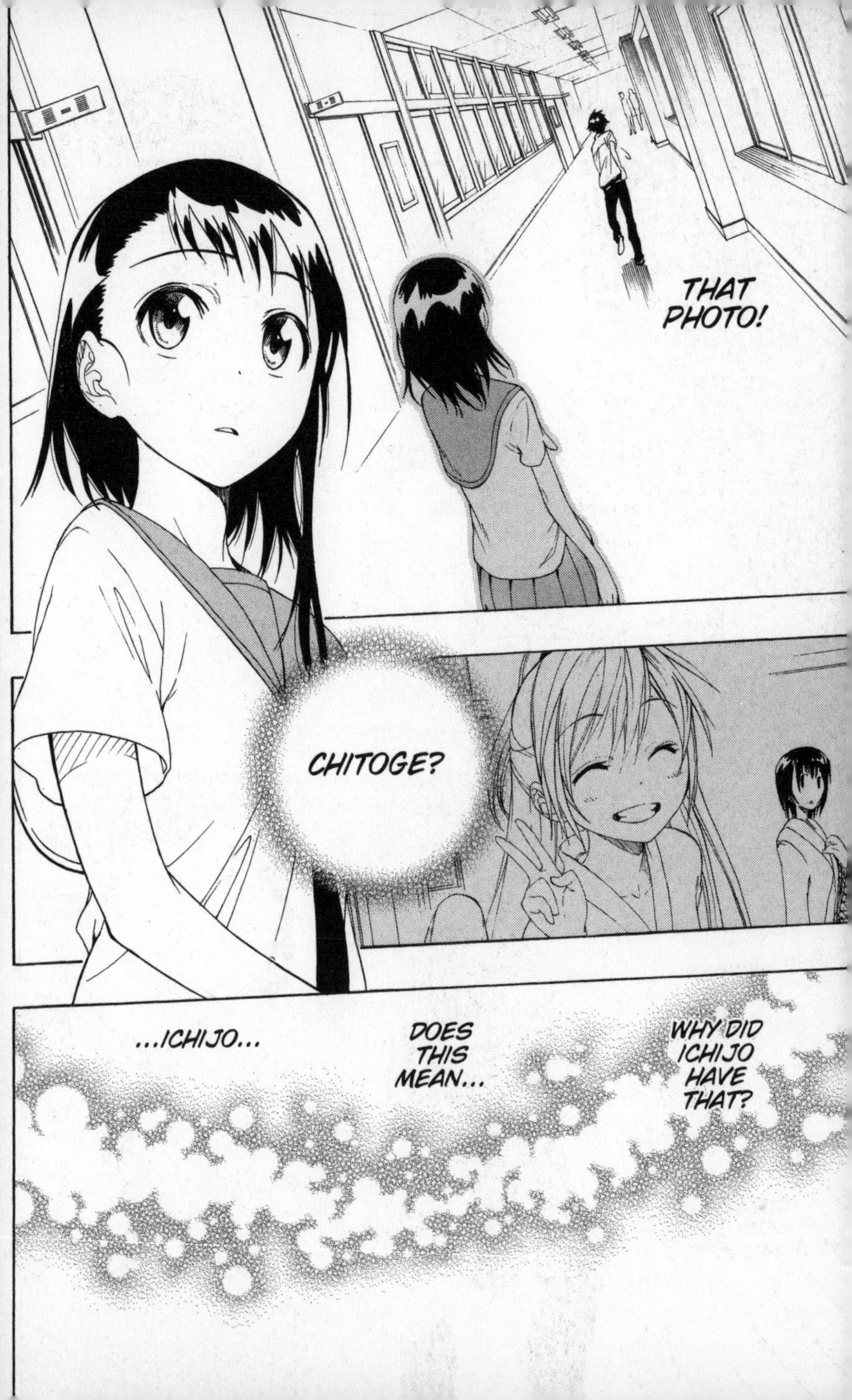
THAT PHOTO!
CHITOGE?
WHY DID ICHIJO HAVE THAT?
DOES THIS MEAN...
...ICHIJO...

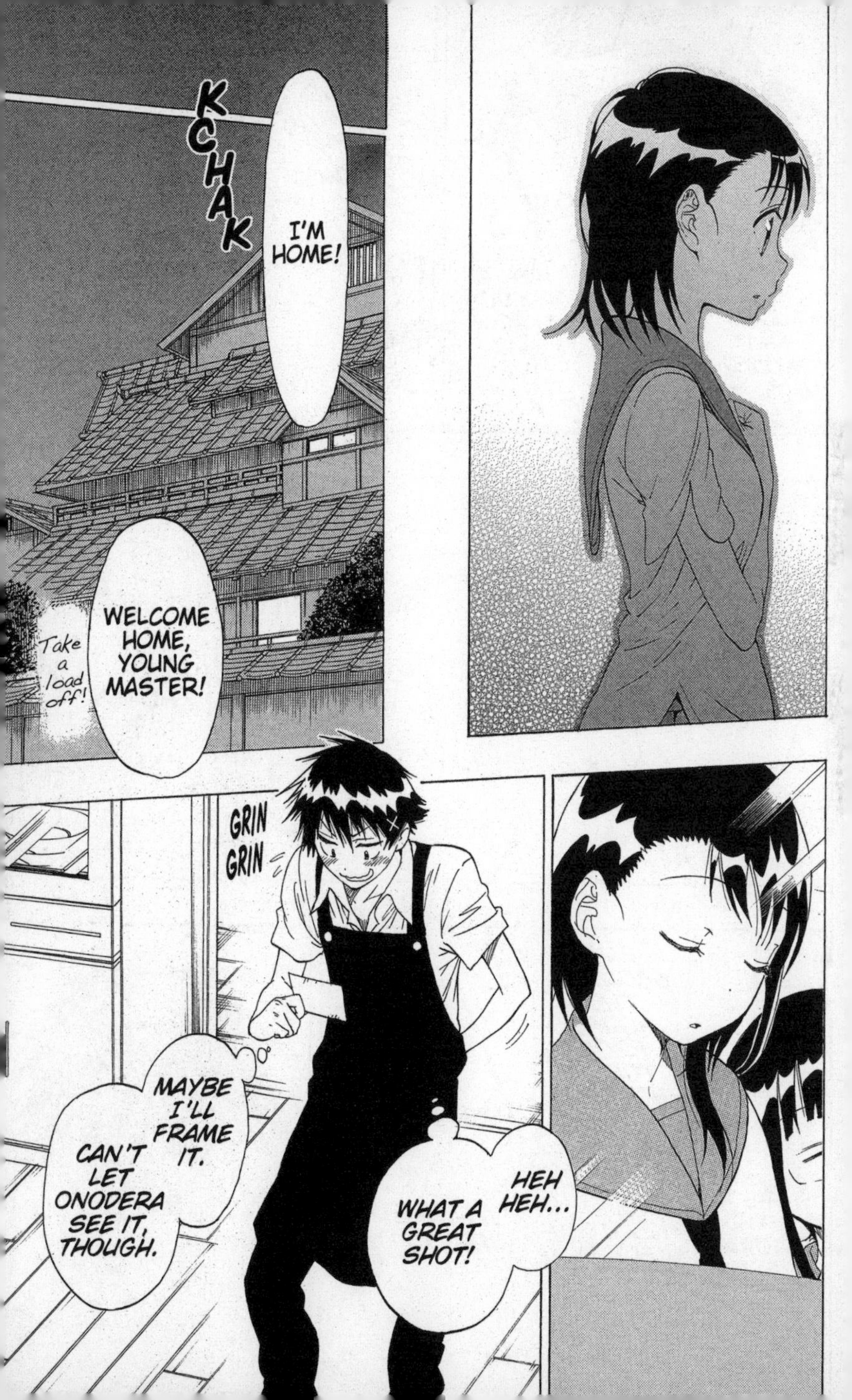
KCHAK
I'M HOME!
WELCOME HOME, YOUNG MASTER!
Take a load off!
GRIN GRIN
HEH HEH...
WHAT A GREAT SHOT!
MAYBE I'LL FRAME IT.
CAN'T LET ONODERA SEE IT, THOUGH.

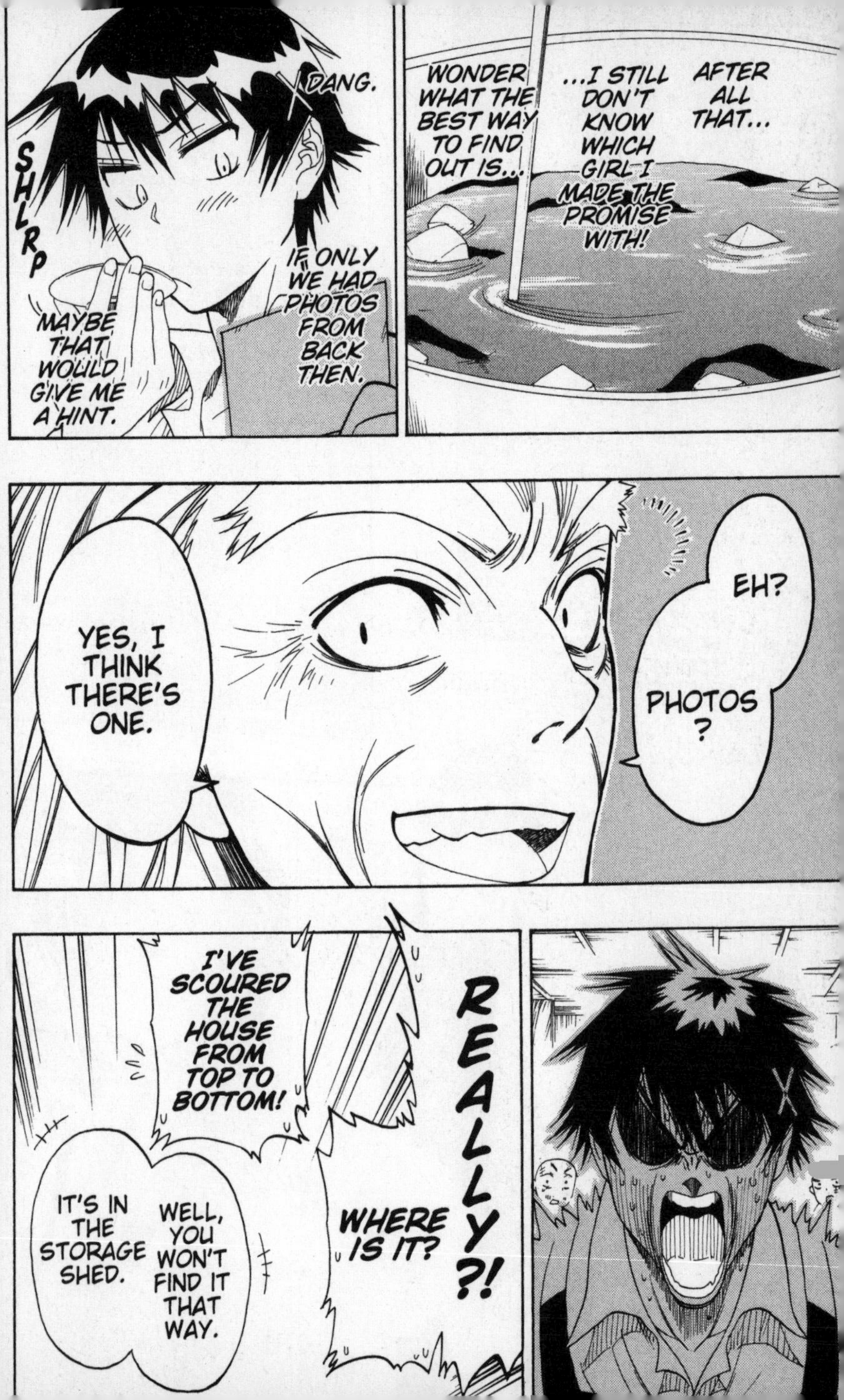
AFTER ALL THAT...
...I STILL DON'T KNOW WHICH GIRL I MADE THE PROMISE WITH!
WONDER WHAT THE BEST WAY TO FIND OUT IS...
DANG.
SHLRP
IF ONLY WE HAD PHOTOS FROM BACK THEN.
MAYBE THAT WOULD GIVE ME A HINT.
EH?
PHOTOS?
YES, I THINK THERE'S ONE.
REALLY?!
I'VE SCOURED THE HOUSE FROM TOP TO BOTTOM!
WHERE IS IT?
WELL, YOU WON'T FIND IT THAT WAY.
IT'S IN THE STORAGE SHED.

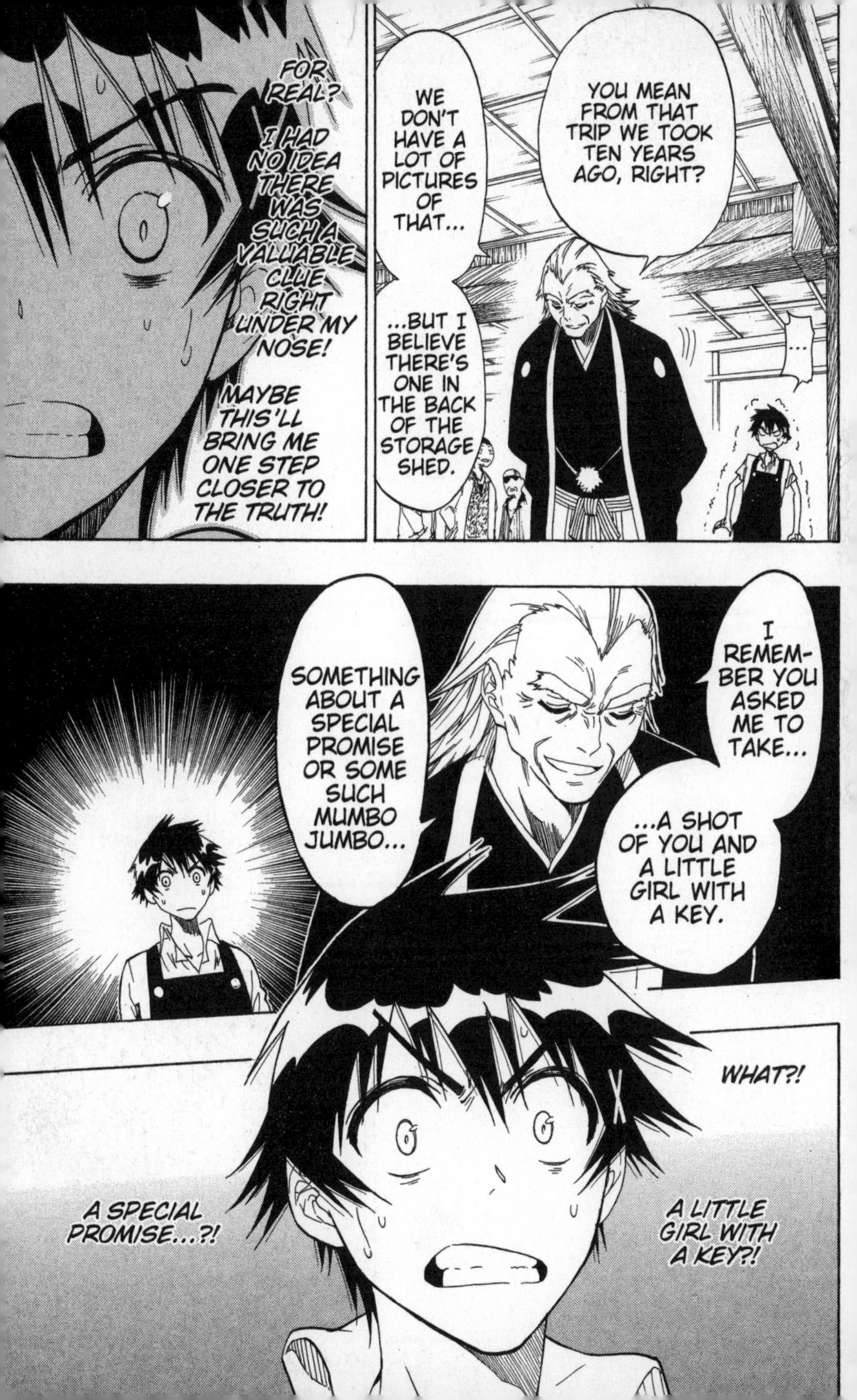
YOU MEAN FROM THAT TRIP WE TOOK TEN YEARS AGO, RIGHT?
WE DON'T HAVE A LOT OF PICTURES OF THAT...
...BUT I BELIEVE THERE'S ONE IN THE BACK OF THE STORAGE SHED.
...
FOR REAL?
I HAD NO IDEA THERE WAS SUCH A VALUABLE CLUE RIGHT UNDER MY NOSE!
MAYBE THIS'LL BRING ME ONE STEP CLOSER TO THE TRUTH!
I REMEMBER YOU ASKED ME TO TAKE...
...A SHOT OF YOU AND A LITTLE GIRL WITH A KEY.
SOMETHING ABOUT A SPECIAL PROMISE OR SOME SUCH MUMBO JUMBO...
WHAT?!
A LITTLE GIRL WITH A KEY?!
A SPECIAL PROMISE...?!

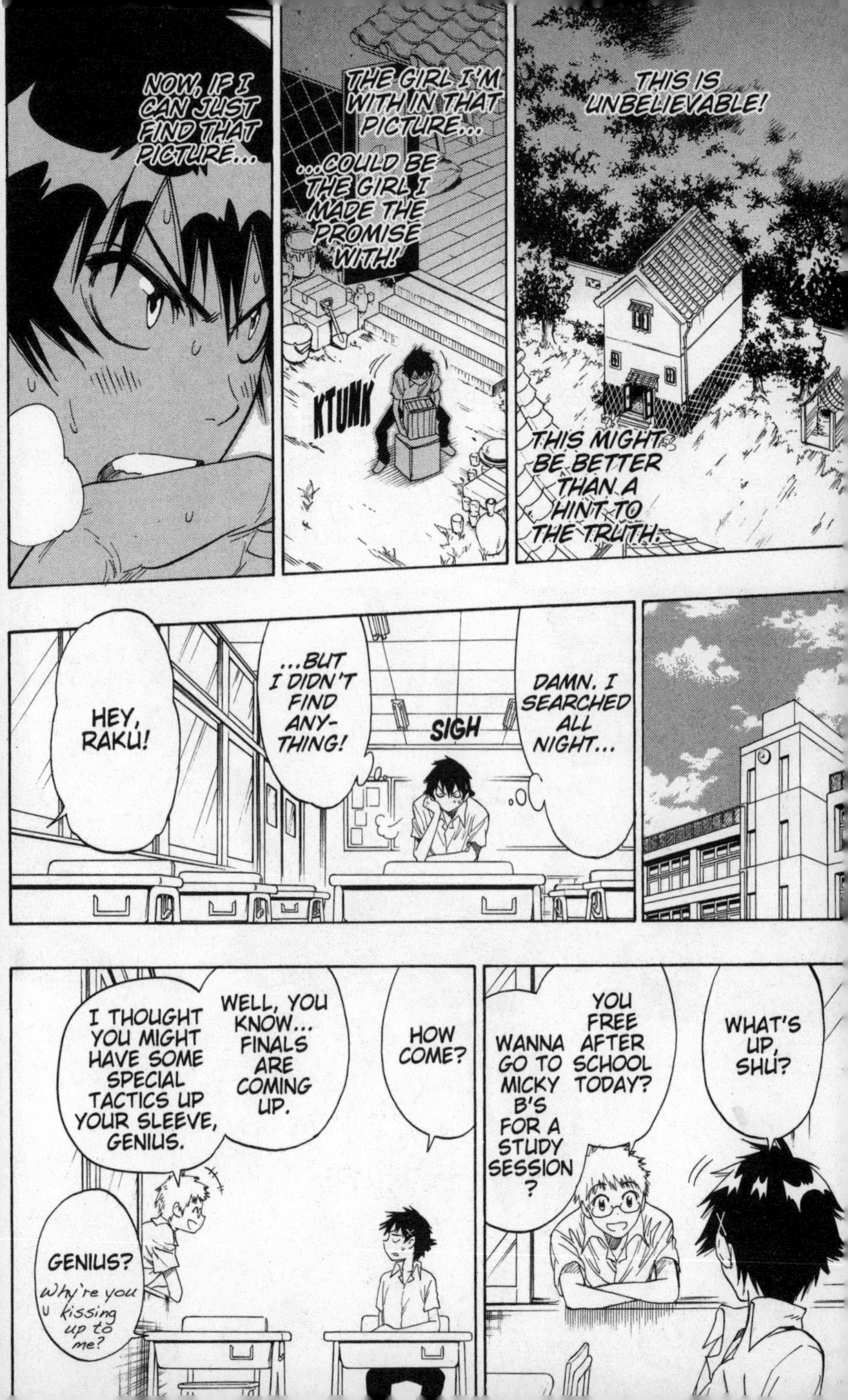
THIS IS UNBELIEVABLE!
THIS MIGHT BE BETTER THAN A HINT TO THE TRUTH.
THE GIRL I'M WITH IN THAT PICTURE...
...COULD BE THE GIRL I MADE THE PROMISE WITH!
KTUNK
NOW, IF I CAN JUST FIND THAT PICTURE...
DAMN. I SEARCHED ALL NIGHT...
SIGH
...BUT I DIDN'T FIND ANYTHING!
HEY, RAKU!
WHAT'S UP, SHU?
YOU FREE AFTER SCHOOL TODAY?
WANNA GO TO MICKY B'S FOR A STUDY SESSION?
HOW COME?
WELL, YOU KNOW... FINALS ARE COMING UP.
I THOUGHT YOU MIGHT HAVE SOME SPECIAL TACTICS UP YOUR SLEEVE, GENIUS.
GENIUS? Why're you kissing up to me?

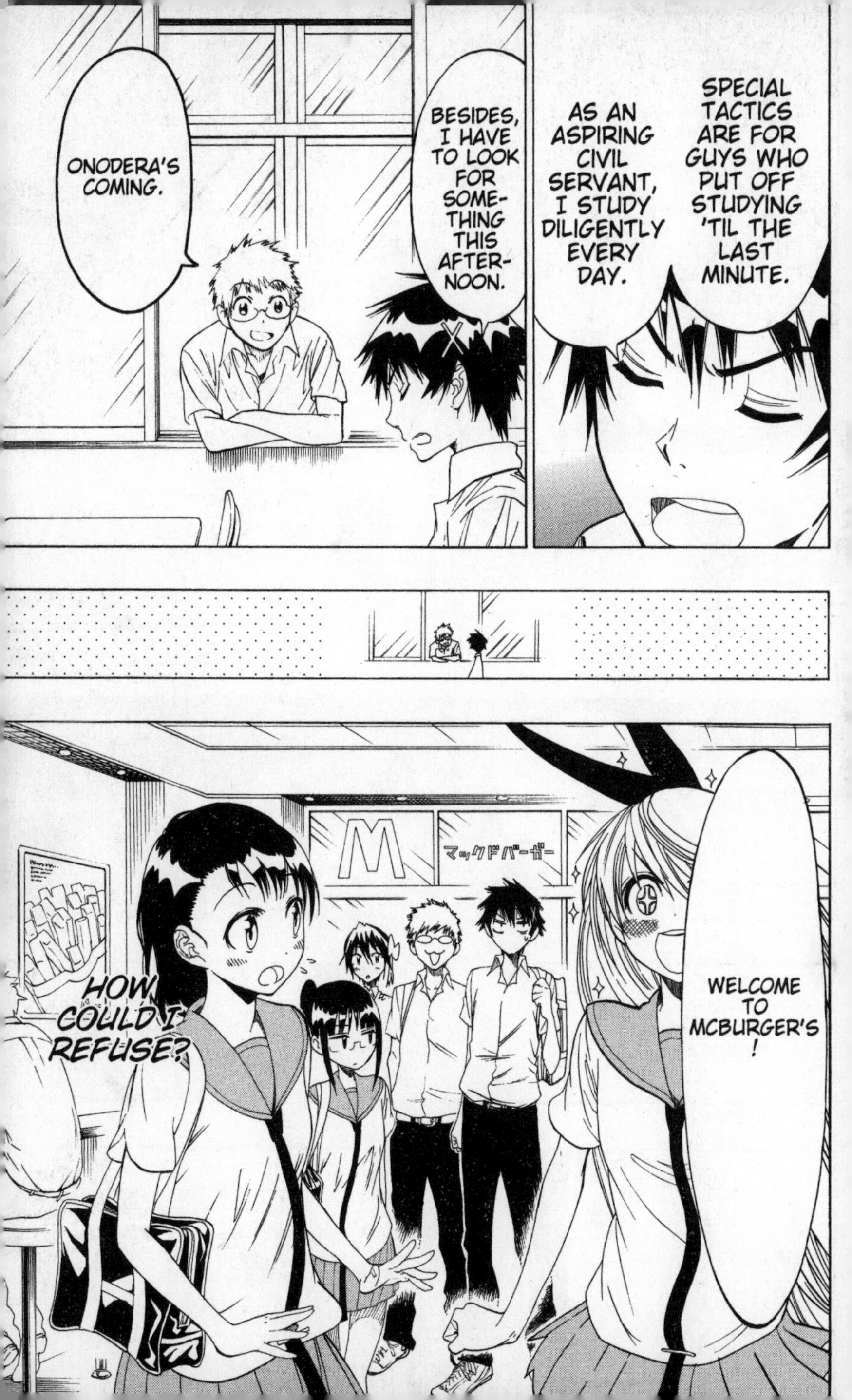
SPECIAL TACTICS ARE FOR GUYS WHO PUT OFF STUDYING 'TIL THE LAST MINUTE.
AS AN ASPIRING CIVIL SERVANT, I STUDY DILIGENTLY EVERY DAY.
BESIDES, I HAVE TO LOOK FOR SOMETHING THIS AFTERNOON.
ONODERA'S COMING.
WELCOME TO MCBURGER'S!
マックドバーガー
HOW COULD I REFUSE?

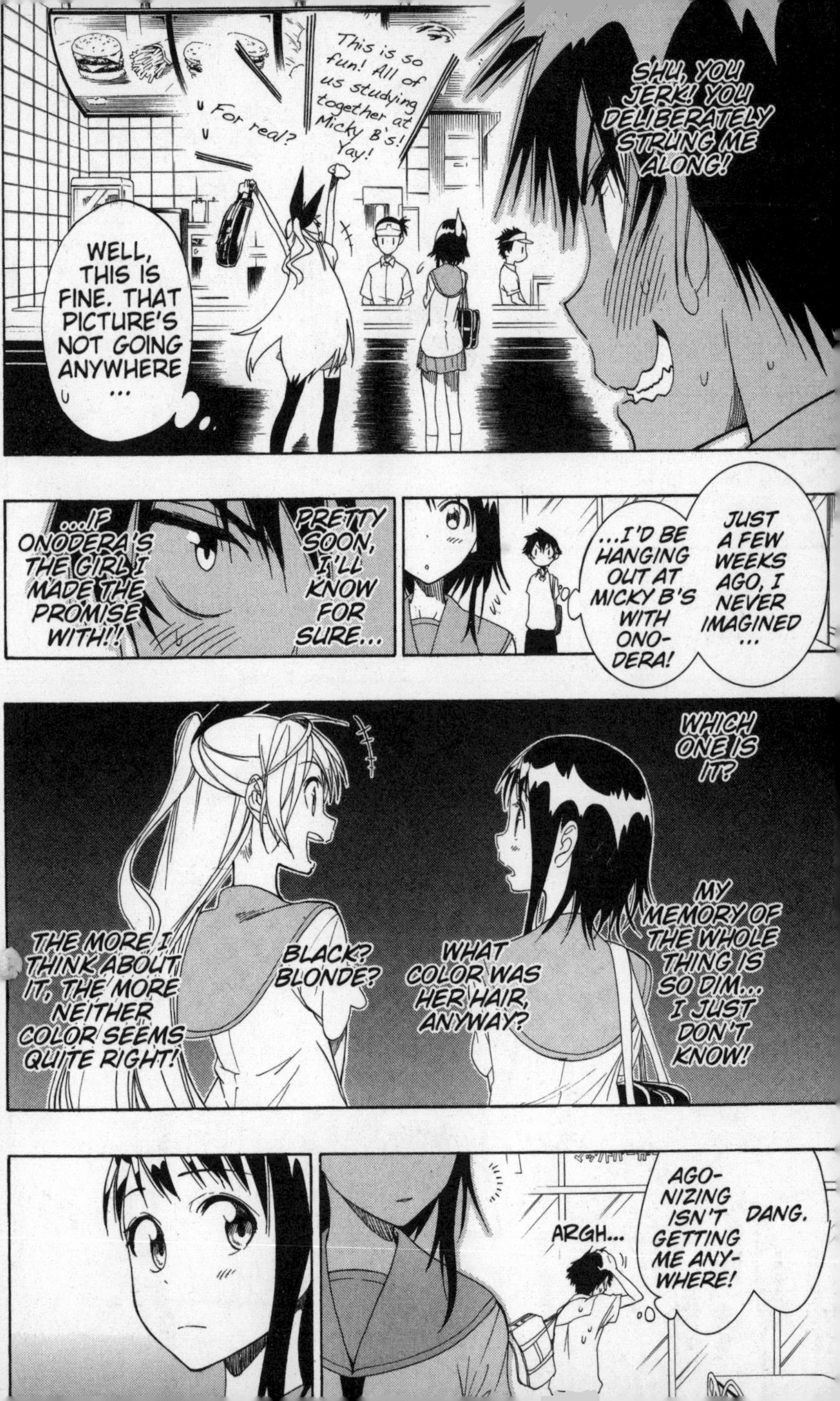
SHU, YOU JERK! YOU DELIBERATELY STRUNG ME ALONG!
This is so fun! All of us studying together at Micky B's! Yay!
For real?
WELL, THIS IS FINE. THAT PICTURE'S NOT GOING ANYWHERE...
JUST A FEW WEEKS AGO, I NEVER IMAGINED...
...I'D BE HANGING OUT AT MICKY B'S WITH ONODERA!
PRETTY SOON, I'LL KNOW FOR SURE...
...IF ONODERA'S THE GIRL I MADE THE PROMISE WITH!!
WHICH ONE IS IT?
MY MEMORY OF THE WHOLE THING IS SO DIM... I JUST DON'T KNOW!
WHAT COLOR WAS HER HAIR, ANYWAY?
BLACK? BLONDE?
THE MORE I THINK ABOUT IT, THE MORE NEITHER COLOR SEEMS QUITE RIGHT!
DANG.
AGONIZING ISN'T GETTING ME ANYWHERE!
ARGH...

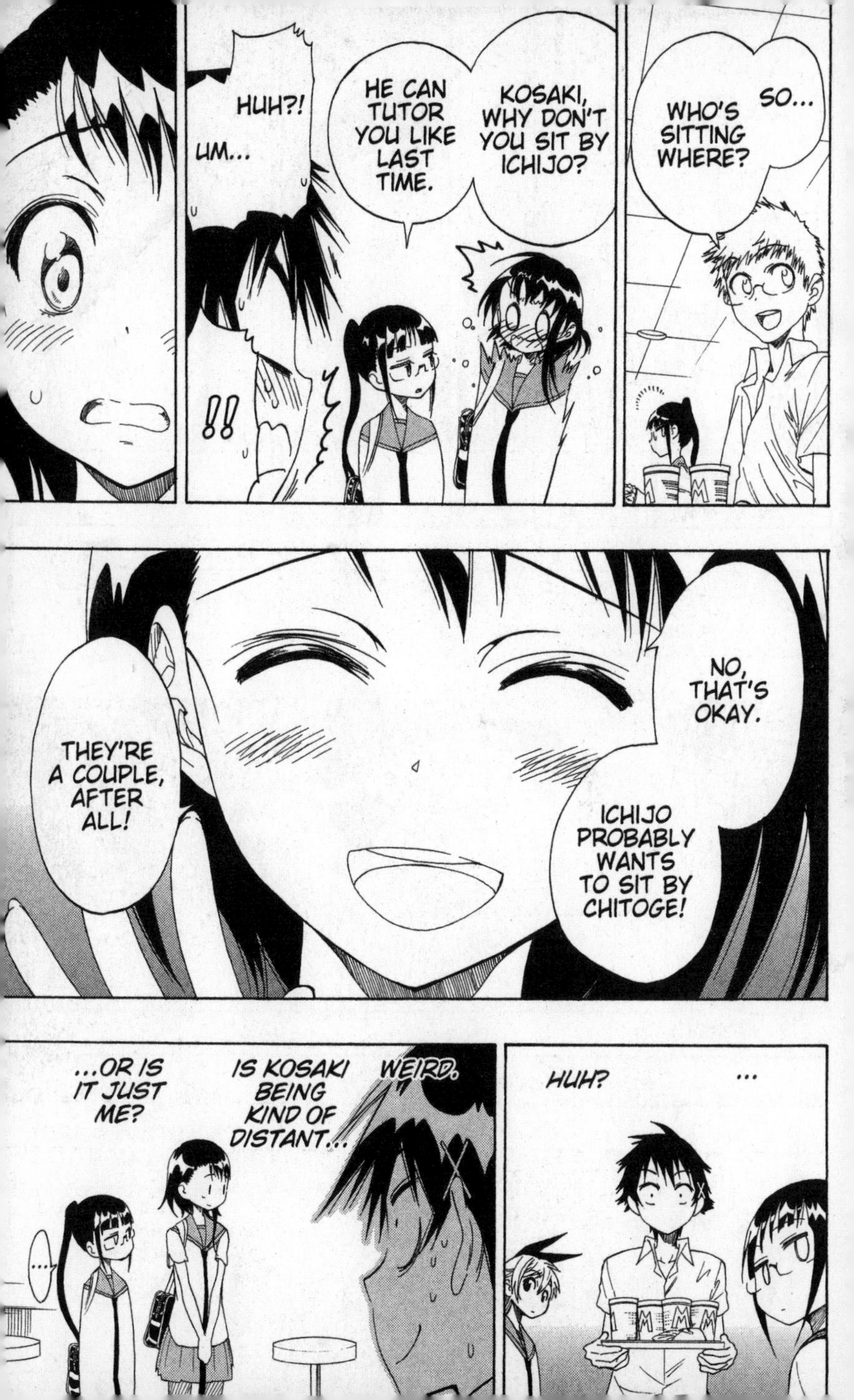
SO...
WHO'S SITTING WHERE?
KOSAKI, WHY DON'T YOU SIT BY ICHIJO?
HE CAN TUTOR YOU LIKE LAST TIME.
HUH?!
UM...
!!
NO, THAT'S OKAY.
ICHIJO PROBABLY WANTS TO SIT BY CHITOGE!
THEY'RE A COUPLE, AFTER ALL!
...
HUH?
WEIRD.
IS KOSAKI BEING KIND OF DISTANT...
...OR IS IT JUST ME?
...

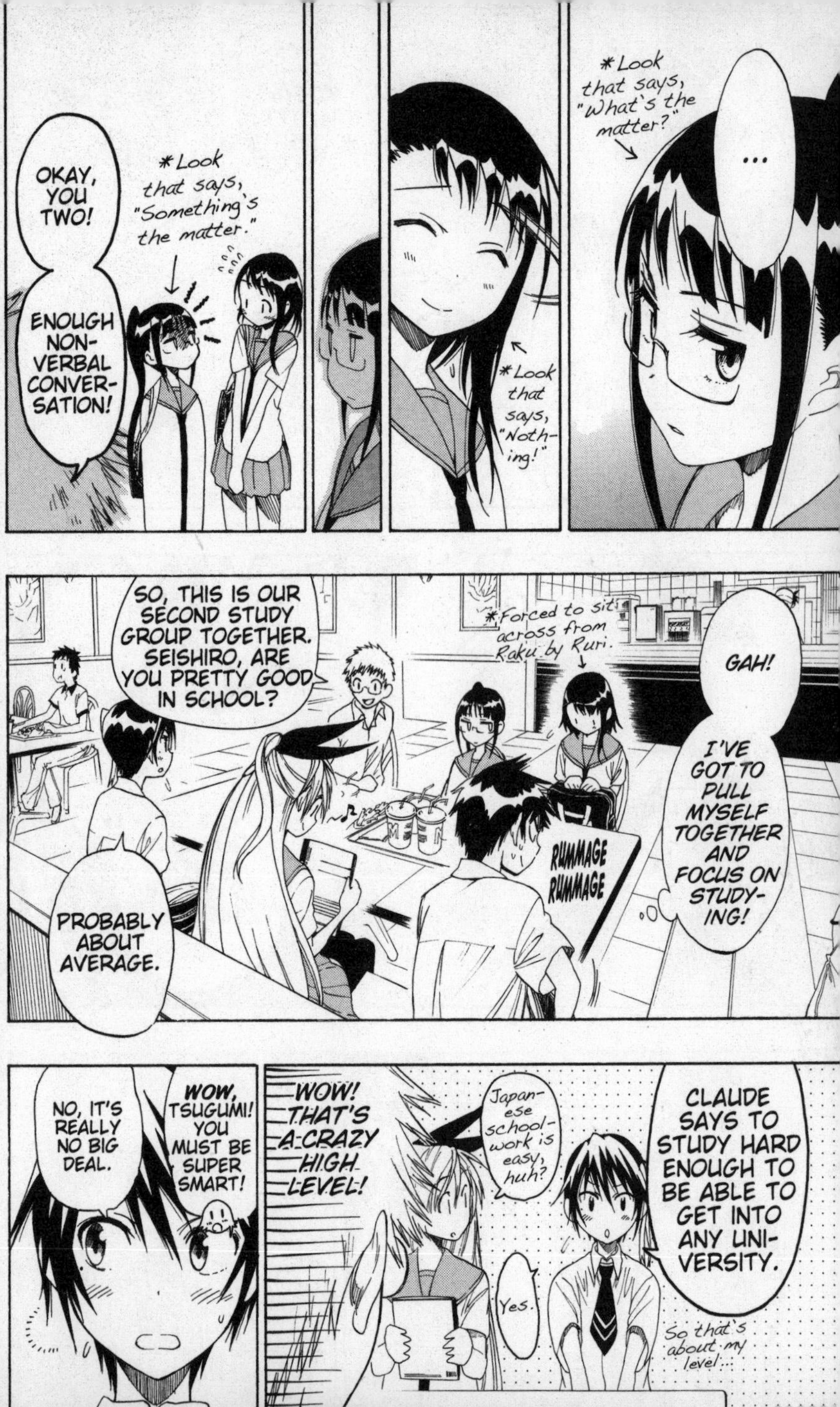

...
*Look that says, "What's the matter?"
*Look that says, "Nothing!"
OKAY, YOU TWO! ENOUGH NON-VERBAL CONVERSATION!
*Look that says, "Something's the matter."
GAH! I'VE GOT TO PULL MYSELF TOGETHER AND FOCUS ON STUDYING!
*Forced to sit across from Raku by Ruri.
SO, THIS IS OUR SECOND STUDY GROUP TOGETHER. SEISHIRO, ARE YOU PRETTY GOOD IN SCHOOL?
RUMMAGE RUMMAGE
PROBABLY ABOUT AVERAGE.
CLAUDE SAYS TO STUDY HARD ENOUGH TO BE ABLE TO GET INTO ANY UNIVERSITY.
Japanese schoolwork is easy, huh?
Yes.
So that's about my level...
WOW! THAT'S A CRAZY HIGH LEVEL!
WOW, TSUGUMI! YOU MUST BE SUPER SMART!
NO, IT'S REALLY NO BIG DEAL.

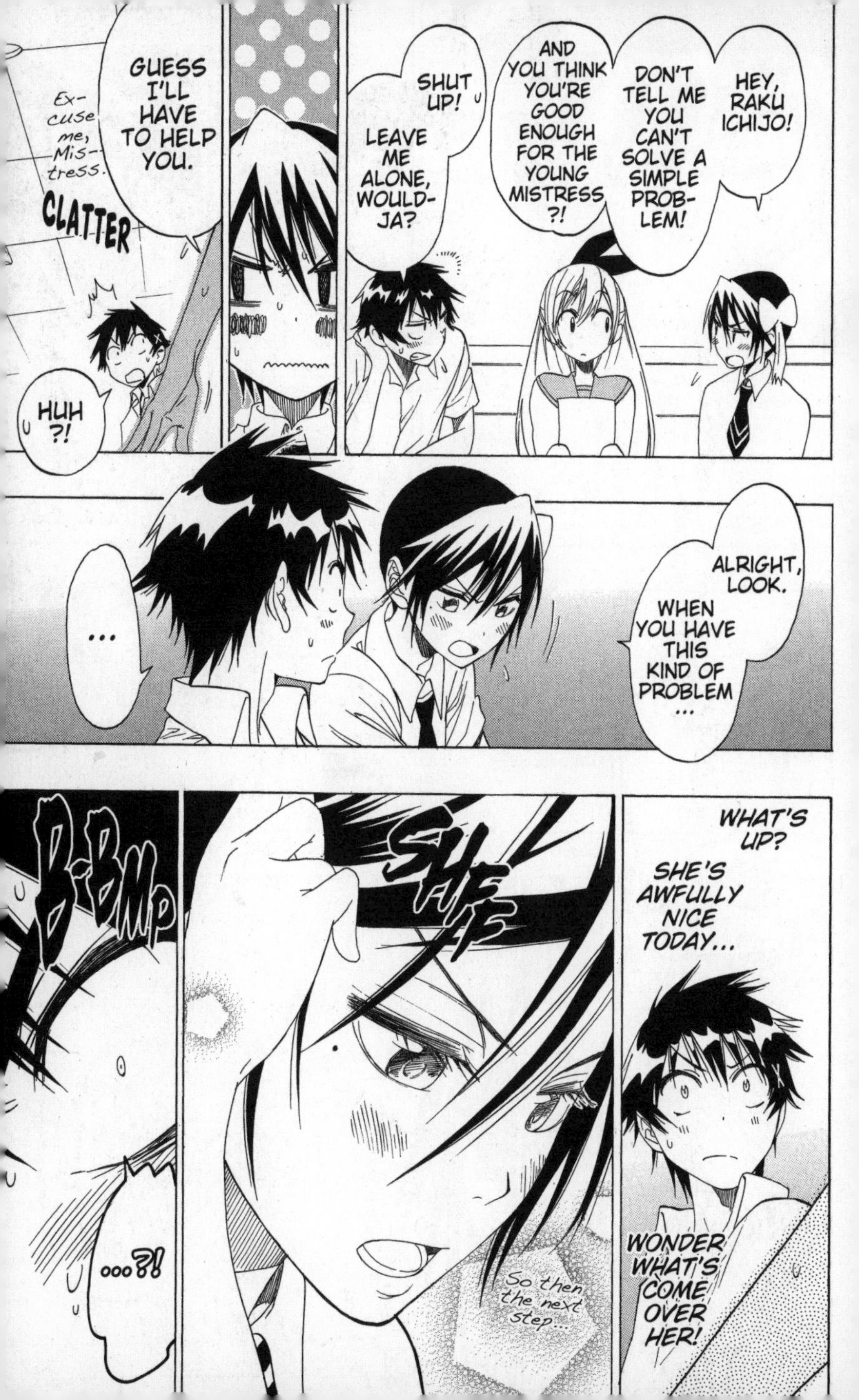
HEY, RAKU ICHIJO!
DON'T TELL ME YOU CAN'T SOLVE A SIMPLE PROBLEM!
AND YOU THINK YOU'RE GOOD ENOUGH FOR THE YOUNG MISTRESS ?!
SHUT UP!
LEAVE ME ALONE, WOULD-JA?
GUESS I'LL HAVE TO HELP YOU.
Excuse me, Mistress.
CLATTER
HUH ?!
ALRIGHT, LOOK.
WHEN YOU HAVE THIS KIND OF PROBLEM ...
...
WHAT'S UP?
SHE'S AWFULLY NICE TODAY...
WONDER WHAT'S COME OVER HER!
SHFF
So then the next step...
B-BMP
ooo?!

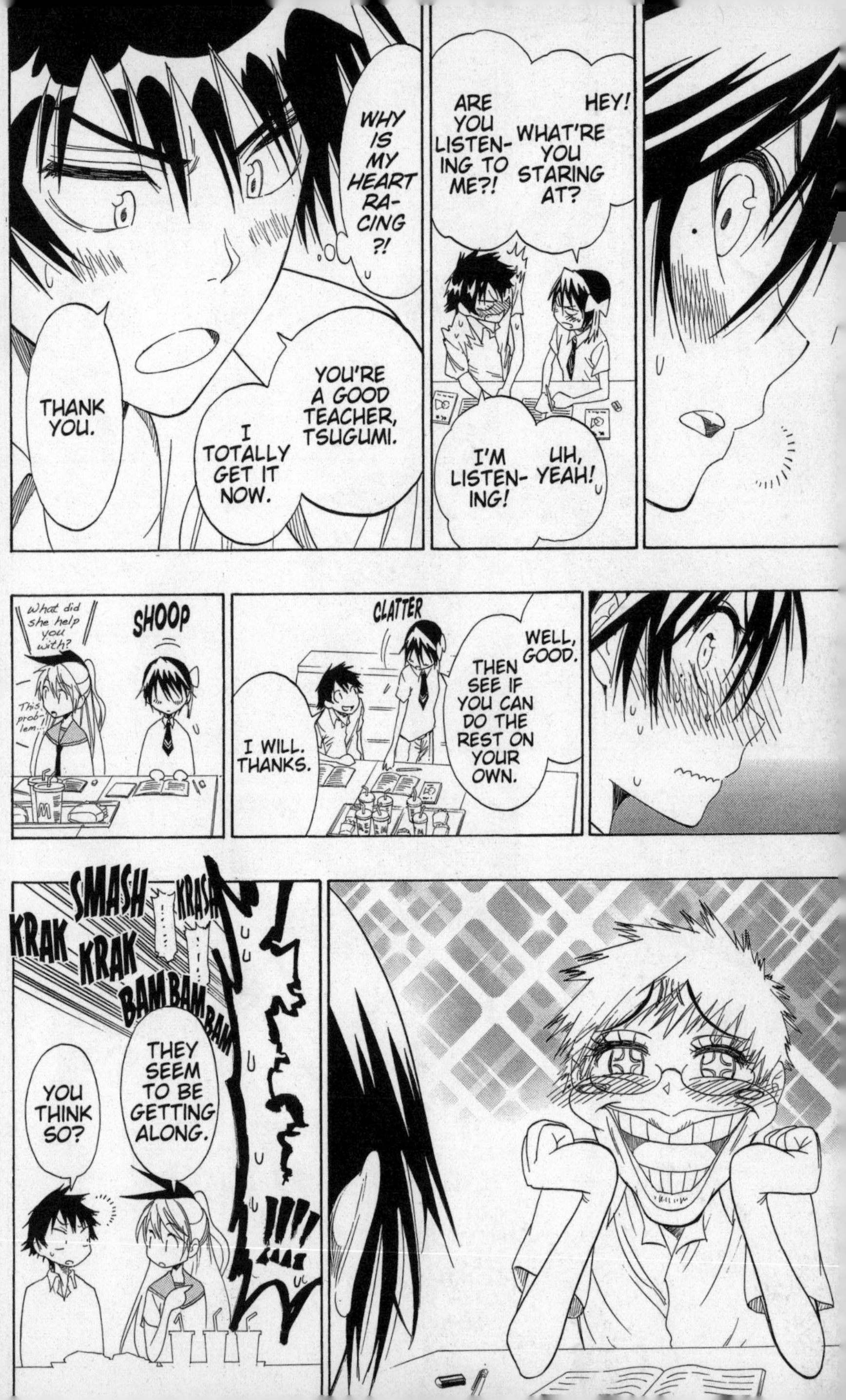
HEY! WHAT'RE YOU STARING AT?
ARE YOU LISTEN-ING TO ME?!
UH, YEAH! I'M LISTEN-ING!
WHY IS MY HEART RA-CING ?!
YOU'RE A GOOD TEACHER, TSUGUMI.
I TOTALLY GET IT NOW.
THANK YOU.
WELL, GOOD.
THEN SEE IF YOU CAN DO THE REST ON YOUR OWN.
CLATTER
I WILL. THANKS.
SHOOP
What did she help you with?
This prob-lem...
KRASH
SMASH
KRAK
KRAK
BAM BAM BAM
THEY SEEM TO BE GETTING ALONG.
YOU THINK SO?

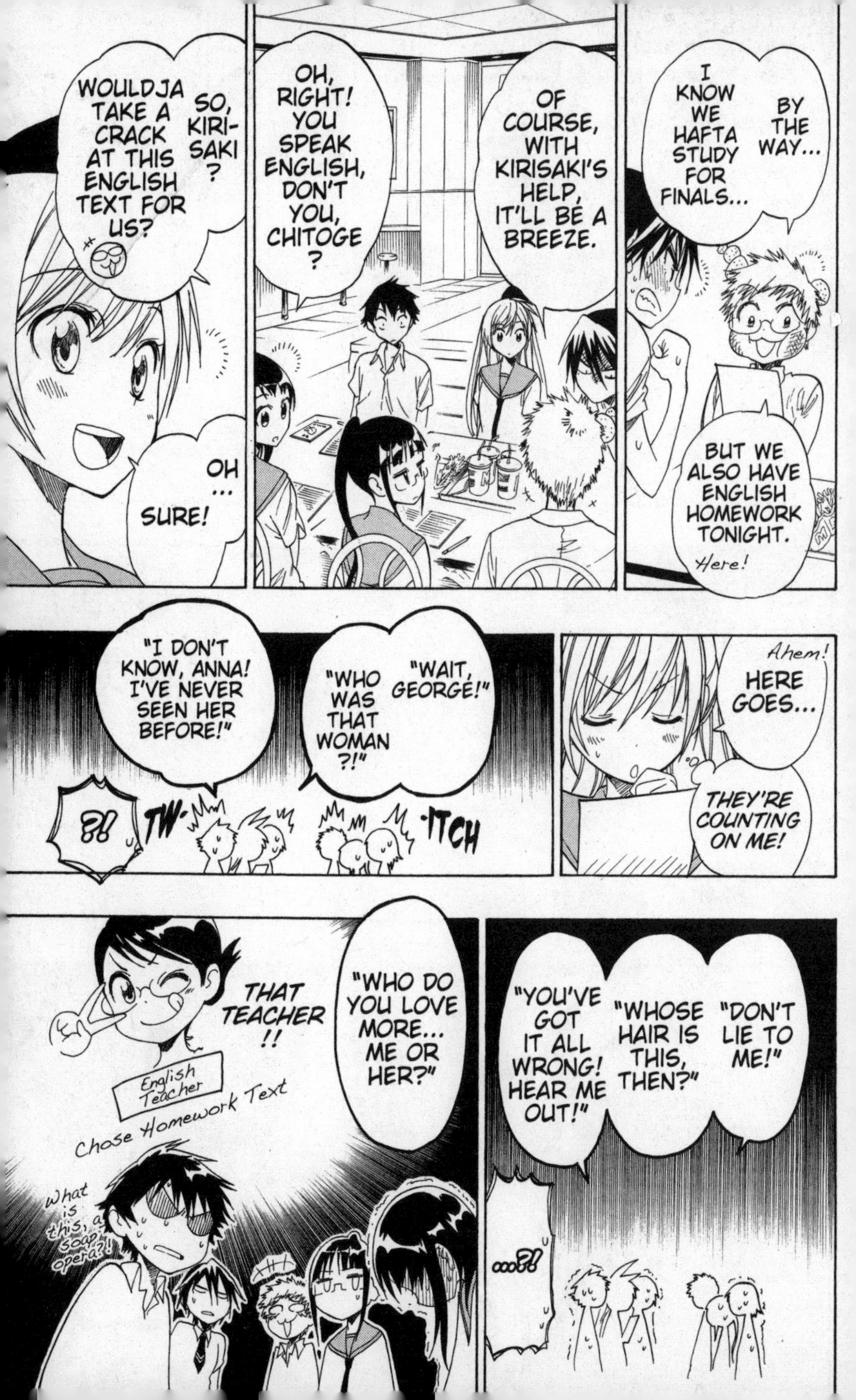
BY THE WAY...
I KNOW WE HAFTA STUDY FOR FINALS...
BUT WE ALSO HAVE ENGLISH HOMEWORK TONIGHT.
Here!
OF COURSE, WITH KIRISAKI'S HELP, IT'LL BE A BREEZE.
OH, RIGHT! YOU SPEAK ENGLISH, DON'T YOU, CHITOGE?
SO, KIRI-SAKI?
WOULDJA TAKE A CRACK AT THIS ENGLISH TEXT FOR US?
OH ... SURE!
Ahem!
HERE GOES...
THEY'RE COUNTING ON ME!
"WAIT, GEORGE!"
"WHO WAS THAT WOMAN?!"
"I DON'T KNOW, ANNA! I'VE NEVER SEEN HER BEFORE!"
?!
TW-ITCH
"DON'T LIE TO ME!"
"WHOSE HAIR IS THIS, THEN?"
"YOU'VE GOT IT ALL WRONG! HEAR ME OUT!"
...?!
"WHO DO YOU LOVE MORE... ME OR HER?"
THAT TEACHER!!
English Teacher
Chose Homework Text
What is this, a soap opera?!

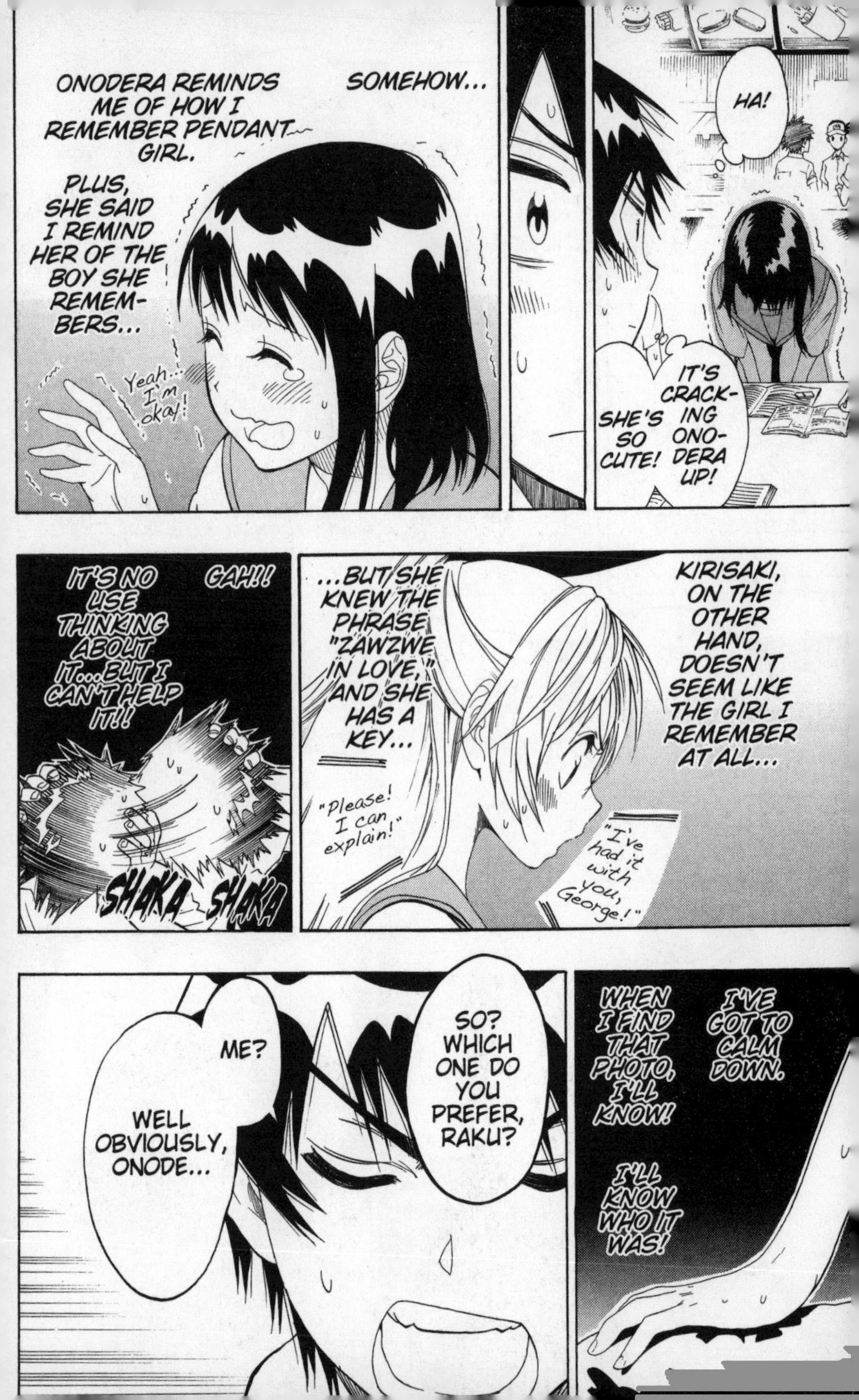
HA!
IT'S CRACKING ONODERA UP!
SHE'S SO CUTE!
SOMEHOW...
ONODERA REMINDS ME OF HOW I REMEMBER PENDANT GIRL.
PLUS, SHE SAID I REMIND HER OF THE BOY SHE REMEMBERS...
Yeah... I'm okay!
KIRISAKI, ON THE OTHER HAND, DOESN'T SEEM LIKE THE GIRL I REMEMBER AT ALL...
...BUT SHE KNEW THE PHRASE "ZAWZWE IN LOVE," AND SHE HAS A KEY...
"I've had it with you, George!"
"Please! I can explain!"
GAH!!
IT'S NO USE THINKING ABOUT IT...BUT I CAN'T HELP IT!!
SHAKA SHAKA
I'VE GOT TO CALM DOWN.
WHEN I FIND THAT PHOTO, I'LL KNOW!
I'LL KNOW WHO IT WAS!
SO? WHICH ONE DO YOU PREFER, RAKU?
ME?
WELL OBVIOUSLY, ONODE...

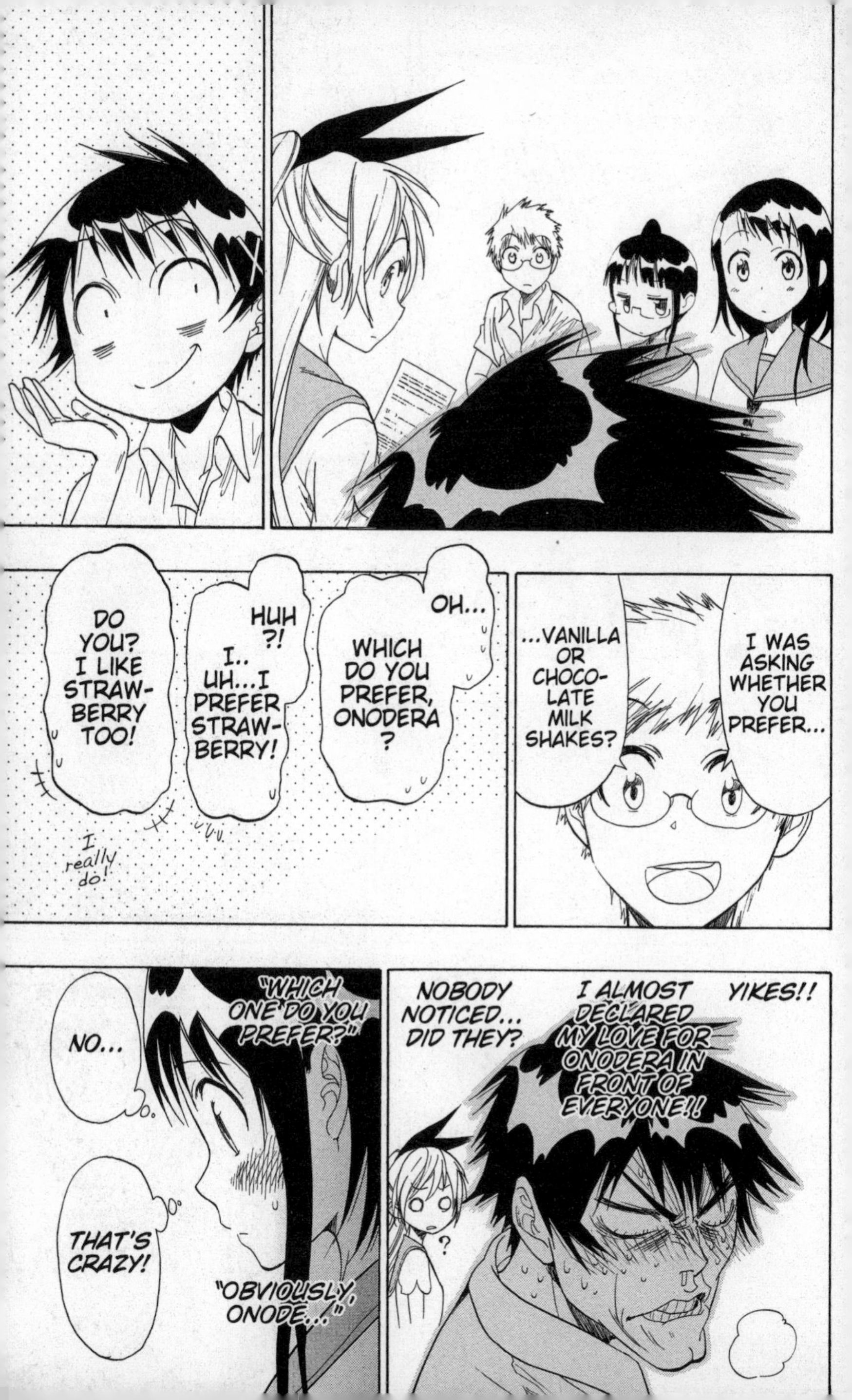
I WAS ASKING WHETHER YOU PREFER...
...VANILLA OR CHOCOLATE MILK SHAKES?
OH...
WHICH DO YOU PREFER, ONODERA?
HUH?!
I.. UH...I PREFER STRAWBERRY!
DO YOU? I LIKE STRAWBERRY TOO!
I really do!
YIKES!!
I ALMOST DECLARED MY LOVE FOR ONODERA IN FRONT OF EVERYONE!!
NOBODY NOTICED... DID THEY?
?
"WHICH ONE DO YOU PREFER?"
NO...
"OBVIOUSLY, ONODE..."
THAT'S CRAZY!

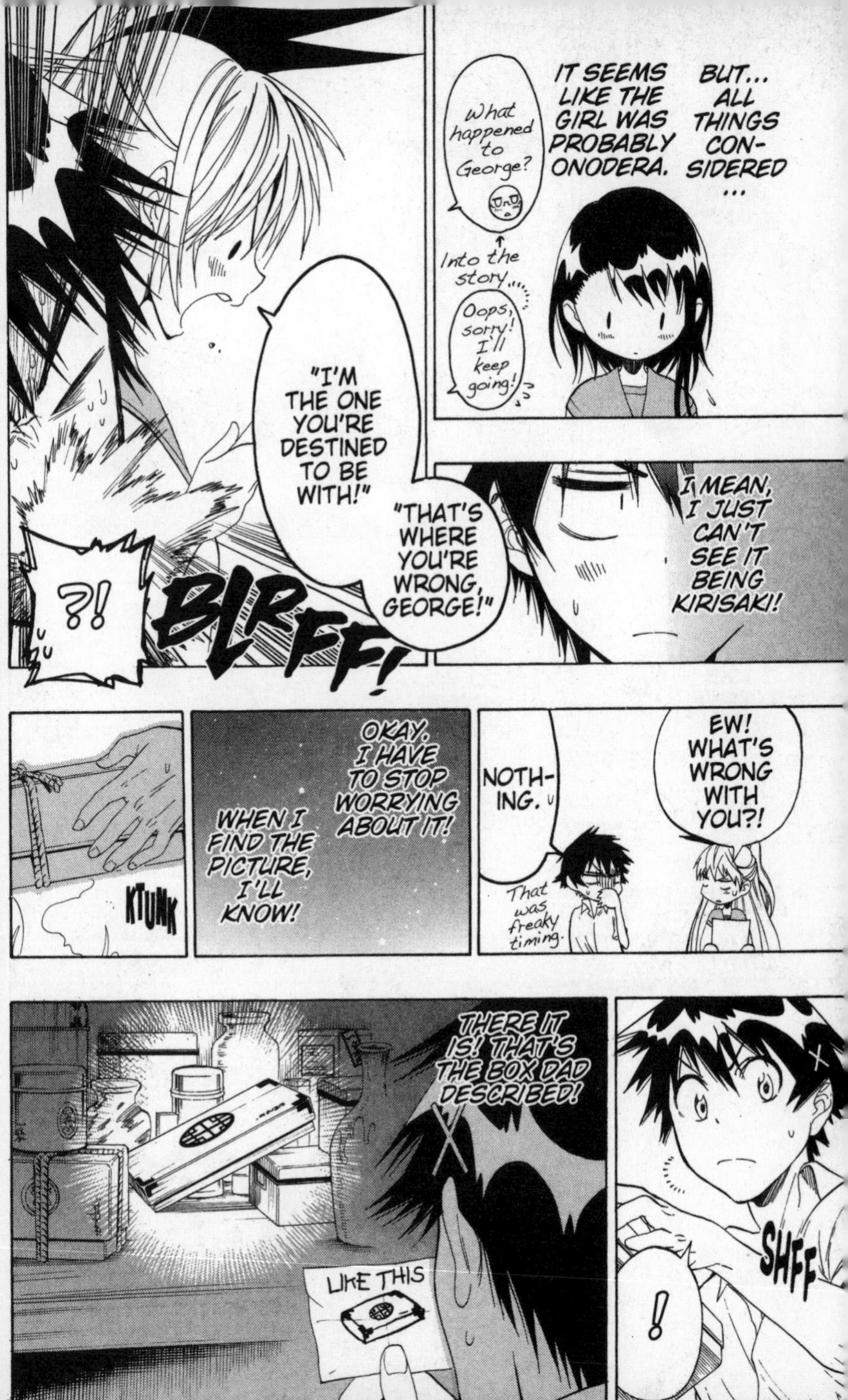
IT SEEMS LIKE THE GIRL WAS PROBABLY ONODERA.
BUT... ALL THINGS CONSIDERED...
What happened to George?
Into the story...
Oops, sorry! I'll keep going!
I MEAN, I JUST CAN'T SEE IT BEING KIRISAKI!
"THAT'S WHERE YOU'RE WRONG, GEORGE!"
"I'M THE ONE YOU'RE DESTINED TO BE WITH!"
?!
BLRFF!
EW! WHAT'S WRONG WITH YOU?!
NOTHING.
That was freaky timing.
OKAY. I HAVE TO STOP WORRYING ABOUT IT!
WHEN I FIND THE PICTURE, I'LL KNOW!
KTUNK
SHFF
!
THERE IT IS! THAT'S THE BOX DAD DESCRIBED!
LIKE THIS

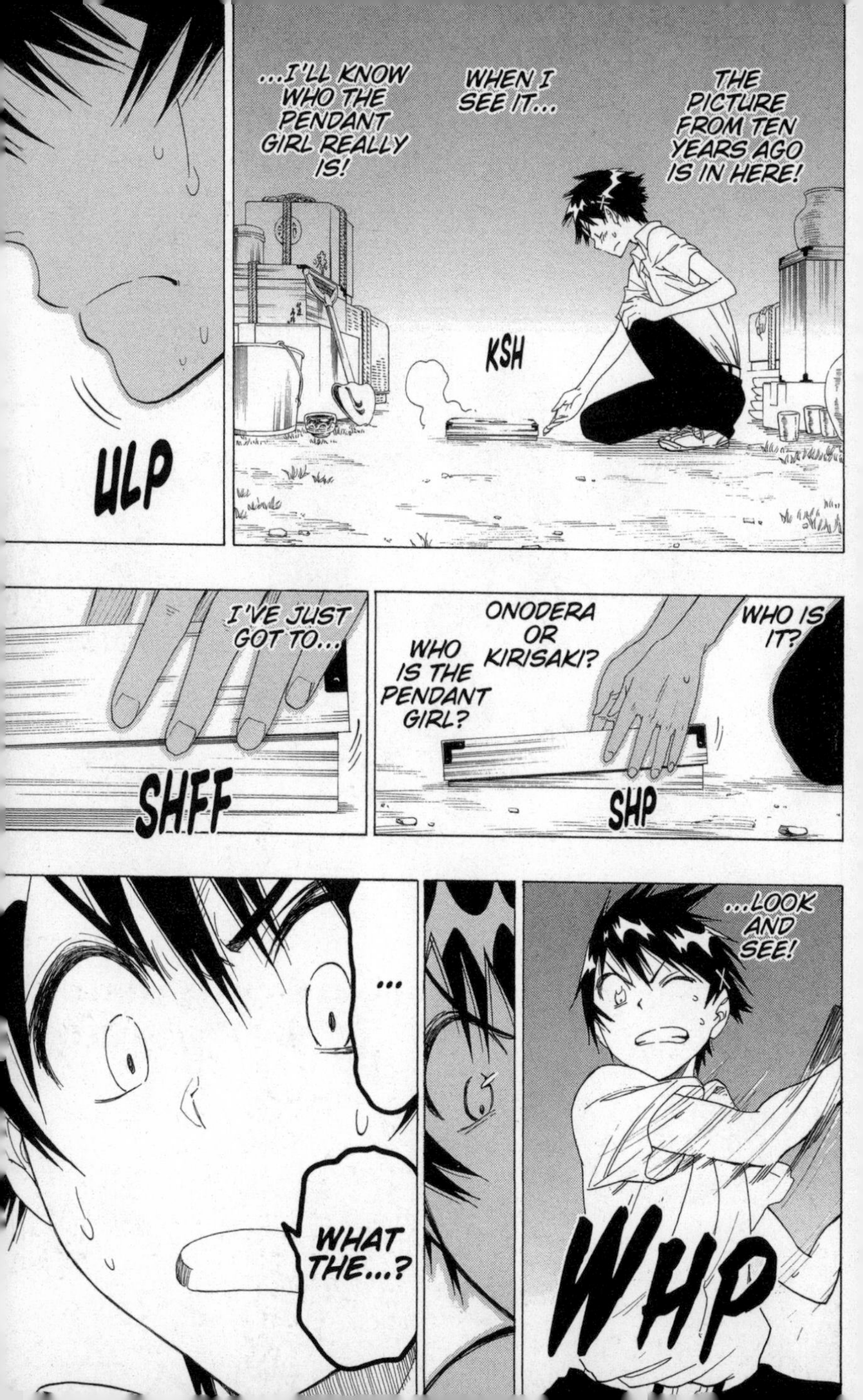
THE PICTURE FROM TEN YEARS AGO IS IN HERE!
WHEN I SEE IT...
...I'LL KNOW WHO THE PENDANT GIRL REALLY IS!
KSH
ULP
WHO IS IT?
ONODERA OR KIRISAKI?
WHO IS THE PENDANT GIRL?
SHP
I'VE JUST GOT TO...
SHFF
...LOOK AND SEE!
WHP
...
WHAT THE...?

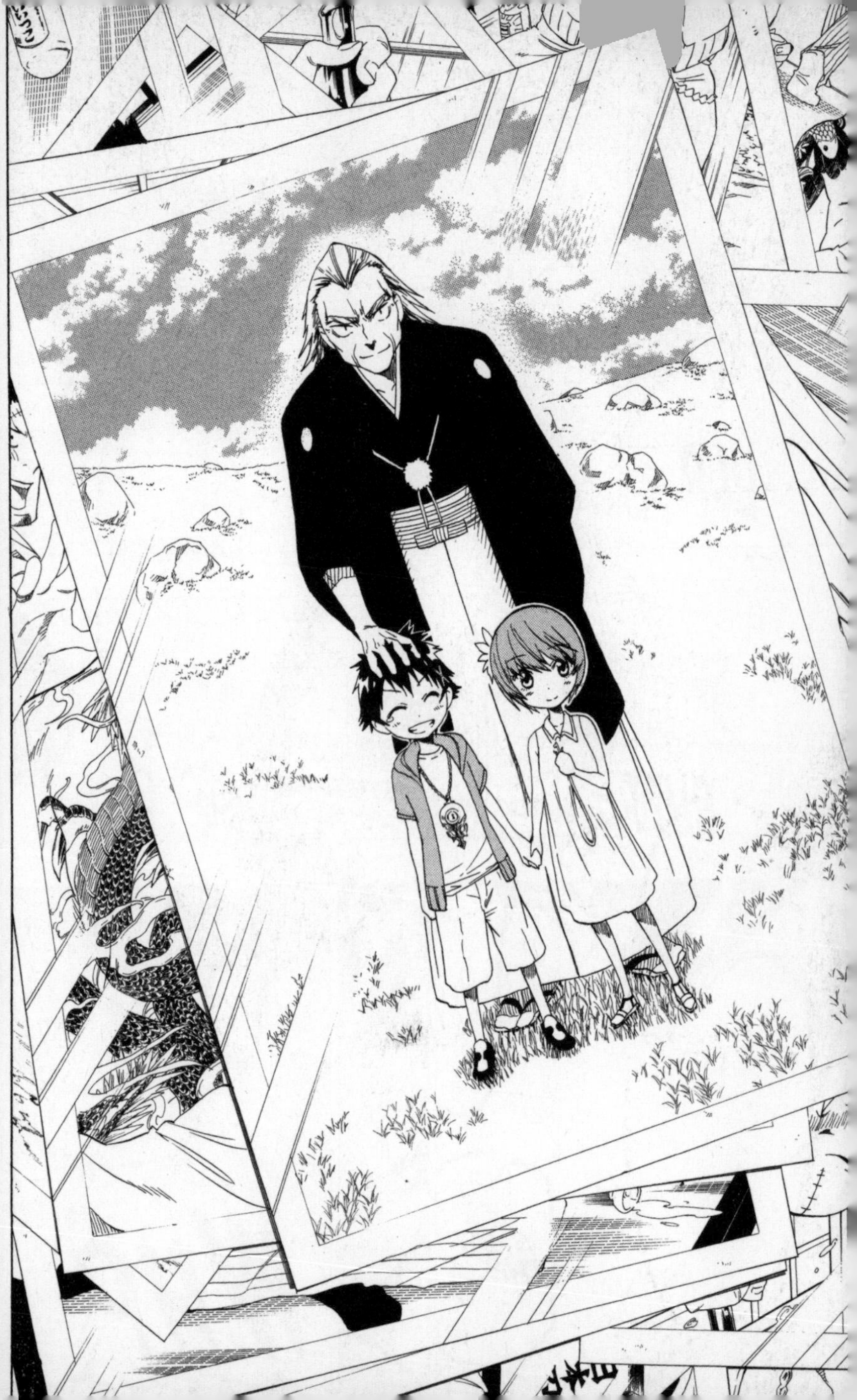

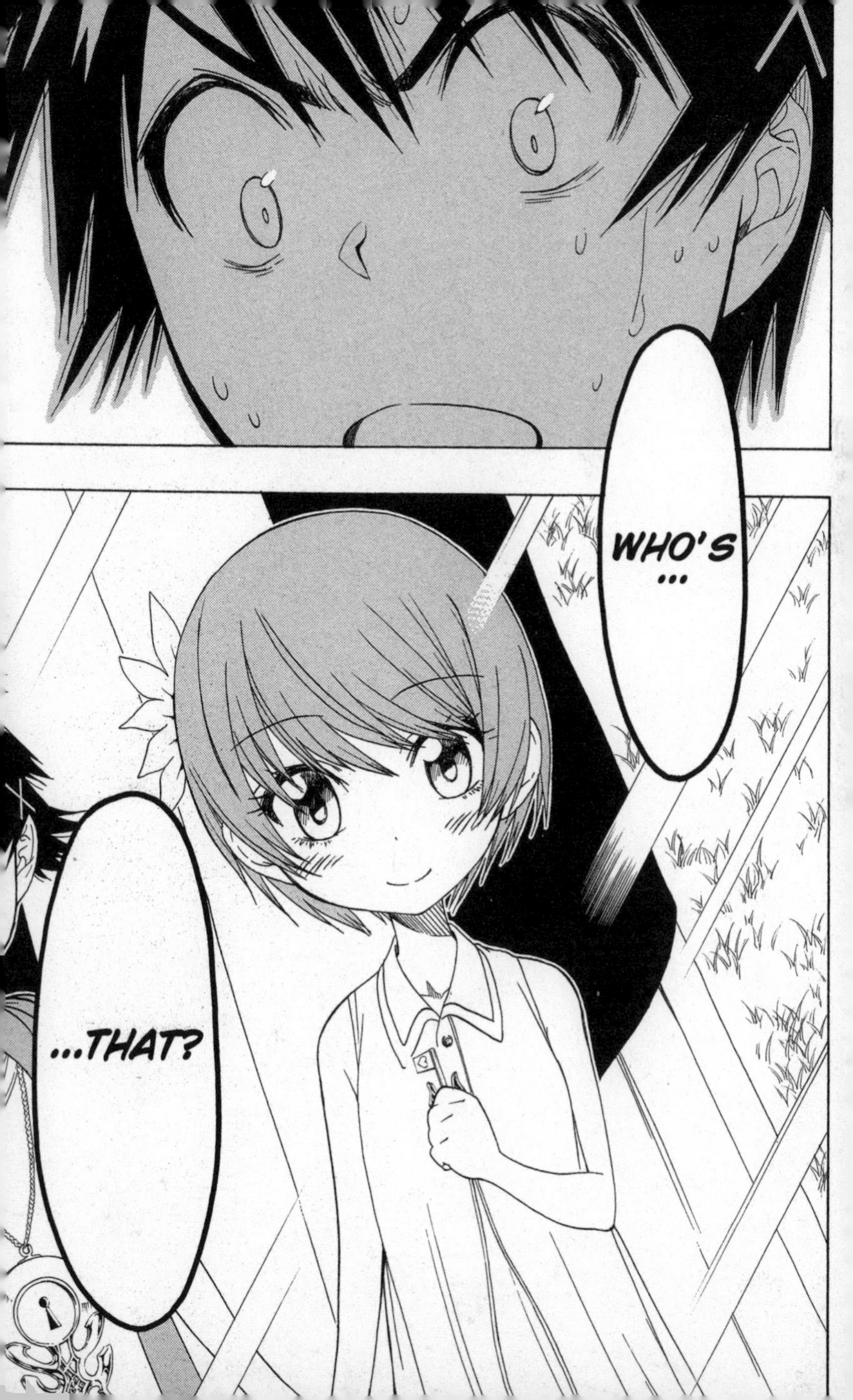
WHO'S ...
...THAT?

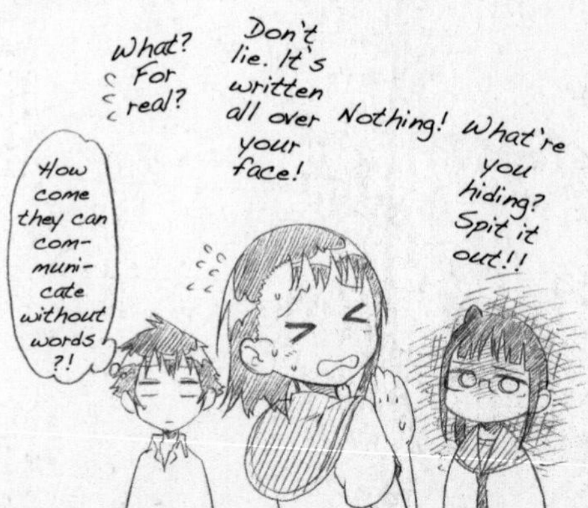
What're you hiding? Spit it out!!
Nothing!
Don't lie. It's written all over your face!
What? For real?
How come they can communicate without words?!

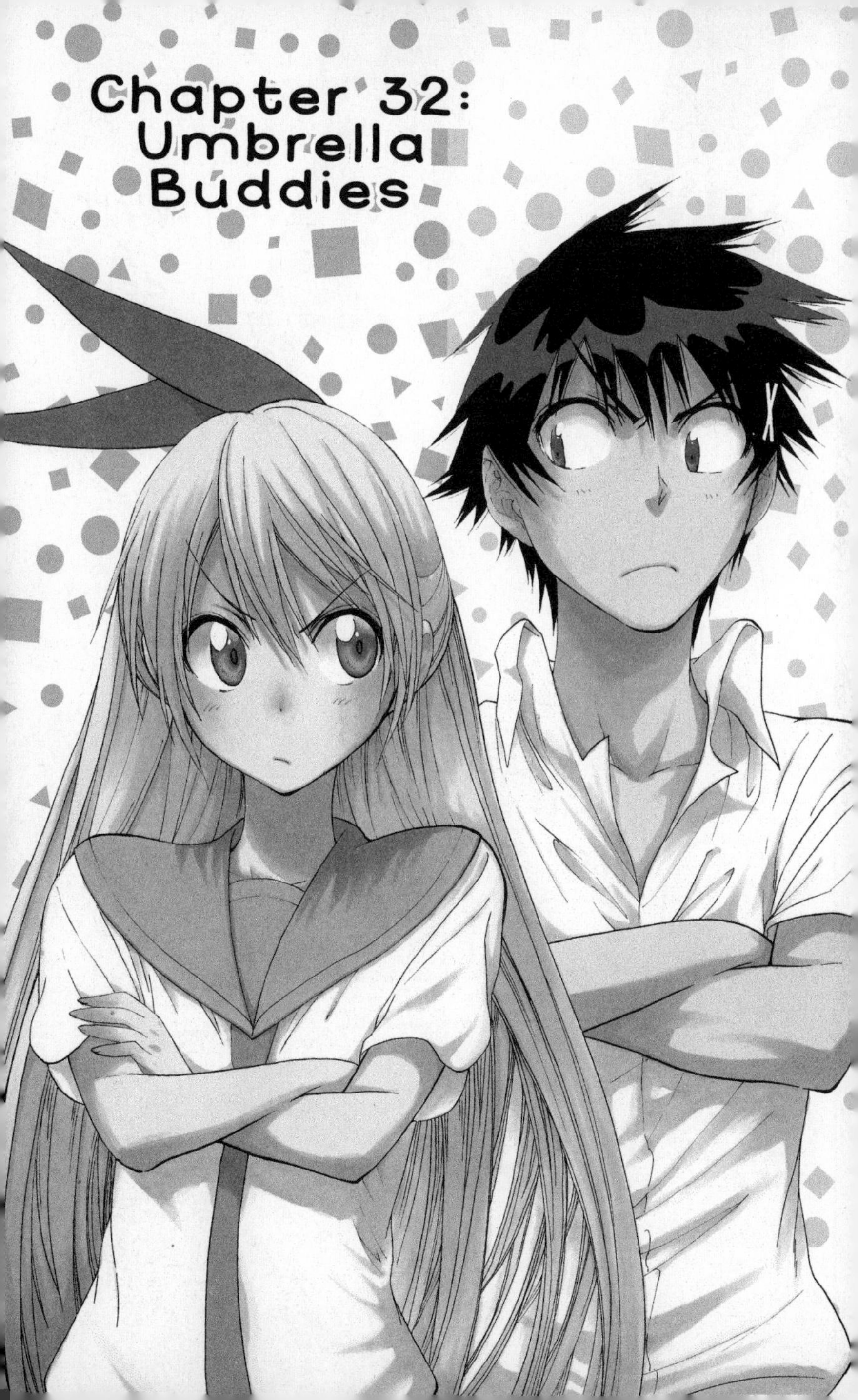
Chapter 32:
Umbrella
Buddies

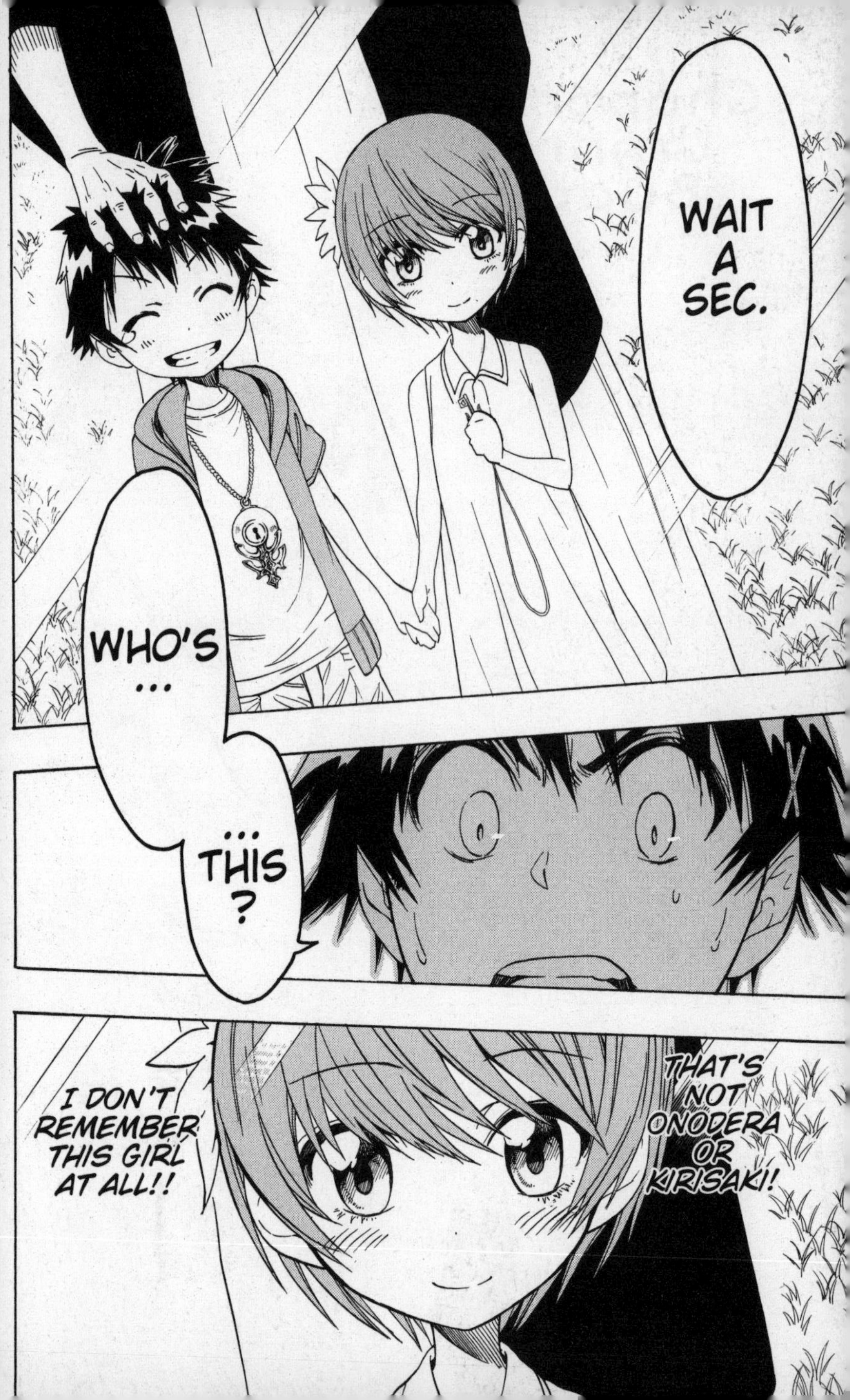
WAIT A SEC.
WHO'S ...
... THIS?
THAT'S NOT ONODERA OR KIRISAKI!
I DON'T REMEMBER THIS GIRL AT ALL!!

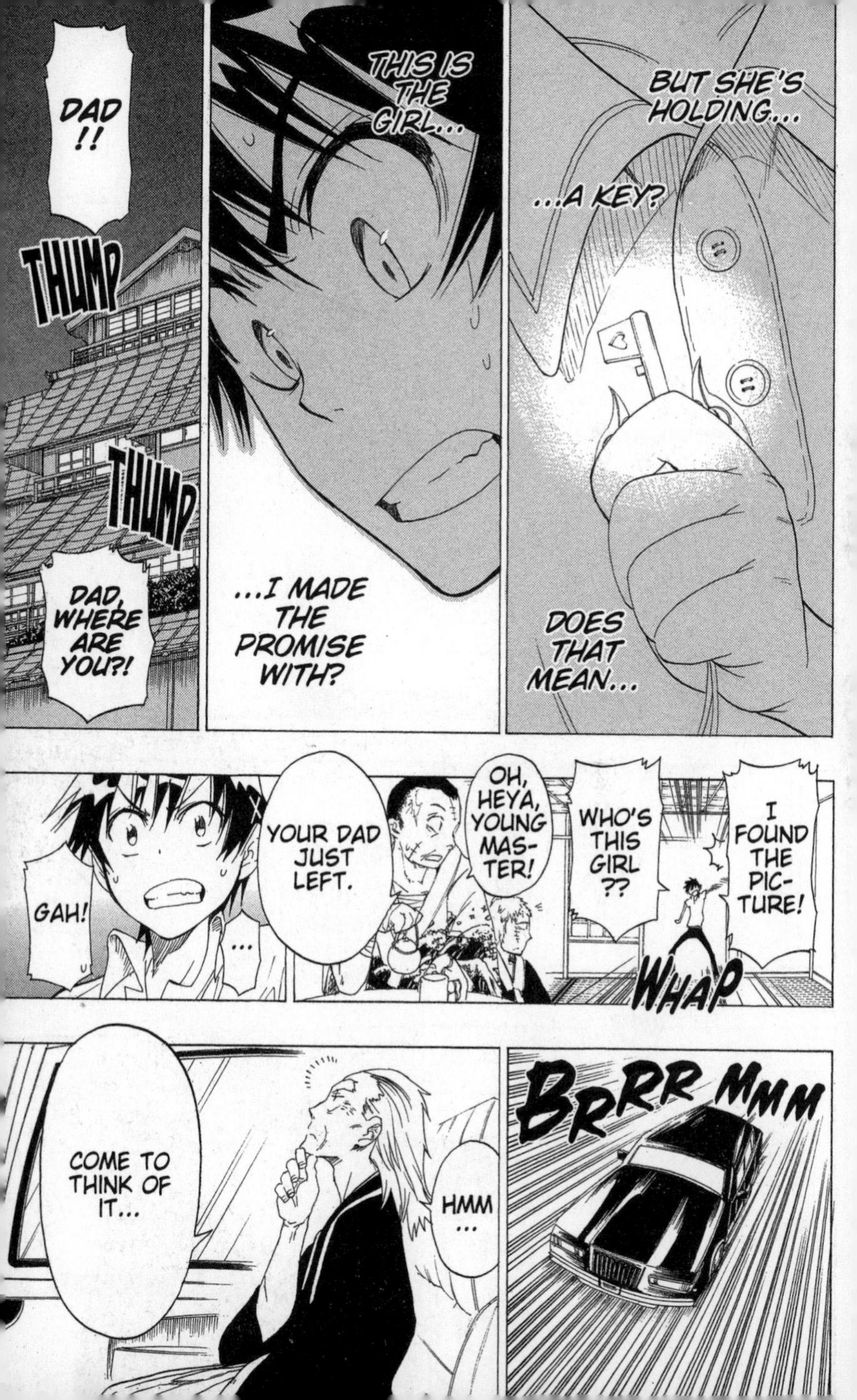
BUT SHE'S HOLDING...
...A KEY?
DOES THAT MEAN...
THIS IS THE GIRL...
...I MADE THE PROMISE WITH?
DAD !!
THUMP
THUMP
DAD, WHERE ARE YOU?!
I FOUND THE PIC-TURE!
WHO'S THIS GIRL ??
WHAP
OH, HEYA, YOUNG MAS-TER!
YOUR DAD JUST LEFT.
...
GAH!
BRRR MMM
HMM ...
COME TO THINK OF IT...

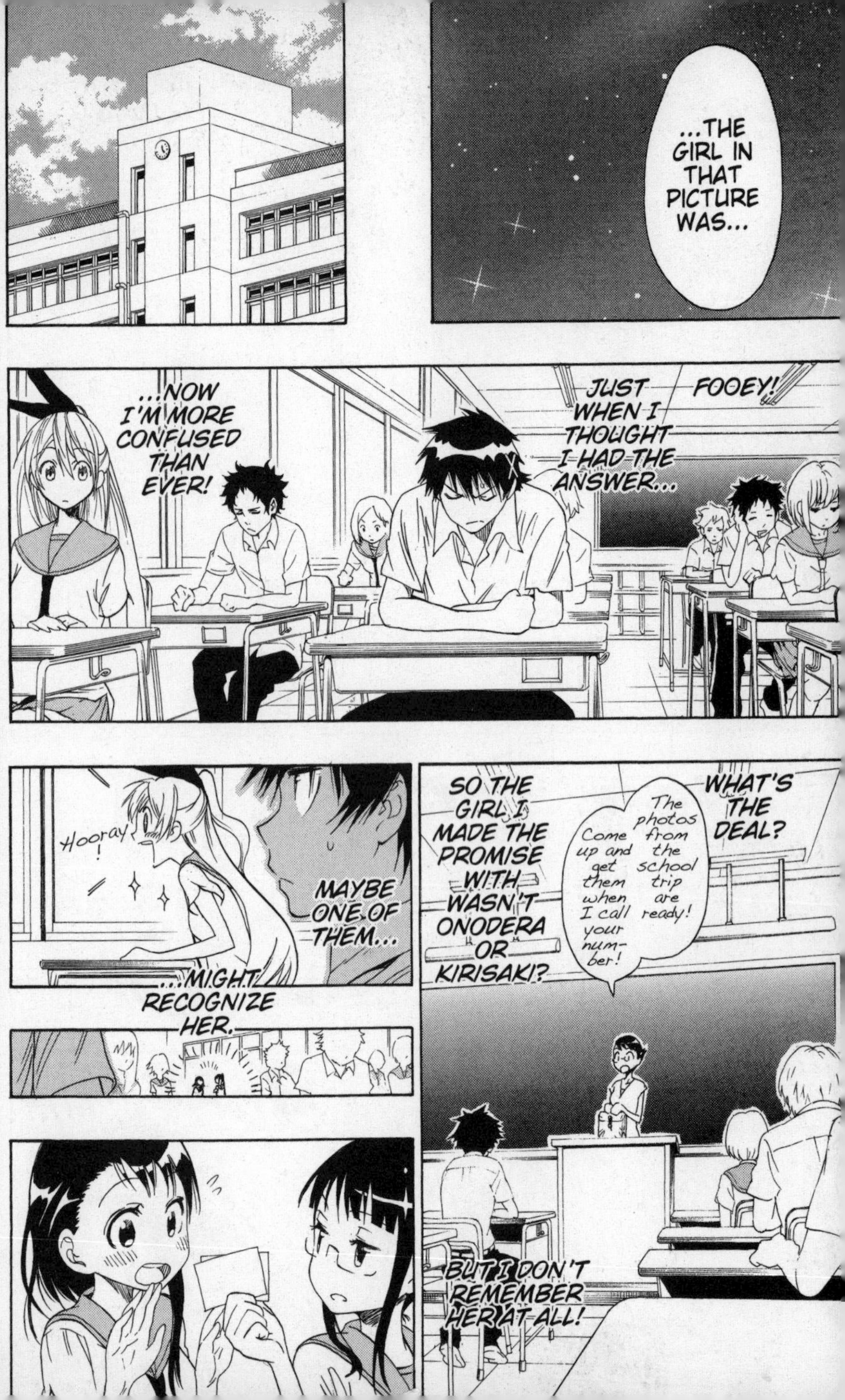
...THE GIRL IN THAT PICTURE WAS...
FOOEY!
JUST WHEN I THOUGHT I HAD THE ANSWER...
...NOW I'M MORE CONFUSED THAN EVER!
WHAT'S THE DEAL?
The photos from the school trip are ready! Come up and get them when I call your number!
SO THE GIRL I MADE THE PROMISE WITH WASN'T ONODERA OR KIRISAKI?
BUT I DON'T REMEMBER HER AT ALL!
Hooray!
MAYBE ONE OF THEM...
...MIGHT RECOGNIZE HER.

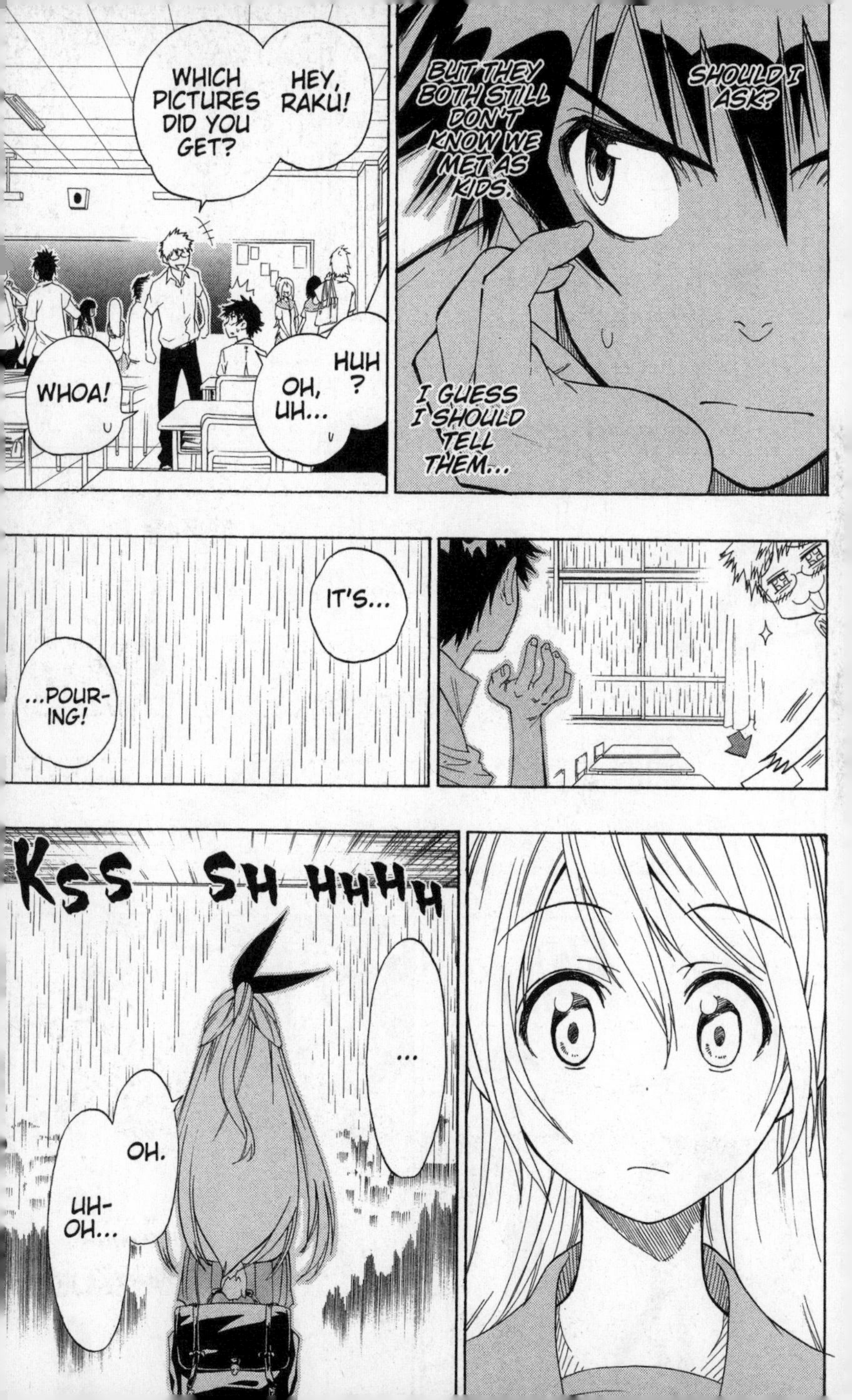
SHOULD I ASK?
BUT THEY BOTH STILL DON'T KNOW WE MET AS KIDS.
I GUESS I SHOULD TELL THEM...
HEY, RAKU!
WHICH PICTURES DID YOU GET?
HUH?
OH, UH...
WHOA!
IT'S...
...POURING!
KSS SH HHHH
...
OH.
UH-OH...

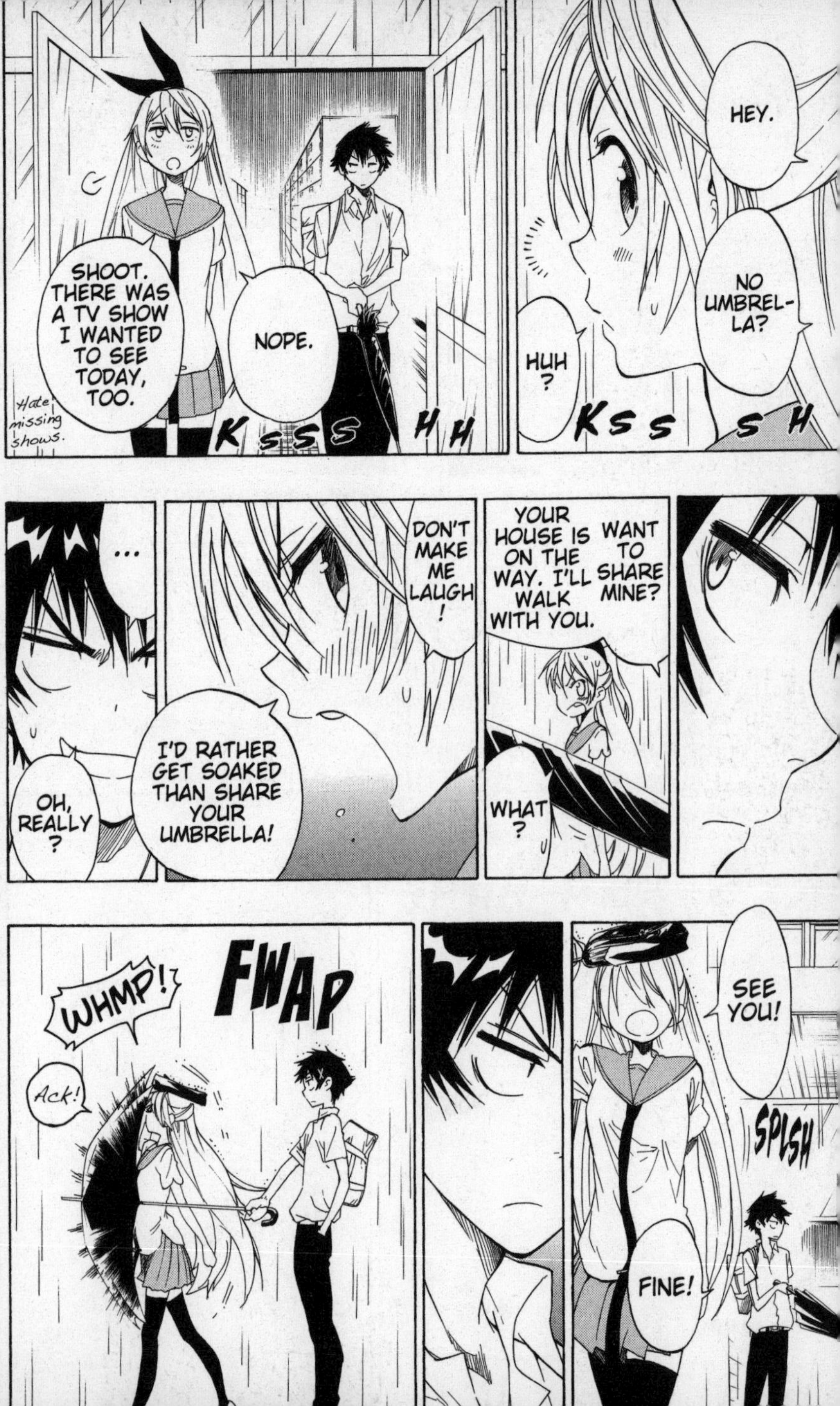
HEY.
NO UMBREL-LA?
HUH?
KSSSH
NOPE.
SHOOT. THERE WAS A TV SHOW I WANTED TO SEE TODAY, TOO.
Hate missing shows.
KSSSHH
WANT TO SHARE MINE?
YOUR HOUSE IS ON THE WAY. I'LL WALK WITH YOU.
WHAT?
DON'T MAKE ME LAUGH!
I'D RATHER GET SOAKED THAN SHARE YOUR UMBRELLA!
...
OH, REALLY?
SEE YOU!
SPLSH
FINE!
FWAP
WHMP!
Ack!

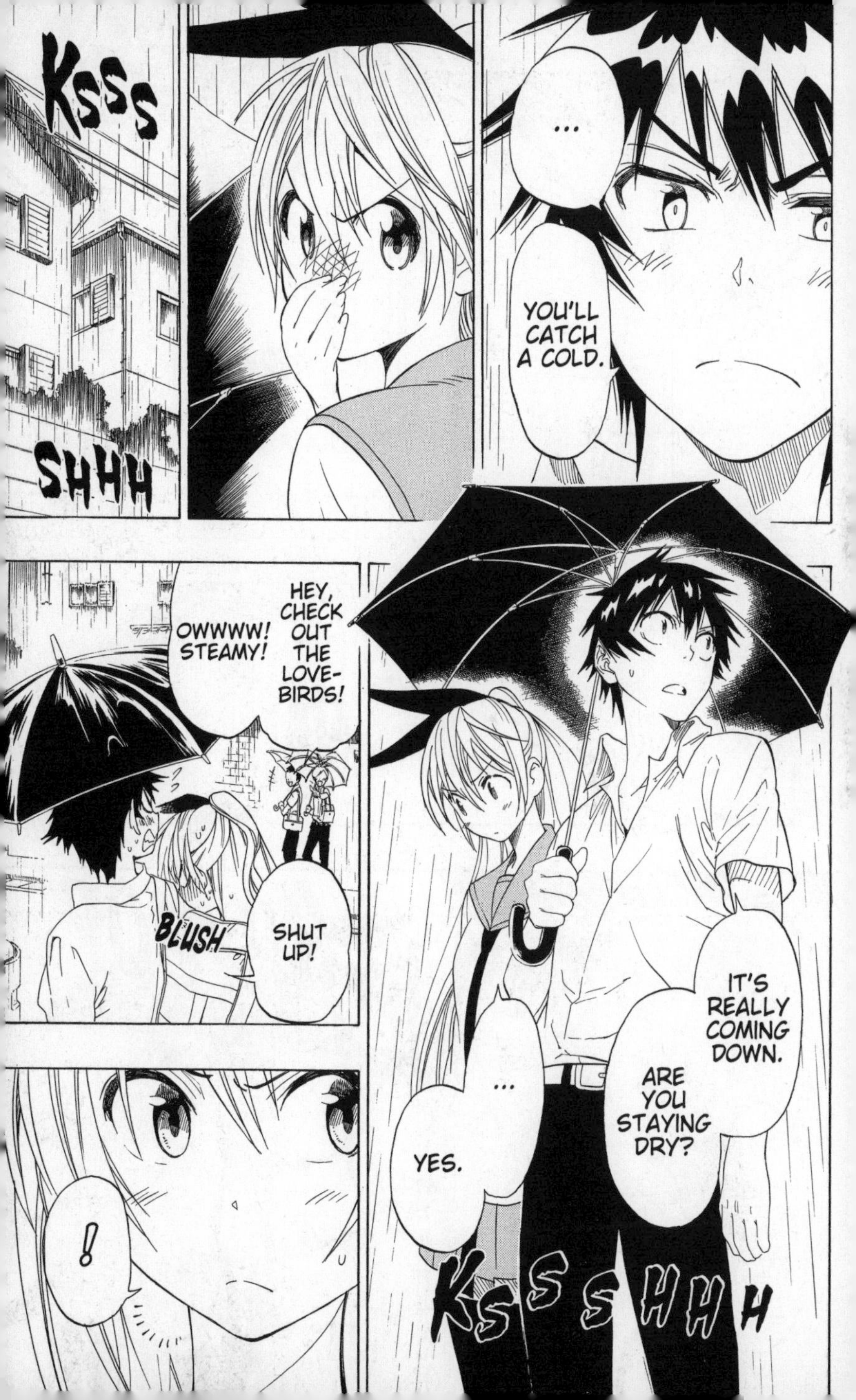
...
YOU'LL CATCH A COLD.
KSSS
SHHH
IT'S REALLY COMING DOWN.
ARE YOU STAYING DRY?
...
YES.
KSSSSHHHH
HEY, CHECK OUT THE LOVE-BIRDS!
OWWWW! STEAMY!
SHUT UP!
BLUSH
!

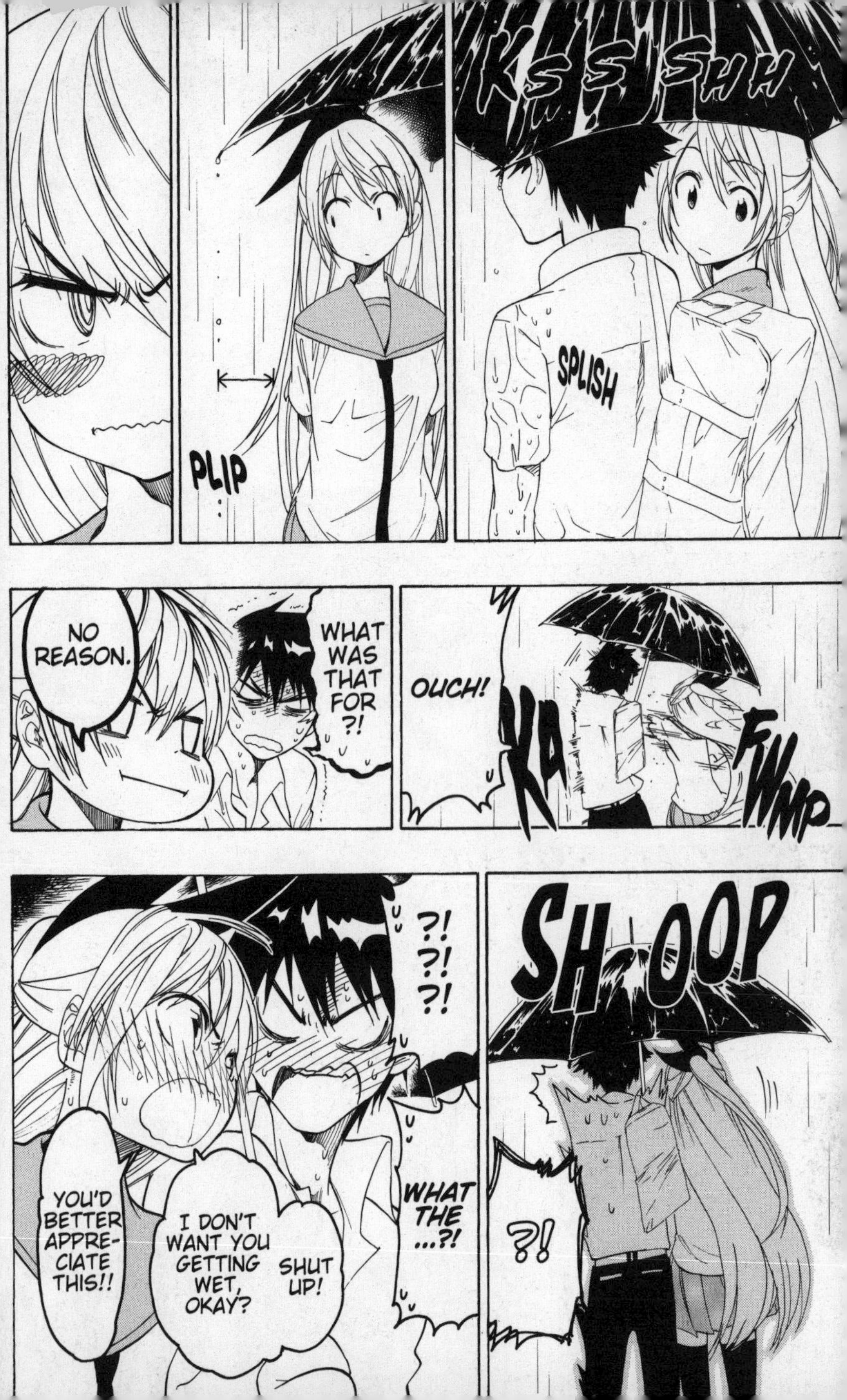
KSSSHH
SPLISH
PLIP
FWMP
KA
OUCH!
WHAT WAS THAT FOR?!
NO REASON.
SHOOP
?!
?! ?! ?!
WHAT THE ...?!
SHUT UP!
I DON'T WANT YOU GETTING WET, OKAY?
YOU'D BETTER APPRECIATE THIS!!

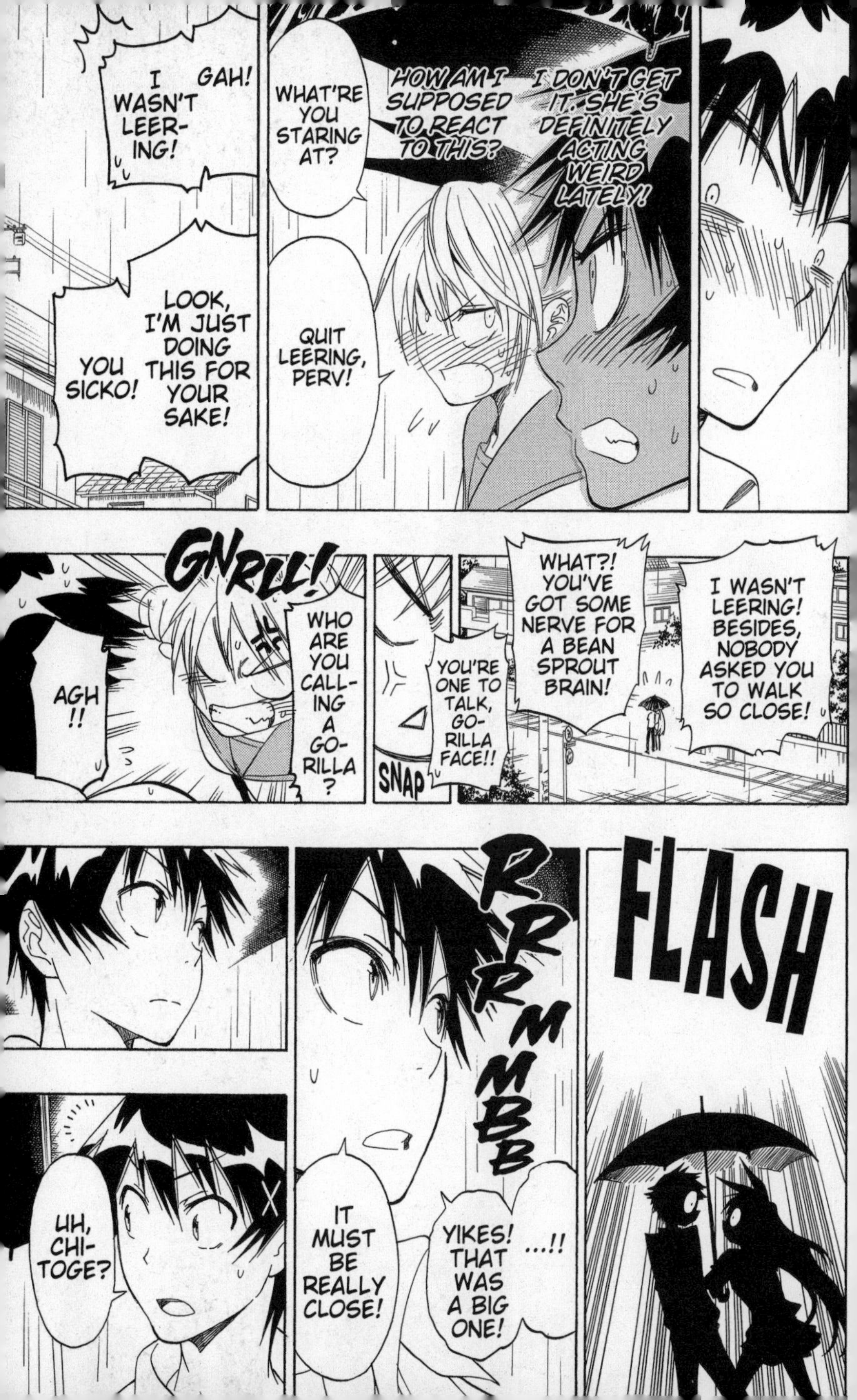
I DON'T GET IT. SHE'S DEFINITELY ACTING WEIRD LATELY!
HOW AM I SUPPOSED TO REACT TO THIS?
WHAT'RE YOU STARING AT?
QUIT LEERING, PERV!
GAH! I WASN'T LEERING!
LOOK, I'M JUST DOING THIS FOR YOUR SAKE!
YOU SICKO!
I WASN'T LEERING! BESIDES, NOBODY ASKED YOU TO WALK SO CLOSE!
WHAT?! YOU'VE GOT SOME NERVE FOR A BEAN SPROUT BRAIN!
YOU'RE ONE TO TALK, GORILLA FACE!!
SNAP
GNRLL!
WHO ARE YOU CALLING A GORILLA?
AGH!!
FLASH
RRRRMMMBB
...!!
YIKES! THAT WAS A BIG ONE!
IT MUST BE REALLY CLOSE!
UH, CHITOGE?

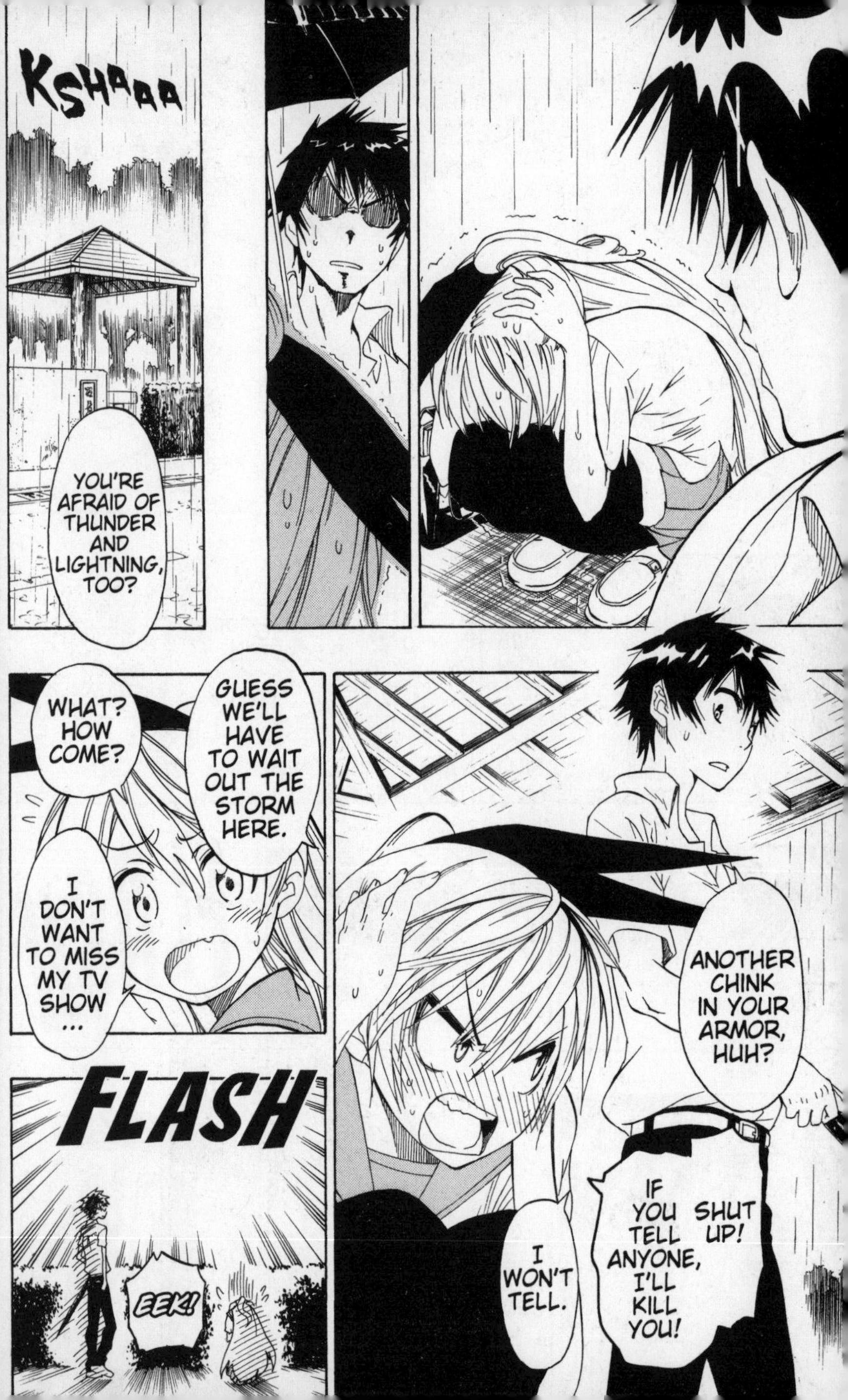
KSHAAA
YOU'RE AFRAID OF THUNDER AND LIGHTNING, TOO?
ANOTHER CHINK IN YOUR ARMOR, HUH?
SHUT UP! IF YOU TELL ANYONE, I'LL KILL YOU!
I WON'T TELL.
GUESS WE'LL HAVE TO WAIT OUT THE STORM HERE.
WHAT? HOW COME?
I DON'T WANT TO MISS MY TV SHOW ...
FLASH
EEK!

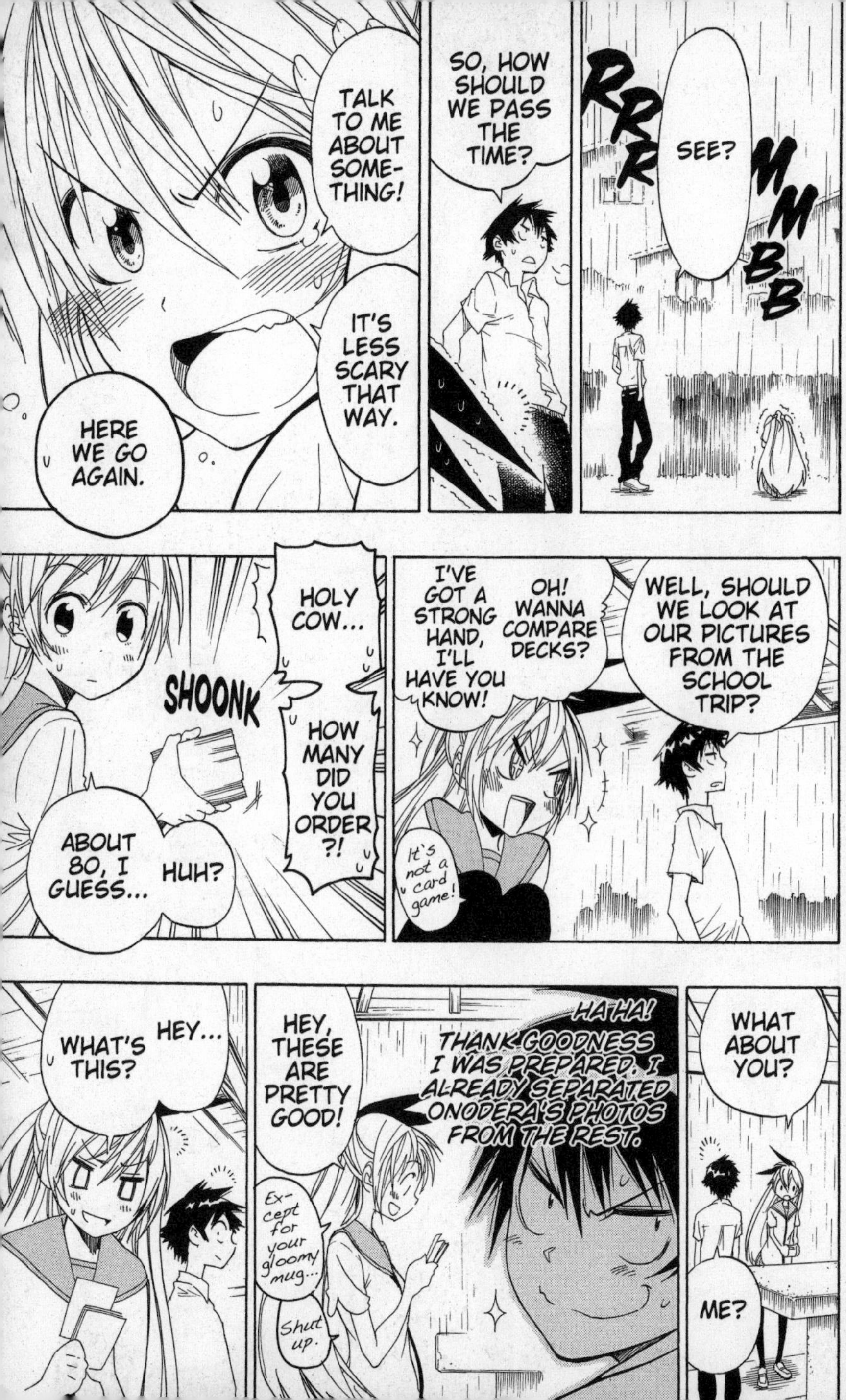
RRR
MMBB
SEE?
SO, HOW SHOULD WE PASS THE TIME?
TALK TO ME ABOUT SOME-THING!
IT'S LESS SCARY THAT WAY.
HERE WE GO AGAIN.
WELL, SHOULD WE LOOK AT OUR PICTURES FROM THE SCHOOL TRIP?
OH! WANNA COMPARE DECKS?
I'VE GOT A STRONG HAND, I'LL HAVE YOU KNOW!
It's not a card game!
HOLY COW...
SHOONK
HOW MANY DID YOU ORDER?!
HUH?
ABOUT 80, I GUESS...
WHAT ABOUT YOU?
ME?
HA HA! THANK GOODNESS I WAS PREPARED. I ALREADY SEPARATED ONODERA'S PHOTOS FROM THE REST.
HEY, THESE ARE PRETTY GOOD!
Ex-cept for your gloomy mug...
Shut up.
HEY...
WHAT'S THIS?

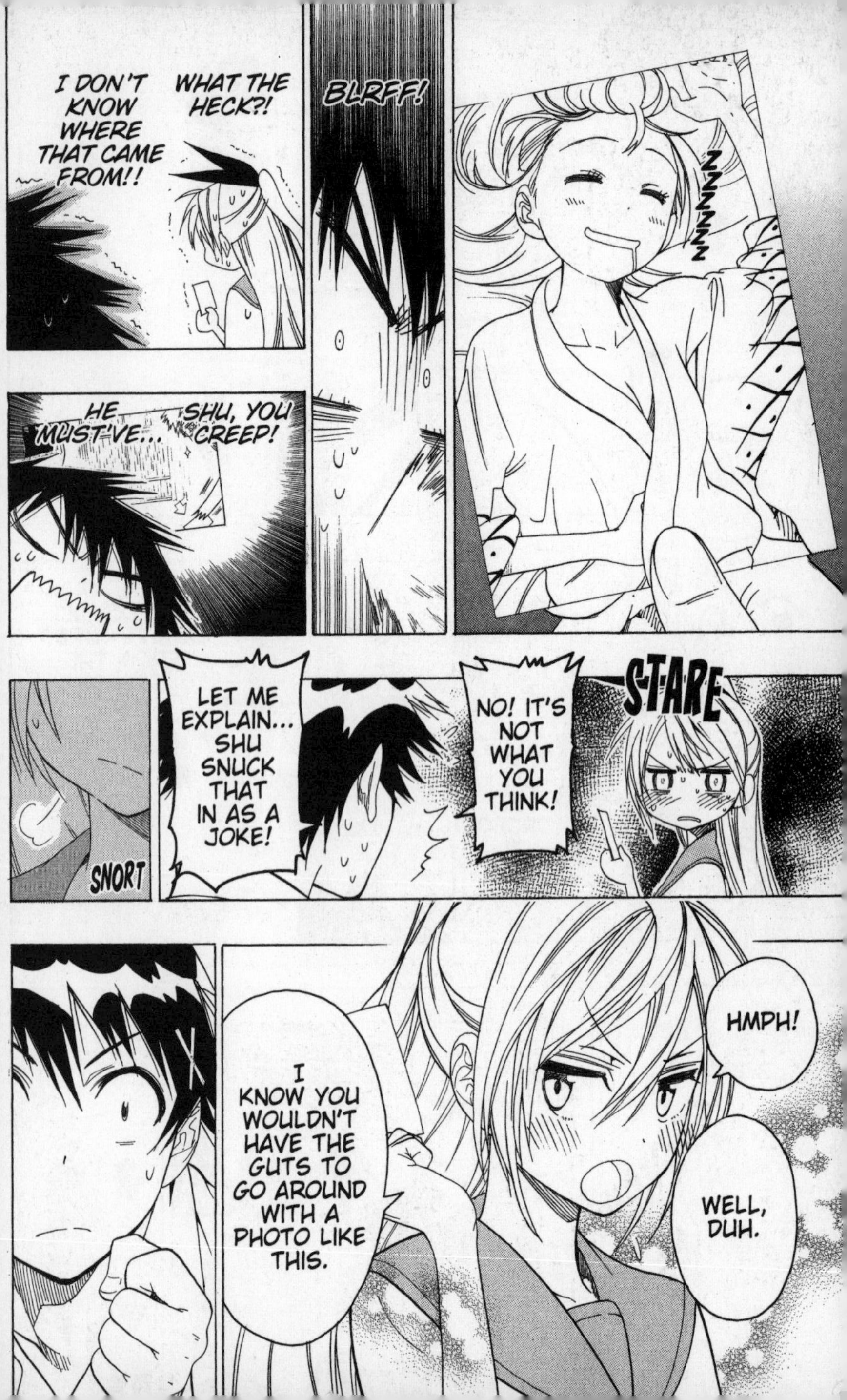
ZZZZZ
BLRFF!
WHAT THE HECK?!
I DON'T KNOW WHERE THAT CAME FROM!!
SHU, YOU CREEP!
HE MUST'VE...
STARE
NO! IT'S NOT WHAT YOU THINK!
LET ME EXPLAIN... SHU SNUCK THAT IN AS A JOKE!
SNORT
HMPH!
I KNOW YOU WOULDN'T HAVE THE GUTS TO GO AROUND WITH A PHOTO LIKE THIS.
WELL, DUH.

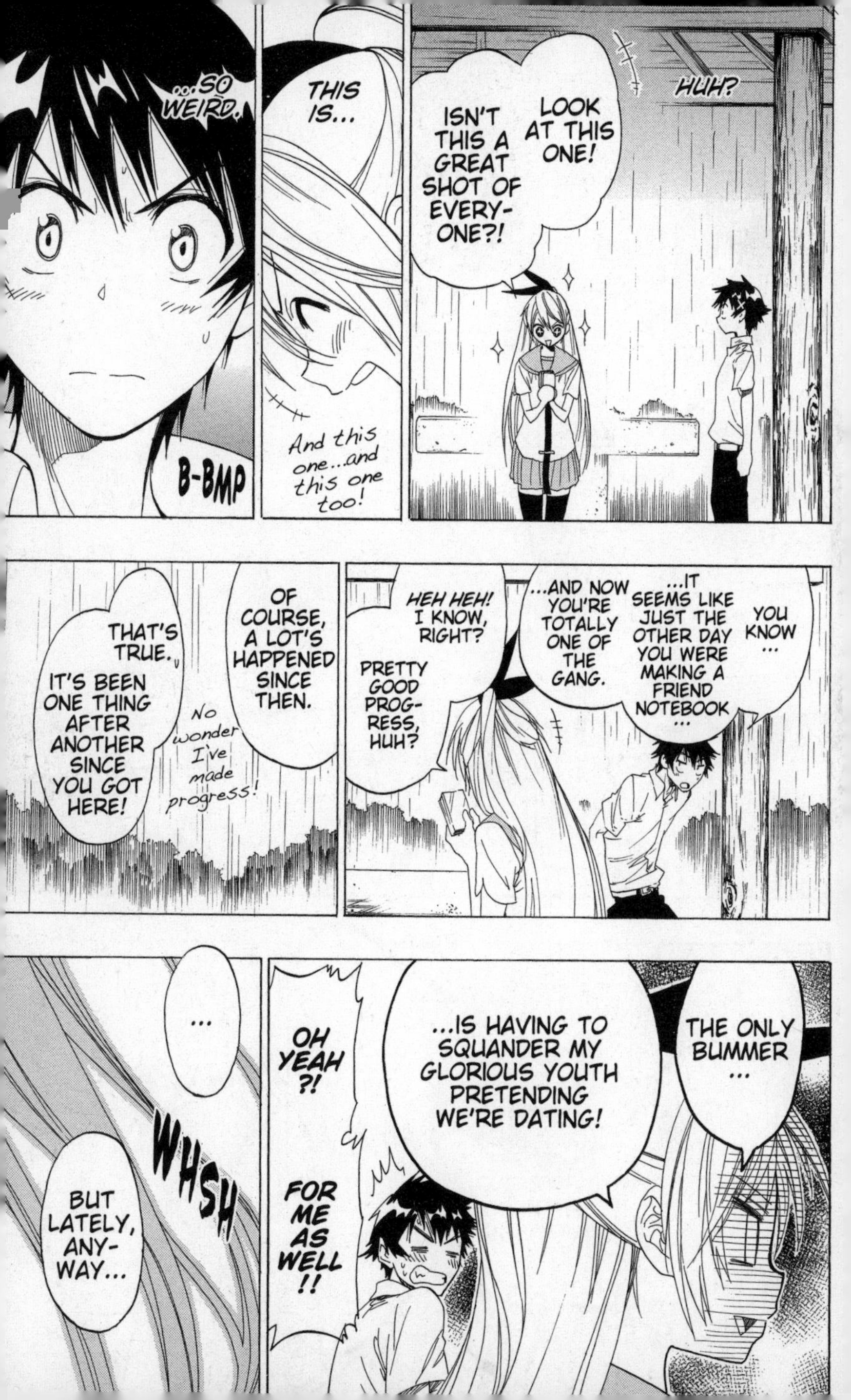
HUH?
LOOK AT THIS ONE!
ISN'T THIS A GREAT SHOT OF EVERY-ONE?!
THIS IS...
And this one...and this one too!
...SO WEIRD.
B-BMP
YOU KNOW ...
...IT SEEMS LIKE JUST THE OTHER DAY YOU WERE MAKING A FRIEND NOTEBOOK ...
...AND NOW YOU'RE TOTALLY ONE OF THE GANG.
HEH HEH! I KNOW, RIGHT?
PRETTY GOOD PROG-RESS, HUH?
OF COURSE, A LOT'S HAPPENED SINCE THEN.
THAT'S TRUE.
IT'S BEEN ONE THING AFTER ANOTHER SINCE YOU GOT HERE!
No wonder I've made progress!
THE ONLY BUMMER ...
...IS HAVING TO SQUANDER MY GLORIOUS YOUTH PRETENDING WE'RE DATING!
OH YEAH?!
FOR ME AS WELL!!
...
WHSH
BUT LATELY, ANY-WAY...

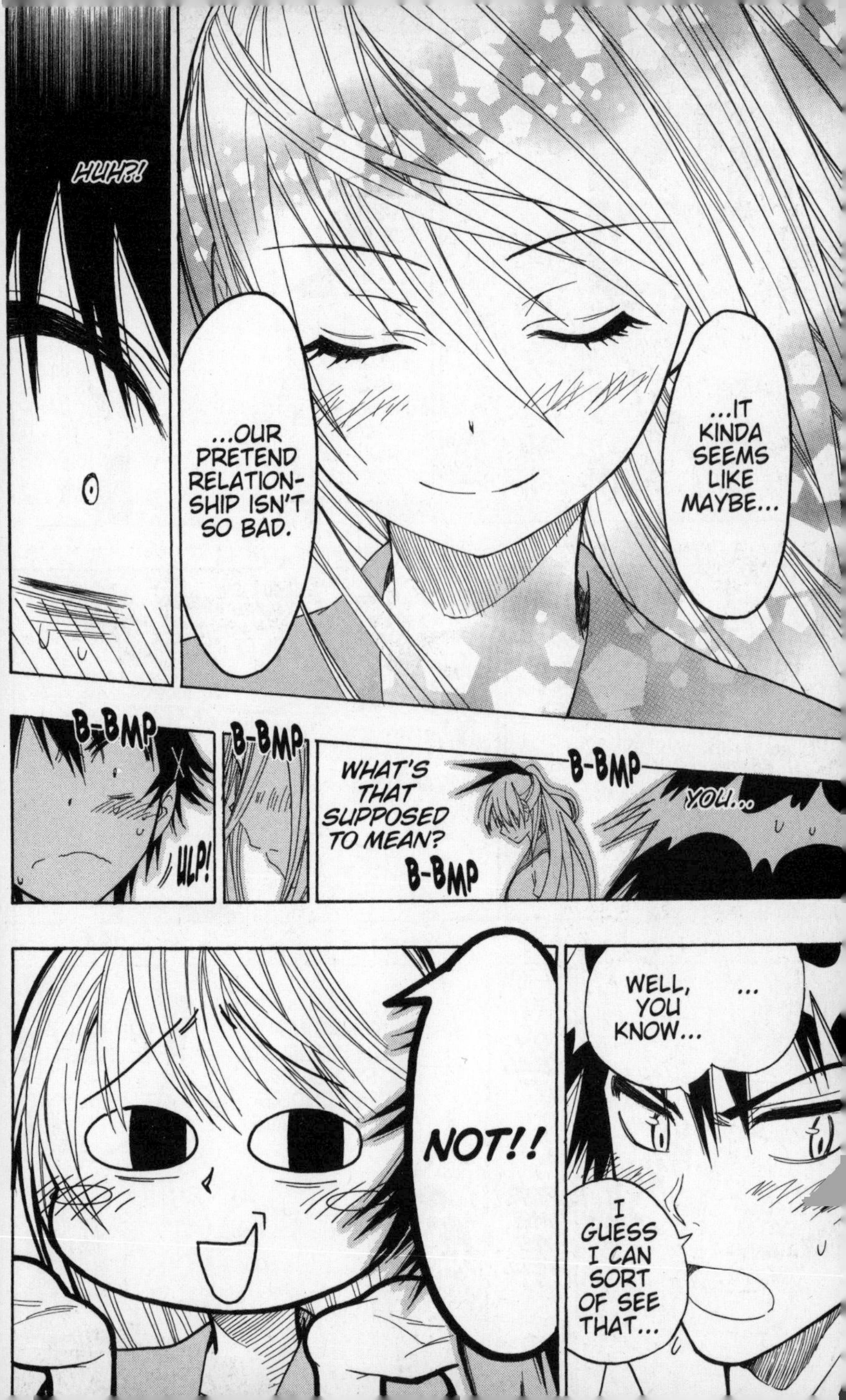
...IT KINDA SEEMS LIKE MAYBE...
...OUR PRETEND RELATION-SHIP ISN'T SO BAD.
HUH?!
YOU...
B-BMP
WHAT'S THAT SUPPOSED TO MEAN?
B-BMP
B-BMP
B-BMP
ULP!
WELL, YOU KNOW...
...
I GUESS I CAN SORT OF SEE THAT...
NOT!!

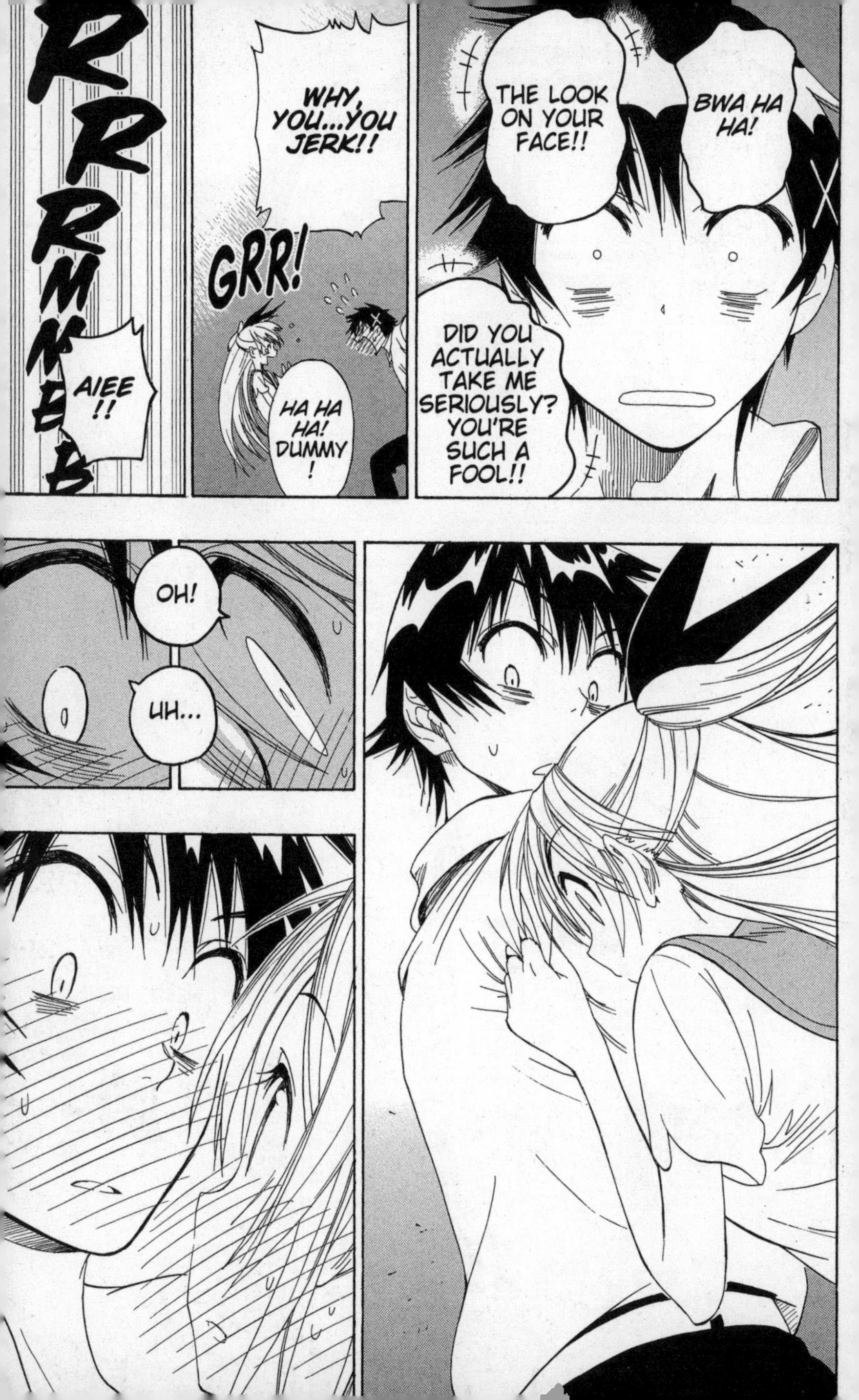
BWA HA HA!
THE LOOK ON YOUR FACE!!
DID YOU ACTUALLY TAKE ME SERIOUSLY? YOU'RE SUCH A FOOL!!
WHY, YOU...YOU JERK!!
GRR!
HA HA HA! DUMMY!
RRRMMBB
AIEE!!
OH!
UH...

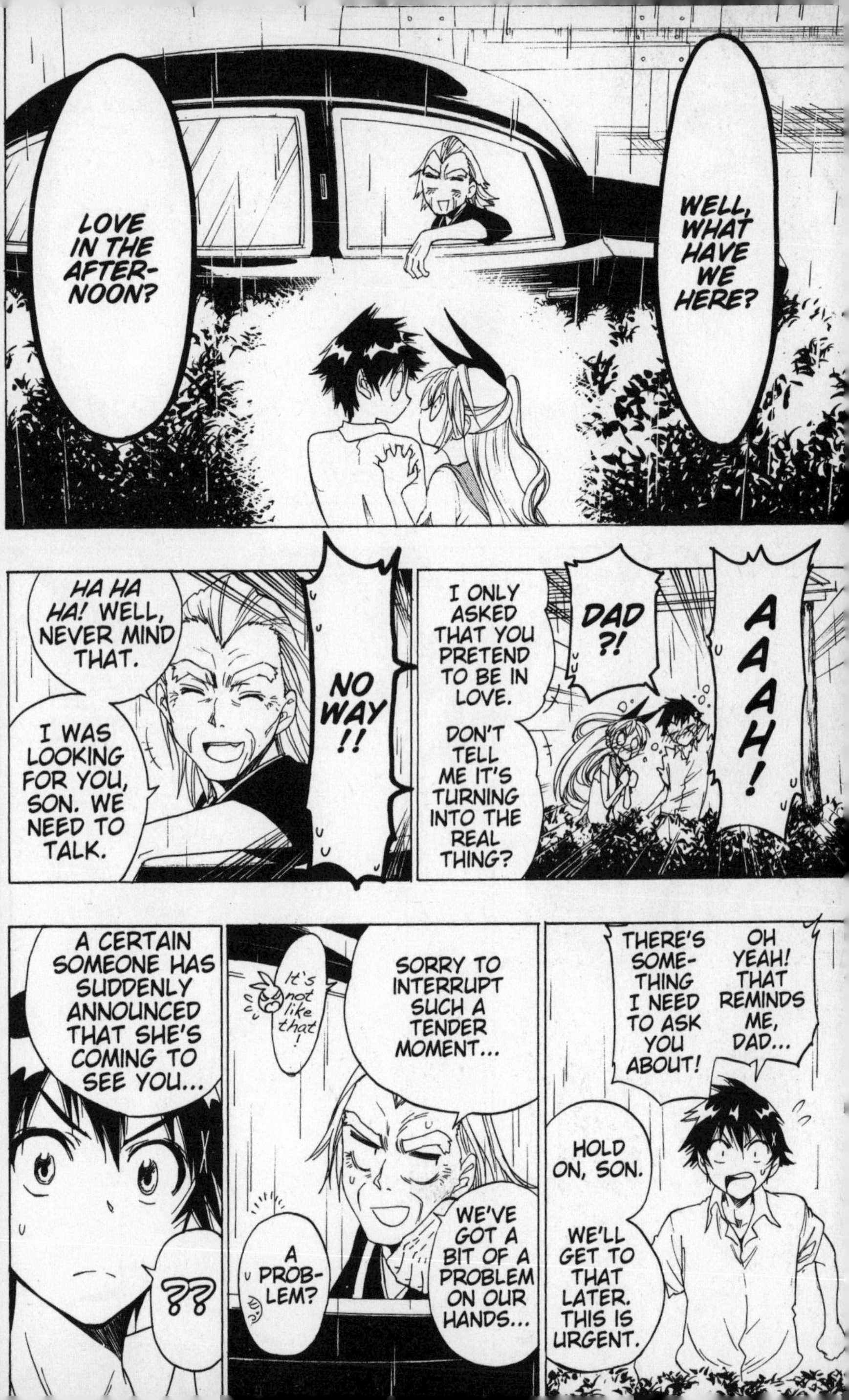
WELL, WHAT HAVE WE HERE?
LOVE IN THE AFTERNOON?
AAAH!
DAD?!
I ONLY ASKED THAT YOU PRETEND TO BE IN LOVE.
DON'T TELL ME IT'S TURNING INTO THE REAL THING?
NO WAY!!
HA HA HA! WELL, NEVER MIND THAT.
I WAS LOOKING FOR YOU, SON. WE NEED TO TALK.
OH YEAH! THAT REMINDS ME, DAD...
THERE'S SOMETHING I NEED TO ASK YOU ABOUT!
HOLD ON, SON.
WE'LL GET TO THAT LATER. THIS IS URGENT.
SORRY TO INTERRUPT SUCH A TENDER MOMENT...
It's not like that!
WE'VE GOT A BIT OF A PROBLEM ON OUR HANDS...
A PROBLEM?
A CERTAIN SOMEONE HAS SUDDENLY ANNOUNCED THAT SHE'S COMING TO SEE YOU...
??

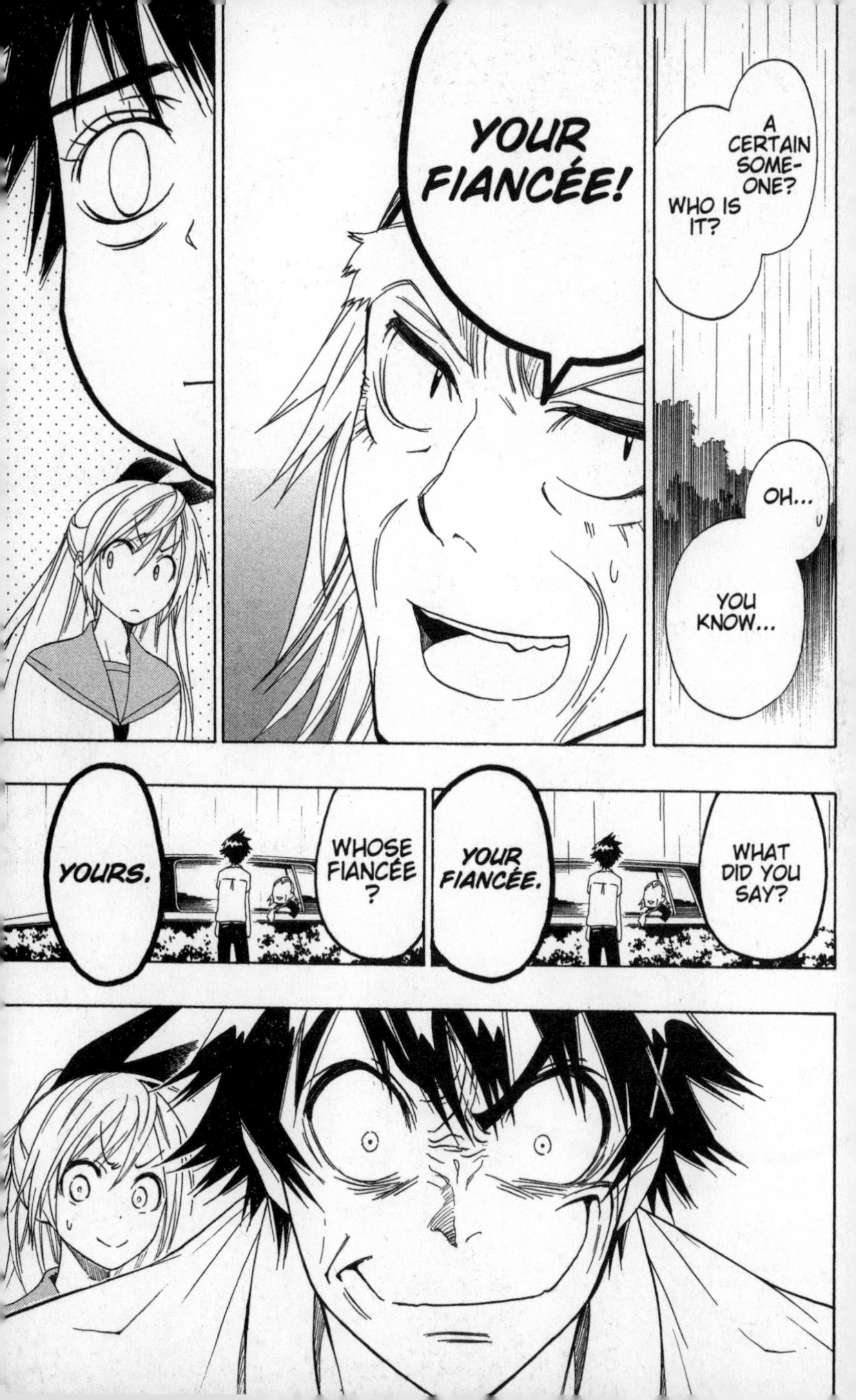
A CERTAIN SOME-ONE? WHO IS IT?
OH... YOU KNOW...
YOUR FIANCÉE!
WHAT DID YOU SAY?
YOUR FIANCÉE.
WHOSE FIANCÉE?
YOURS.

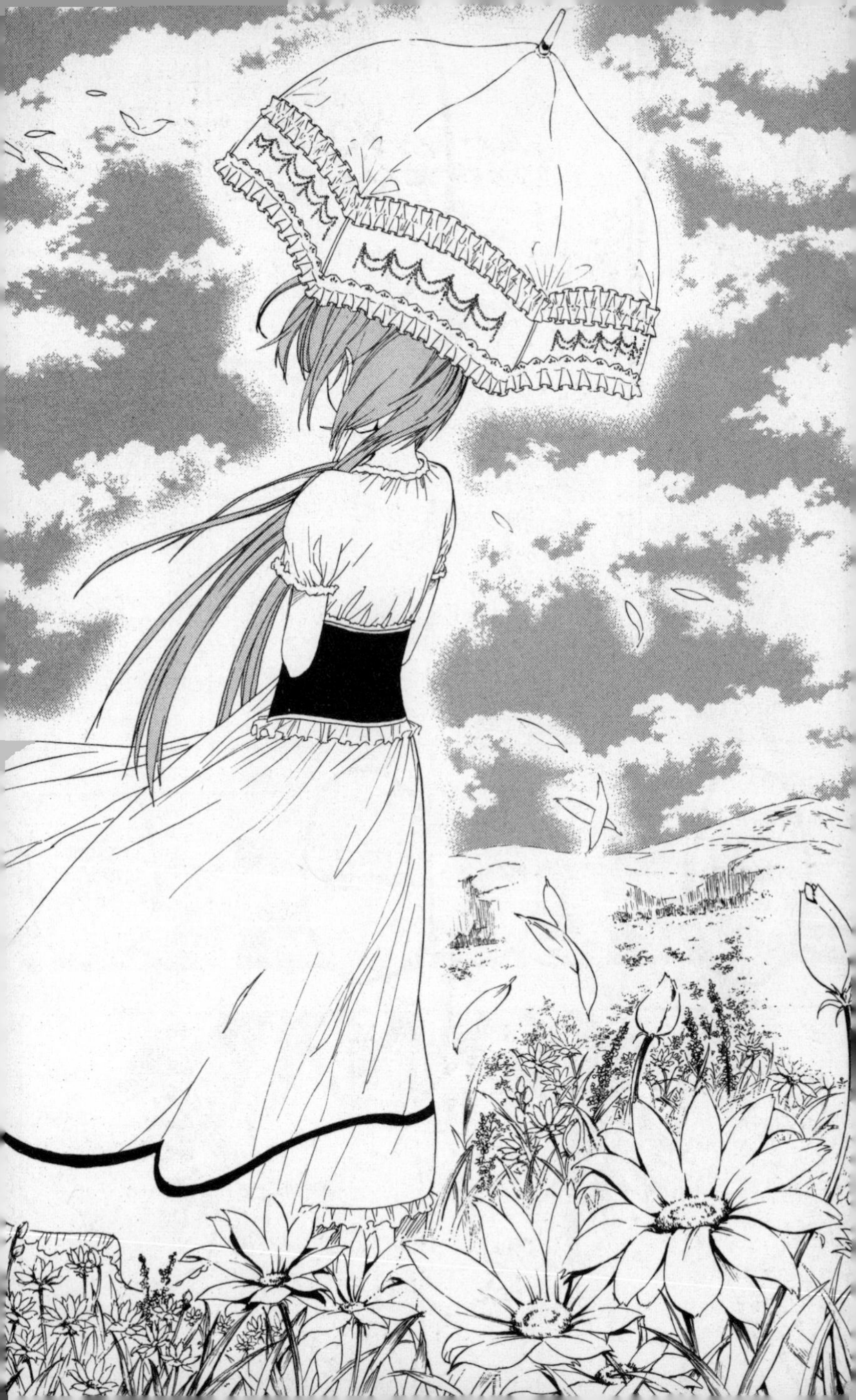

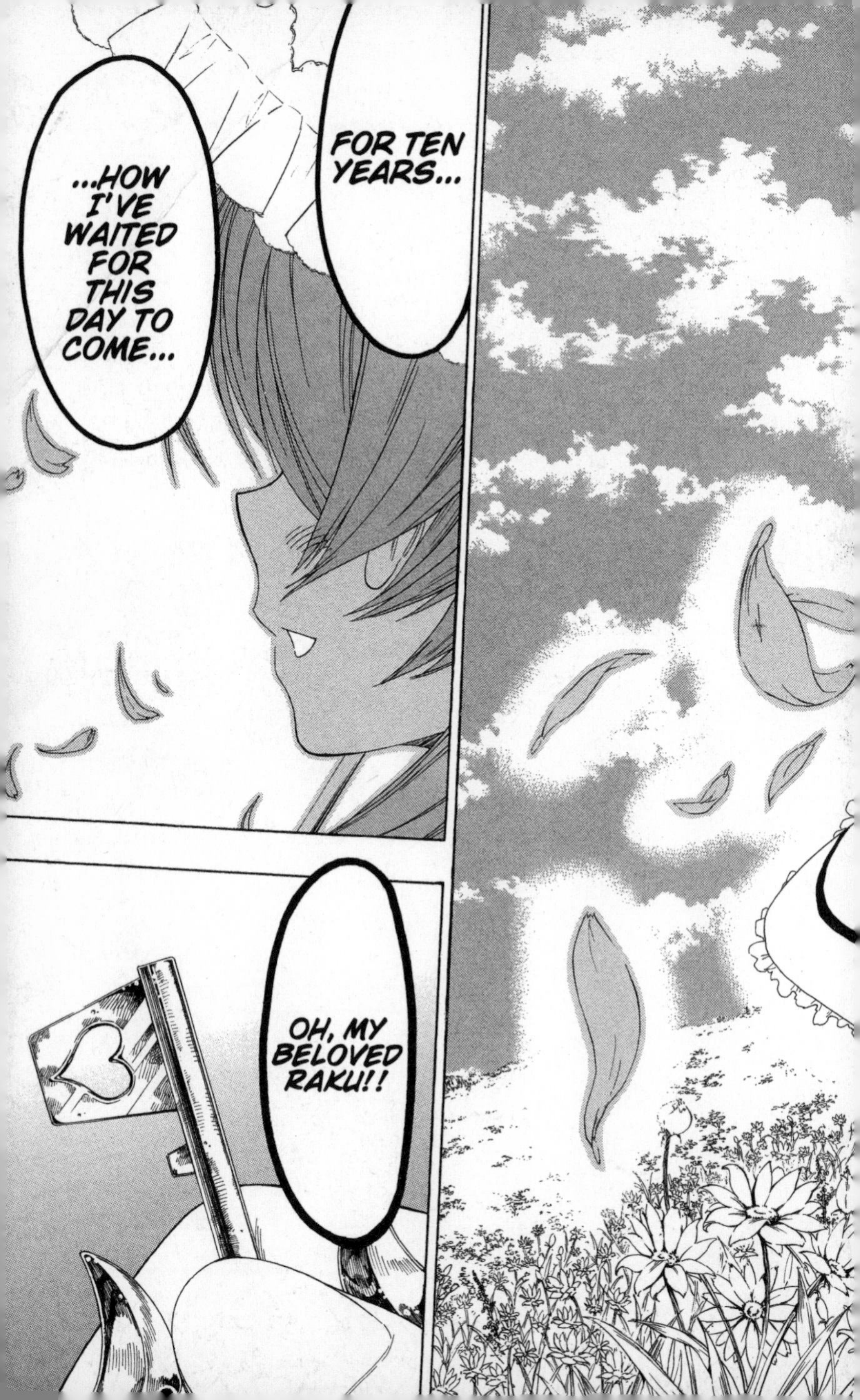
FOR TEN YEARS...
...HOW I'VE WAITED FOR THIS DAY TO COME...
OH, MY BELOVED RAKU!!

Prized Possession

The photos from the school trip are ready!
Come up and get them when I call your number!
What're you grinning about?
I wasn't!
SHOOP
Ono-dera's secret pur-chase!

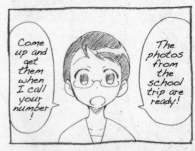

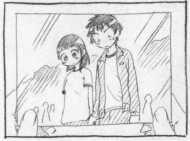

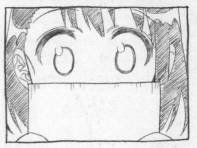

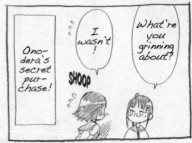

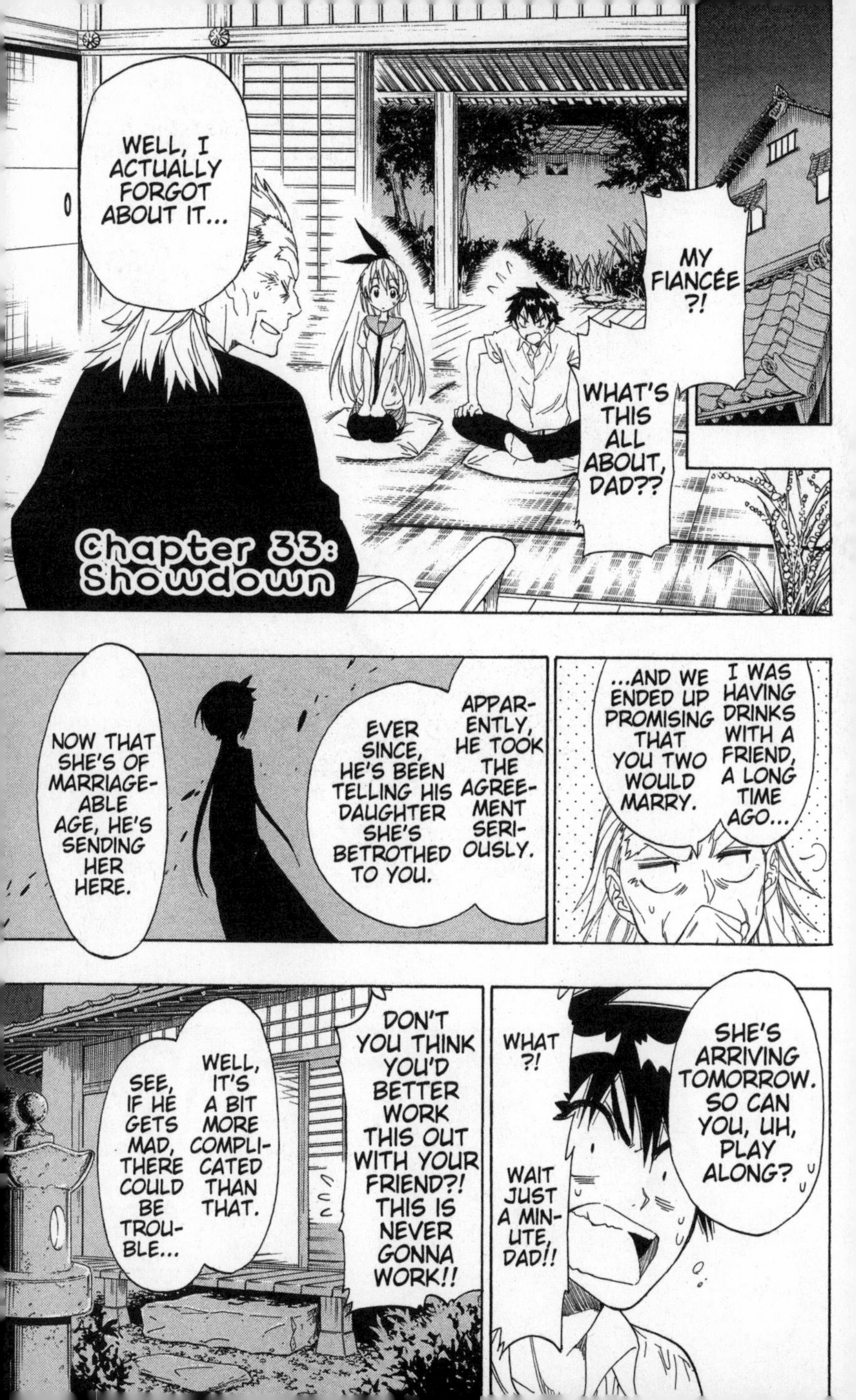
MY FIANCÉE?!
WHAT'S THIS ALL ABOUT, DAD??
WELL, I ACTUALLY FORGOT ABOUT IT...
Chapter 33: Showdown
I WAS HAVING DRINKS WITH A FRIEND, A LONG TIME AGO...
...AND WE ENDED UP PROMISING THAT YOU TWO WOULD MARRY.
APPARENTLY, HE TOOK THE AGREEMENT SERIOUSLY.
EVER SINCE, HE'S BEEN TELLING HIS DAUGHTER SHE'S BETROTHED TO YOU.
NOW THAT SHE'S OF MARRIAGEABLE AGE, HE'S SENDING HER HERE.
SHE'S ARRIVING TOMORROW. SO CAN YOU, UH, PLAY ALONG?
WHAT?!
WAIT JUST A MINUTE, DAD!!
DON'T YOU THINK YOU'D BETTER WORK THIS OUT WITH YOUR FRIEND?! THIS IS NEVER GONNA WORK!!
WELL, IT'S A BIT MORE COMPLICATED THAN THAT.
SEE, IF HE GETS MAD, THERE COULD BE TROUBLE...

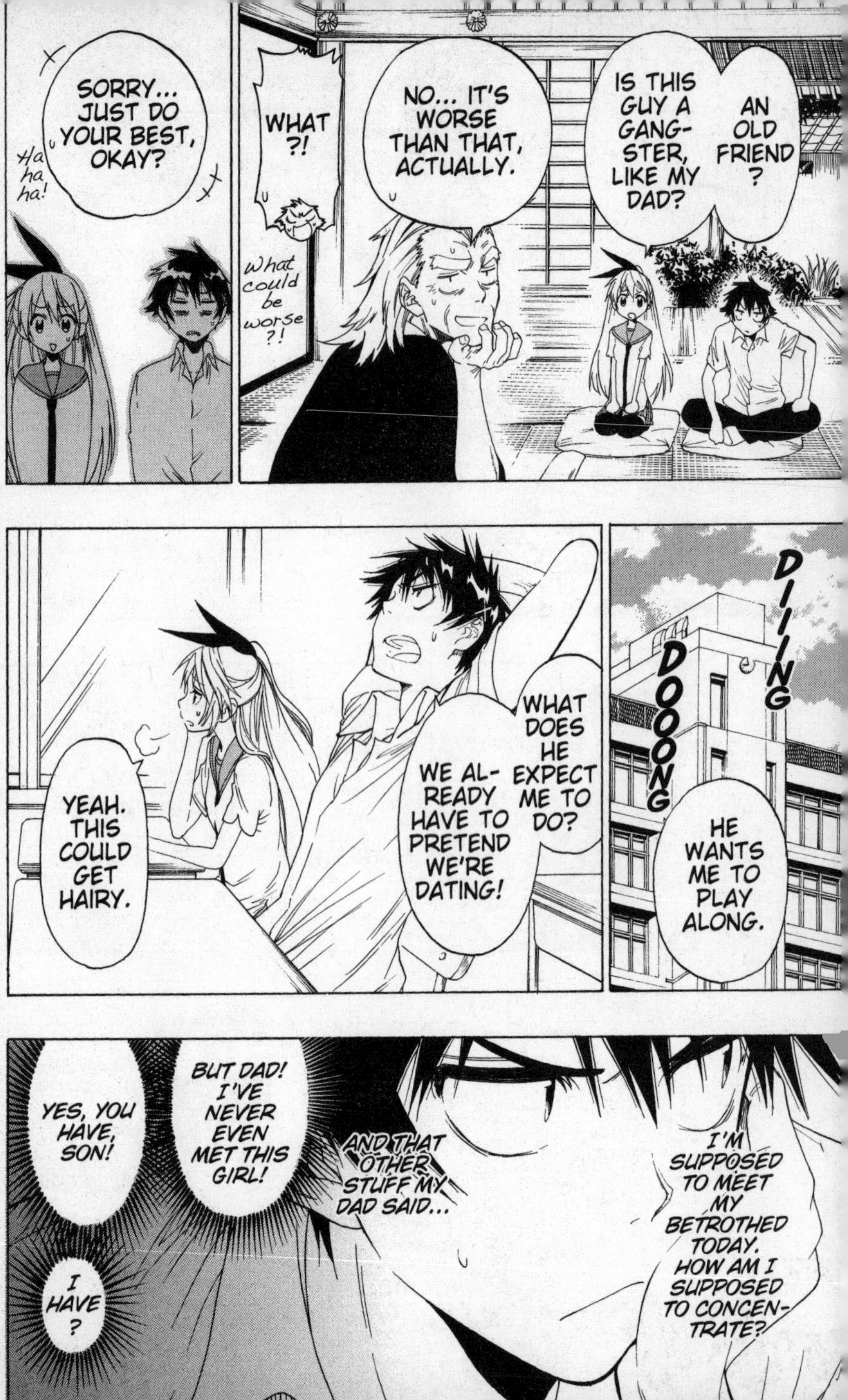
AN OLD FRIEND?
IS THIS GUY A GANGSTER, LIKE MY DAD?
NO... IT'S WORSE THAN THAT, ACTUALLY.
WHAT?!
What could be worse?!
SORRY... JUST DO YOUR BEST, OKAY?
Ha ha ha!
DIIING
DOOOONG
HE WANTS ME TO PLAY ALONG.
WHAT DOES HE EXPECT ME TO DO?
WE ALREADY HAVE TO PRETEND WE'RE DATING!
YEAH. THIS COULD GET HAIRY.
I'M SUPPOSED TO MEET MY BETROTHED TODAY. HOW AM I SUPPOSED TO CONCENTRATE?
AND THAT OTHER STUFF MY DAD SAID...
BUT DAD! I'VE NEVER EVEN MET THIS GIRL!
YES, YOU HAVE, SON!
I HAVE?

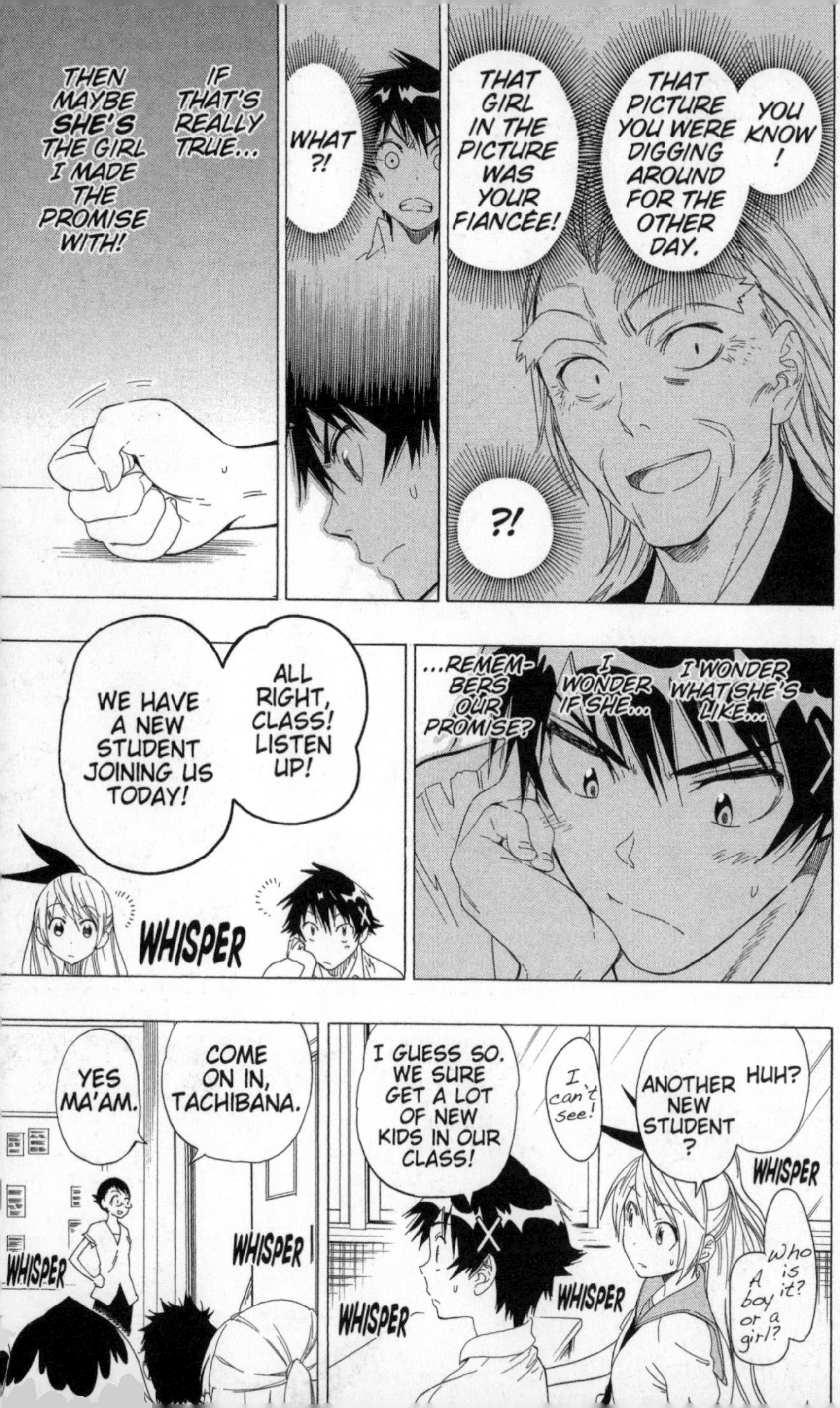
YOU KNOW!
THAT PICTURE YOU WERE DIGGING AROUND FOR THE OTHER DAY.
THAT GIRL IN THE PICTURE WAS YOUR FIANCÉE!
?!
WHAT ?!
IF THAT'S REALLY TRUE...
THEN MAYBE SHE'S THE GIRL I MADE THE PROMISE WITH!
I WONDER WHAT SHE'S LIKE...
I WONDER IF SHE...
...REMEMBERS OUR PROMISE?
ALL RIGHT, CLASS! LISTEN UP!
WE HAVE A NEW STUDENT JOINING US TODAY!
WHISPER
HUH?
ANOTHER NEW STUDENT?
I can't see!
I GUESS SO. WE SURE GET A LOT OF NEW KIDS IN OUR CLASS!
WHISPER
Who is it? A boy or a girl?
WHISPER
WHISPER
COME ON IN, TACHIBANA.
YES MA'AM.
WHISPER
WHISPER

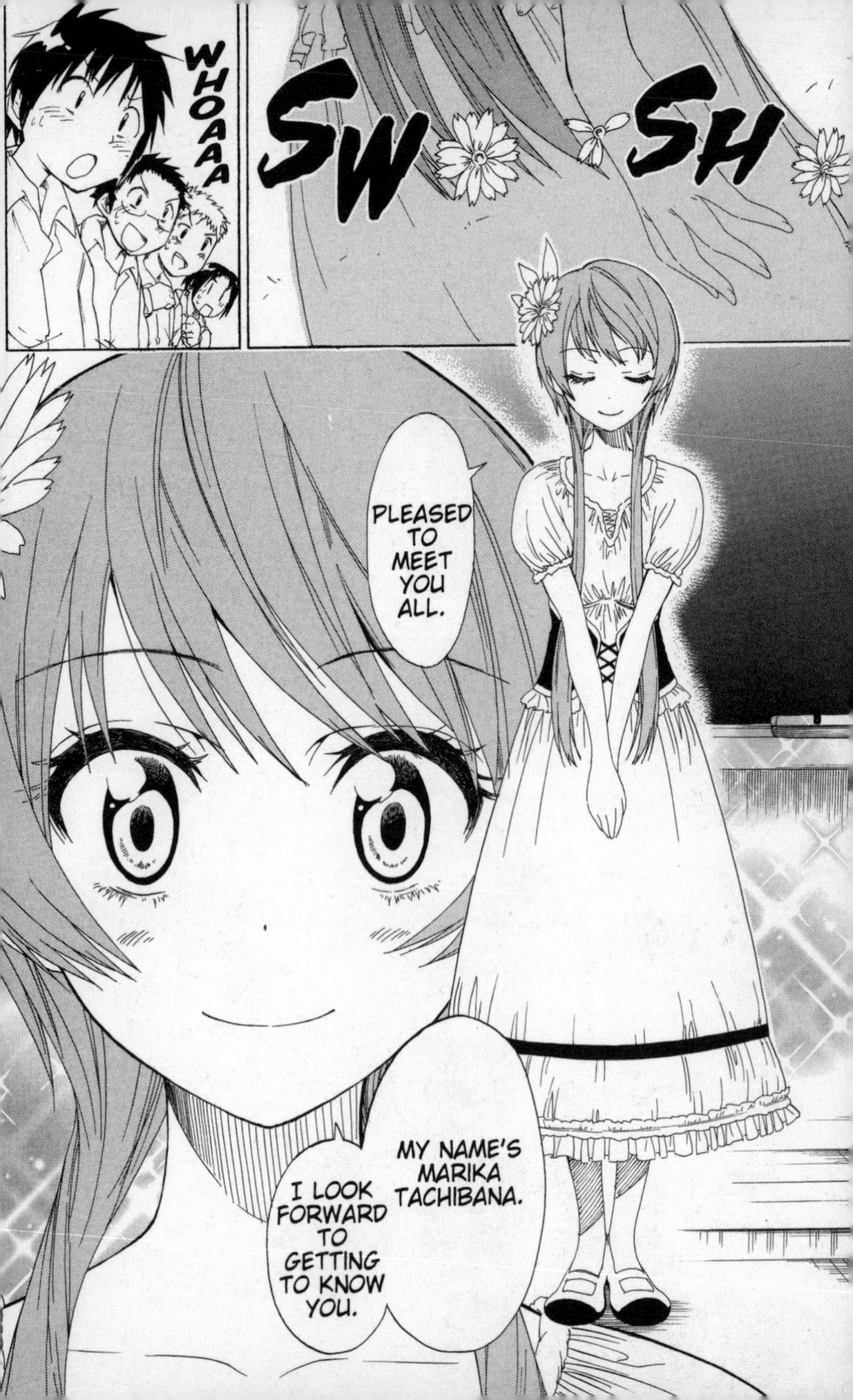
SW SH
WHOAAA
PLEASED TO MEET YOU ALL.
MY NAME'S MARIKA TACHIBANA.
I LOOK FORWARD TO GETTING TO KNOW YOU.

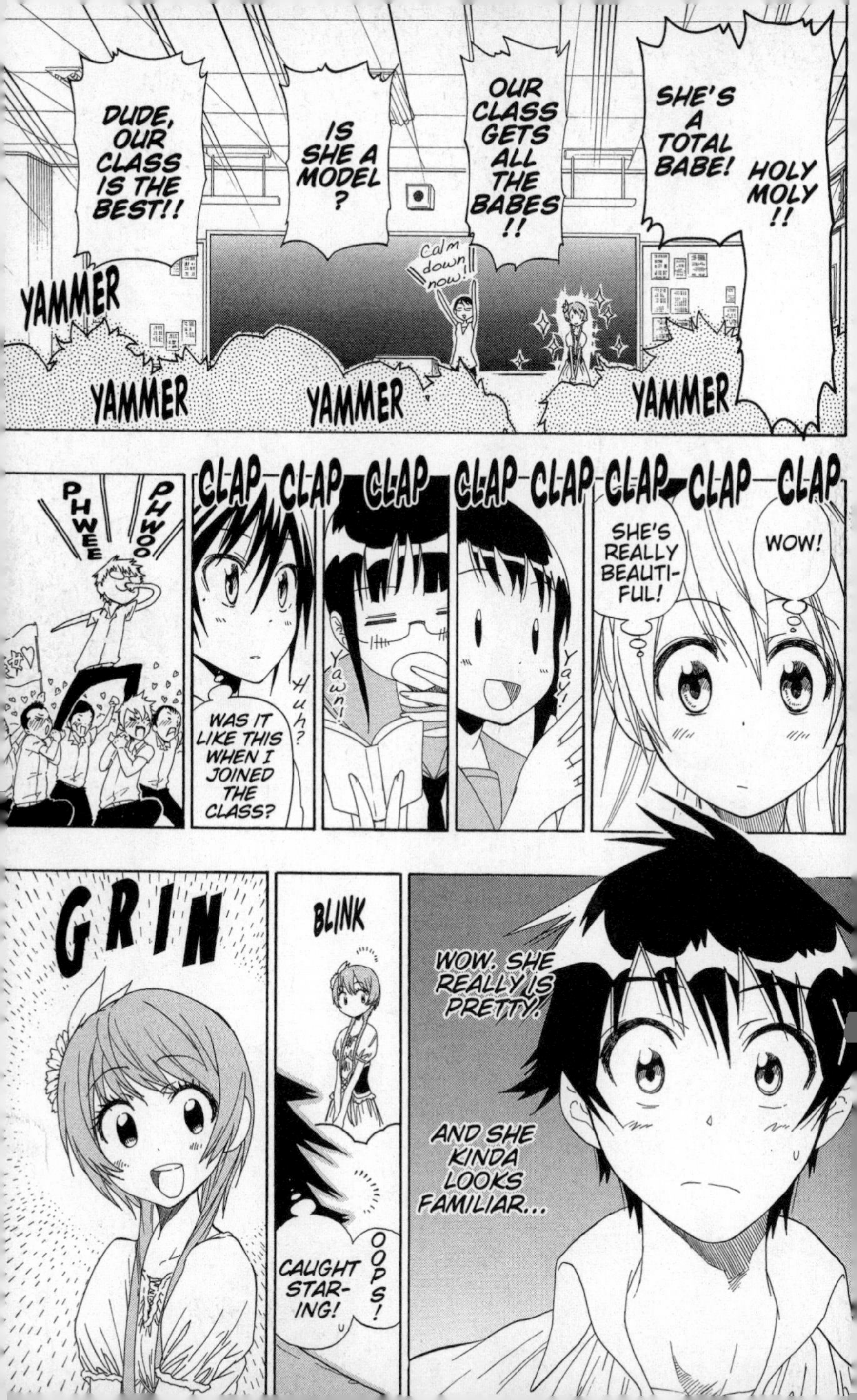
HOLY MOLY!!
SHE'S A TOTAL BABE!
OUR CLASS GETS ALL THE BABES!!
IS SHE A MODEL?
DUDE, OUR CLASS IS THE BEST!!
Calm down now!
YAMMER
YAMMER
YAMMER
YAMMER
CLAP CLAP CLAP CLAP CLAP CLAP CLAP CLAP
WOW!
SHE'S REALLY BEAUTIFUL!
Yay!
Yawn!
Huh?
WAS IT LIKE THIS WHEN I JOINED THE CLASS?
PHWOO
PHWEE
WOW. SHE REALLY IS PRETTY.
AND SHE KINDA LOOKS FAMILIAR...
BLINK
OOPS!
CAUGHT STARING!
GRIN

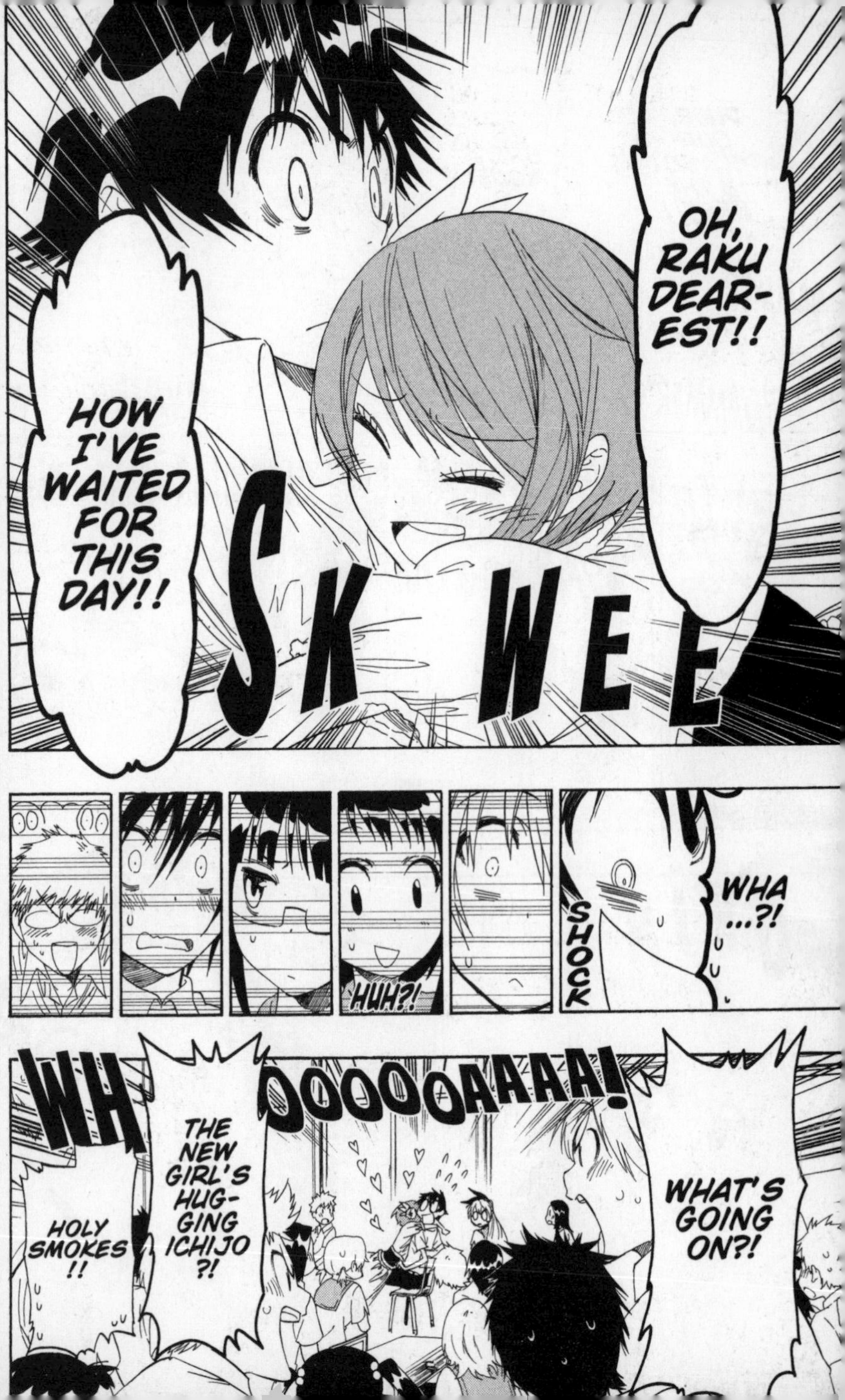
OH, RAKU DEAREST!!
HOW I'VE WAITED FOR THIS DAY!!
SKWEE
WHA ...?!
SHOCK
HUH?!
WHOOOOOAAAA!
WHAT'S GOING ON?!
THE NEW GIRL'S HUGGING ICHIJO?!
HOLY SMOKES!!

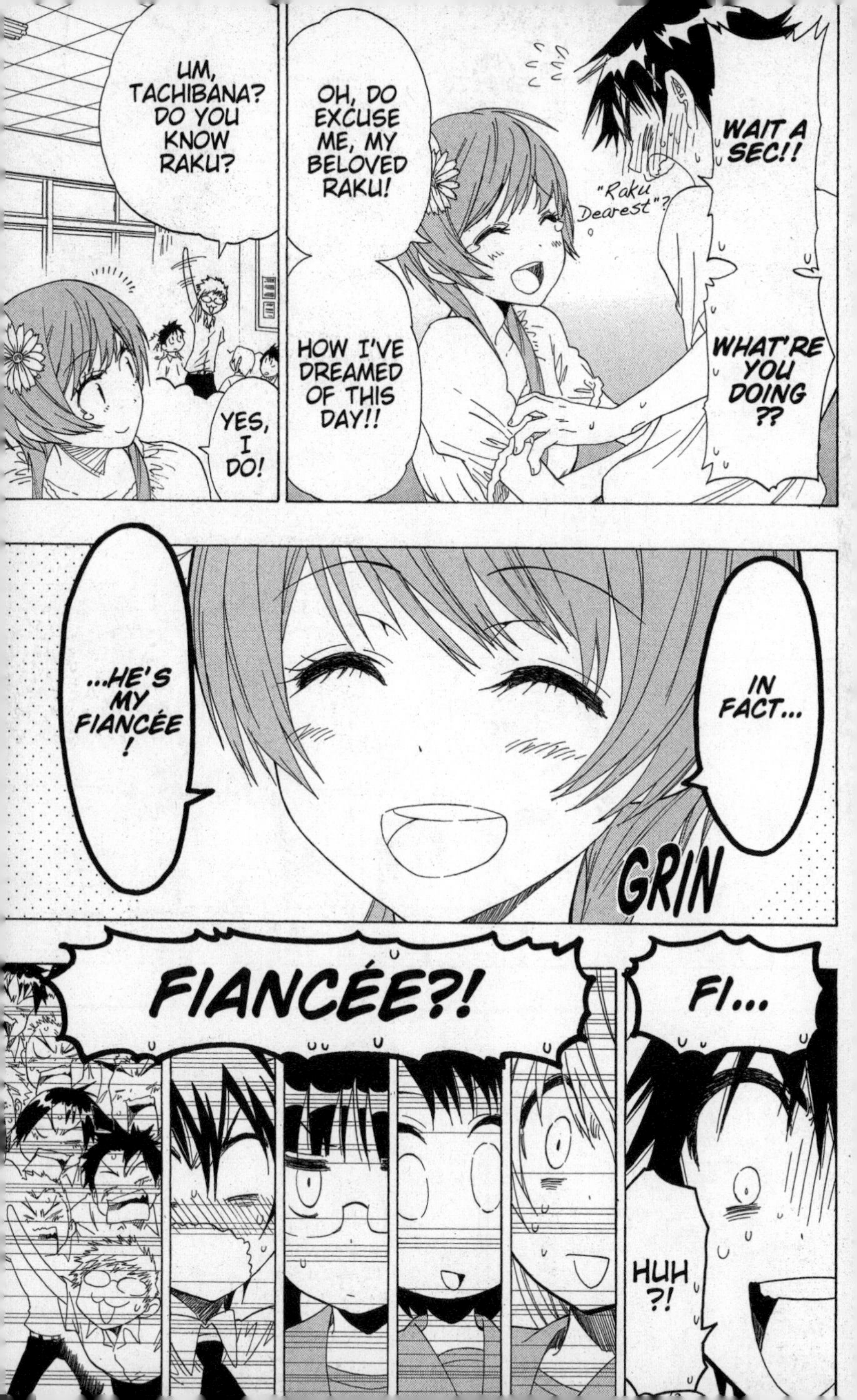
WAIT A SEC!!
"Raku Dearest"?
WHAT'RE YOU DOING??
OH, DO EXCUSE ME, MY BELOVED RAKU!
HOW I'VE DREAMED OF THIS DAY!!
UM, TACHIBANA? DO YOU KNOW RAKU?
YES, I DO!
IN FACT...
...HE'S MY FIANCÉE!
GRIN
FI...
HUH?!
FIANCÉE?!

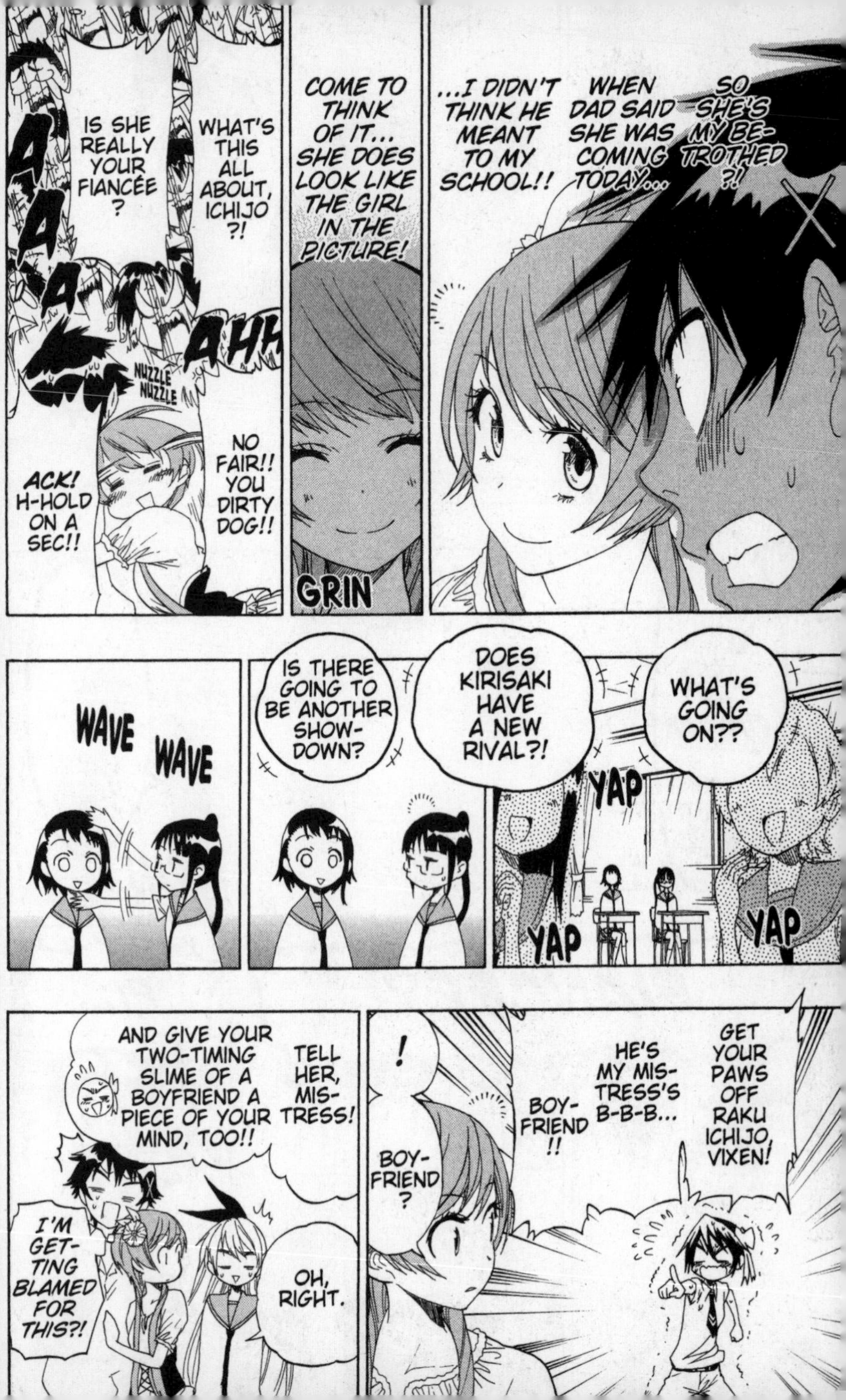
SO SHE'S MY BETROTHED?!
WHEN DAD SAID SHE WAS COMING TODAY...
...I DIDN'T THINK HE MEANT TO MY SCHOOL!!
COME TO THINK OF IT... SHE DOES LOOK LIKE THE GIRL IN THE PICTURE!
GRIN
WHAT'S THIS ALL ABOUT, ICHIJO?!
IS SHE REALLY YOUR FIANCÉE?
AAAAHH
NUZZLE NUZZLE
NO FAIR!! YOU DIRTY DOG!!
ACK! H-HOLD ON A SEC!!
WHAT'S GOING ON??
YAP
YAP
DOES KIRISAKI HAVE A NEW RIVAL?!
YAP
IS THERE GOING TO BE ANOTHER SHOWDOWN?
WAVE
WAVE
GET YOUR PAWS OFF RAKU ICHIJO, VIXEN!
HE'S MY MISTRESS'S B-B-B...
BOYFRIEND!!
!
BOYFRIEND?
TELL HER, MISTRESS!
AND GIVE YOUR TWO-TIMING SLIME OF A BOYFRIEND A PIECE OF YOUR MIND, TOO!!
OH, RIGHT.
I'M GETTING BLAMED FOR THIS?!

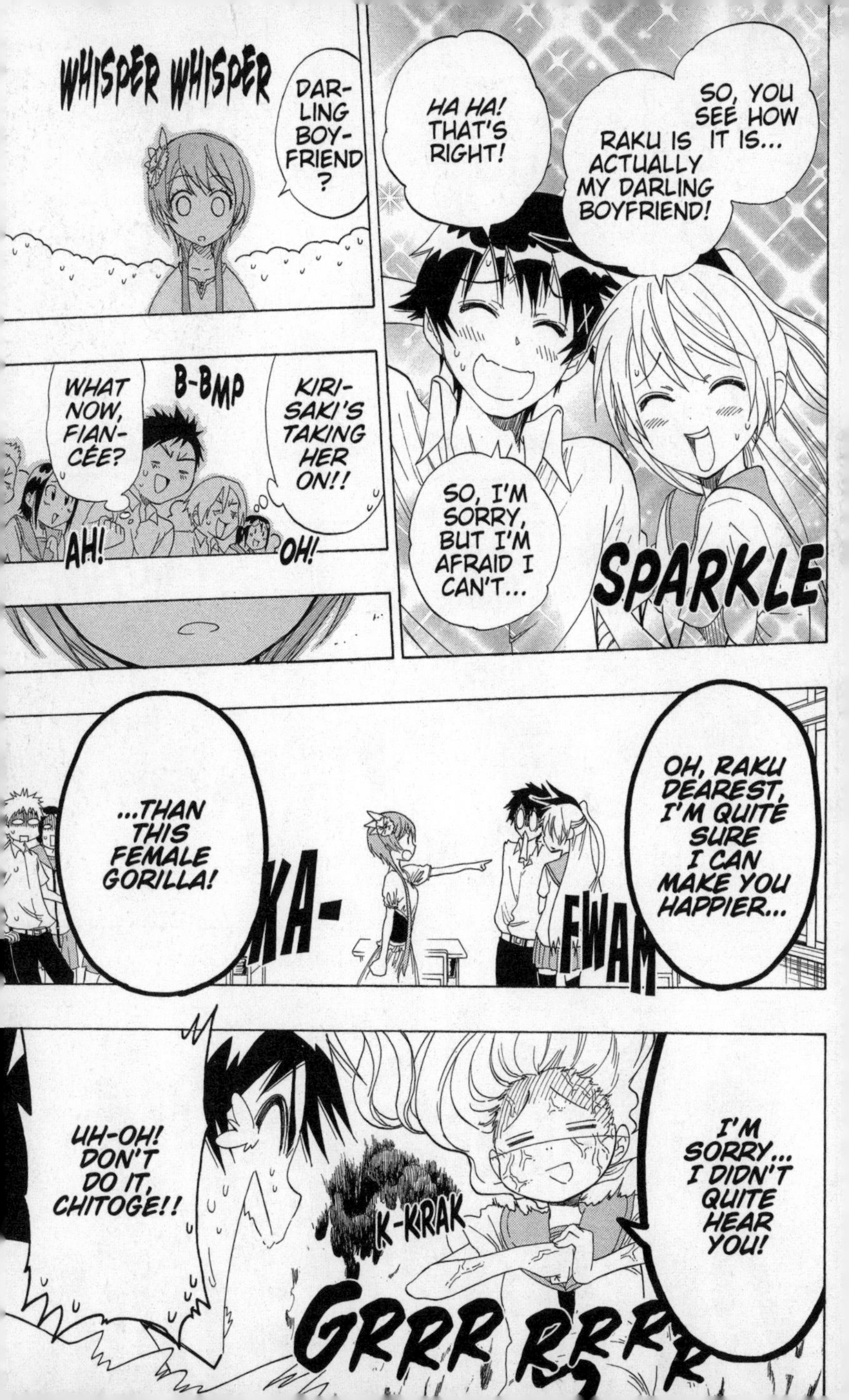
SO, YOU SEE HOW IT IS... RAKU IS ACTUALLY MY DARLING BOYFRIEND!
HA HA! THAT'S RIGHT!
SO, I'M SORRY, BUT I'M AFRAID I CAN'T...
SPARKLE
DARLING BOYFRIEND?
WHISPER WHISPER
KIRISAKI'S TAKING HER ON!!
B-BMP
OH!
WHAT NOW, FIANCÉE?
AH!
OH, RAKU DEAREST, I'M QUITE SURE I CAN MAKE YOU HAPPIER...
FWAM
KA-
...THAN THIS FEMALE GORILLA!
I'M SORRY... I DIDN'T QUITE HEAR YOU!
GRRR RRRR
K-KRAK
UH-OH! DON'T DO IT, CHITOGE!!

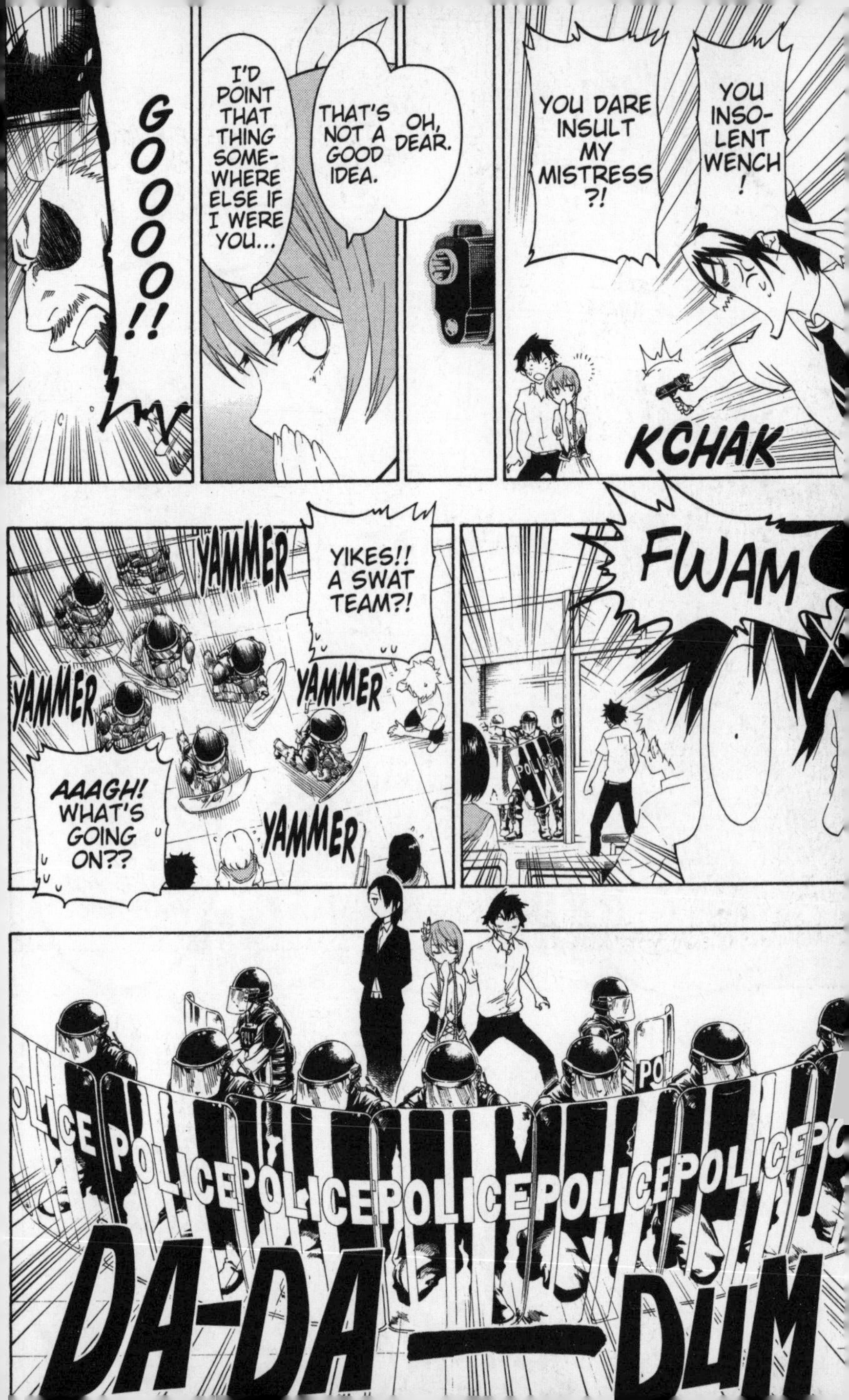
YOU INSO-LENT WENCH!
YOU DARE INSULT MY MISTRESS?!
KCHAK
OH, DEAR.
THAT'S NOT A GOOD IDEA.
I'D POINT THAT THING SOME-WHERE ELSE IF I WERE YOU...
GOOOOO!!
FWAM
POLICE
YIKES!! A SWAT TEAM?!
YAMMER
YAMMER
YAMMER
AAAGH! WHAT'S GOING ON??
YAMMER
PO
POLICEPOLICEPOLICEPOLICEPOLICEPOLICEPO
DA-DA—DUM

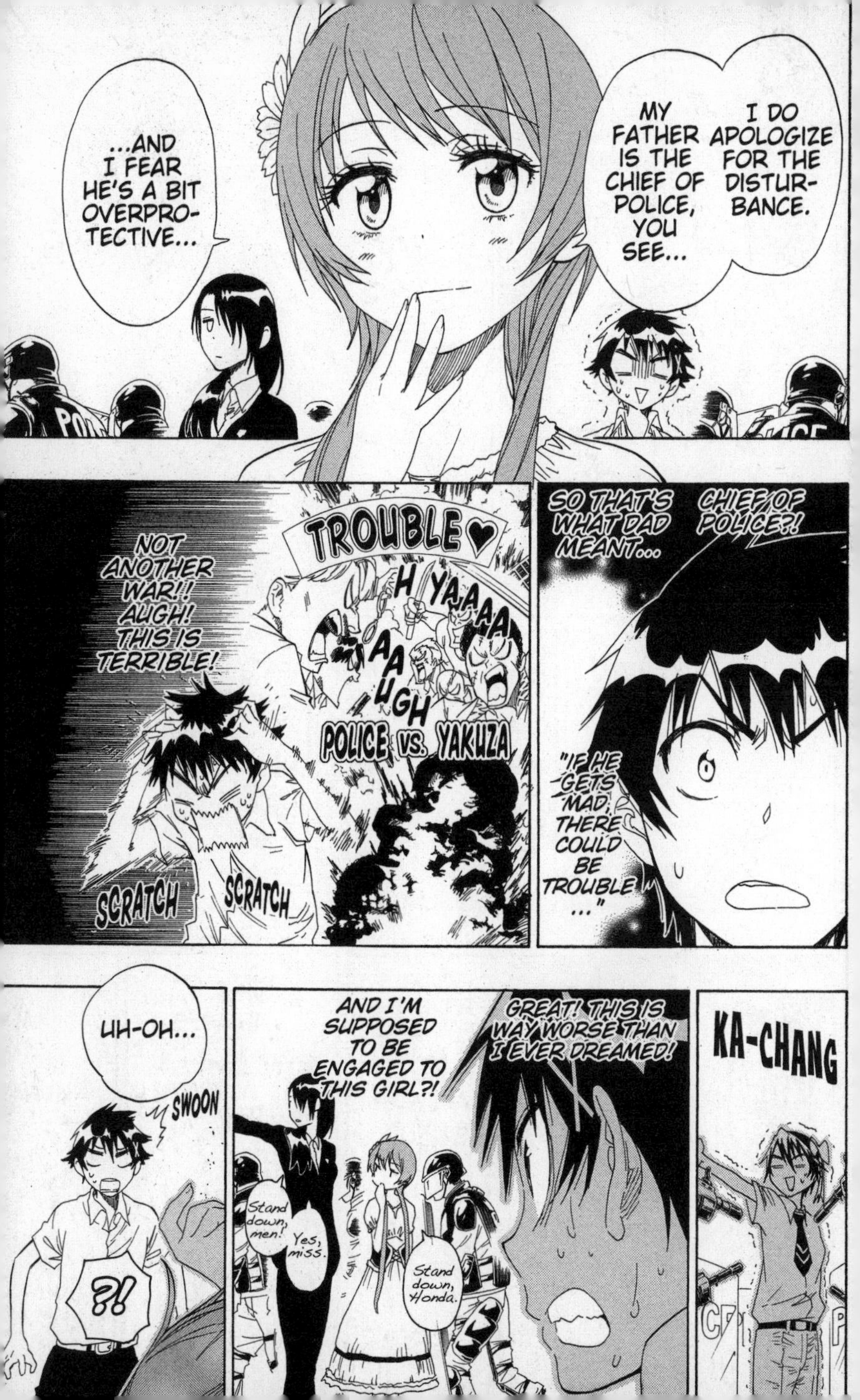
I DO APOLOGIZE FOR THE DISTURBANCE.
MY FATHER IS THE CHIEF OF POLICE, YOU SEE...
...AND I FEAR HE'S A BIT OVERPROTECTIVE...
CHIEF OF POLICE?!
SO THAT'S WHAT DAD MEANT...
"IF HE GETS MAD, THERE COULD BE TROUBLE..."
TROUBLE♥
HYAAAAA
AAAUGH
POLICE VS. YAKUZA
NOT ANOTHER WAR!! AUGH! THIS IS TERRIBLE!
SCRATCH
SCRATCH
KA-CHANG
GREAT! THIS IS WAY WORSE THAN I EVER DREAMED!
AND I'M SUPPOSED TO BE ENGAGED TO THIS GIRL?!
Stand down, Honda.
Stand down, men!
Yes, miss.
UH-OH...
SWOON
?!

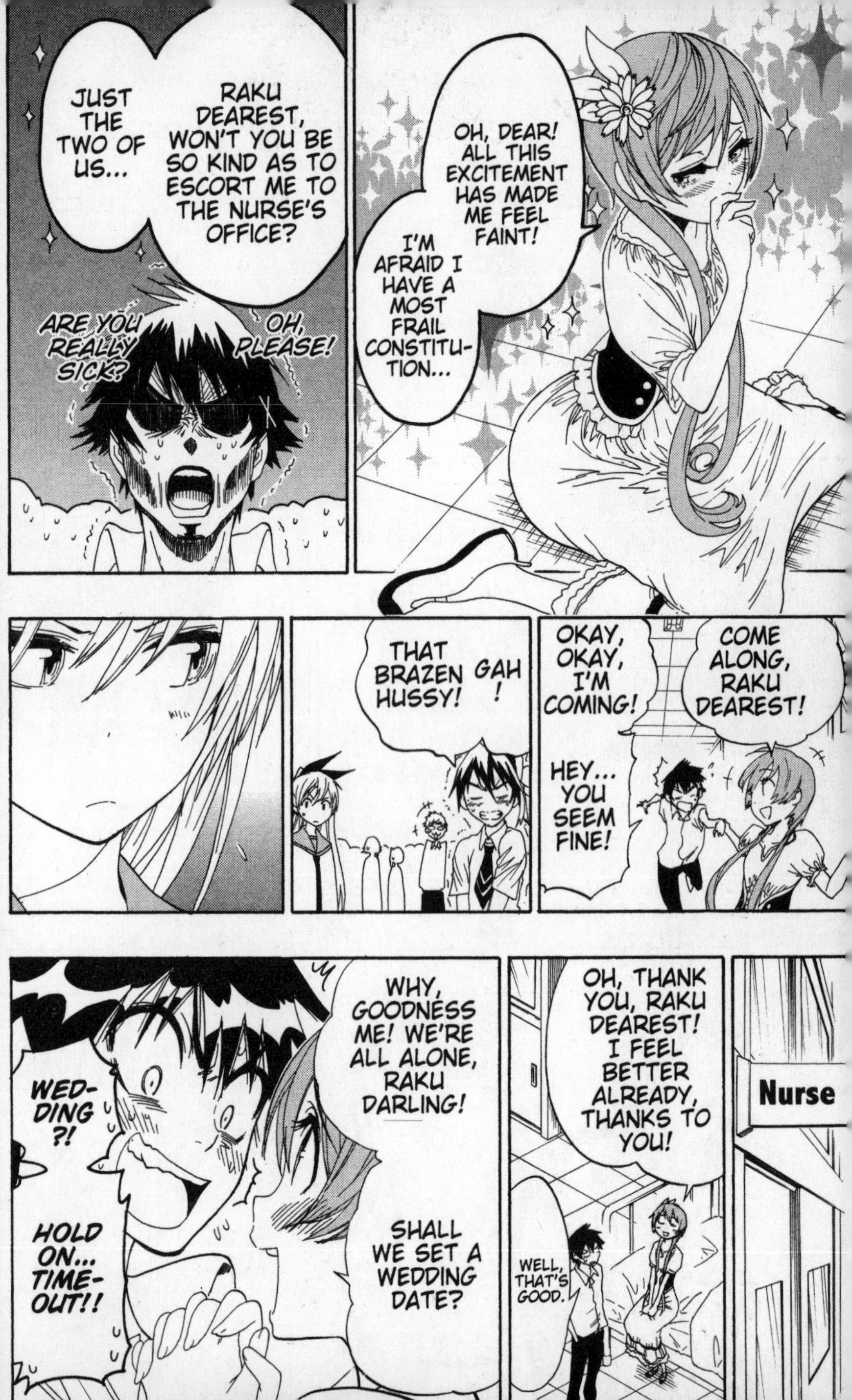
OH, DEAR! ALL THIS EXCITEMENT HAS MADE ME FEEL FAINT!
I'M AFRAID I HAVE A MOST FRAIL CONSTITUTION...
RAKU DEAREST, WON'T YOU BE SO KIND AS TO ESCORT ME TO THE NURSE'S OFFICE?
JUST THE TWO OF US...
OH, PLEASE!
ARE YOU REALLY SICK?
COME ALONG, RAKU DEAREST!
OKAY, OKAY, I'M COMING!
HEY... YOU SEEM FINE!
GAH!
THAT BRAZEN HUSSY!
Nurse
OH, THANK YOU, RAKU DEAREST! I FEEL BETTER ALREADY, THANKS TO YOU!
WELL, THAT'S GOOD.
WHY, GOODNESS ME! WE'RE ALL ALONE, RAKU DARLING!
SHALL WE SET A WEDDING DATE?
WEDDING?!
HOLD ON... TIME-OUT!!

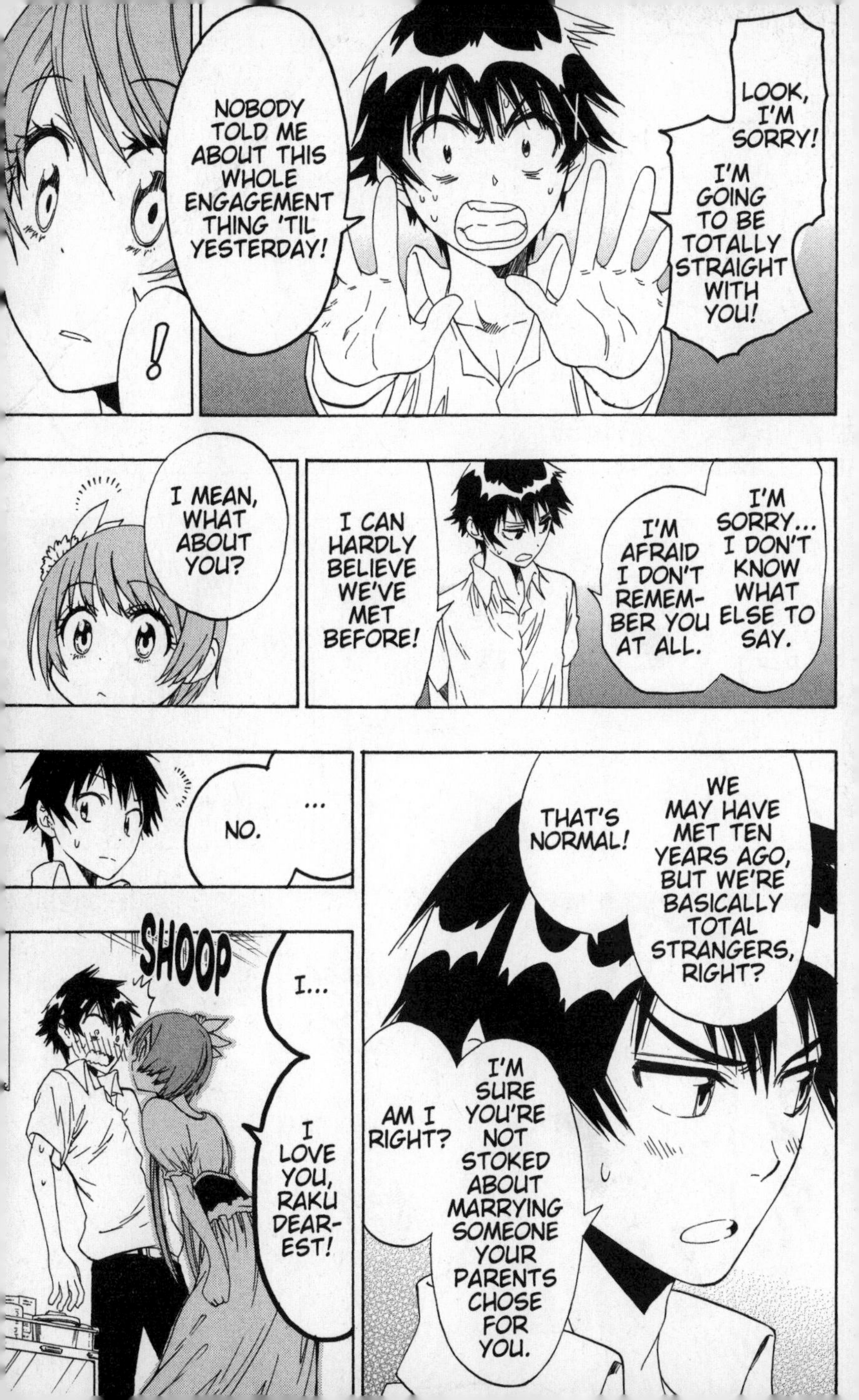
LOOK, I'M SORRY!
I'M GOING TO BE TOTALLY STRAIGHT WITH YOU!
NOBODY TOLD ME ABOUT THIS WHOLE ENGAGEMENT THING 'TIL YESTERDAY!
!
I'M SORRY... I DON'T KNOW WHAT ELSE TO SAY.
I'M AFRAID I DON'T REMEMBER YOU AT ALL.
I CAN HARDLY BELIEVE WE'VE MET BEFORE!
I MEAN, WHAT ABOUT YOU?
WE MAY HAVE MET TEN YEARS AGO, BUT WE'RE BASICALLY TOTAL STRANGERS, RIGHT?
THAT'S NORMAL!
I'M SURE YOU'RE NOT STOKED ABOUT MARRYING SOMEONE YOUR PARENTS CHOSE FOR YOU.
AM I RIGHT?
... NO.
SHOOP
I...
I LOVE YOU, RAKU DEAREST!

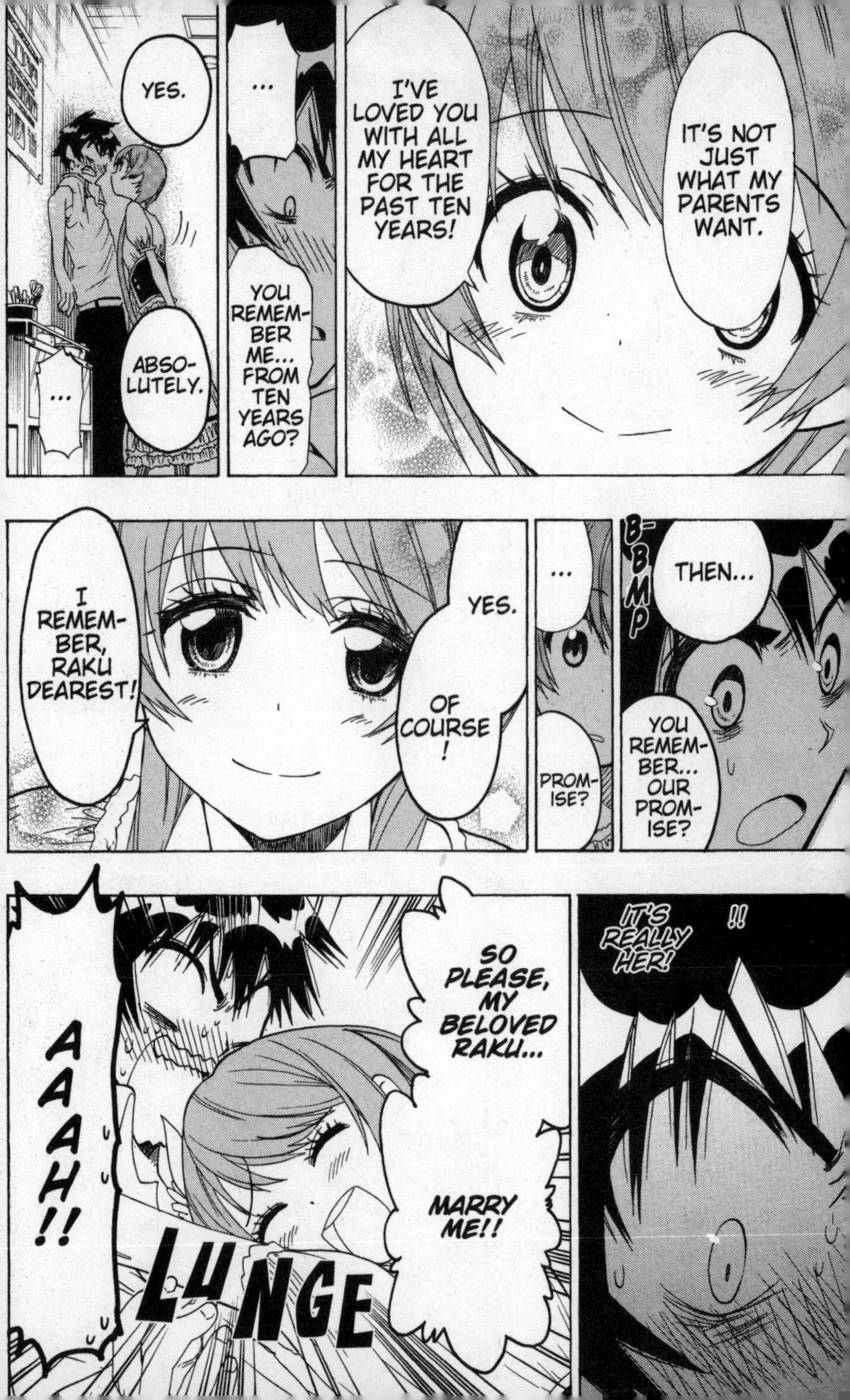
IT'S NOT JUST WHAT MY PARENTS WANT.
I'VE LOVED YOU WITH ALL MY HEART FOR THE PAST TEN YEARS!
...
YOU REMEMBER ME... FROM TEN YEARS AGO?
YES.
ABSOLUTELY.
...
THEN...
B-BMP
YOU REMEMBER... OUR PROMISE?
...
PROMISE?
YES.
OF COURSE!
I REMEMBER, RAKU DEAREST!
IT'S REALLY HER!
!!
SO PLEASE, MY BELOVED RAKU...
MARRY ME!!
AAAAH!!
LUNGE

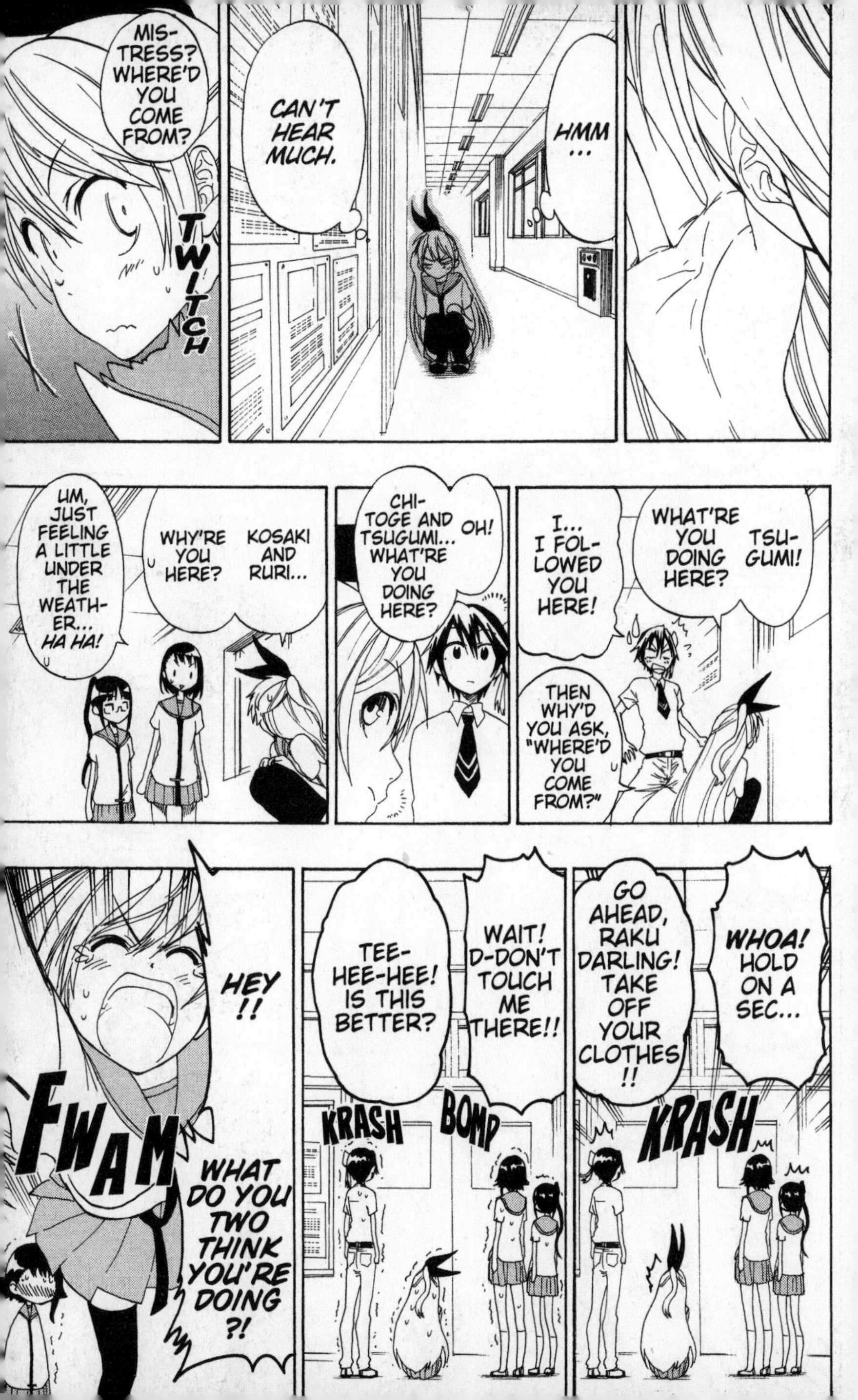
HMM...
CAN'T HEAR MUCH.
MIS-TRESS? WHERE'D YOU COME FROM?
TWITCH
TSU-GUMI!
WHAT'RE YOU DOING HERE?
I... I FOL-LOWED YOU HERE!
THEN WHY'D YOU ASK, "WHERE'D YOU COME FROM?"
OH!
CHI-TOGE AND TSUGUMI... WHAT'RE YOU DOING HERE?
KOSAKI AND RURI...
WHY'RE YOU HERE?
UM, JUST FEELING A LITTLE UNDER THE WEATH-ER... HA HA!
WHOA! HOLD ON A SEC...
GO AHEAD, RAKU DARLING! TAKE OFF YOUR CLOTHES!!
KRASH
WAIT! D-DON'T TOUCH ME THERE!!
BOMP
TEE-HEE-HEE! IS THIS BETTER?
KRASH
HEY!!
FWAM
WHAT DO YOU TWO THINK YOU'RE DOING?!

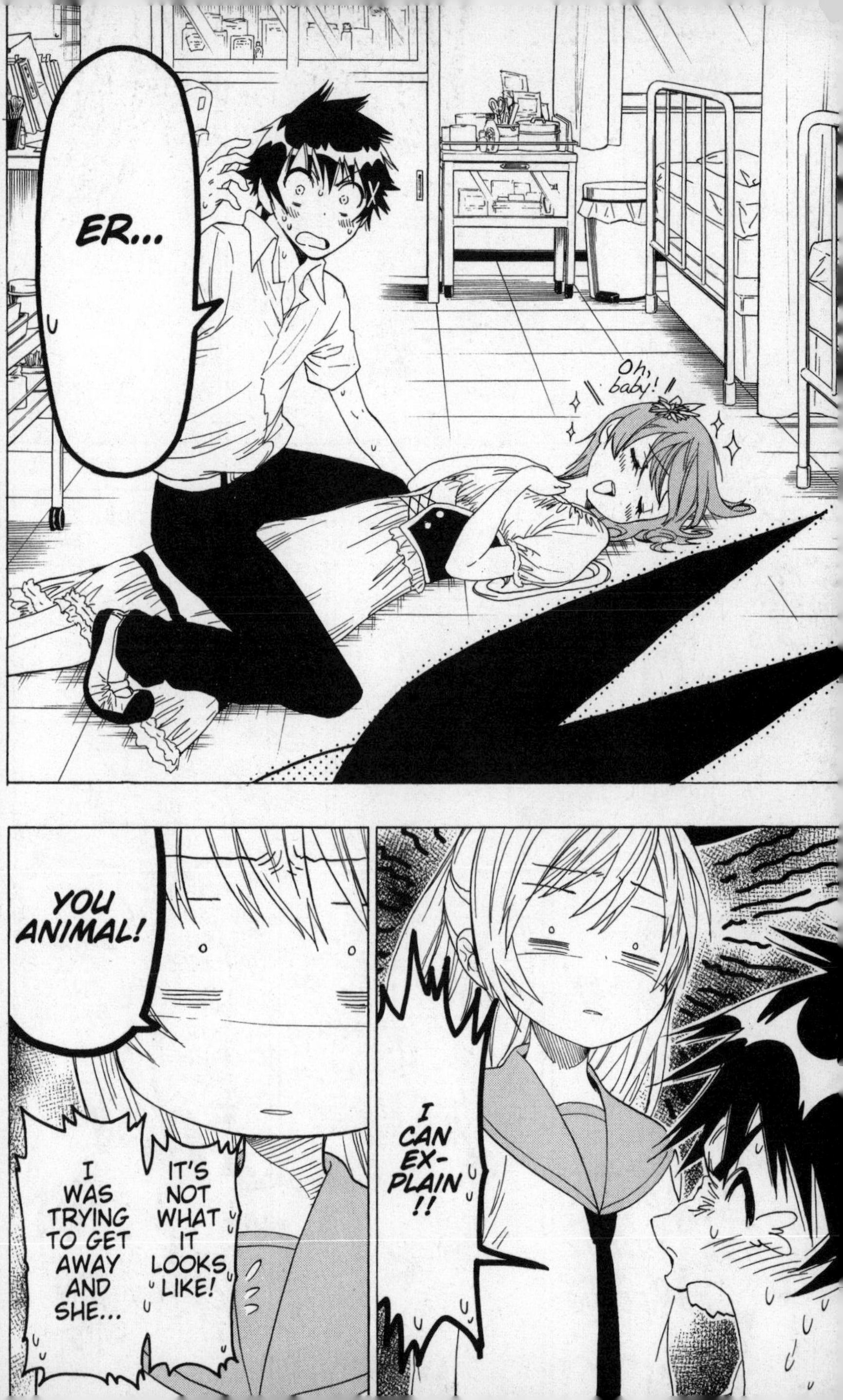

ER...
Oh, baby!
I CAN EX-PLAIN!!
YOU ANIMAL!
IT'S NOT WHAT IT LOOKS LIKE!
I WAS TRYING TO GET AWAY AND SHE...

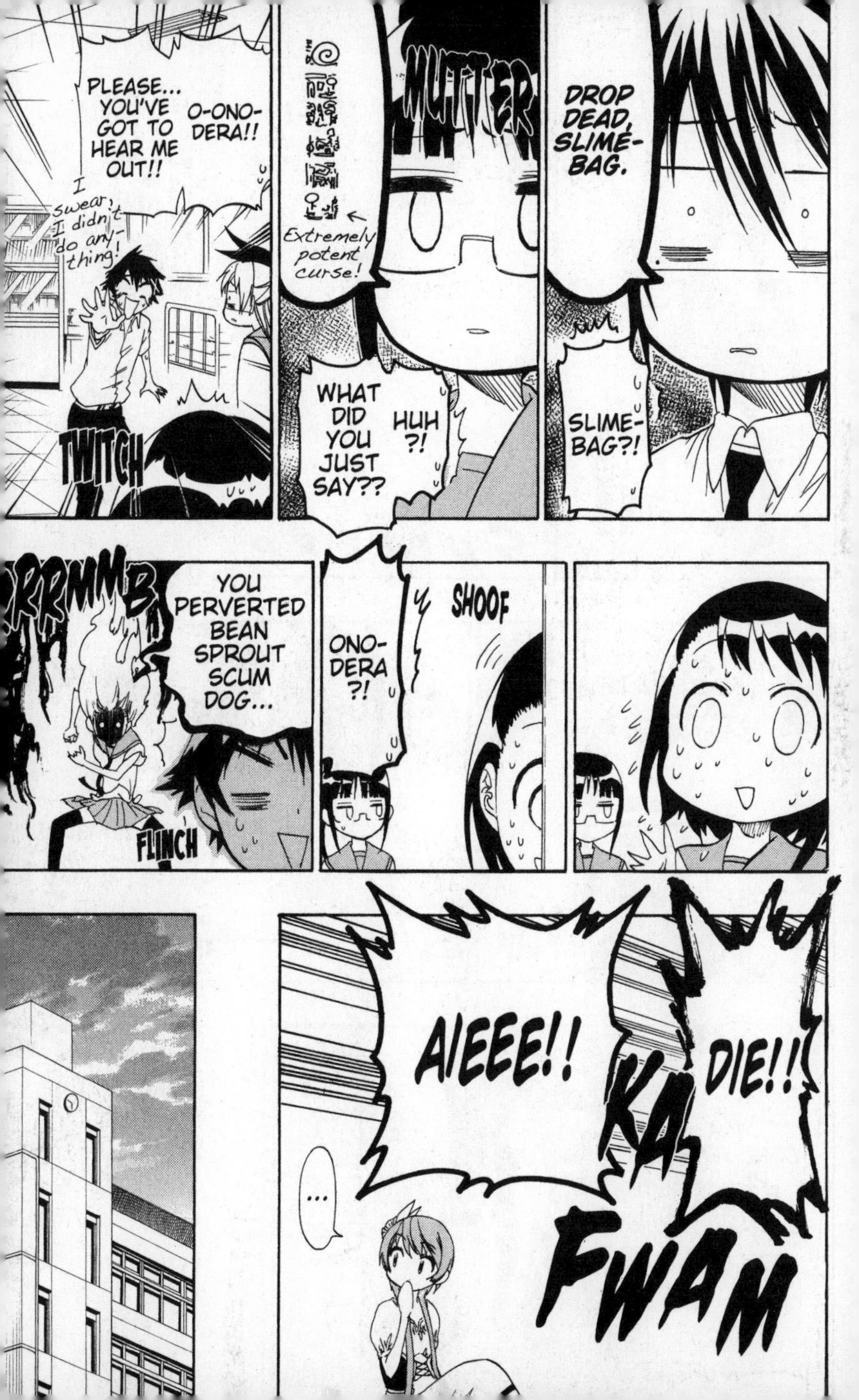
DROP DEAD, SLIME-BAG.
SLIME-BAG?!
MUTTER
Extremely potent curse!
HUH?!
WHAT DID YOU JUST SAY??
O-ONO-DERA!!
PLEASE... YOU'VE GOT TO HEAR ME OUT!!
I swear, I didn't do any-thing!
TWITCH
SHOOF
ONO-DERA?!
RRMMB
YOU PERVERTED BEAN SPROUT SCUM DOG...
FLINCH
DIE!!
KA
FWAM
AIEEE!!
...

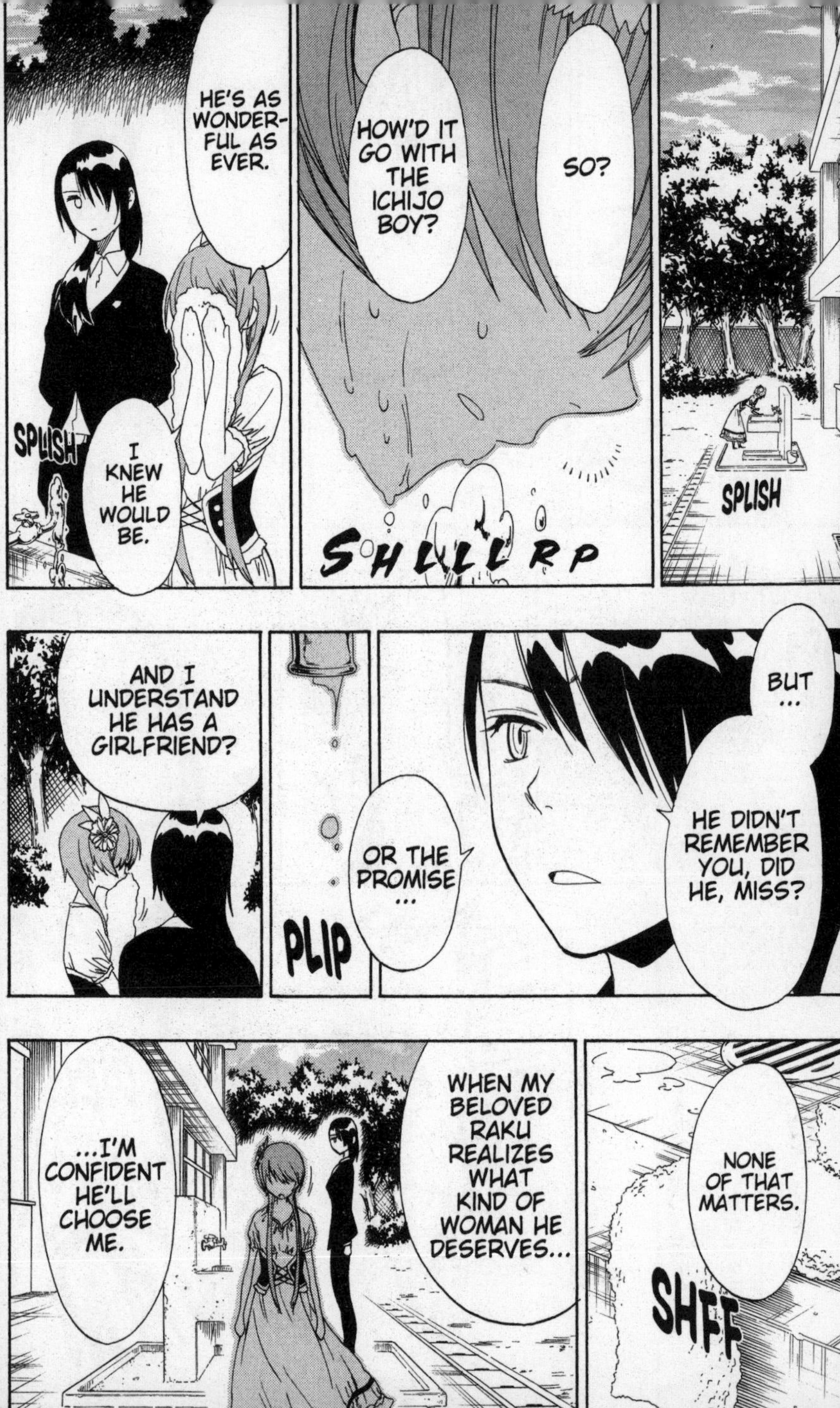
SPLISH
SO?
HOW'D IT GO WITH THE ICHIJO BOY?
SHLLLRP
HE'S AS WONDERFUL AS EVER.
I KNEW HE WOULD BE.
SPLISH
BUT ...
HE DIDN'T REMEMBER YOU, DID HE, MISS?
OR THE PROMISE ...
PLIP
AND I UNDERSTAND HE HAS A GIRLFRIEND?
NONE OF THAT MATTERS.
SHFF
WHEN MY BELOVED RAKU REALIZES WHAT KIND OF WOMAN HE DESERVES...
...I'M CONFIDENT HE'LL CHOOSE ME.

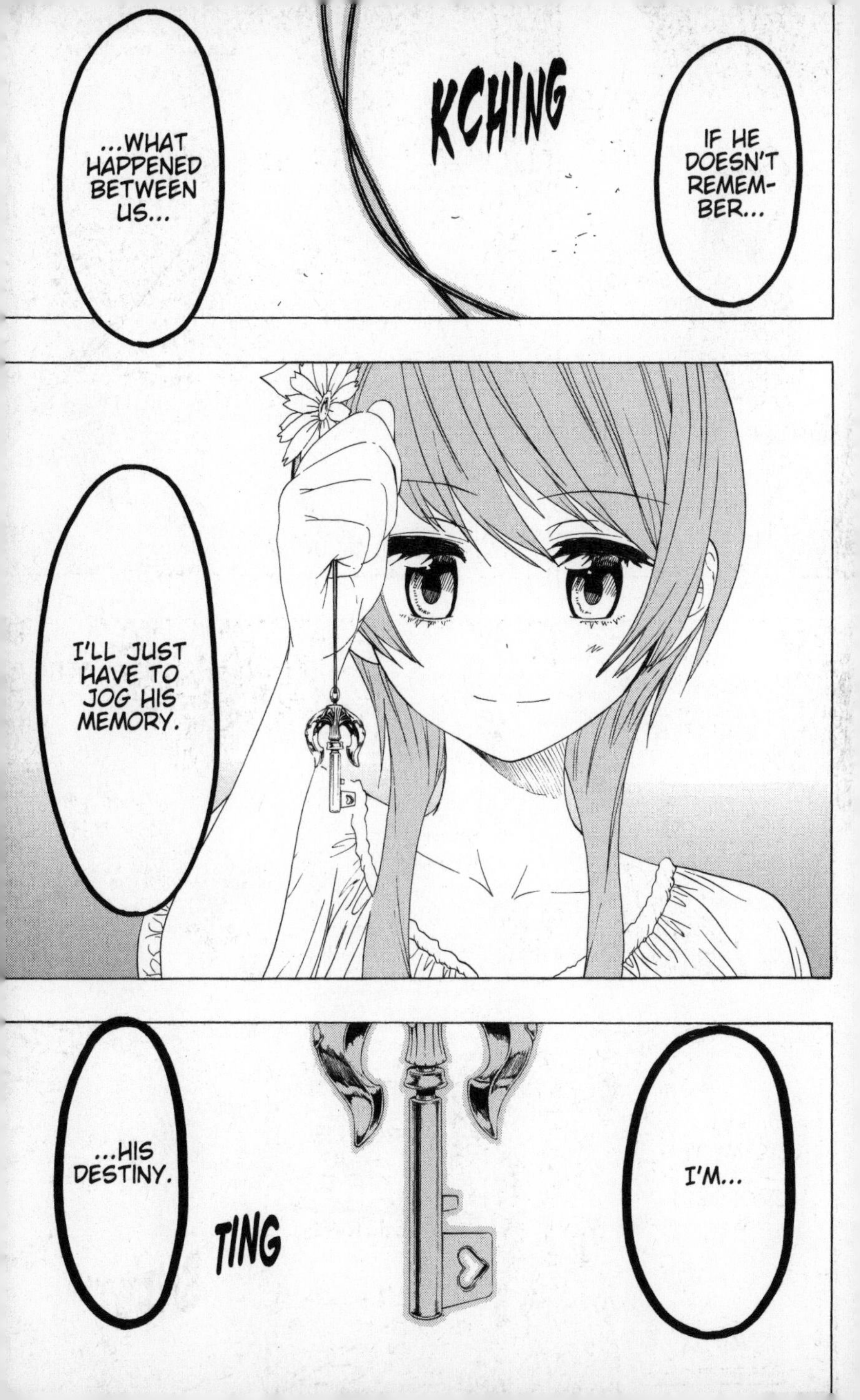
IF HE DOESN'T REMEMBER...
KCHING
...WHAT HAPPENED BETWEEN US...
I'LL JUST HAVE TO JOG HIS MEMORY.
I'M...
TING
...HIS DESTINY.

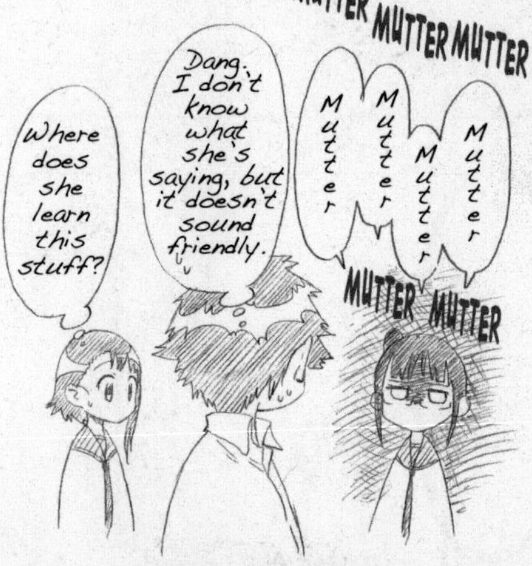
MUTTER MUTTER MUTTER
Mutter
Mutter
Mutter
Mutter
MUTTER MUTTER
Dang. I don't know what she's saying, but it doesn't sound friendly.
Where does she learn this stuff?

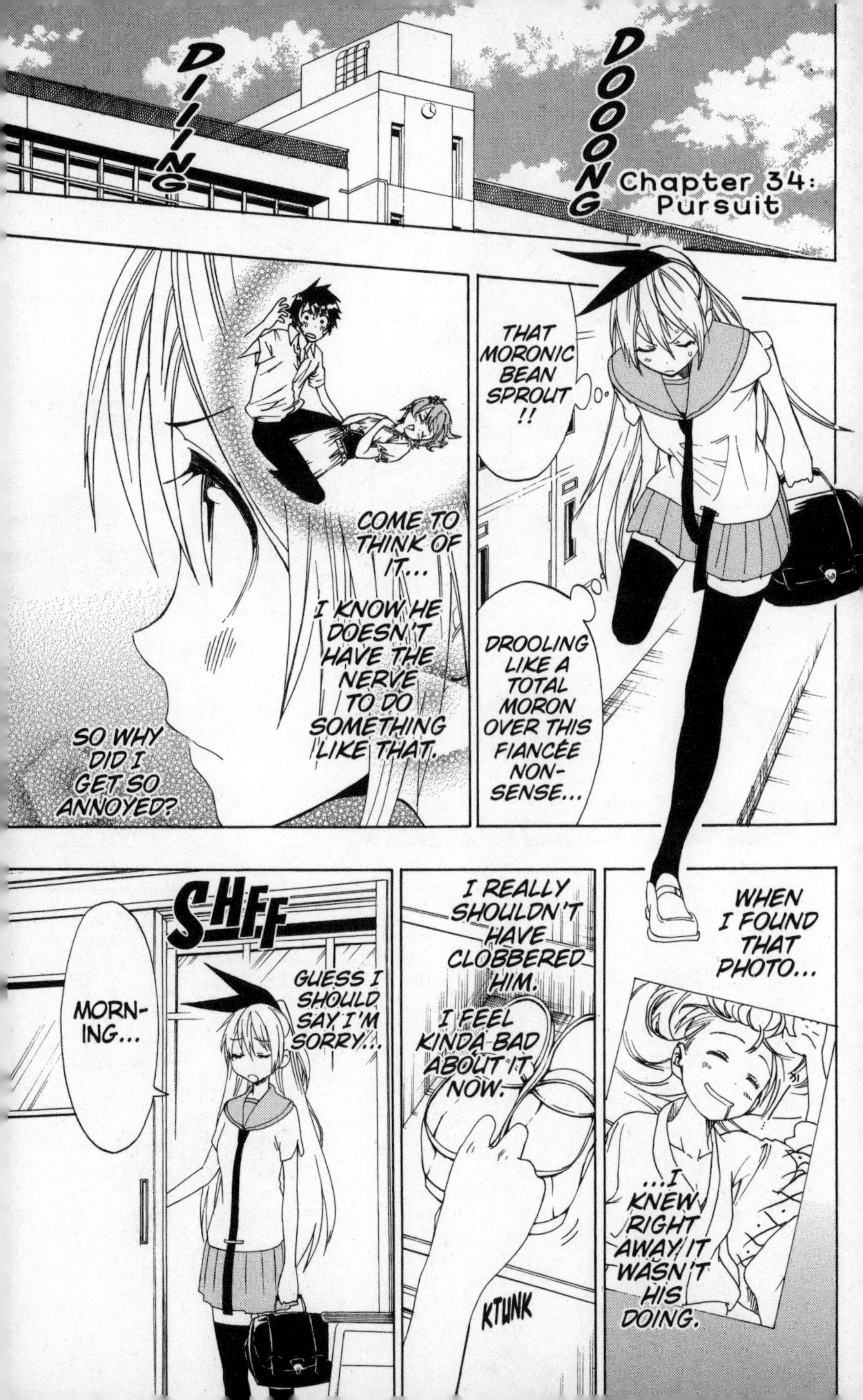
DIIING
DOOOONG
Chapter 34: Pursuit
THAT MORONIC BEAN SPROUT !!
DROOLING LIKE A TOTAL MORON OVER THIS FIANCÉE NON-SENSE...
COME TO THINK OF IT...
I KNOW HE DOESN'T HAVE THE NERVE TO DO SOMETHING LIKE THAT.
SO WHY DID I GET SO ANNOYED?
WHEN I FOUND THAT PHOTO...
...I KNEW RIGHT AWAY IT WASN'T HIS DOING.
I REALLY SHOULDN'T HAVE CLOBBERED HIM.
I FEEL KINDA BAD ABOUT IT NOW.
KTUNK
SHFF
GUESS I SHOULD SAY I'M SORRY...
MORN-ING...

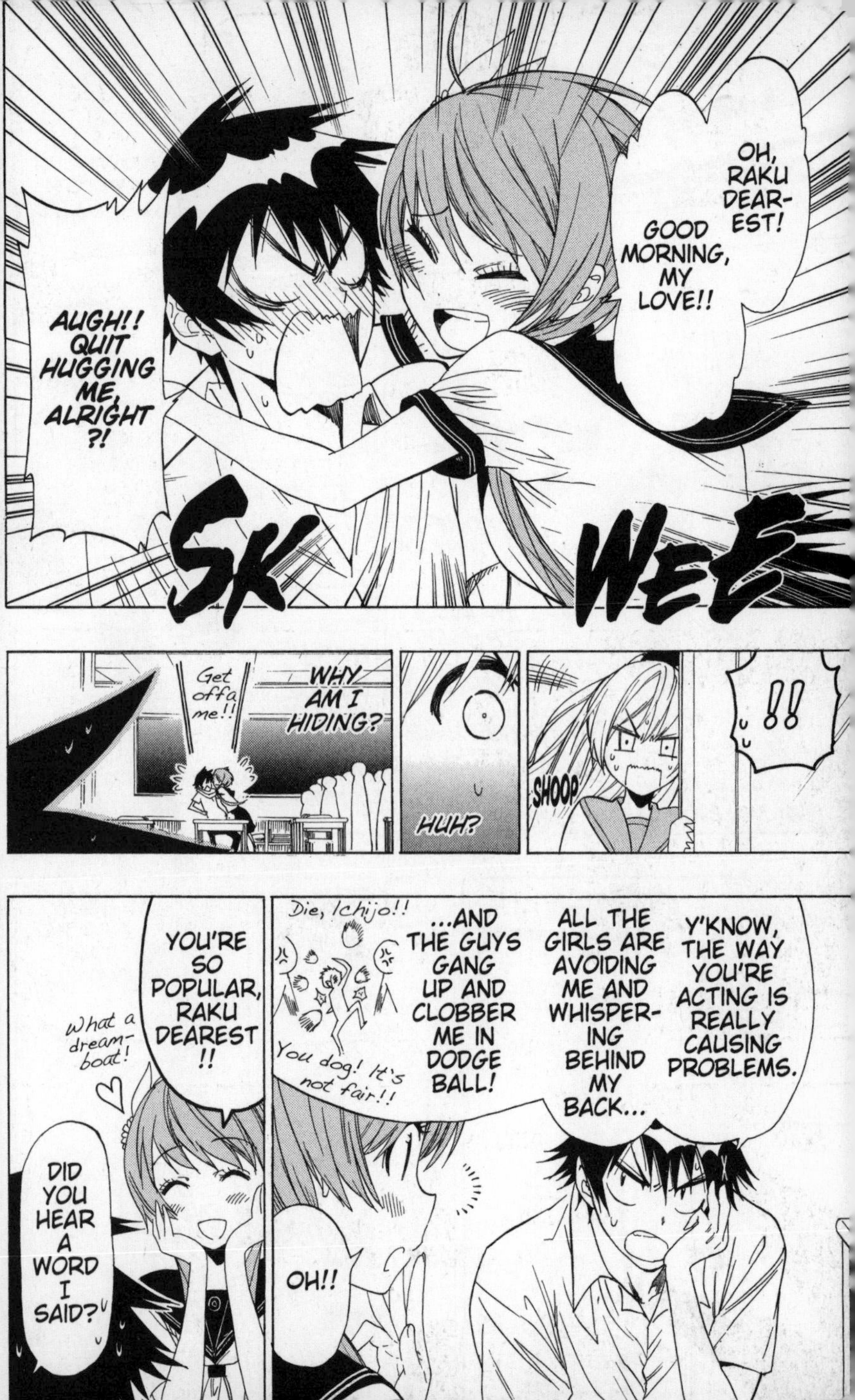
OH, RAKU DEAREST!
GOOD MORNING, MY LOVE!!
AUGH!! QUIT HUGGING ME, ALRIGHT?!
SKWEE
!!
SHOOP
HUH?
WHY AM I HIDING?
Get offa me!!
Y'KNOW, THE WAY YOU'RE ACTING IS REALLY CAUSING PROBLEMS.
ALL THE GIRLS ARE AVOIDING ME AND WHISPERING BEHIND MY BACK...
...AND THE GUYS GANG UP AND CLOBBER ME IN DODGE BALL!
Die, Ichijo!!
You dog! It's not fair!!
OH!!
YOU'RE SO POPULAR, RAKU DEAREST!!
What a dreamboat!
DID YOU HEAR A WORD I SAID?

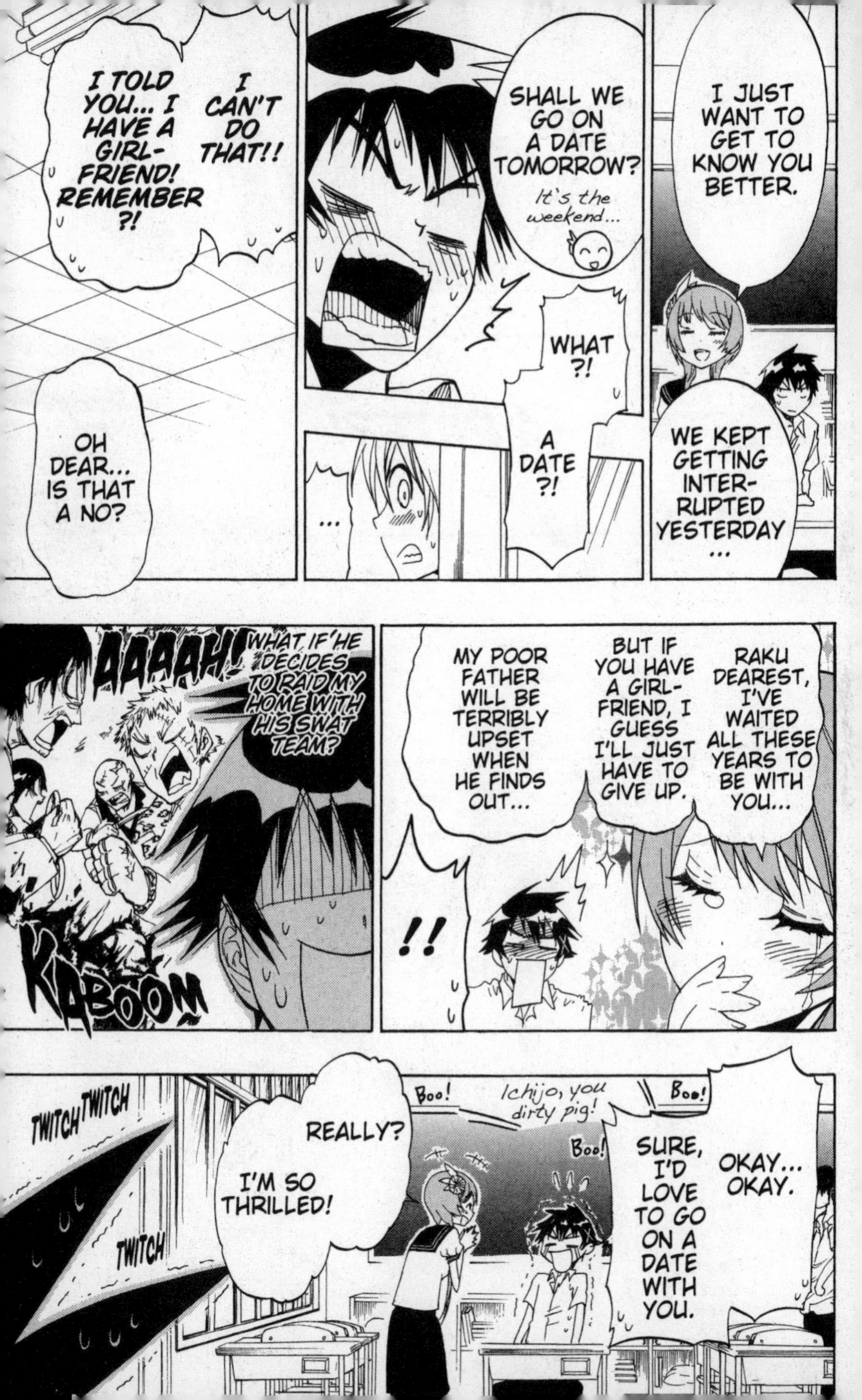
I JUST WANT TO GET TO KNOW YOU BETTER.
WE KEPT GETTING INTER-RUPTED YESTERDAY...
SHALL WE GO ON A DATE TOMORROW?
It's the weekend...
WHAT?!
A DATE?!
...
I CAN'T DO THAT!!
I TOLD YOU... I HAVE A GIRL-FRIEND! REMEMBER?!
OH DEAR... IS THAT A NO?
RAKU DEAREST, I'VE WAITED ALL THESE YEARS TO BE WITH YOU...
BUT IF YOU HAVE A GIRL-FRIEND, I GUESS I'LL JUST HAVE TO GIVE UP.
MY POOR FATHER WILL BE TERRIBLY UPSET WHEN HE FINDS OUT...
!!
WHAT IF HE DECIDES TO RAID MY HOME WITH HIS SWAT TEAM?
AAAAH!
KABOOM
OKAY... OKAY.
SURE, I'D LOVE TO GO ON A DATE WITH YOU.
Boo!
Ichijo, you dirty pig!
Boo!
Boo!
REALLY?
I'M SO THRILLED!
TWITCH TWITCH
TWITCH

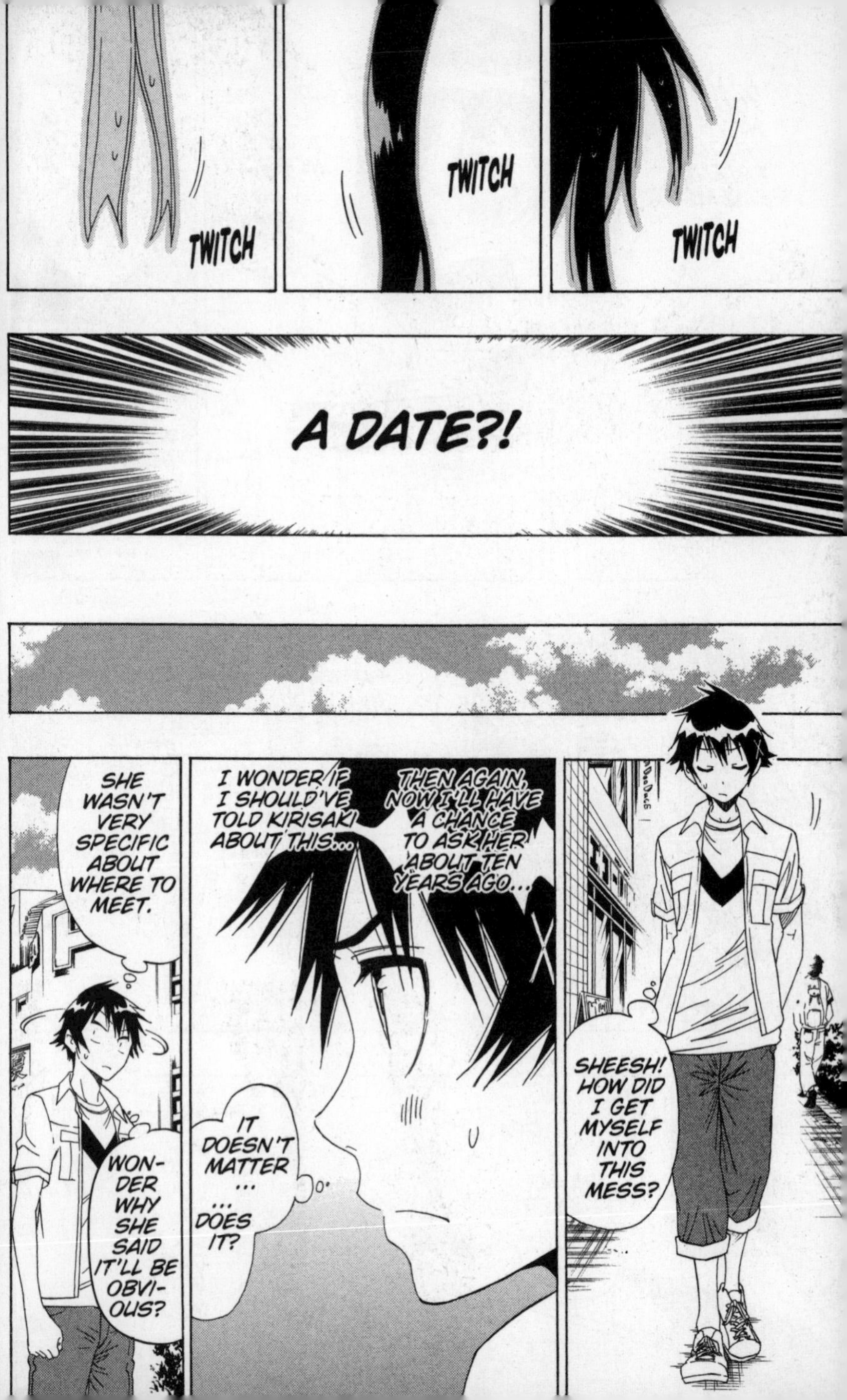
TWITCH
TWITCH
TWITCH
A DATE?!
SHEESH! HOW DID I GET MYSELF INTO THIS MESS?
THEN AGAIN, NOW I'LL HAVE A CHANCE TO ASK HER ABOUT TEN YEARS AGO...
I WONDER IF I SHOULD'VE TOLD KIRISAKI ABOUT THIS...
IT DOESN'T MATTER ... ... DOES IT?
SHE WASN'T VERY SPECIFIC ABOUT WHERE TO MEET.
WONDER WHY SHE SAID IT'LL BE OBVIOUS?

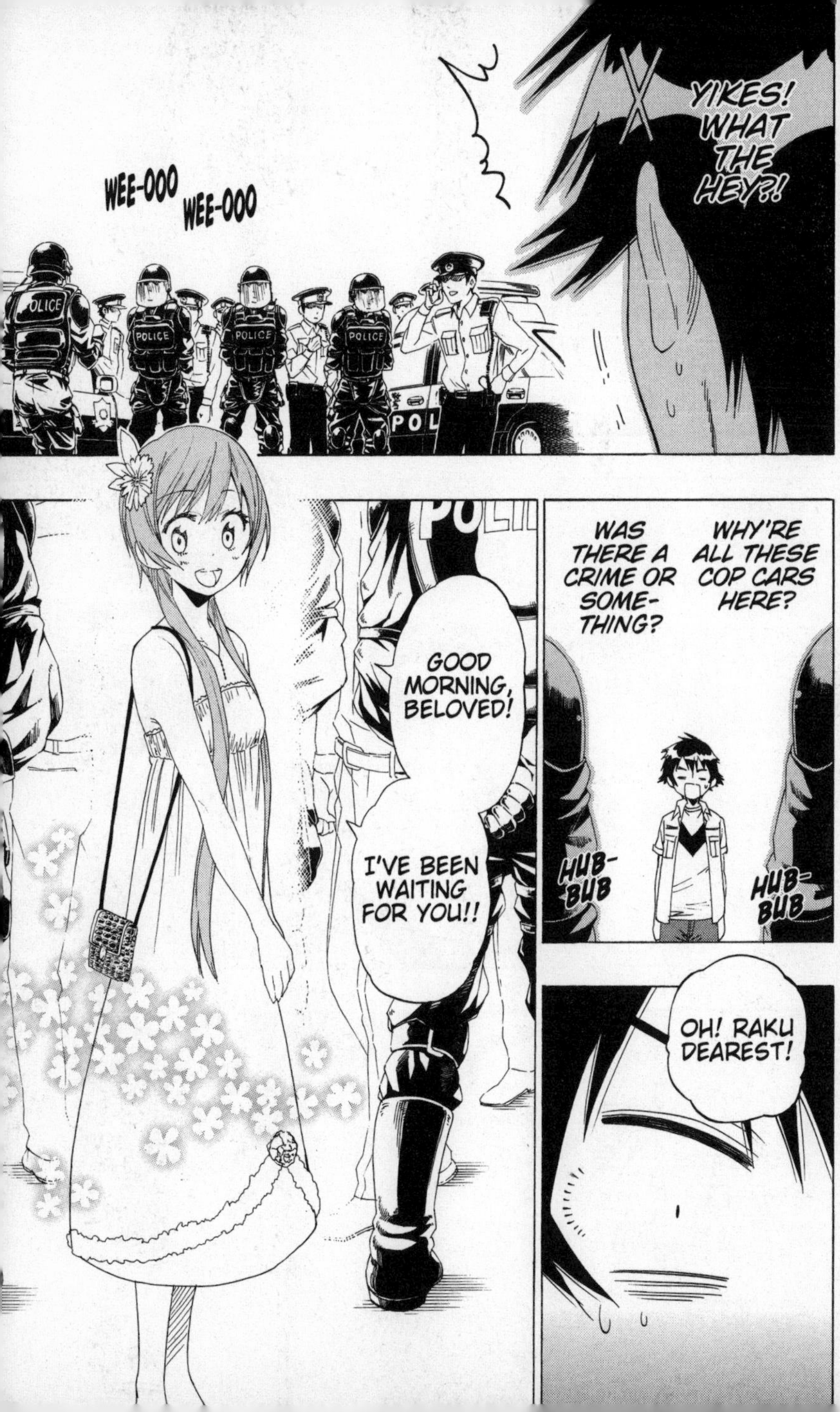
YIKES! WHAT THE HEY?!
WEE-OOO WEE-OOO
POLICE
POLICE
POLICE
POLICE
POL
WHY'RE ALL THESE COP CARS HERE?
WAS THERE A CRIME OR SOME-THING?
HUB-BUB
HUB-BUB
OH! RAKU DEAREST!
POLI
GOOD MORNING, BELOVED!
I'VE BEEN WAITING FOR YOU!!

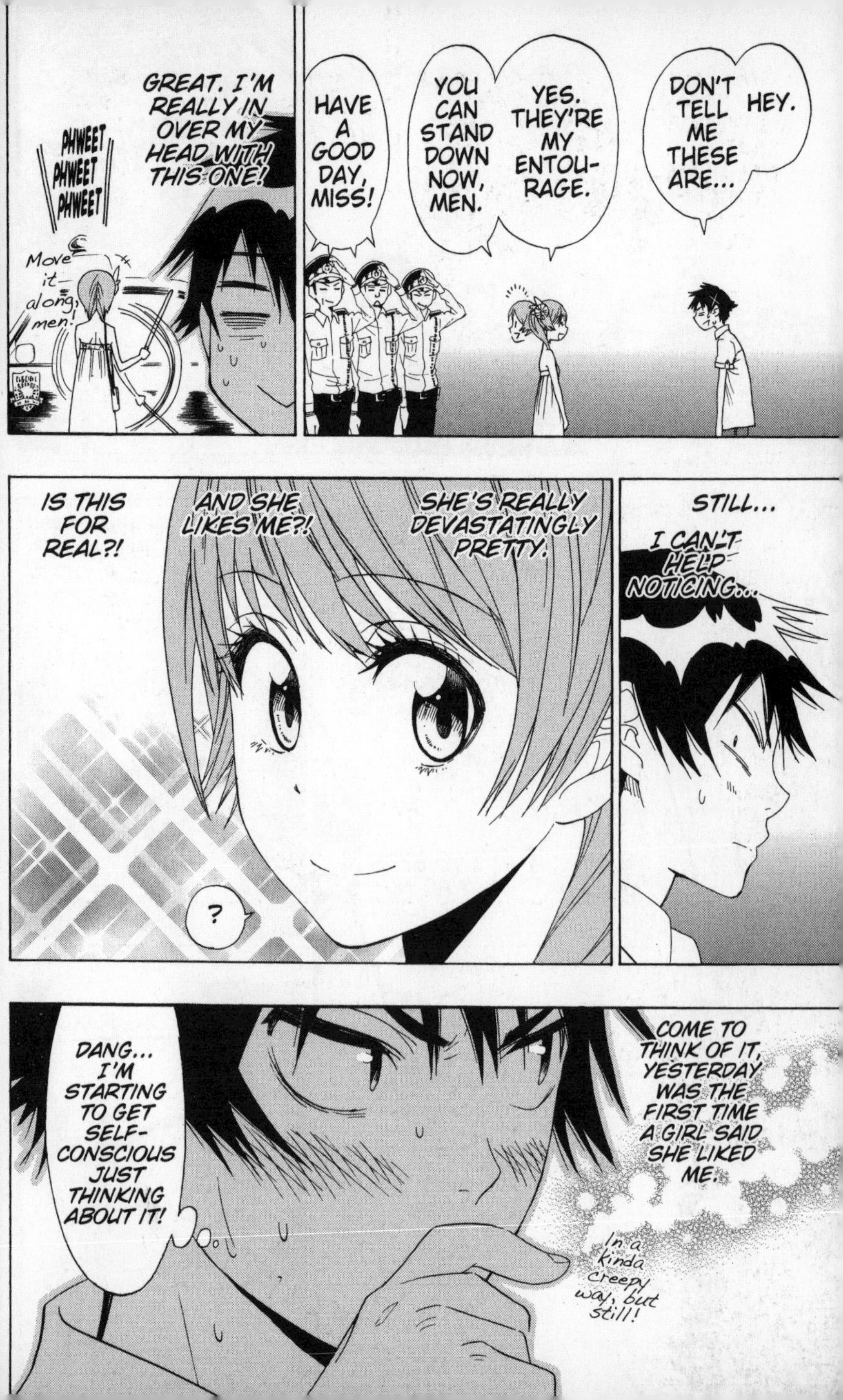
HEY.
DON'T TELL ME THESE ARE...
YES. THEY'RE MY ENTOURAGE.
YOU CAN STAND DOWN NOW, MEN.
HAVE A GOOD DAY, MISS!
GREAT. I'M REALLY IN OVER MY HEAD WITH THIS ONE!
PHWEET PHWEET PHWEET
Move it along, men!
STILL...
I CAN'T HELP NOTICING...
SHE'S REALLY DEVASTATINGLY PRETTY.
AND SHE LIKES ME?!
IS THIS FOR REAL?!
?
COME TO THINK OF IT, YESTERDAY WAS THE FIRST TIME A GIRL SAID SHE LIKED ME.
In a kinda creepy way, but still!
DANG... I'M STARTING TO GET SELF-CONSCIOUS JUST THINKING ABOUT IT!

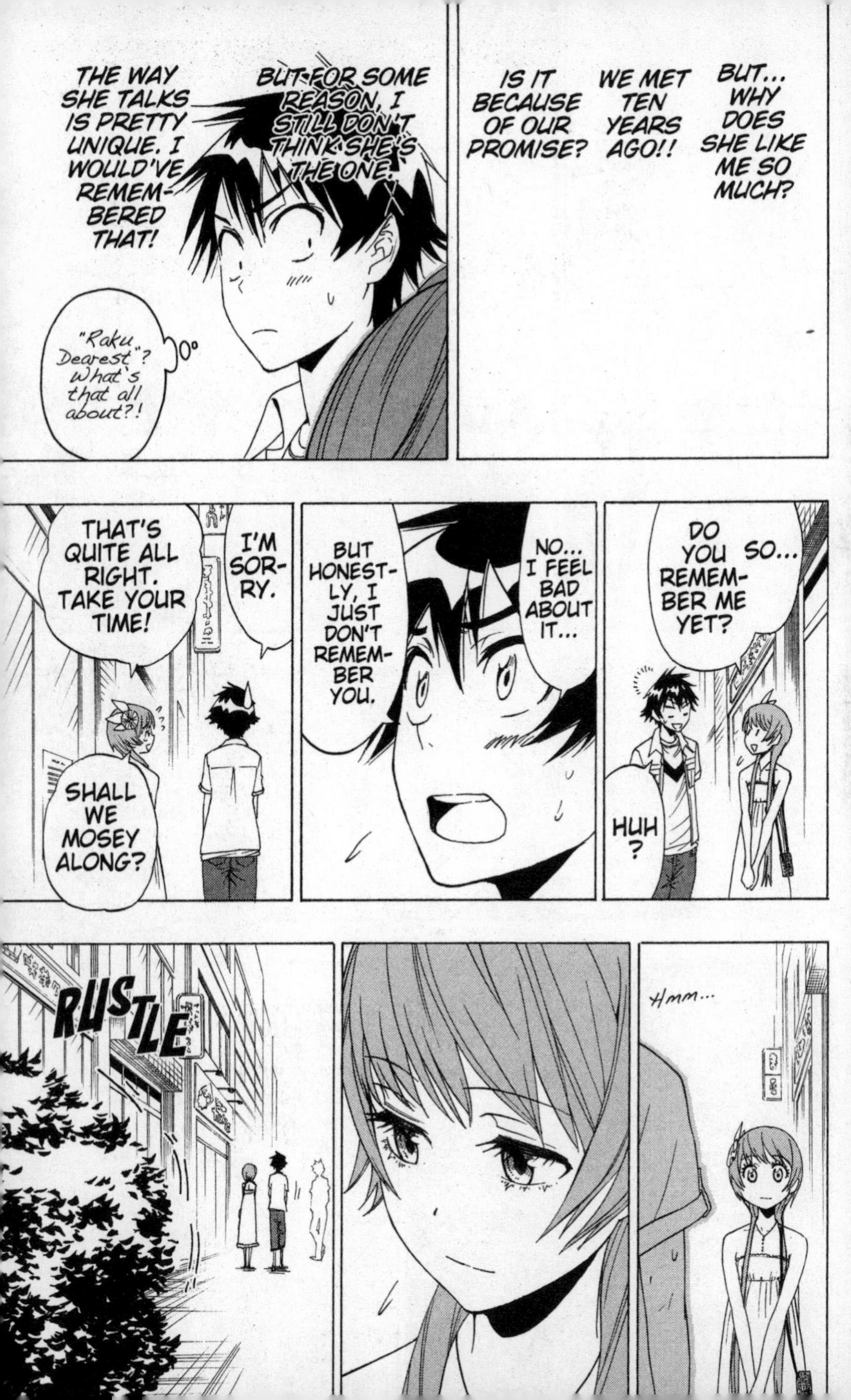
BUT... WHY DOES SHE LIKE ME SO MUCH?
WE MET TEN YEARS AGO!!
IS IT BECAUSE OF OUR PROMISE?
BUT FOR SOME REASON, I STILL DON'T THINK SHE'S THE ONE.
THE WAY SHE TALKS IS PRETTY UNIQUE. I WOULD'VE REMEMBERED THAT!
"Raku Dearest"? What's that all about?!
SO...
DO YOU REMEMBER ME YET?
HUH?
NO... I FEEL BAD ABOUT IT...
BUT HONESTLY, I JUST DON'T REMEMBER YOU.
I'M SORRY.
THAT'S QUITE ALL RIGHT. TAKE YOUR TIME!
SHALL WE MOSEY ALONG?
Hmm...
RUSTLE

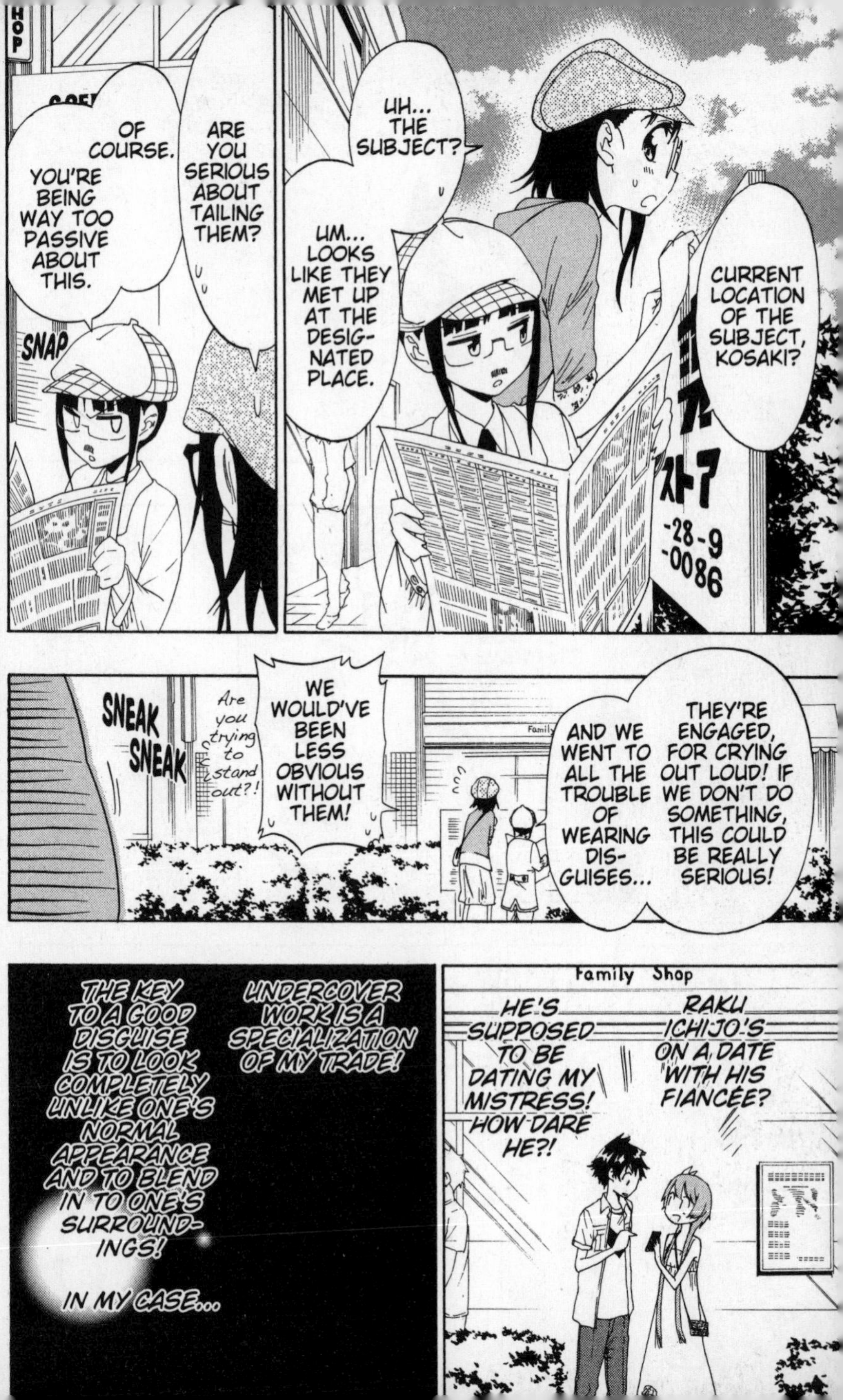
CURRENT LOCATION OF THE SUBJECT, KOSAKI?
UH... THE SUBJECT?
UM... LOOKS LIKE THEY MET UP AT THE DESIG-NATED PLACE.
-28-9
-0086
ARE YOU SERIOUS ABOUT TAILING THEM?
OF COURSE. YOU'RE BEING WAY TOO PASSIVE ABOUT THIS.
SNAP
THEY'RE ENGAGED, FOR CRYING OUT LOUD! IF WE DON'T DO SOMETHING, THIS COULD BE REALLY SERIOUS!
AND WE WENT TO ALL THE TROUBLE OF WEARING DIS-GUISES...
WE WOULD'VE BEEN LESS OBVIOUS WITHOUT THEM!
Are you trying to stand out?!
SNEAK SNEAK
Family Shop
RAKU ICHIJO'S ON A DATE WITH HIS FIANCÉE?
HE'S SUPPOSED TO BE DATING MY MISTRESS! HOW DARE HE?!
UNDERCOVER WORK IS A SPECIALIZATION OF MY TRADE!
THE KEY TO A GOOD DISGUISE IS TO LOOK COMPLETELY UNLIKE ONE'S NORMAL APPEARANCE AND TO BLEND IN TO ONE'S SURROUND-INGS!
IN MY CASE...

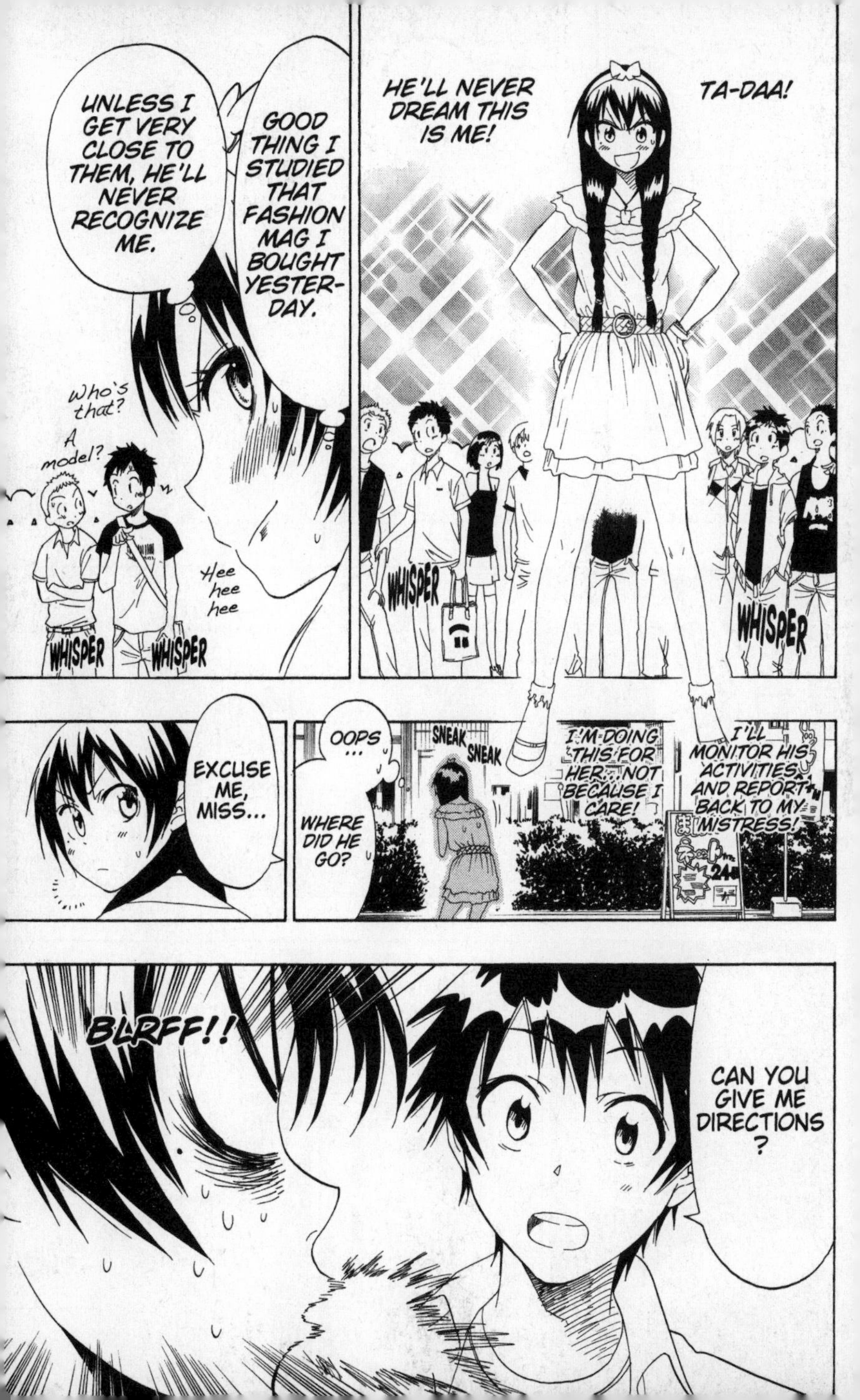
TA-DAA!
HE'LL NEVER DREAM THIS IS ME!
WHISPER
WHISPER
GOOD THING I STUDIED THAT FASHION MAG I BOUGHT YESTER-DAY.
UNLESS I GET VERY CLOSE TO THEM, HE'LL NEVER RECOGNIZE ME.
Hee hee hee
Who's that?
A model?
WHISPER
WHISPER
I'LL MONITOR HIS ACTIVITIES AND REPORT BACK TO MY MISTRESS!
I'M DOING THIS FOR HER...NOT BECAUSE I CARE!
SNEAK
SNEAK
OOPS...
WHERE DID HE GO?
EXCUSE ME, MISS...
CAN YOU GIVE ME DIRECTIONS?
BLRFF!!

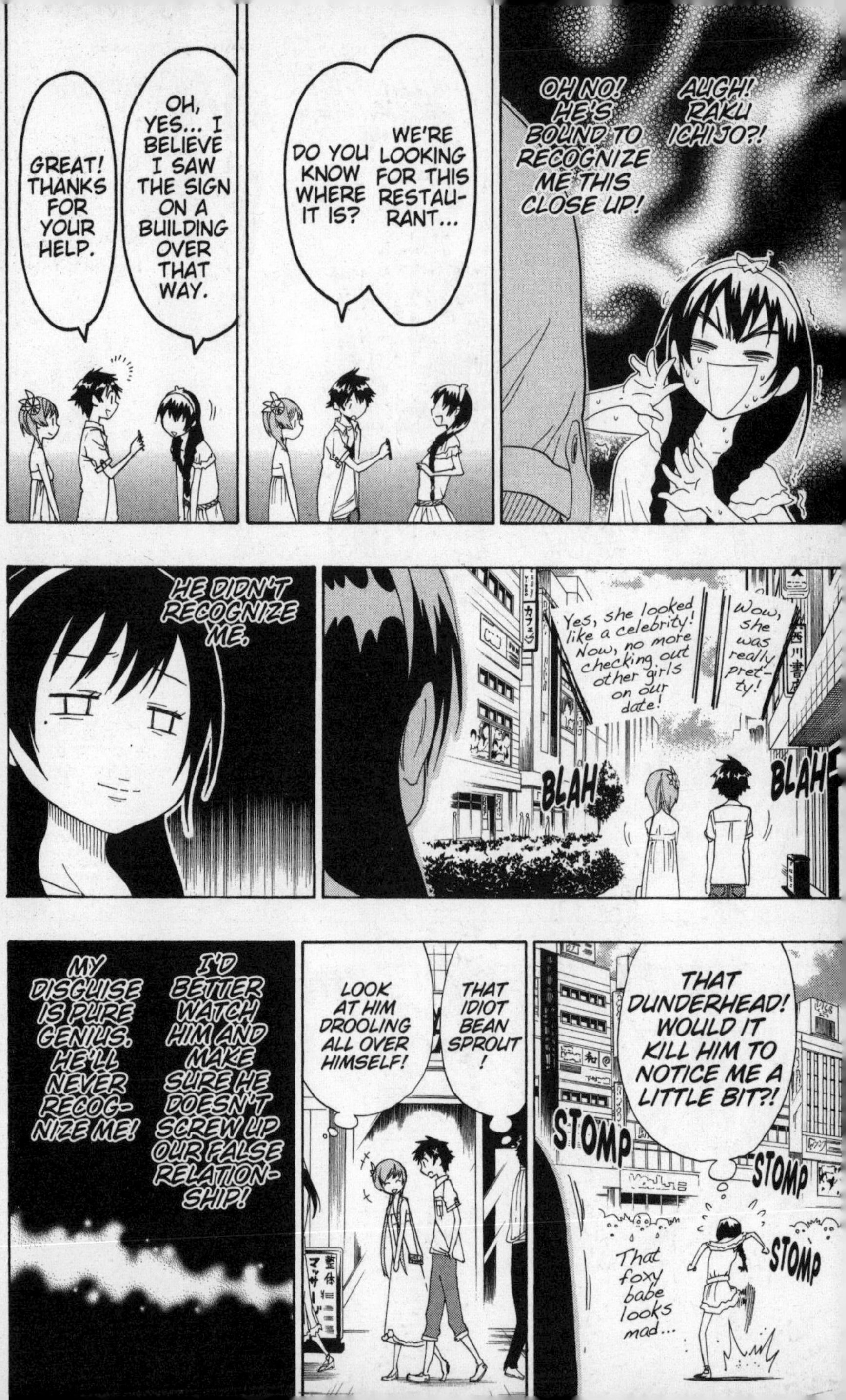
AUGH! RAKU ICHIJO?!
OH NO! HE'S BOUND TO RECOGNIZE ME THIS CLOSE UP!
WE'RE LOOKING FOR THIS RESTAURANT...
DO YOU KNOW WHERE IT IS?
OH, YES... I BELIEVE I SAW THE SIGN ON A BUILDING OVER THAT WAY.
GREAT! THANKS FOR YOUR HELP.
Wow, she was really pretty!
Yes, she looked like a celebrity! Now, no more checking out other girls on our date!
BLAH
BLAH
HE DIDN'T RECOGNIZE ME.
THAT DUNDERHEAD! WOULD IT KILL HIM TO NOTICE ME A LITTLE BIT?!
STOMP
STOMP
STOMP
That foxy babe looks mad...
THAT IDIOT BEAN SPROUT!
LOOK AT HIM DROOLING ALL OVER HIMSELF!
I'D BETTER WATCH HIM AND MAKE SURE HE DOESN'T SCREW UP OUR FALSE RELATIONSHIP!
MY DISGUISE IS PURE GENIUS. HE'LL NEVER RECOGNIZE ME!

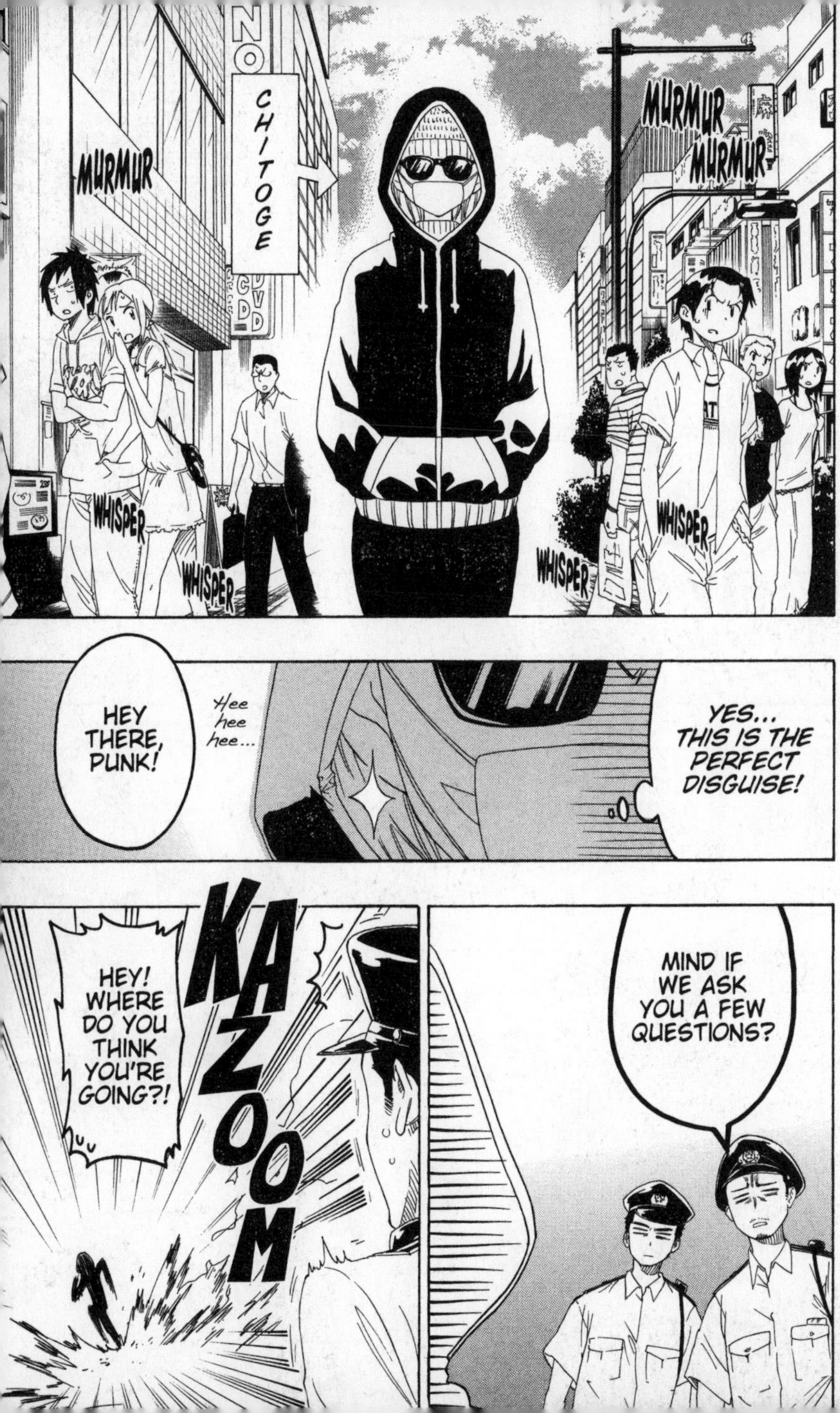
MURMUR
MURMUR
WHISPER
WHISPER
NO
CHITOGE
CD
DVD
MURMUR
WHISPER
WHISPER
YES... THIS IS THE PERFECT DISGUISE!
Hee hee hee...
HEY THERE, PUNK!
MIND IF WE ASK YOU A FEW QUESTIONS?
KAZOOM
HEY! WHERE DO YOU THINK YOU'RE GOING?!

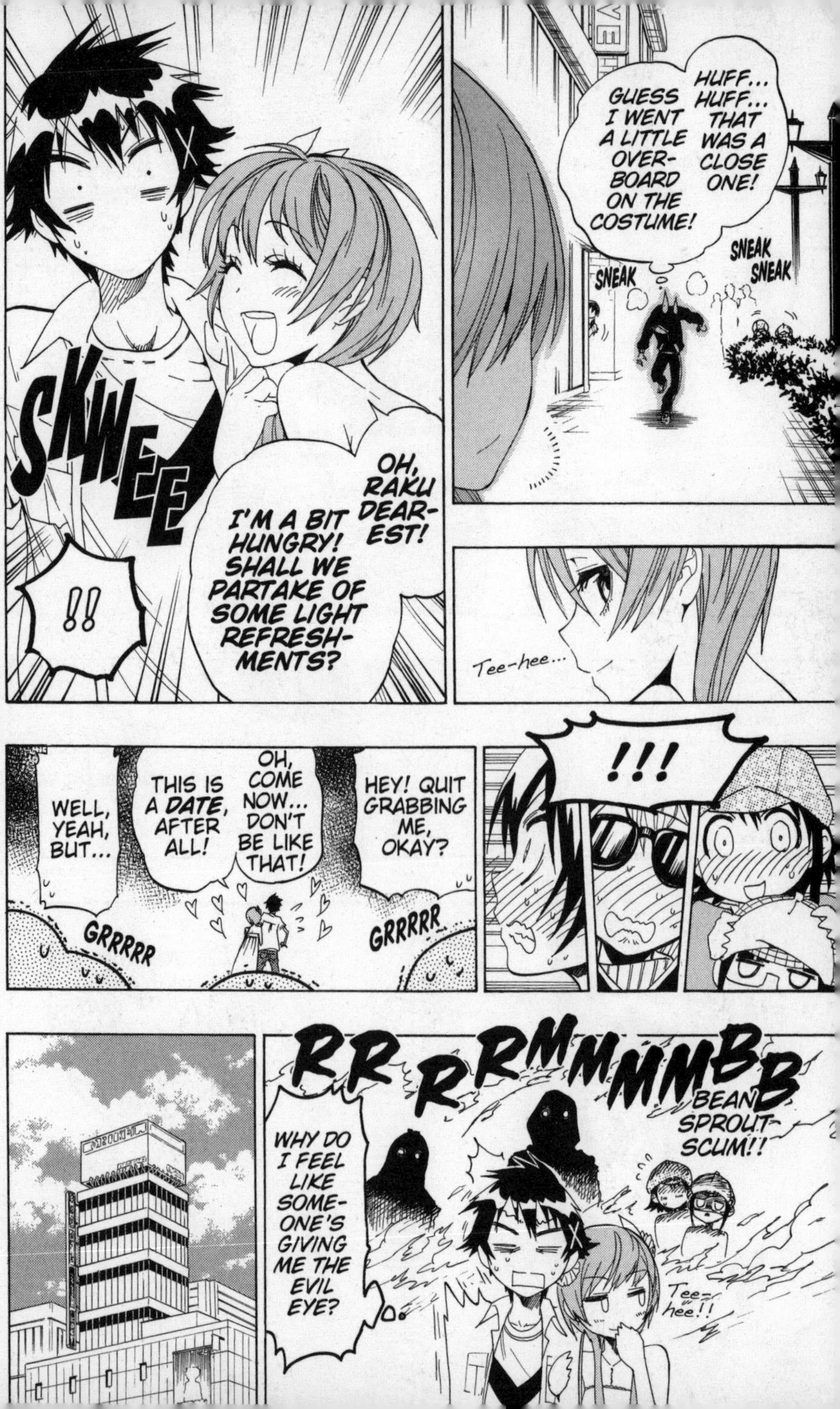
HUFF... HUFF... THAT WAS A CLOSE ONE!
GUESS I WENT A LITTLE OVER-BOARD ON THE COSTUME!
SNEAK SNEAK
SNEAK
Tee-hee...
OH, RAKU DEAR-EST!
I'M A BIT HUNGRY! SHALL WE PARTAKE OF SOME LIGHT REFRESH-MENTS?
SKWEE
!!
!!!
HEY! QUIT GRABBING ME, OKAY?
OH, COME NOW... DON'T BE LIKE THAT!
THIS IS A *DATE*, AFTER ALL!
WELL, YEAH, BUT...
GRRRRR
GRRRRR
RRRRMMMMMBB
BEAN SPROUT-SCUM!!
WHY DO I FEEL LIKE SOME-ONE'S GIVING ME THE EVIL EYE?
Tee-hee!!

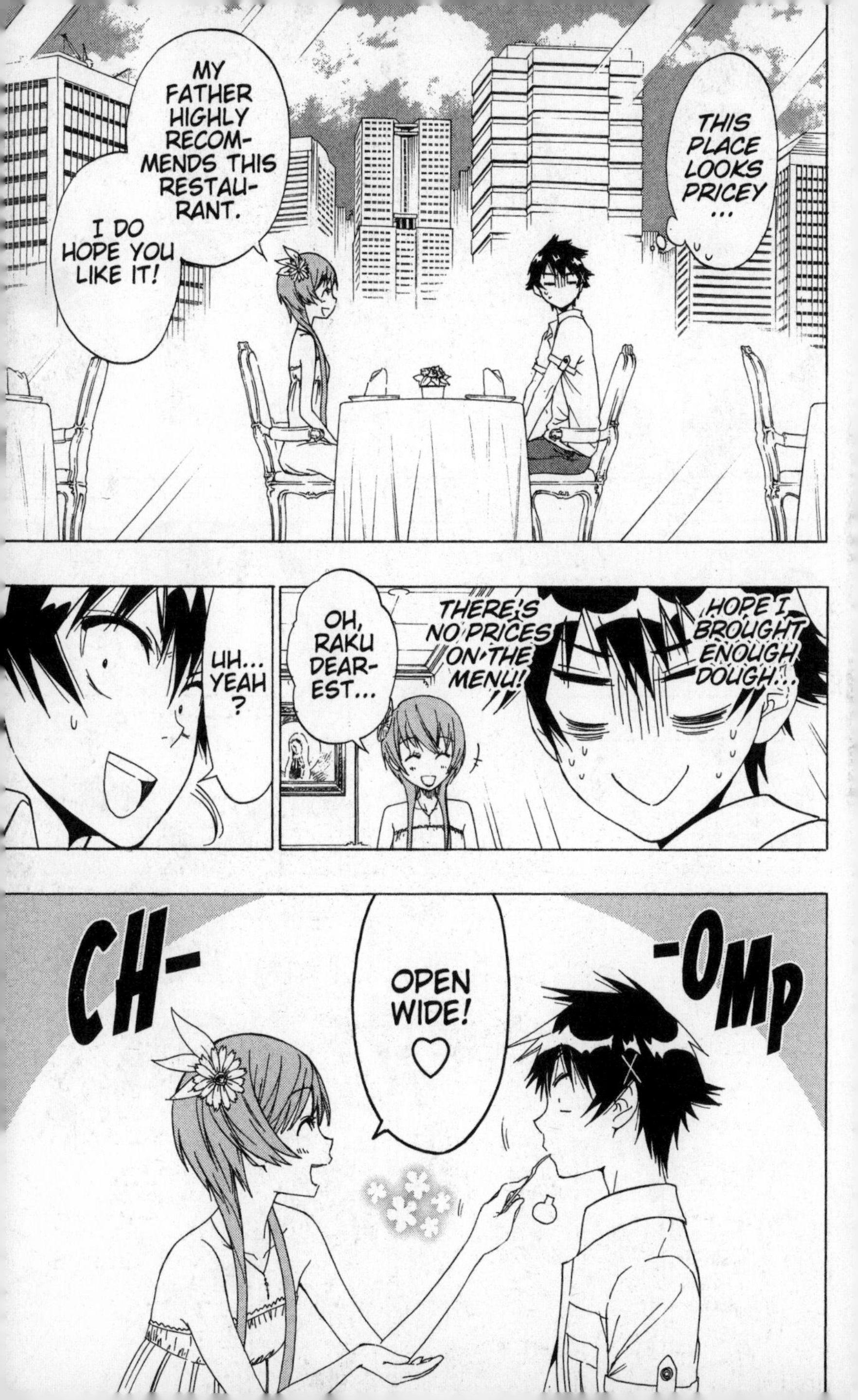
THIS PLACE LOOKS PRICEY...
MY FATHER HIGHLY RECOMMENDS THIS RESTAURANT.
I DO HOPE YOU LIKE IT!
HOPE I BROUGHT ENOUGH DOUGH...
THERE'S NO PRICES ON THE MENU!
OH, RAKU DEAREST...
UH... YEAH?
OPEN WIDE! ♥
CH- -OMP

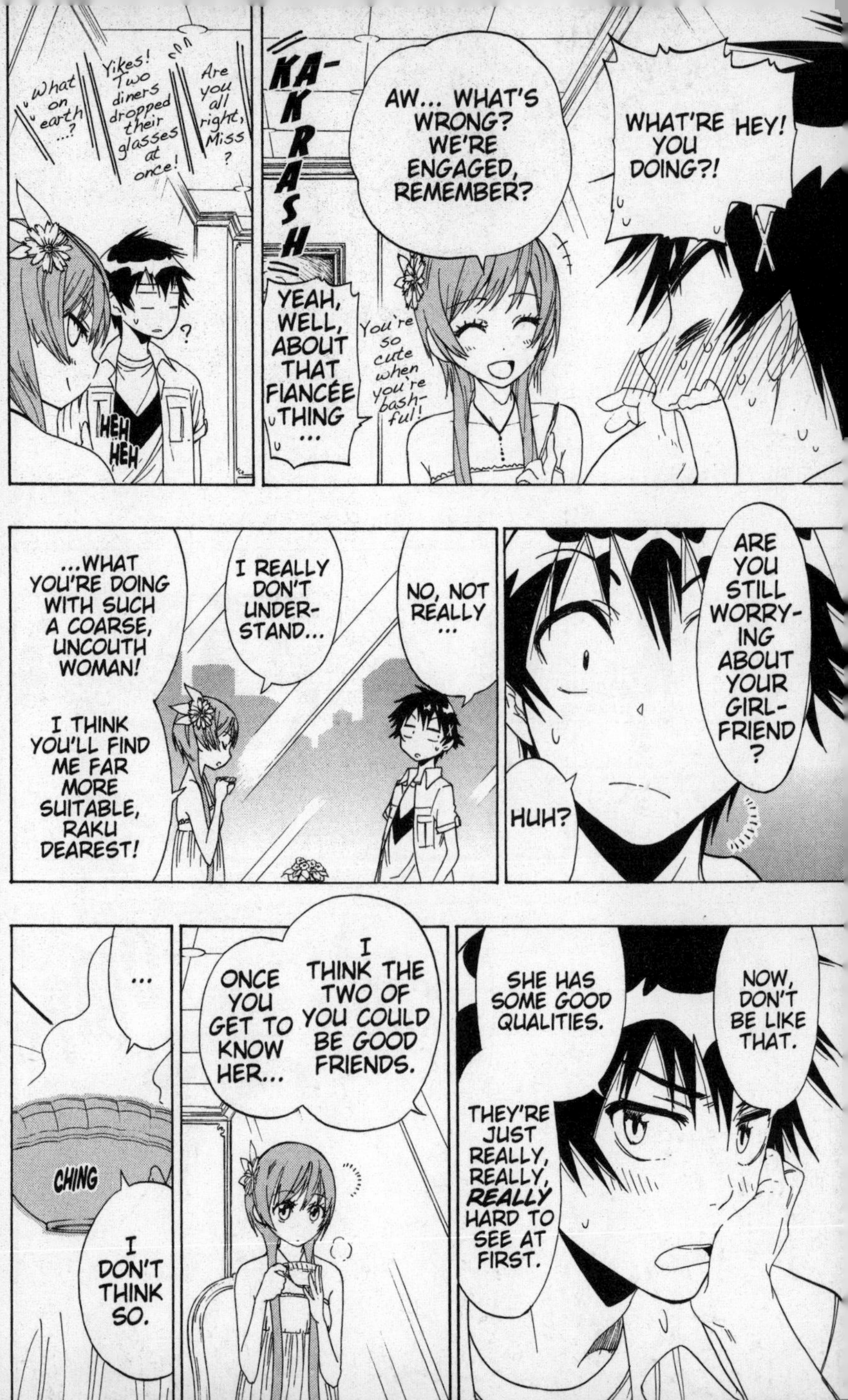
HEY! WHAT'RE YOU DOING?!
AW... WHAT'S WRONG? WE'RE ENGAGED, REMEMBER?
You're so cute when you're bashful!
KA-KRASH
YEAH, WELL, ABOUT THAT FIANCÉE THING...
Are you all right, Miss?
Yikes! Two diners dropped their glasses at once!
What on earth...?
?
HEH HEH
ARE YOU STILL WORRYING ABOUT YOUR GIRLFRIEND?
HUH?
NO, NOT REALLY...
I REALLY DON'T UNDERSTAND...
...WHAT YOU'RE DOING WITH SUCH A COARSE, UNCOUTH WOMAN!
I THINK YOU'LL FIND ME FAR MORE SUITABLE, RAKU DEAREST!
NOW, DON'T BE LIKE THAT.
SHE HAS SOME GOOD QUALITIES.
THEY'RE JUST REALLY, REALLY, REALLY HARD TO SEE AT FIRST.
I THINK THE TWO OF YOU COULD BE GOOD FRIENDS.
ONCE YOU GET TO KNOW HER...
...
CHING
I DON'T THINK SO.

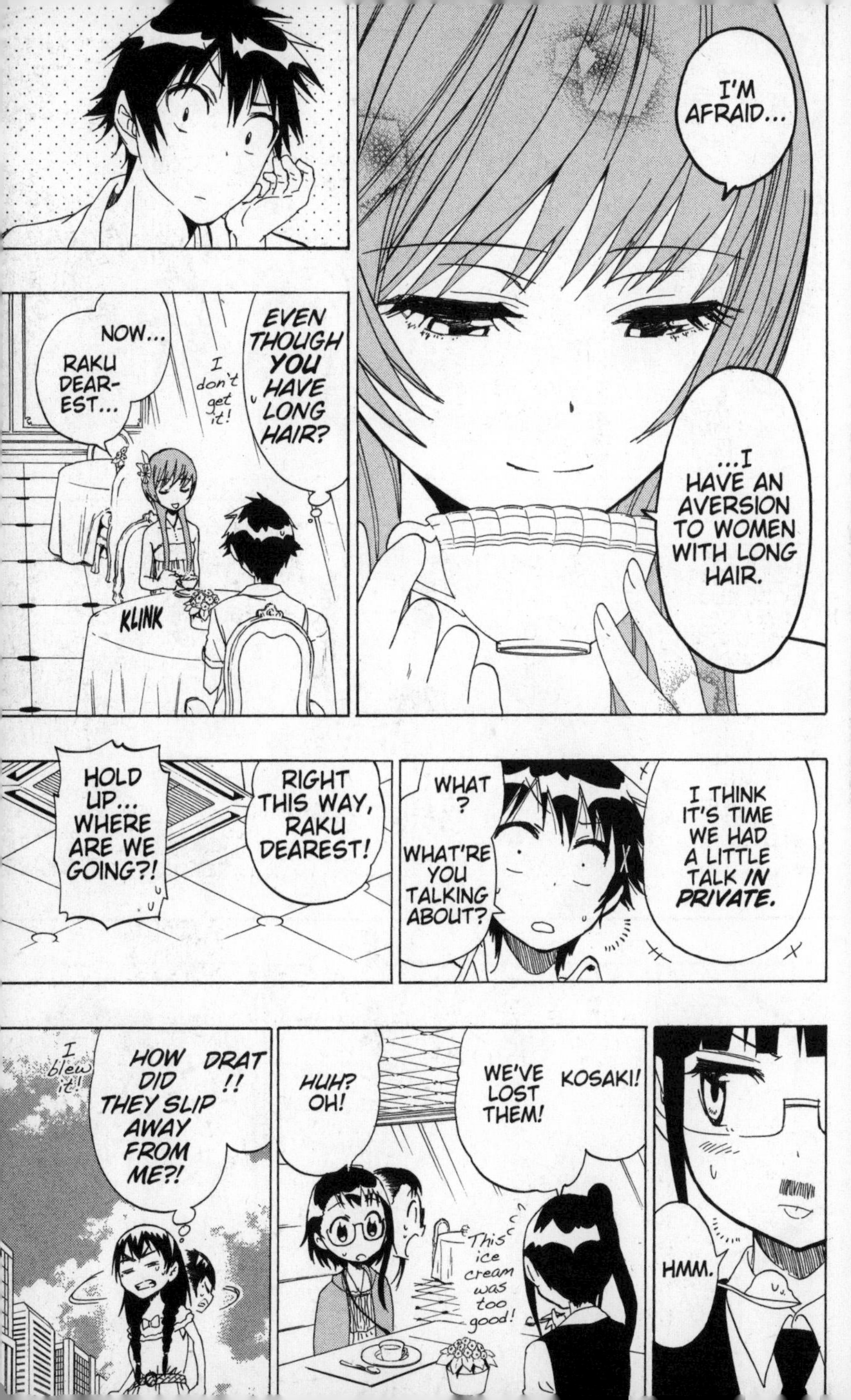
I'M AFRAID...
...I HAVE AN AVERSION TO WOMEN WITH LONG HAIR.
EVEN THOUGH YOU HAVE LONG HAIR?
I don't get it!
NOW... RAKU DEAREST...
KLINK
I THINK IT'S TIME WE HAD A LITTLE TALK IN PRIVATE.
WHAT?
WHAT'RE YOU TALKING ABOUT?
RIGHT THIS WAY, RAKU DEAREST!
HOLD UP... WHERE ARE WE GOING?!
HMM.
KOSAKI!
WE'VE LOST THEM!
HUH? OH!
This ice cream was too good!
DRAT!!
HOW DID THEY SLIP AWAY FROM ME?!
I blew it!

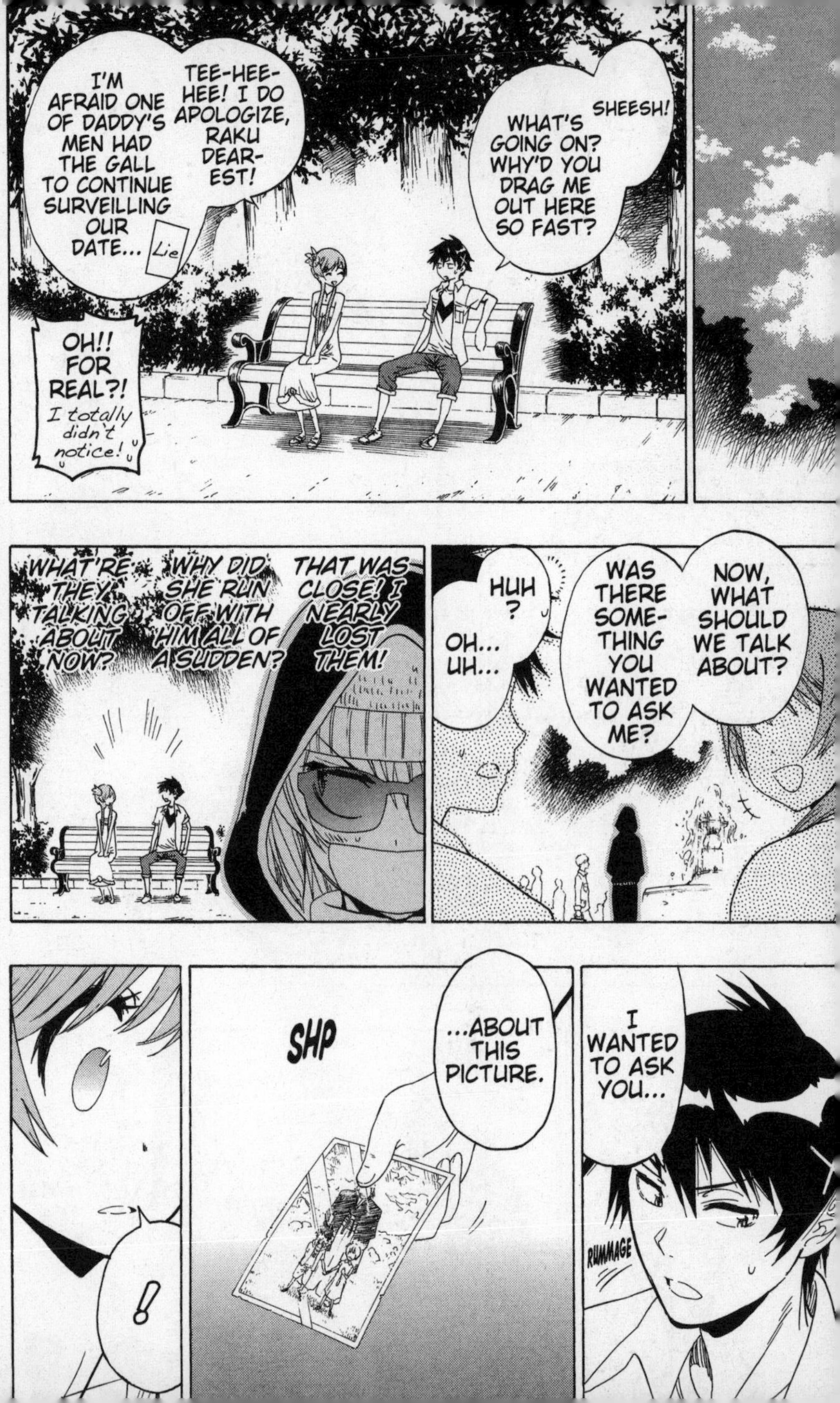
SHEESH!
WHAT'S GOING ON? WHY'D YOU DRAG ME OUT HERE SO FAST?
TEE-HEE-HEE! I DO APOLOGIZE, RAKU DEAREST!
I'M AFRAID ONE OF DADDY'S MEN HAD THE GALL TO CONTINUE SURVEILLING OUR DATE...
Lie
OH!! FOR REAL?!
I totally didn't notice!
NOW, WHAT SHOULD WE TALK ABOUT?
WAS THERE SOMETHING YOU WANTED TO ASK ME?
HUH?
OH... UH...
THAT WAS CLOSE! I NEARLY LOST THEM!
WHY DID SHE RUN OFF WITH HIM ALL OF A SUDDEN?
WHAT'RE THEY TALKING ABOUT NOW?
I WANTED TO ASK YOU...
RUMMAGE
...ABOUT THIS PICTURE.
SHP
!

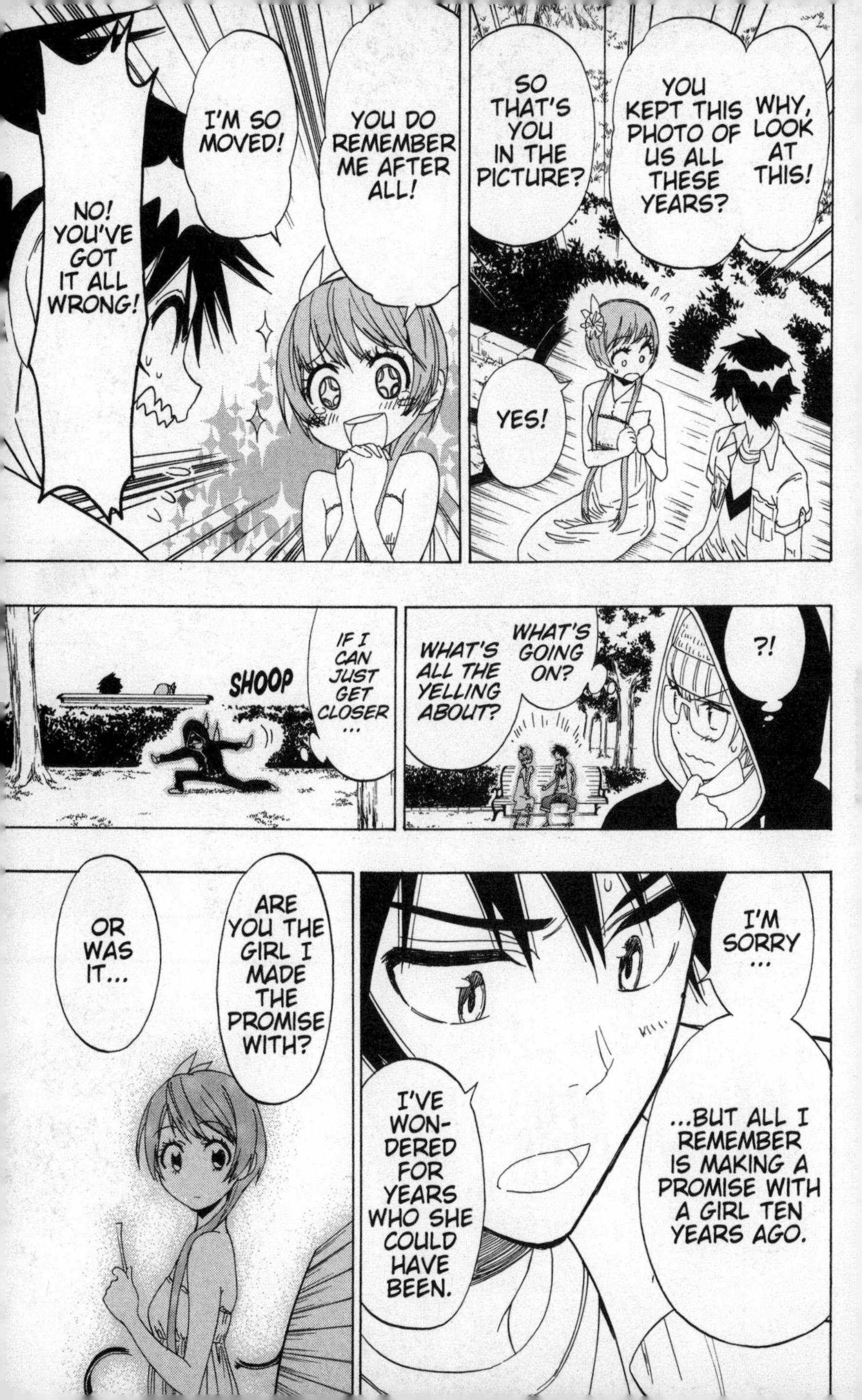
WHY, LOOK AT THIS!
YOU KEPT THIS PHOTO OF US ALL THESE YEARS?
SO THAT'S YOU IN THE PICTURE?
YES!
YOU DO REMEMBER ME AFTER ALL!
I'M SO MOVED!
NO! YOU'VE GOT IT ALL WRONG!
?!
WHAT'S GOING ON?
WHAT'S ALL THE YELLING ABOUT?
IF I CAN JUST GET CLOSER...
SHOOP
I'M SORRY...
...BUT ALL I REMEMBER IS MAKING A PROMISE WITH A GIRL TEN YEARS AGO.
I'VE WONDERED FOR YEARS WHO SHE COULD HAVE BEEN.
ARE YOU THE GIRL I MADE THE PROMISE WITH?
OR WAS IT...

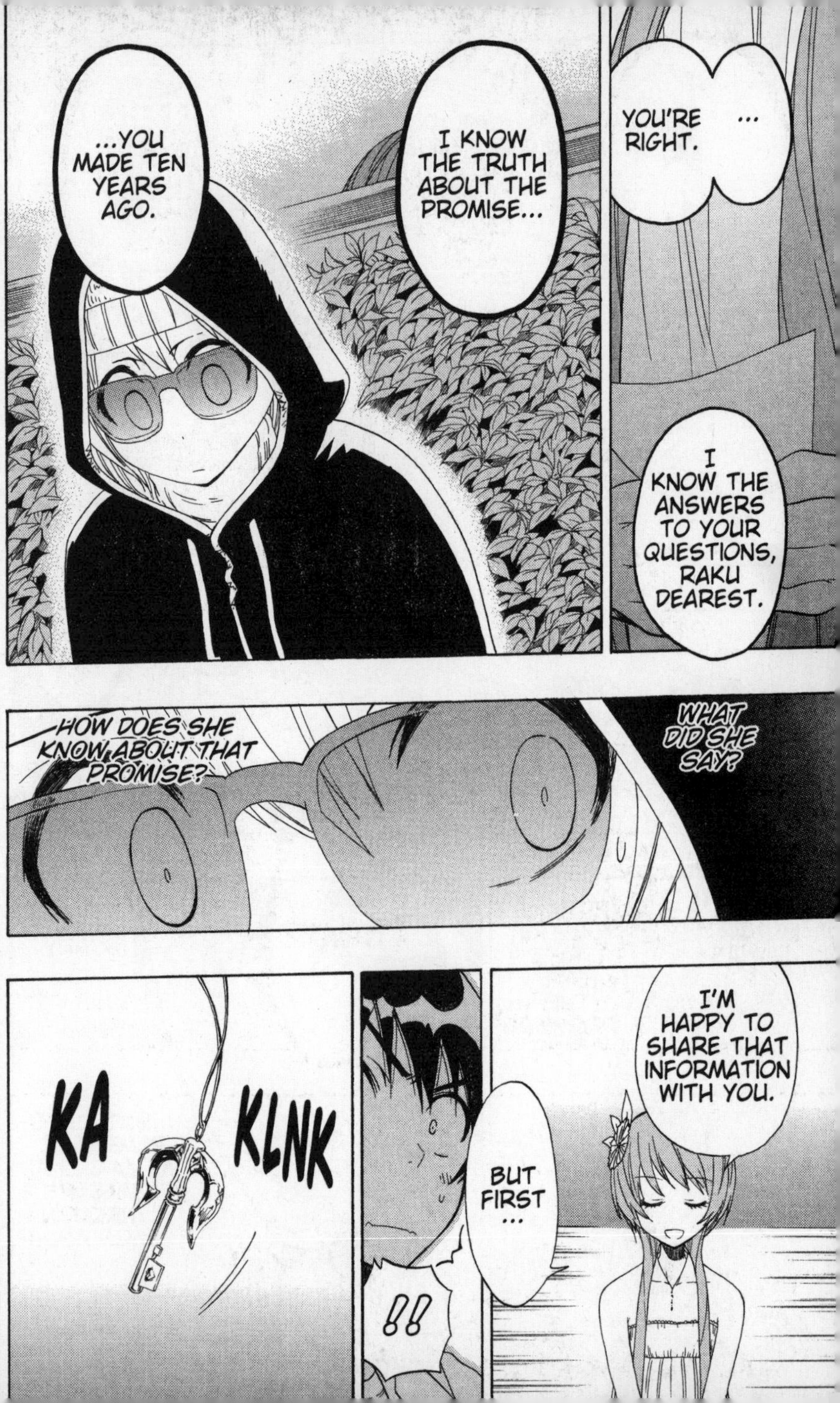
YOU'RE RIGHT. ...
I KNOW THE ANSWERS TO YOUR QUESTIONS, RAKU DEAREST.
I KNOW THE TRUTH ABOUT THE PROMISE...
...YOU MADE TEN YEARS AGO.
WHAT DID SHE SAY?
HOW DOES SHE KNOW ABOUT THAT PROMISE?
I'M HAPPY TO SHARE THAT INFORMATION WITH YOU.
BUT FIRST ...
!!
KA KLNK

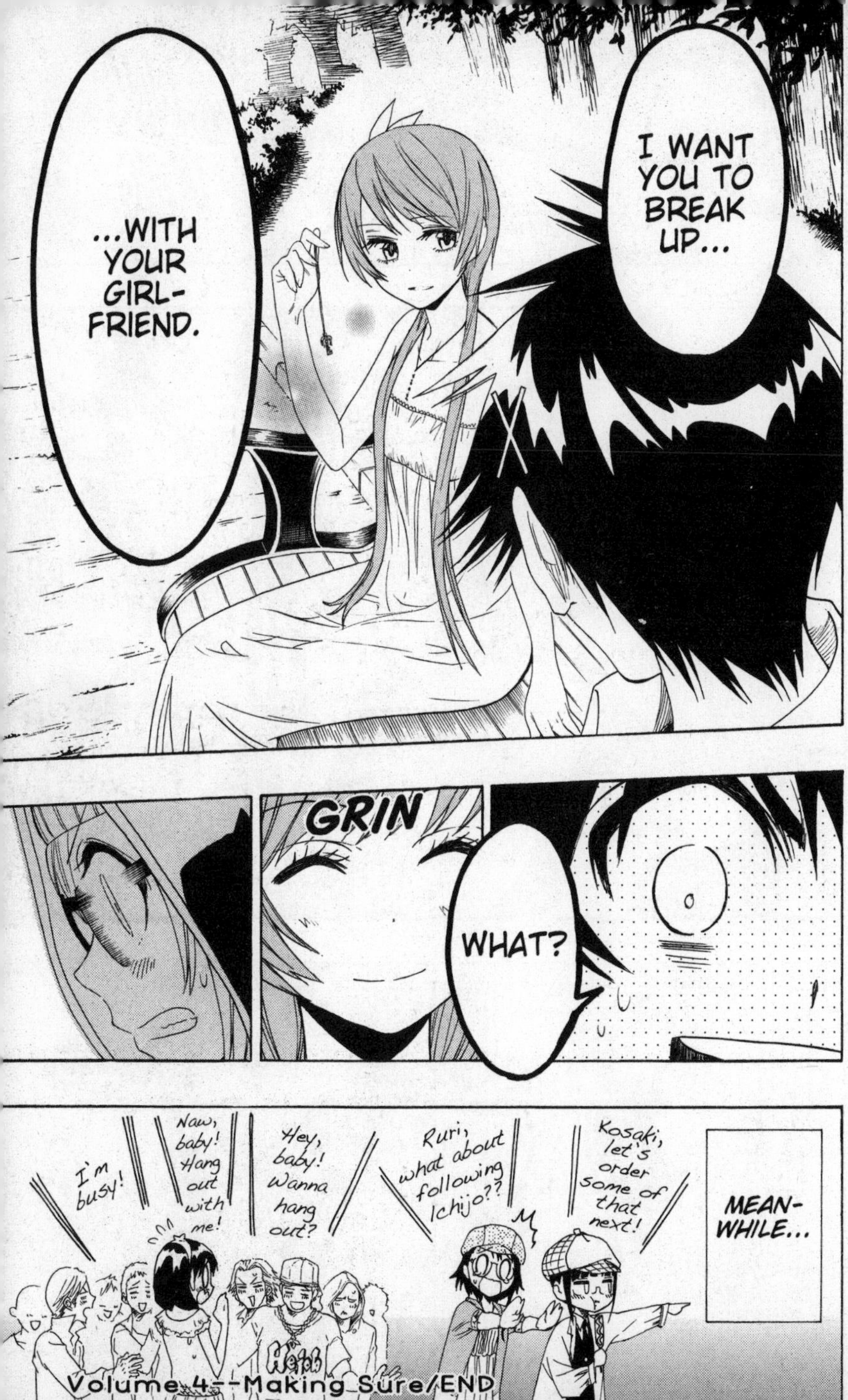
I WANT YOU TO BREAK UP...
...WITH YOUR GIRL-FRIEND.
WHAT?
GRIN
MEAN-WHILE...
Kosaki, let's order some of that next!
Ruri, what about following Ichijo??
Hey, baby! Wanna hang out?
Naw, baby! Hang out with me!
I'm busy!
Volume 4--Making Sure/END

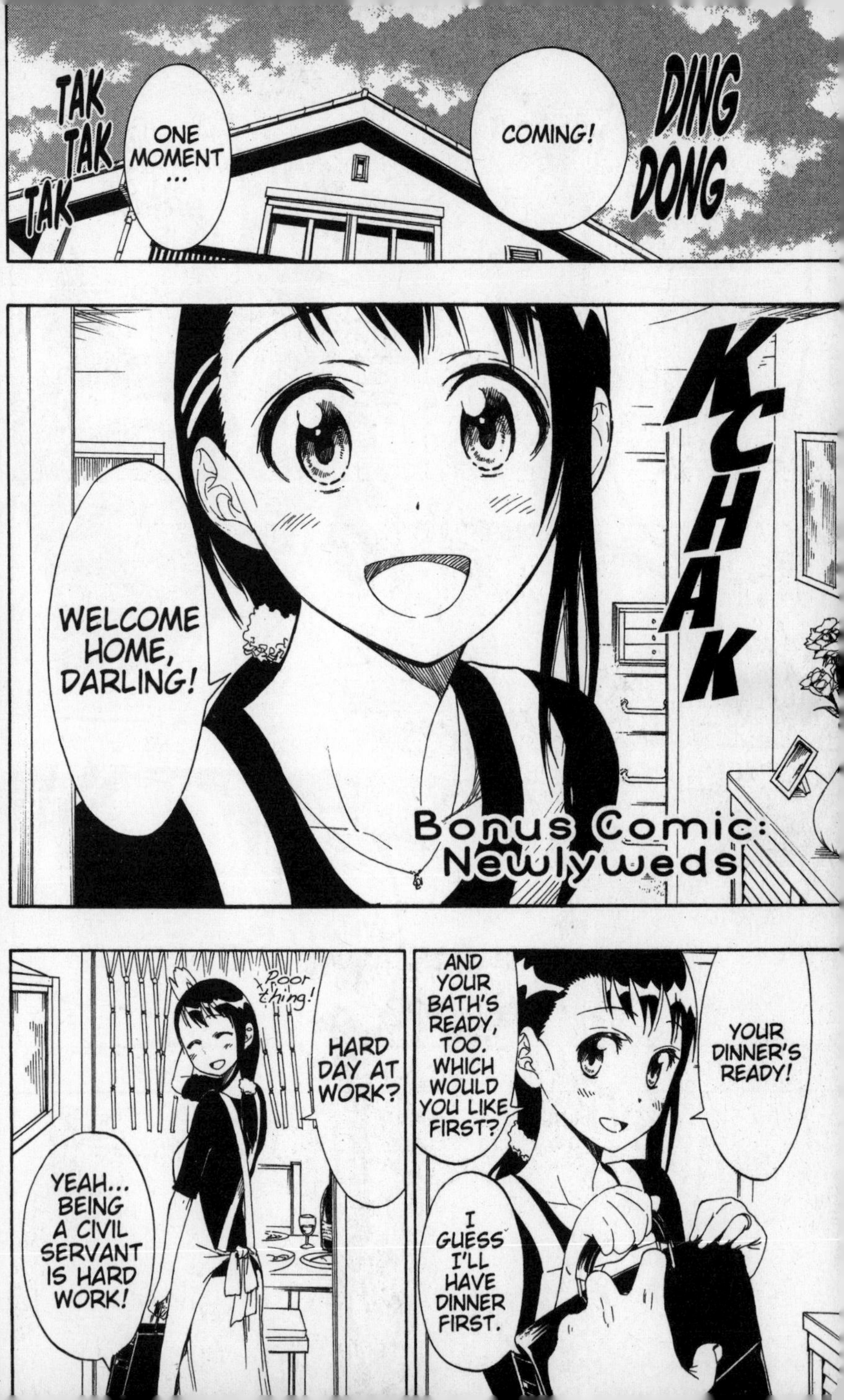
DING DONG
COMING!
ONE MOMENT...
TAK TAK TAK
KCHAK
WELCOME HOME, DARLING!
Bonus Comic: Newlyweds
YOUR DINNER'S READY!
AND YOUR BATH'S READY, TOO. WHICH WOULD YOU LIKE FIRST?
I GUESS I'LL HAVE DINNER FIRST.
HARD DAY AT WORK?
Poor thing!
YEAH... BEING A CIVIL SERVANT IS HARD WORK!

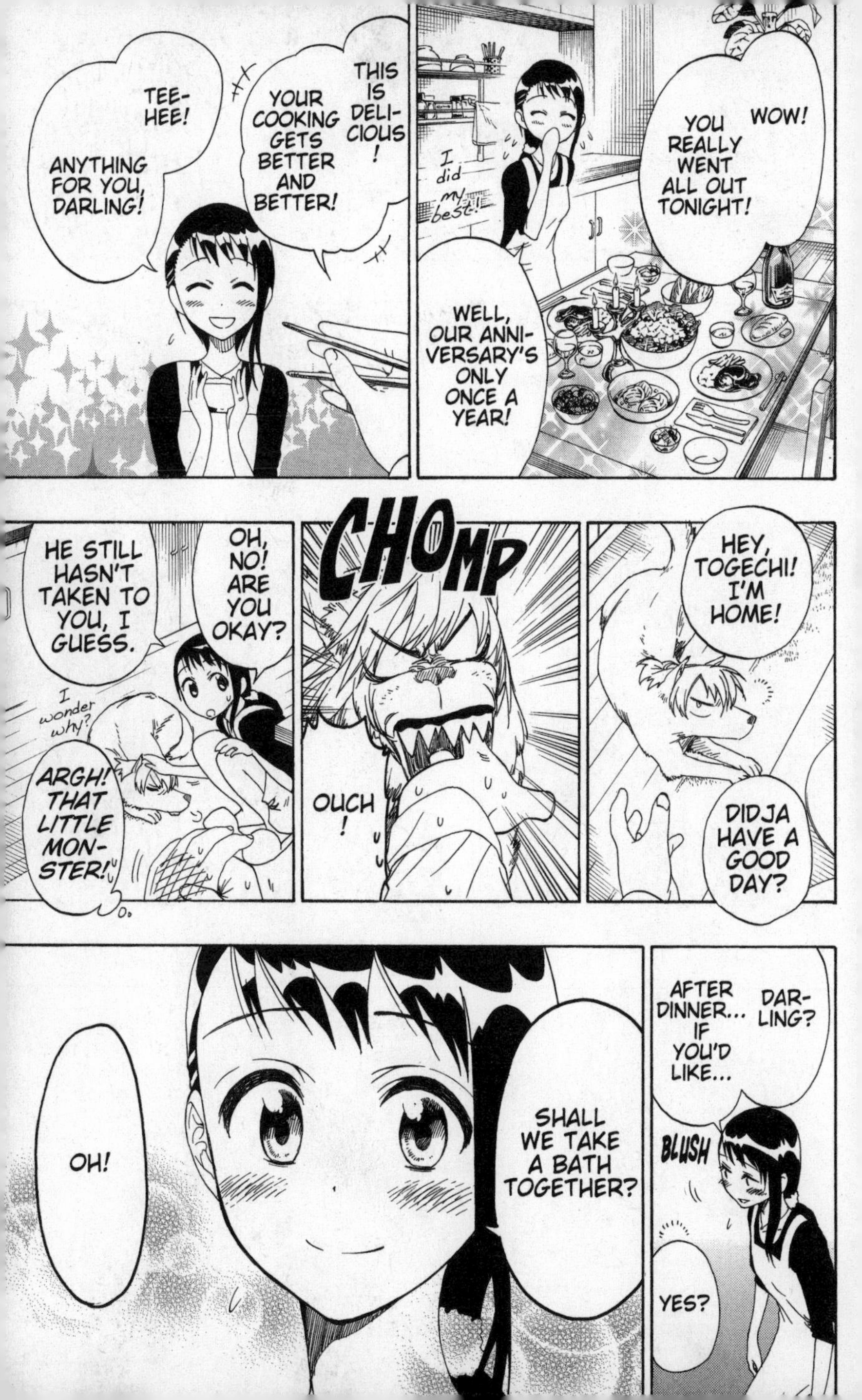
WOW!
YOU REALLY WENT ALL OUT TONIGHT!
I did my best!
WELL, OUR ANNIVERSARY'S ONLY ONCE A YEAR!
THIS IS DELICIOUS!
YOUR COOKING GETS BETTER AND BETTER!
TEE-HEE!
ANYTHING FOR YOU, DARLING!
HEY, TOGECHI! I'M HOME!
DIDJA HAVE A GOOD DAY?
CHOMP
OUCH!
OH, NO! ARE YOU OKAY?
HE STILL HASN'T TAKEN TO YOU, I GUESS.
I wonder why?
ARGH! THAT LITTLE MONSTER!
DARLING?
YES?
AFTER DINNER... IF YOU'D LIKE...
BLUSH
SHALL WE TAKE A BATH TOGETHER?
OH!

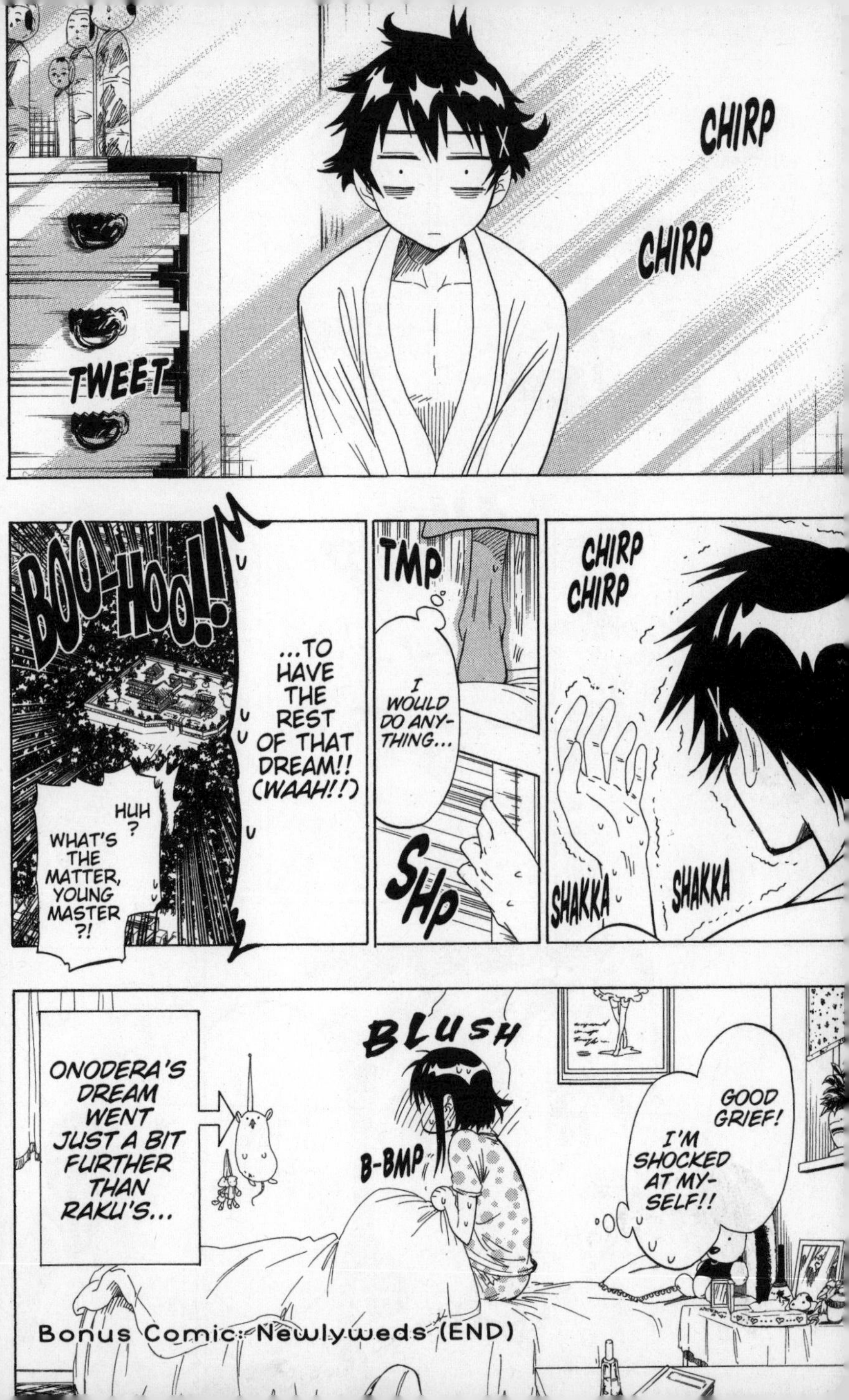
CHIRP
CHIRP
TWEET
CHIRP CHIRP
SHAKKA
SHAKKA
TMP
I WOULD DO ANYTHING...
SHp
...TO HAVE THE REST OF THAT DREAM!! (WAAH!!)
BOO-HOO!!
HUH? WHAT'S THE MATTER, YOUNG MASTER?!
BLUSH
GOOD GRIEF! I'M SHOCKED AT MYSELF!!
B-BMP
ONODERA'S DREAM WENT JUST A BIT FURTHER THAN RAKU'S...
Bonus Comic: Newlyweds (END)

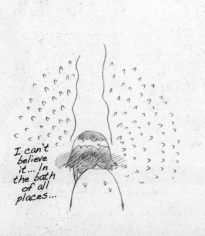

I can't believe it... In the bath of all places...

You're Reading the WRONG WAY!

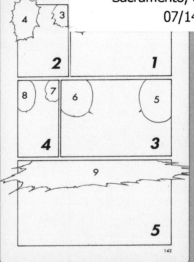

NISEKOI reads from right to left, starting in the upper-right corner. Japanese is read from right to left, meaning that action, sound effects, and word-balloon order are completely reversed from English order.